'This is a timely volume that nurtures a nuanced understanding of the ways that cultures, markets, marketing and consumption "give birth" to experiences of motherhood. A particular strength is the multidisciplinarity of the contributors, and the diversity of the types of motherhoods that are explored. For established and aspiring scholars interested in the intersection of gender, consumption, and markets, this book provides an invaluable resource.'

Eileen Fischer, Professor,
York University, Canada

'What does motherhood mean, and how does contemporary culture understand it? This comprehensive volume explores these compelling questions. Its expert roster of multidisciplinary, multinational contributors offers a thought-provoking panoply of perspectives on the experiences and expressions of motherhood around the world.'

Cele Otnes, Professor of Marketing,
University of Illinois at Urbana-Champaign, USA

'This book is essential reading for anyone wishing to explore and understand the multifaceted links between markets and motherhood, and I wholeheartedly recommend it.'

Stefania Borghini, Associate Professor,
Bocconi University, Italy

'With its carefully researched and thoughtfully composed essays, *Motherhoods, Markets and Consumption* demonstrates the depth and ongoing promise of interpretive consumer research. Under the evident, excellent direction of the editors, the book is sure to inspire new pathways of exploration into the politics, economics and pragmatics of gendered, maternal consumption and in its many expressions.'

Daniel Thomas Cook, Associate Professor,
Rutgers University, Camden, USA

'A much-needed book finally arrives. Five eminent scholars have assembled a collection that explores critically motherhood in relation to markets and consumption. We welcome this volume both for its intellectual content and potential impact on the world of practice.'

Alladi Venkatesh, Professor of Management,
University of California, USA

Motherhoods, Markets and Consumption

It takes more than a baby to make a mother, and mothers make more than babies. This edited collection brings together a range of international studies to explore the role of markets and consumption in the making of mothers.

Combining personal accounts from many mothers with different theoretical perspectives and organized into five main sections, this book:

- Considers how advertising, media and consumer culture contribute to myths and stereotypes concerning good and bad mothers;
- Explores how particular consumer choices are bound up with women's identities as mothers;
- Highlights how mothers deal with social expectations, marketing practices and family taste in feeding their families;
- Explores the role of consumption for women entering different phases of their mothering lives, such as pregnancy, early motherhood, and the 'empty nest';
- Considers how women's identities as mothers do not exist in isolation, but are shaped by their interactions with others, both within and beyond the immediate family.

Motherhoods, Markets and Consumption examines how marketing and consumer culture construct particular images of what mothers are, what they should care about and how they should behave; and explores how women's use of consumer goods and services shapes how they mother as well as how they are seen and judged by others.

Stephanie O'Donohoe is Professor of Advertising and Consumer Culture at the University of Edinburgh, UK.

Margaret Hogg is Fulgoni Professor of Consumer Behaviour and Marketing at Lancaster University Management School, UK.

Pauline Maclaran is Professor of Marketing and Consumer Research at Royal Holloway, University of London, UK.

Lydia Martens is Senior Lecturer in Sociology at Keele University, UK.

Lorna Stevens is Senior Lecturer in Marketing at the University of the West of Scotland, UK.

Routledge interpretive marketing research

Edited by Stephen Brown

University of Ulster, Northern Ireland

Recent years have witnessed an 'interpretive turn' in marketing and consumer research. Methodologies from the humanities are taking their place alongside those drawn from the traditional social sciences.

Qualitative and literary modes of marketing discourse are growing in popularity. Art and aesthetics are increasingly firing the marketing imagination.

This series brings together the most innovative work in the burgeoning interpretive marketing research tradition. It ranges across the methodological spectrum from grounded theory to personal introspection, covers all aspects of the postmodern marketing 'mix', from advertising to product development, and embraces marketing's principal sub-disciplines.

Also available in the Routledge interpretive marketing research series:

Motherhoods, Markets and Consumption

The making of mothers in contemporary Western cultures

Edited by Stephanie O'Donohoe, Margaret Hogg, Pauline Maclaran, Lydia Martens and Lorna Stevens

Routledge
Taylor & Francis Group

LONDON AND NEW YORK

First published 2014
by Routledge
2 Park Square, Milton Park, Abingdon, Oxon OX14 4RN

and by Routledge
711 Third Avenue, New York, NY 10017

Routledge is an imprint of the Taylor & Francis Group, an informa business

British Library Cataloguing in Publication Data
A catalogue record for this book is available from the British Library

Library of Congress Cataloging in Publication Data
Motherhoods, markets and consumption : the making of mothers in contemporary western cultures / edited by Stephanie O'Donohoe, Margaret Hogg, Pauline Maclaran, Lydia Martens and Lorna Stevens.
    pages cm. – (Routledge interpretive marketing research ; 18)
    Includes bibliographical references and index.
    1. Motherhood – Economic aspects. 2. Mothers – Economic aspects.
    I. O'Donohoe, Stephanie.
    HQ759.M87429 2013
    306.874′3–dc23   2013011445

ISBN: 978-0-415-51649-5 (hbk)
ISBN: 978-0-203-46972-9 (ebk)

Typeset in Times New Roman
by HWA Text and Data Management, London

Printed and bound in the United States of America by Publishers Graphics, LLC on sustainably sourced paper.

We dedicate this book to our children and grandchildren – Daniel and Robert Hogg, and Zoe Steinhauer-Hogg; Eva and Carina Lucas; Kate and Frank Maclaran; Fergal O'Donohoe; and Saorla Rose, Shane and Marcus Stevens-Houston.

Thank you all for being the making of us (sometimes the breaking of us!), and for teaching us to Keep Calm and Mother On!

Contents

Illustrations

Contributors

Helene Brembeck is Professor of Ethnology and Co-director of the Centre for Consumer Science at the University of Gothenburg. Her research interests are motherhood and childhood in consumer culture, including food and eating, and she has published several articles, books and anthologies in this field. Her latest international publications include 'Cozy Friday: an analysis of family togetherness and ritual overconsumption', in Barbara Czarniawska and Orvar Löfgren (eds) *Managing Overflow in Affluent Societies* (2012), and 'Exploring children's foodscapes', in *Children's Geographies* (with co-authors, 2013).

Benedetta Cappellini is Lecturer in Marketing at Royal Holloway, University of London, UK. Prior to that, she held lecturing posts at the University of Worcester, UK and the University of Florence, Italy. Her research interests include food consumption, material culture and market discourses. Her approach to research is ethnographic and interpretive. She has published her work in several journals including *Consumption, Markets and Culture*, *Journal of Business Research* and *Advances in Consumer Research*.

Alison J. Clarke is Chair of Design History and Theory at the University of Applied Arts, and Director of the Victor J. Papanek Foundation, overseeing the Foundation's contemporary social design research programme. Alison trained as a social anthropologist and design historian, and her research focuses on the social aspects of aesthetics and design. She has carried out numerous academically-funded ethnographies and co-ethnographies and most recently published *Design Anthropology: Object Culture in the 21st Century* (Springer 2010), addressing the interdisciplinary aspects of material culture. She has published widely on aspects of mothers' and children's consumption.

Carolyn F. Curasi is an Associate Professor of Marketing and the Associate Director of the Center for Mature Consumer Studies, both at the J. Mack Robinson College of Business Administration at Georgia State University (GSU). She is also a faculty member at the Gerontology Center, also at GSU. Dr. Curasi's research has been published in numerous academic journals including: *Journal of Consumer Research*, *Journal of Services Marketing*, *International Journal of Marketing Research*, *Journal of Financial Services Marketing*, *Journal of Consumer Marketing* and *Advances in Consumer Research*. Her research has been presented at many national and international academic conferences.

Andrea Davies is Senior Lecturer in Marketing and Consumer Research at University Leicester School of Management. She was co-editor of the *Journal of Consumer Behaviour* (2006–2009) and is joint editor of *Consumer Research Methods* (Volumes I – IV), SAGE Major Works Series (published Spring 2013). Her research interests focus on contemporary and historical aspects of consumers and consumption, including consumer identities and performance, empowerment and consumer ambivalence, motherhood and consumption, consumers and retail technologies, persuasion knowledge in advertising, consumer research methodologies and cross-cultural consumer behaviour.

Teresa Davis is Associate Professor of Marketing, University of Sydney Business School. Her research interests lie in two areas: children as consumers, particularly the marketing of food; and 'cultures of transition' such as consumption of childhood and migrant groups. Her work has been published in *Sociology, Consumption Markets and Culture* and other journals. She teaches consumer behaviour and is the co-convenor of the Australian Food Society and Culture Network and a member of the University of Sydney Research Ethics Committee.

Susan Dobscha earned a BBA and an MBA degree from the University of New Mexico and a PhD from Virginia Tech. She is an Associate Professor of Marketing at Bentley University in Waltham, MA. She conducts research on gender issues such as motherhood, earth/nature connections and female heroes, and sustainability issues such as peer to peer sharing and reverse distribution. She has published in *Journal of Retailing*, *Harvard Business Review* and *Journal of Public Policy and Marketing*.

Caroline J. Gatrell is Senior Lecturer at Lancaster University Management School, where she is also Director of Doctoral Programmes. Caroline's research centres on sociologies of health, work and family, focusing on how the reproductive labour of parenting interconnects with the productive labour of employment. From a sociological perspective she explores how working parents (both mothers and fathers) manage their health, their work-life balance, and the health and nutrition of babies and infant children. Caroline's work has been published in journals including: *Social Science and Medicine, International Journal of Management Reviews, International Journal of Human Resource Management* and *Gender, Work and Organization*. She currently serves on the editorial boards of *International Journal of Management Reviews* and *British Journal of Management*.

Susi Geiger is an Associate Professor of Marketing at University College Dublin Business School. Her research considers market actors and activities in business-to-business and consumer markets, an area she has widely published on in such journals as *Consumption Markets and Culture, European Journal of Marketing, Journal of Marketing Management, Industrial Marketing Management* and others. Most recently, she has led a large research project on the regulation and marketing of green chemistry, and is embarking on a multi-disciplinary project on market shaping of connected health solutions for dementia patients and caregivers.

Malene Gram, PhD, is Associate Professor and Head of the School of Culture and Global Studies at Aalborg University, Denmark. Her main research interests are within consumer culture with a special focus on family, parent and child consumption, motherhood and intergenerational relations. She has a special interest in cross-cultural studies and in gaps between ideals and practice in everyday culture. She has published in *Childhood, Journal of Consumer Culture, Advertising and Society Review*, *International Journal of Consumer Studies*, *Young Consumers* and *Journal of Marketing Communications*.

Lisa Glass is a Volunteer and Service Coordinator at Positive Help, an Edinburgh-based charity providing practical help for people with HIV and Hepatitis C. After receiving a first class MA (Social Sciences) in Psychology and Public Policy from the University of Glasgow, Lisa has worked on the frontline with vulnerable communities experiencing homelessness, financial exclusion and, currently, blood-borne viruses. Lisa has also completed field research on the impact of welfare reform for Hastings Council.

Bente Halkier is Professor in Communication, Department of Communication, Business and Information Technologies, Roskilde University, Denmark. Her research interests are within sociology of consumption and citizen communication. She is the author of *Consumption Challenged: Food in Medialised Everyday Lives* (Ashgate, 2010) and has published in journals including *Critical Public Health*, *Food, Culture & Society* and the *Journal of Consumer Culture*.

Kathy Hamilton is a Senior Lecturer in Marketing at the University of Strathclyde, Glasgow. She has been researching issues relating to consumer vulnerability and poverty for the last ten years. A key focus is the coping strategies employed by low-income families in response to consumer culture. She is also interested in gender and poverty, and researcher vulnerability. Her work has been published in *Sociology*, *Journal of Marketing Management* and *European Journal of Marketing*.

Elizabeth C. Hirschman has published around 230 articles, papers and books in the areas of consumer behaviour, advertising, marketing, psychology, semiotics and religious history. Presently she is splitting her teaching duties between Rutgers University School of Business in New Jersey and the University of Virginia-Wise in the Appalachian Mountains. Her three daughters are either in or have graduated from college and she is basking in the joy of empty-nesthood. Quote: 'At this point in my life and career, everything is gravy!'

Margaret Hogg is Fulgoni Professor of Consumer Behaviour and Marketing at Lancaster University Management School. Margaret's research focuses on inter-relationships between identity, self and consumption. She has researched identity and consumption across different generational (e.g. new mothers; empty nest women) and ethnic (e.g. British Asian) family contexts. She holds degrees in Politics and Modern History (Edinburgh University) as well as an MBA (Lancaster University) and PhD (Manchester University). She has published in the *Journal of Advertising, Journal of Business Research, European Journal of Marketing, Advances in Consumer Research, Consumption, Markets and Culture* and the *Journal of Marketing Management*.

Julia Keenan is a social and cultural geographer with interests in health, risk and governmentality perspectives, the new genetics, family relationships and parenting cultures. Together with Dr Helen Stapleton, she has published findings from research on transitions to motherhood and 'obesity', consumption practices in pregnancy, infant agency in feeding relationships, and the gender and division of labour. She is currently working as a Senior Research Associate at the University of East Anglia.

Mary Jane Kehily is Professor of Gender and Education at The Open University, UK. She has research interests in gender and sexuality, narrative and identity and popular culture and has published widely on these themes. Her books include: *Gender, Sexuality and Schooling, Shifting Agendas in Social Learning* (Routledge 2002), *An Introduction to Childhood Studies* (Open University Press/ McGraw Hill 2008), *Understanding Youth: Perspectives, Identities and Practices* (Sage/The Open University 2007) and, with Anoop Nayak, *Gender, Youth and Culture, Young Masculinities and Femininities* (Palgrave 2008). Her recent work on motherhood is based on a five-year collaboration with Rachel Thomson, Lucy Hadfield and Sue Sharpe, published as Thomson *et al. Making Modern Mothers* (Policy 2011).

Linda L. Layne is Program Director of the Science, Technology and Society Program at the US National Science Foundation, on loan from Rensselaer. She has authored two books: *Home and Homeland: The Dialogics of Tribal and National Identities in Jordan* and *Motherhood Lost: A Feminist Account of Pregnancy Loss in America* and co-produced a television series, 'Motherhood Lost: Conversations'. Her edited or co-edited books include *Transformative Motherhood: On Giving and Getting in a Consumer Culture, Consuming Motherhood, Feminist Technology* (and an associated blog, *Understanding Reproductive Loss*) and *Parenting in Global Perspective*. Her current research is on single mothers by choice, two-mom families, two-dad families and families that include a 'baby' lost through a miscarriage or stillbirth as a family member. She has published a number of articles on this subject and two books are planned: one on absent presences in these emerging families and the other an in-depth case study of one American single mother by choice.

Pauline Maclaran is Professor of Marketing and Consumer Research at Royal Holloway, University of London. Pauline's research interests focus on cultural aspects of contemporary consumption, and she adopts a critical perspective to analyze the ideological assumptions that underpin many marketing activities, particularly in relation to gender issues. Her work has been published in internationally recognized journals including the *Journal of Consumer Research*. She has co-edited various books, including *Marketing and Feminism: Current Issues and Research*. She is also Editor in Chief of *Marketing Theory*, a journal that promotes alternative and critical perspectives in marketing and consumer behaviour.

David Marshall is Professor of Marketing and Consumer Behaviour at the University of Edinburgh Business School. His research interests include food access and availability; consumer food choice and eating rituals; and children's discretionary consumption in relation to food advertising and marketing. He edited *Understanding Children as Consumers* (2010) and *Food Choice and the Consumer* (1995) and has published in journals including *The Sociological Review*, *Journal of Marketing Management*, *Consumption, Markets and Culture*, *Journal of Consumer Behaviour*, *Young Consumers*, *Appetite*, *Food Quality and Preference*, *International Journal of Epidemiology* and *Journal of Human Nutrition*.

Lydia Martens is Senior Lecturer in Sociology at Keele University. Her research examines intersections between consumption and domestic life, with particular focus on children, families and consumer culture. She has conducted fieldwork at The Baby Show and on other market cultures around the young child. Her publications include *Eating Out: Social Differentiation, Consumption and Pleasure* (2000, with Alan Warde) and *Gender and Consumption: Domestic Cultures and the Commercialisation of Everyday Life* (2007, with Emma Casey). She is co-author of 'Bringing children (and parents) into the sociology of consumption' (*Journal of Consumer Culture*, 2004) and has also published in the journals *Sociology*, *Consumption, Markets and Culture*, and *Home Cultures*. Lydia co-convened the European Sociological Association Consumption Network between 2007 and 2010, and was an expert on the DCSF panel that pulled together evidence on the impact of the commercial world on children's wellbeing in 2008–2009. She is a member of the Food Standards Agency's Register of Specialists.

Tina Miller is a Professor of Sociology at Oxford Brookes University. Her research and teaching interests include motherhood and fatherhood transitions, gender and identities, reproductive health, narratives, qualitative research methods and ethics, and she has published in all these areas. Tina has lived and worked in the Solomon Islands and Bangladesh as well as Oxford. She has been engaged as an expert advisor by the World Health Organisation and presented her work at UNICEF headquarters (New York). She has also been engaged as an adviser to political parties and think tanks and participated in various TV and radio programmes in relation to her research and publications on motherhood and fatherhood.

Stephanie O'Donohoe is Professor of Advertising and Consumer Culture at the University of Edinburgh. A member of The VOICE Group and co-organizer of the ESRC Seminar Series on Motherhoods, Markets and Consumption, her research interests include consumption experiences in the transition to motherhood, bereaved people's interactions with the marketplace, child and young adult consumers, and advertising creatives' working lives. Her work has been published in journals including *Human Relations*, *Journal of Marketing Management* and *Consumption, Markets and Culture*.

Lisa O'Malley has published widely in the marketing field. She has been interested in research on motherhood and consumption for over a decade, and has undertaken a number of research projects in this space including work with colleagues in VOICE – an international research collaboration. Publications include *Consumption, Markets & Culture*, *Advertising & Society Review*, *Marketing Theory* and the *Journal of Macromarketing*. Lisa is on the Editorial Boards of *Marketing Theory* and the *Journal of Marketing Management*.

Elizabeth Parsons is Professor of Marketing at the University of Liverpool. Her research explores a range of topics pertinent to consumer culture, critical marketing and gender studies. Recent projects explore families and food, antique dealing and gender in the workplace. She has published in a range of outlets including the *Journal of Marketing* and *Gender, Work and Organisation*. She is joint editor of *Marketing Theory*, a journal that promotes alternative and critical approaches to the study of markets and marketing.

Maurice Patterson is a Consumer Researcher with a particular focus on embodiment, though he has also contributed work within the fields of branding and advertising. He has co-written two textbooks in the field of direct and relationship marketing, and has over 30 peer-reviewed publications. These publications have appeared in journals such as *Consumption, Markets & Culture, European Journal of Marketing, Journal of Marketing Management* and *Marketing Theory*. He is on the editorial board of the *Journal of Consumer Behaviour*.

Helle D. Pedersen, MA, is Teaching Assistant at Aalborg University, Denmark. She has worked with consumer culture and issues related to motherhood and consumption.

Alan Petersen is Professor of Sociology in the School of Political and Social Inquiry at Monash University, Melbourne. He has researched and published extensively in the sociology of health and illness, science and technology studies, and gender studies. His most recent book is *Aging Men, Masculinities and Modern Medicine* (Routledge, 2013), edited with Antje Kampf and Barbara Marshall.

Andrea Prothero is Associate Dean of Academic Affairs at University College Dublin, Ireland. She has previously lectured at universities in Wales and Scotland and spent a sabbatical at Arizona State University. Her research explores marketing in society, with specific research projects including advertising to children, motherhood and consumption, sustainability marketing and sustainable consumption; she has published widely in these areas. In 2005 Andy received a President's Research Fellowship award to explore 'Motherhood: Identity, Experience and Consumption' with colleagues in Denmark, Ireland, the UK and the USA. Andy also received a UCD President's Teaching Award in 2012 to explore ethics in business education. She is Associate Editor for the *Journal of Macromarketing* and *Journal of Marketing Management*.

Tanja Schneider is a Research Fellow in Science and Technology Studies at the University of Oxford and a Research Fellow at Green Templeton College, Oxford. Her areas of expertise include social studies of markets and marketing, media and consumer culture as well as the politics and practices of food governance. She has published on these topics in *Consumption, Markets & Culture, Health Sociology Review* and *Science as Culture*.

Elin Brandi Sørensen is Associate Professor of Marketing, Department of Entrepreneurship and Relationship Management, University of Southern Denmark. Her research interests are mainly within consumer behaviour, with particular attention to consumers in transition, motherhood and consumption.

Helen Stapleton is a Senior Research Fellow at Australian Catholic University and Mater Medical Research Institute. Helen has a clinical background in midwifery and medical herbalism and research interests which include the social context of reproduction; transitions to motherhood and mothering practices; family life and relationships; and maternity service provision. Her approach is informed by the disciplines of sociology and medical anthropology. Prior to relocation in Brisbane (2009) Helen worked at the University of Sheffield.

Lorna Stevens is a Senior Lecturer in Marketing at the University of the West of Scotland. She is interested in gender issues and feminist perspectives on marketing, consumer behaviour, experiential consumption and media consumption. Her work often explores the wider, ideological forces that shape consumers' experiences, and thus takes a critical, socio-cultural approach to marketing and consumption. She is co-editor of *Marketing and Feminism: Current Issues and Research*, and her work has been published in a range of national and international edited books and marketing, advertising and consumer behaviour journals.

Thyra Uth Thomsen is Associate Professor at the Department of Marketing, Copenhagen Business School. Her research focuses on consumer behaviour. Moreover, she has a special interest in the link between consumption and identity construction. Her articles have been published in journals including the *Journal of Consumer Behaviour* and the *Journal of Marketing Management*.

Amy E. Traver has been an Assistant Professor of Sociology at CUNY's Queensborough Community College since 2008. Her research, which has been published in journals including *Qualitative Sociology*, *Sociological Focus* and the *International Journal of Sociology of the Family*, focuses on intersections of race/ethnicity and gender in American families and schools. Amy is currently directing a study of American primary- and secondary-school-aged girls' interactions across physical abilities.

Katherine Trebeck is Policy and Advocacy Manager for Oxfam's UK Programme. Prior to this role she led Oxfam's Humankind Index, a measure of Scotland's real prosperity developed through wide ranging community consultation. She also managed Oxfam's 'Whose Economy?' project which asked why, despite decades of economic growth, Scotland's poverty has not been addressed and inequalities have deepened. Katherine has a PhD in political science from the Australian National University and is also an Honorary Research Fellow at the University of Glasgow.

Acknowledgements

This book arose from our ESRC-funded seminar series, *Motherhoods, Markets and Consumption*, and we are grateful to the ESRC and its reviewers for the opportunity this provided for us to reflect on motherhood in consumer culture and to exchange ideas with a wonderful range of scholars working in this area. We are grateful to our co-organizer Linda Scott, University of Oxford, all the speakers at the six seminars and the delegates who shared their perspectives with us. Many of the speakers also contributed chapters to this book; we thank all our contributors for sharing their insightful work with us. We would also like to thank Sue Humphries, Keele University, for her efficient administration of the seminar series.

We are grateful to Stephen Brown, Interpretive Marketing Research Series Editor, for his support and encouragement as we developed this book, Jacqueline Curthoys, Alexander Krause and, latterly, Holly Knapp at Routledge, for guiding us so helpfully and patiently through the production of the manuscript, the reviewers for their constructive feedback on the book proposal, and Aliette Ferns, University of Edinburgh, for her assistance in editing chapters.

The authors and publishers also thank the following for permission to reproduce copyright material:

- The Trustees of the National Library of Scotland and of Hearst Magazines, Princes Group and Alpro UK for permission to reproduce the Crosse and Black-well advertisement (Figure 6.1) the Alpro Soya advertisement (Figure 6.2).
- Springer for permission to reproduce portions of Amy E. Traver's (2007) article in *Qualitative Sociology*, 'Home(land) décor: China adoptive parents' consumption of Chinese cultural objects for display in their homes'.

As ever, a book takes time to bring together and we are grateful to our families and friends for bearing with us as we laboured over this particular delivery.

Stephanie O'Donohoe
Margaret Hogg
Pauline Maclaran
Lydia Martens
Lorna Stevens

1   The making of mothers

*Stephanie O'Donohoe, Margaret Hogg,
Pauline Maclaran, Lydia Martens and
Lorna Stevens*

In Korean author Kyung-sook Shin's best-selling novel, *Please Look After Mom*, when an elderly mother goes missing in Seoul, her family are desperate to find her, but to no avail. The book revolves around their search, with each chapter narrated by a different family member and, finally, by the mother herself. As the chapters unfold, we realise that no-one in her family ever really knew her as a person: their relationship with her was based only on their own needs and the role she played, as wife or mother, in fulfilling these needs. The mother's chapter makes a surprising revelation: she too had desires, dreams and feelings that were secret from her family. In a poignant moment she admits that she also 'desperately needed a mother' her whole life.

For all that her novel is grounded in Korean life and culture, Shin's evocative account of the mother's predicament reminds us of the work of Nancy Chodorow, the American feminist sociologist and psychoanalyst, who wrote in 1978 about women's lot to be relational, focused on the needs of others, but expecting little nurturing in return. More recently, she has written that 'for many women the personal and emotional investment and sense of what it means to an individual unique woman to be a mother should be recognized' (in Metzl 2003). Above all, then, Chodorow's work over the past 30 years culminates in a plea for maternal subjectivity and maternal identity, and as such it complements this book's focus on what it means to be a mother, and what place the self has in constructions of motherhood in contemporary consumer culture.

In keeping with Shin's novel, this book highlights the universal yet multifaceted nature of motherhood (or motherhoods, a term we see as better reflecting the diversity and complexity it entails). Individually and collectively, the chapters in this book unpick the mothering role in its many different guises, exploring the tensions women encounter and the negotiations they make when mothering in contemporary consumer culture.

Put simply, it takes more than a baby to make a mother, and mothers make more than babies.

Marketing and consumer culture construct particular images of what mothers are, what they should care about and how they should behave. Women's use of consumer goods and services shapes how they mother as well as how they are seen and judged by others. Mothering practices also inevitably involve others –

children, fathers, grandparents and wider social networks (Oakley 1992; Miller 2005; Miller 2011). Relationships between mothers and others are shaped at least in part by societal norms and values, regardless of whether these have been absorbed, reproduced or resisted, and they are often enacted through material goods. Thus, it is important to understand how intersections between people, norms and values are played out in marketplace interactions and consumption practices surrounding motherhood. In this chapter, we briefly explore both the making of mothers and what mothers make, before outlining key themes across the contributions in this book and introducing its four main sections and individual chapters.

What makes a mother?

Marketers have long been interested in family life over time, and the knowledge they have generated on domestic personae, like the housewife, has fed into product innovation, commercialization and marketing practices (Friedan 1963). As consumer culture has established itself as a normalized aspect of everyday life, markets play an important role in shaping cultural discussions about domestic practices, cultures and identities. Films, magazines, books, advertising and social media all contribute to the construction of motherhood and offer stereotypical maternal scripts (Commuri *et al.* 2002; Johnston and Swanson 2003; Douglas and Michaels 2004; VOICE Group 2010).

Ideas about motherhood, and everyday mothering practices, are also played out through consumer goods themselves, through a sedimented consumer consciousness, and even through forms of consumer citizenship (Clarke 2004, 2007; Cook 1995; Chin 2001; Miller 2011). Early feminist scholars highlighted the implications of new domestic goods and technologies for domestic life (Cowan 1983; Myrdal and Klein 1956). More recent work by anthropologists (Clarke 2007), sociologists (Warde 1997), and consumer researchers (Banister and Hogg 2007) has documented how at least some women resist the 'encroachment' of the market in everyday life and the stereotypical maternal scripts offered by the marketplace, their social position and their relationships with others. This raises questions about how (or whether) commercial scripts relate to women's cultural understandings of motherhood and practices of care (Hochschild 2001, 2003).

What do mothers make?

Mothers have long been characterized as 'homemakers', but mothering also involves the making of identities and relationships as well as more tangible entities such as family meals.

At this point, there is a body of work exploring how women perform their mothering roles in the context of pervasive cultural prescriptions, their more immediate material and social relations, and their life course experiences and life stages (Martens 2010; Hogg *et al.* 2004; Layne 1999). Against this broader cultural discourse about motherhood, women create and develop their own particular maternal identities, experiences and relationships through everyday consumption practices and rituals. Previous research has explored, for example, how mothers create normalized and localized mothering cultures by adopting similar consumption orientations around children's birthday parties (Clarke 2007); how differential access to monetary resources shapes mothers' participation in consumerism (Pugh 2004; Vincent and Ball 2007); and how mothers and children negotiate around fashion (Boden *et al.* 2004). Taken together, such studies highlight the many different ways there are of 'doing' motherhood, and the necessity for women to choose their own path through the diverse, often conflicting, cultural scripts and social norms surrounding mothers and mothering.

Contemporary research on motherhoods, markets and consumption

Although motherhoods, markets and consumption have each been subjected to considerable research attention from many different disciplines, few books have considered the relationship between them, and fewer still have taken an interdisciplinary perspective. Building on our recent ESRC-funded seminar series *Motherhoods, Markets and Consumption*, this book brings together a range of studies, spanning many disciplines within the humanities and social sciences and drawing on a wide range of theoretical frameworks and qualitative research methods. These diverse chapters explore the role of markets and consumption in the making of mothers and, importantly, in the experience of mothers. Many of the following chapters are based on research undertaken with women in Western, developed markets, but some are based on research with women less closely related to mainstream (consumer) culture in those countries, such as low-income mothers in Britain and Northern Ireland, or Bosnian refugees living in Sweden. Other chapters explore discourses and representations of mothers and motherhood in films, advertising and popular culture, and we suggest that even if these discourses do not do justice to the great diversity of mothers' lives and relationships, they circulate constantly in contemporary consumer culture, shaping to some degree women's experiences of motherhood and mothering.

We see this book as making a distinctive contribution to knowledge in three respects. First, it draws on a wide range of disciplines in exploring the connections between motherhoods, markets and consumption in contemporary Western culture. In addition to marketing/ consumer researchers, contributors are drawn from disciplines including sociology, anthropology, ethnology, geography, political science, design, communication and cultural studies. Second, this book examines the making of mothers in two respects: how mothers are 'made' through representations of motherhood in historical narratives, cultural practices and marketing discourses in consumer culture, and how this relates to what mothers 'make' – the identities and relationships that they construct through their everyday consumption practices. Third, the chapters draw on a wide range of methodologies. In addition to in-depth individual interviews – in some cases longitudinal – and focus groups, our contributors have used diaries, visual discourse analysis, ethnographic studies, netnography and participant-driven photo elicitation. Individually and collectively, the contributions to this book offer many insights into how a wide range of qualitative methods give voice to mothers' experiences and enhance understanding of the relationship between motherhoods, markets and consumption.

Part I, *Motherhood as an Ideological, Mediated Project*, deals with cultural and market ideologies of motherhood. Myths endure around maternal archetypes that imply certain behaviours, norms and taboos (Thurer 1994; Forna 1998; Douglas and Michaels 2004), and social and cultural constructions about what constitutes a 'good mother' proliferate in the marketplace (Thompson 1996; Prothero 2002). Furthermore, significant markets have grown up around the ideology of the nuclear family and the central role of the mother in maintaining it. Contributors in this section consider maternal archetypes and stereotypes in culture, marketing discourse and consumer culture, showing how they are articulated not only in advertising and the media, but also through the goods bought and used by them as part of their motherhood projects.

The section commences with Elizabeth C. Hirschman's chapter on 'Motherhood in the movies'. Locating her discussion in the historical, social and cultural landscape, she firstly demonstrates how the concept of motherhood is a complex historical phenomenon, surrounded by taboos, superstitions and elemental, primal associations. Turning her attention to the twentieth and twenty-first centuries, she then offers a detailed deconstruction of motherhood in motion pictures. The movie genre has served as a cultural marker of motherhood, feminism, work and the home. Beginning with *Mrs Miniver* in 1942, Hirschman traces the impact of the Second World War on representations of motherhood, taking us through seven decades depicting motherhood in a series of classic Hollywood films. Her analysis culminates with *The Kids are Alright* in 2010, by which time concepts of motherhood, feminism, work and the home had changed beyond recognition, at least on the face of it. According to Hirschman, the new emphasis is on issues of self-fulfilment, often in the context of a non-traditional family unit. The self is a central issue in motherhood as an ideology, and it is a thread running throughout this section. Hirschman argues that the old archetypes of sacrificing Madonna and 'phallic mother' (Kaplan 1992) still persist, evidence of the power of ideologies and their cyclic, normative and pervasive nature in culture. The rise of consumer culture has also meant that economic imperatives and material culture have a significant effect on how one 'does' mothering, with gender inequality and the dilemmas facing working mothers very much to the fore. Contemporary motherhood is thus located in the troubling domain of love, work, relationships and self-determination, with gender inequalities in terms of work, childcare and the home continuing to frame the experience of motherhood in the twenty-first century.

In 'How to be a mother: expert advice and the material subject', Mary Jane Kehily continues to explore what it is to be a mother, the on-going construction or the material project of motherhood. Her focus is on the role of experts in helping expectant mothers 'do' motherhood. Expertise comes in many forms: advice literature, pregnancy magazines and childcare manuals; family, friends and other mothers; and medical experts such as doctors and midwives. All contribute to the body of knowledge gathered by acquisitive and inquisitive expectant mothers. Based on a study of 144 mothers in the UK, the chapter reveals the vast amount of expertise that has helped create conflicting, competing and often moral and pathological layers to the vast body of expertise available. Beginning with pregnancy and childcare manuals in the early twentieth century, it then turns an inward, psychological gaze on motherhood. Increasingly a democratic approach to wisdom, advice and expertise became evident, accelerated by the advent of the internet. The chapter analyses pregnancy magazines and their part in helping expectant mothers and new mothers adapt to their roles, as well as the vast array and various waves of books and childcare manuals available. The chapter ultimately argues that motherhood is a complex interplay between mediated knowledge, fashion, self-identity, social class, age, choice, taste and, above all, the 'common culture' of mothering that permeates contemporary culture. It also points to the key roles of coupledom, career and consumption in constructing motherhood, which act as key reference points for women that help them map out their 'motherhood projects'.

The question of how one 'does' mothering is also addressed by Alison J. Clarke in 'Designing mothers and the market: social class and material culture'. She discusses the specific role of modes of mothering in a hyper-consumptive context of objects, brands and goods. Drawing on contemporary models of motherhood in terms of taste, fashion and material practices, she explores how motherhood and its norms are shaped by social class as well as access to material goods. Aside from 'yummy mummy' and 'slummy mummy' stereotypes, the most popular amongst these various modes of motherhood is essentially the 'consumptive mother', defined according to her material acts. A new variant on the consumptive mother is the glamorous mother, a stereotype driven by consumption practices, consumer projects, expressive consumption and high fashion. The glamorous mother model transcends class, and is mediated and driven by popular culture forms, such as the gossip media and 'fabloids'. She also locates motherhood in the context of self-expression, a concept that has always sat uneasily with that of mother in most cultures, as Chodorow (1978) has noted. New ideals of 'achieved motherhood' including its pinnacle, reproductive technologies, are also discussed in this chapter, demonstrating how material practices intersect with normative mothering prerogatives. Drawing on consumption practices in Greece, India and the UK, Clarke argues that whatever it takes to be a good mother is being remade as new, mediated, material practices of mothering and motherhood evolve alongside older, persistent cultural ideologies of normative motherhood. Significantly, however, the on-going project of motherhood is now located within a consumer culture of marketing practices, consumption and fashion, what Clarke evocatively terms 'the cosmology of goods and taste knowledges'.

The final chapter in this section, 'Negotiations of motherhood – between ideals and practice', by Malene Gram and Helle D. Pedersen, explores the expectations and anxieties that ideals of motherhood may create. Focussing on Danish expectant mothers, the chapter illustrates how they negotiate the tensions arising from the conflicting choices and decisions they must make on the road to motherhood. Here again, rather than women striving to be perfectionist, the findings reveal more pragmatic approaches as women seek to see themselves as competent mothers. To some extent these Danish women contest many motherhood ideals, seeing themselves as responsible yet far from perfect mothers-to-be. In this respect they develop their own personal 'navigation maps' which enable them to compare themselves favourably to other pregnant women and to overcome many anxieties that marketplace ideals engender during this transitional period.

Part II, *Feeding Motherhood*, acknowledges the centrality of food to family health, identity and relationships (DeVault 1991). The contributions in this section offer insights into how mothers' food and feeding practices are outcomes of the intermediation between medical and marketing pedagogies, social and cultural norms, and the motherly responsibility towards the nurturing and maintenance of intimate familial relationships. In the research reported here, this intermediation is never 'easily' experienced, but conveys the range of contradictory priorities that are intrinsic to mothering in affluent contemporary societies. The discussion offered here throws light on these intermediations from different perspectives in that the first three chapters explore the standpoint of mothers, with the final chapter considering commercial constructions of mothers and mothering.

This section opens with a chapter by Julia Keenan and Helen Stapleton. '"It won't do her any harm" they said...' draws on their research with new mothers in England, who provided feeding narratives as their children moved from early babyhood into toddlerhood. The paper thus demonstrates an interesting longitudinal qualitative approach, that is particularly suited to this phase of the life-course, when young children and their perceived needs change so quickly, drawing mothers into a lifestyle where routines are hard to establish in the context of continuously changing demands. The paper illustrates how individual mothers' infant feeding decisions take place in a strong moralistic environment, that finds its origin in the medical-state-market interactional complex, and that confront new mothers when making decisions about feeding infants (e.g. Murphy 2000). The contemporary duality between 'breast is best' and 'bottle feeding' illustrates the contradictions confronting the motherly citizen-consumer subject, with imperatives for mothers to do 'what is best for their babies' and to give voice to the freedom of choice ideology that also pervades the neo-liberal subject. Keenan and Stapleton draft their analysis through the accounts of two new mothers, and in doing so include some of the photographic materials these mothers made during this stage of their lives. The photographic material pays witness to the contradictions these mothers grappled with and their associated emotional experiences.

The emotional qualities of mothers' food and feeding work also come through very strongly in the papers presented by Bente Halkier and Helene Brembeck, although they achieve this in different ways. Thus, in 'Contesting food – contesting motherhood?' Halkier examines the empirical materials from two recent projects that investigate different dimensions of contested food in Denmark through a practice theory lens (Halkier 2010). This essentially means a shift in focus from 'mothers as individuals' to 'mothering as a practice'. Halkier's research materials still come from individual women. However, their stories may be treated as discursive enactments of mothering, not only of mothers' own mothering practices, but also of those of other mothers. In this way, Halkier derives three dimensions of mothering: mothering as loving; mothering as protecting; and mothering as identifying. In all three dimensions, contestation is evident and Halkier discusses in what ways this makes it hard for mothers to practice 'good' mothering.

In 'Food, cooking and motherhood amongst Bosnian refugees in Sweden', Brembeck adopts an ethnological approach to illustrate the ways emotion, love, intimacy, loss and gains enter into food and feeding narrations. This chapter illustrates how the Bosnian food culture that is part of the mother's cultural and embodied heritage is located in relation to Swedish food culture. Brembeck shows how the mothers continue to cook in the Bosnian way, and find in their cooking practices a sense of purpose and solace that is strongly focused on their children's futures and embodies their sense of cultural and personal loss. The women's cooking activities, and their attempts to share this with their young children, are therefore not solely about sharing Bosnian cultural memories and heritage. These practices and purposes in turn are mediated by the preferences of the children, who become more outspoken as they grow older. In wielding their agency, the children convey a desire to eat more in the Swedish way, adopting also the more commercialized and convenience forms of eating that are common amongst young people in wealthier countries today. The paper finishes with an analysis of how the Bosnian mothers accept a hybridization or synchronization of these diverse food tastes, influences and priorities in an effort to maintain close and intimate familial connections.

Finally, in 'Images of motherhood: food advertising in *Good Housekeeping* Magazine 1950–2010', David Marshall, Margaret Hogg, Teresa Davis, Tanja Schneider and Alan Petersen trace how mothers are portrayed in food advertising in a popular British women's magazine. Using visual discourse analysis, they explore how advertisers link food to mothering, and to domesticity, over six decades. In the 1950s, for example, food ads tended to position mothers as nurturers located in the home. Later ads allowed them to leave the kitchen or the house, and even to play with their children, but still positioned mothers as responsible for meals and food. The theme of 'mother knows best' was evident in ads from the 1960s and 1970s, with advertising presented as fuelling their food expertise, while ads from the 1980s positioned mothers as guardians of their children's health. It is thus interesting to see that the enactments of mothering as protecting and loving move between commercial and personal terrains.

Just as there are many ways of doing motherhood at any one time, maternal practices, identities and relationships themselves involve many transitions (Bialschki and Michener 1994; Miller 2005; Hogg *et al.* 2004). In Part III, *Motherhood, Consumption and Transitions*, researchers explore the role of consumption for women entering different phases of their lives as mothers, such as pregnancy, early motherhood, changing employment status and the 'empty nest'. Chapter authors examine in particular the public and private performances of pregnancy, early motherhood, coping with career transitions and the empty nest phase when children are grown and leave home. Each chapter explores the role of consumption practices and marketplace interactions as women negotiate these transitions, absorbing them into their ongoing and idiosyncratic projects of the self (Giddens 1991; Smith 1994; Bailey 2000).

The section opens with Maurice Patterson and Lisa O'Malley's chapter, 'Bouncing back: reclaiming the body from pregnancy'. These authors examine how pregnant bodies become contested sites, witnessing the struggle between seduction and production (Price 1988), between ornamentation and function (Charles and Kerr 1986); and between sexuality and maternity (Stearns 1999). Using phenomenological-type interviews with ten mothers who had recently given birth, Patterson and O'Malley explore their sense of losing control of their bodies whilst pregnant; strategies for re-asserting control over their bodies during pregnancy and post-partum; and the excitement, once their babies were born, of getting their bodies back to themselves and thus 'bouncing back' to their earlier sense of self before they became pregnant (although not necessarily back to the same body shape, unlike 'yummy mummies' in the media). In conclusion, Patterson and O'Malley identify how women are now challenged to 'manage' their bodies in order to '(i) provide the optimal environment for their growing foetus; (ii) maintain an appropriate aesthetic throughout the pregnancy; and (iii) ensure that their bodies *bounce back* as quickly as possible' and thus how pregnant women and new mothers face two distinct and sometimes mutually exclusive ideologies.

In 'Managing pregnancy work: consumption, emotion and embeddedness', Caroline J. Gatrell identifies a disparity between the view of pregnancy as a project for mothers to manage (Brewis and Warren 2001) and the cultural narratives which present the work of mothering as natural (Miller 2005). From here, Gatrell argues that expectant mothers' consumption of health advice, along with the management of their pregnant bodies, is a form of maternal body work. Gatrell draws particularly on the third dimension of Glucksmann's *Total Social Organization of Labour* (TSOL) concept (1995, 2005), namely the *articulation of work activities* to demonstrate the relationship between pregnancy work and the maternal consumption of health advice. *Articulation of work activities* involves a three-part framework linked to consumption work, emotion work and embeddedness – and these provide the basis for Gatrell's six-year netnographic study of women's experiences of pregnancy and maternity. Gatrell concludes by arguing that pregnancy work should be seen as more than natural and instinctive, and as involving 'unrecorded body work'.

Tina Miller's chapter, 'Engaging with the maternal: tentative mothering acts and the props of performance' discusses how performing the new identity of a first time, embodied mother is complex, challenging and problematic. She argues that Goffman's (1969) concept of impression management offers a valuable lens for examining the transition to first-time motherhood. Her chapter draws on a qualitative, longitudinal study with UK mothers which explored women's expectations, birth, mothering experiences, information-seeking, perceptions of self and others, and work intentions via pre- and post-birth interviews. By focusing on transitions to first-time motherhood, Miller examines both these women's personal identity projects and the public manifestations employed via consumption, most notably the acquisition of the appropriate props of mothering such as the right pram, cot, or changing bag, as well as 'consuming' the normative discourses around appropriate behaviours, such as attending ante-natal appointments; watching their diet, dress and behaviours; and engaging with baby books and expert information.

In 'Whose work is it anyway? The shifting dynamics of "doing mothering"', Benedetta Cappellini and Elizabeth Parsons draw on feminist theorizations of doing gender to analyse changes over time in one mother's household. This single longitudinal case study documents how Tracey has managed her career transitions during a three-year period to reflect her ideas of 'good mothering' and to maintain control of the task management in the household. Using concepts of 'accountability' and 'entitlement', Cappellini and Parsons explore how these changes have impacted on the division of task performances in the home, as well as on the mothering identity. Their findings demonstrate how it is often painful for Tracey to juggle between work and family commitments as she tries to pursue her career, yet balance this with her own and others' expectations of her as a mother. Overall the study reveals the many power struggles continually in operation between family members and the shifting dynamics of 'doing mothering' that take place in response to mothering transitions.

In 'Transitioning into the empty nest: the experiences of mothers as they enter a new life stage', Carolyn F. Curasi, Pauline Maclaran and Margaret Hogg take the empty-nest stage of family life as the empirical context for examining women's experience of changes in their mothering selves over time. This chapter tells women's stories drawn from a mixed-method qualitative study combining in-depth face-to-face interviews with 22 women whose children had recently left home, follow-up interviews with ten of these original informants, and participant observation on online bulletin boards over a year. Focusing on mothers' emotional labour in managing the re-negotiation of family relationships, Curasi, Maclaran and Hogg employ Worden's (1991) four tasks of grief and mourning (accepting the reality of the loss; working through the pain of grief and dealing with the resulting feelings; adjusting to the environment in which the departed is missing; and emotionally relocating the departed and moving on) to show how mothers' consumption practices in this transition might be interpreted.

The final part of the book, *Consumption and Contested Motherhood Identities,* explores some of the struggles involved in becoming, or being seen to be, a 'real' or 'good' mother in difficult – and perhaps less difficult – circumstances, and how material culture and consumption practices are drawn into those struggles.

In 'Mothering, poverty and consumption', Lisa Glass, Kathy Hamilton, and Katherine Trebeck explore the experiences of mothers living in poverty who seek to provide for their children materially and emotionally. Drawing on individual interviews in Northern Ireland and focus groups in Scotland, these authors highlight the challenges of engaging with a problematic labour market and a consumer culture which marginalizes both mothers and their children who can ill afford to participate in it. Glass, Hamilton and Trebeck describe not only how mothers living in poverty sought to stretch their limited resources, but also how they engaged in self-sacrifice to provide material goods for their children and how some of their purchases were designed to mask their poverty, both within and beyond the family. One important difference between the two studies reported here concerns the extent of community support experienced by low income mothers, and the chapter concludes by drawing policy-makers' attention to the importance of living wages and working hours that create space for family and community engagement.

The following three chapters focus on mothers whose economic situation is much more privileged than those who spoke to Glass, Hamilton and Trebeck, but still found aspects of their mothering identities contested. Amy E. Traver's chapter, 'On markets and motherhood: the case of American mothers of children adopted from China', explores how the mothers she interviewed navigate apparent tensions between markets, care and kinship in constructing their identity as mothers. Drawing on interviews with women at different stages of the adoption process, she explores how they used the logic and language of the market to recount their decision to adopt from China, and how, after adoption, they consumed Chinese cultural objects to normalize the bonds of adoptive and multi-ethnic/multi-racial kinship. In this way, Traver argues, 'discourses and practices of care and consumption are both informed by and reliant on each other'.

Linda Layne's chapter, 'Spectacular pregnancy loss – the public private lives of the Santorums and Duggars at the intersection of politics, religion and tabloid culture', examines the case of two highly privileged American women who have been criticized in the media for their 'excessive' mothering. In addition to marrying high-profile, right-wing, anti-abortion politicians, Karen Santorum and Michelle Duggar each have large families; Santorum has 8 and Duggar has 19 children, compared with the 2011 US family average of 2.06. In this chapter, Layne focuses on the media storm surrounding the ways in which they (and their husbands) mourned their second-trimester pregnancy losses. Drawing on Freud's notion of the 'uncanny' and a wealth of newspaper articles, TV shows, blogs and online discussions, she highlights the unease and even disgust aroused by their response to loss. Although both families engaged in practices – such as holding, photographing and spending time with their dead babies – recommended by health professionals, Layne suggests that the public (or publicity-courting) way in which they mourned created public aversion rather than a 'teachable moment' for others encountering such tragic loss.

In the book's final chapter, 'Pregnancy, privacy and personhood in the consumer socialization of expectant mothers', The VOICE Group highlights the pervasiveness of contested motherhood identities. Drawing on interviews with 'ordinary' middle-class expectant mothers in Britain, Ireland, Denmark and America, these authors argue that identity struggles and anxieties about being a 'good' or 'proper' mother are part of women's socialization into motherhood. Thus, although participants in this study acknowledged their relatively privileged economic and social position, and their pleasure in anticipating the birth of their babies, they also identified, and struggled with, wider social and cultural discourses around expectant mothers as sacrificing privacy and as one-dimensional, lesser beings whose autonomy and sense of personal style diminished as their pregnancy progressed.

References

Bailey, L. (2000) 'Bridging home and work in the transition to motherhood: a discursive study', *European Journal of Women's Studies*, 7, 153-70.

Banister E. and Hogg, M. (2007) 'Getting the body back (or not): exploring women's expectations of their body before, during and after birth', *Birth: The Cultural Politics of Reproduction,* Institute for Advanced Studies Workshop (Lancaster University), March.

Bialschki, B. and Michener, S. (1994) 'Re-entering leisure: transition within the role of motherhood', *Journal of Leisure Research*, 26, 57–74.

Boden, S., Pole, P., Pilcher, J. and Edwards, T. (2004) 'New consumers? The social and cultural significance of children's fashion consumption', *Cultures of Consumption Working Paper Series*, 16, 1–26.

Brewis, J. and Warren, S. (2001) 'Pregnancy as project: organising reproduction', *Administrative Theory and Praxis*, 23, 383–406.

Charles, N. and Kerr, M. (1986) 'Food for feminist thought', *The Sociological Review*, 34, 537–72.

Clarke, A. (2004) 'Maternity and materiality: becoming a mother in consumer culture', in J. Taylor, L. Layne and D. Wozniak (eds) *Consuming Motherhood*, New Brunswick: Rutgers University Press, 55–71.

Clarke, A. (2007) 'Making sameness: mothering, commerce and the culture of children's birthday parties', in E. Casey and L. Martens (eds) *Gender and Consumption: Domestic Culture and the Commercialisation of Everyday Life,* Hampshire: Ashgate, 79–96.

Chin, E. (2001) *Purchasing Power: Black Kids and American Consumer Culture*, Minneapolis: University of Minnesota Press.

Chodorow, N. J. (1978/1999) *The Reproduction of Mothering: Psychoanalysis and the Sociology of Gender*, LA and London: University of California Press.

Commuri, S., Ekici, A. and Kennedy, P. (2002) 'Historical review of advertising targeting mothers: content analysis under sociological imagination of ads in 1920s, 1950s, and 1980s', in S. Broniarczyk and K. Nakamoto (eds), *Advances in Consumer Research* 29, Valdosta, GA: Association for Consumer Research,114–23.

Cook, D.T. (1995) 'The mother as consumer – insights from the children wear industry, 1917–1929', *Sociological Quarterly,* 36:3, 505–22.

Cowan (1983) *More Work for Mother: the Ironies of Household Technology from the Open Hearth to the Microwave*, New York: Basic Books.

DeVault, M. (1991) *Feeding the Family: the Social Organization of Caring as Gendered Work*, Chicago: Chicago University Press.

Douglas, S. and Michaels, M. (2004) *The Mommy Myth: the Idealization of Motherhood and How It Has Undermined All Women*, New York: The Free Press.

Forna, A. (1998) *Mother of All Myths: How Society Molds and Constrains Mothers*, London: HarperCollins Publishers.

Friedan, B (1963) *The Feminine Mystique*, New York: WW. Norton & Co.

Giddens, A. (1991) *Modernity and Self-identity: Self and Society in the Late Modern Age*, Cambridge: Polity Press.

Glucksmann, M. (1995) 'Why "work"? Gender and the "total social organization of labour"', *Gender, Work and Organization,* 63–75.

Glucksmann, M. (2005) 'Shifting boundaries and interconnections: extending the "total social organisation of labour"', *Sociological Review,* 53 (Supplement), 19–36.

Goffman, E. (1969) *The Presentation of Self in Everyday Life,* Harmondsworth: Penguin.

Halkier, B. (2010) *Consumption Challenge: Food in Medialised Everyday Lives,* Farnham: Ashgate Publishing Ltd.

Hochschild, A. (2001) *The Time Bind: when Work Becomes Home and Home Becomes Work,* New York: Holt Paperbacks.

Hochschild, A. (2003) *The Second Shift,* New York: Penguin Books.

Hogg, M., Curasi, C.F. and Maclaran, P. (2004) 'The (re-) configuration of production and consumption in empty nest households/families', *Consumption, Markets and Culture,* 7:3, 329–50.

Johnston, D. and Swanson, D. (2003) 'Invisible mothers: a content analysis of motherhood ideologies and myths in magazines', *Sex Roles,* 49:1–2, 21–33.

Kaplan, E.A. (1992) *Motherhood and Representation: the Mother in Popular Culture and Melodrama,* London: Routledge.

Layne, L. (1999) *Transformative Motherhood: on Giving and Getting in a Consumer Culture,* New York: New York University Press.

Martens, L. (2010) 'The cute, the spectacle and the practical: narratives of new parents and babies at The Baby Show', in D. Buckingham and V. Tingstad (eds) *Childhood and Consumer Culture,* Basingstoke: Palgrave MacMillan, 146–60.

Metzl, M.N. (2003) 'From sociology to psychoanalysis: the works of Nancy J. Chodorow', *Psychoanalysis,* Division 39, American Psychological Association, Winter, 55–60.

Miller, D. (2011) 'Getting THINGS right: motherhood and material culture', *Studies in the Maternal,* 3:2, www.mamsie.bbk.ac.uk. Accessed February 25, 2013.

Miller, T. (2005) *Making Sense of Motherhood: a Narrative Approach,* Cambridge: Cambridge University Press.

Murphy, E. (2000) 'Risk, responsibility, and rhetoric in infant feeding', *Journal of Contemporary Ethnography,* 29(3): 291–325.

Myrdal, A. and Klein, V. (1956) *Women's Two Roles: Home and Work,* London: Routledge & Kegan Paul Ltd.

Oakley, A. (1992) *Social Support and Motherhood,* Oxford: Blackwell.

Price J. (1988) *Motherhood: What It Does to Your Mind,* London: Pandora.

Prothero, A. (2002) 'Consuming motherhood: an introspective journey on consuming to be a good mother', *Gender and Consumption: ACR Gender Conference,* Dublin, June.

Pugh, A. (2004) 'Windfall child rearing: low-income care and consumption', *Journal of Consumer Culture,* 4:2, 229–49.

Shin, K. (2012) *Please Look After Mom,* London: Vintage.

Smith, J. (1994) 'Reconstructing selves: an analysis of discrepancies between women's contemporaneous and retrospective accounts of the transition to motherhood', *British Journal of Psychology,* 85:3, 371–93.

Stearns, C. (1999) 'Breastfeeding and the good maternal body', *Gender and Society,* 13:3, 308–25.

Thompson, C. (1996) 'Caring consumers: gendered consumption meanings and the juggling lifestyle', *Journal of Consumer Research,* 22:4, 388–407.

Thurer, S.L. (1994) *Myths of Motherhood: How Culture Reinvents the Good Mother,* New York: Houghton Mifflin Company.

Vincent, C. and Ball, S. (2007) '"Making up" the middle-class child: families, activities and class dispositions', *Sociology,* 41:6, 1061–77.

VOICE Group (2010) 'Motherhood, marketization and consumer vulnerability', *Journal of Macromarketing,* 30:4, 384–97.

Warde, A. (1997) *Consumption, Food and Taste: Culinary Antinomies and Commodity Culture*, London: Sage.

Worden, J.W. (1991) *Grief Counselling and Grief Therapy: A Handbook For the Mental Health Practitioner*, 2nd edn. London: Routledge.

Part I

Motherhood as an ideological, mediated project

2 Motherhood in the movies – 1942 to 2010

Social class mobility and economic power

Elizabeth C. Hirschman

Images of motherhood have been present in human culture since at least the Aurignacian culture of 36,000 – 30,000 BCE. The carved statuette of the Venus of Willendorf (Figure 2.1) depicts a typical fecund female figure dating from 20,000 – 24,000 BCE whose swollen breasts and enlarged pelvis suggest she will shortly give birth (Whitcombe 2003).

At the time this image was made, human female fecundity was crucial to the survival of the species (Prat *et al.* 2011). And yet, apart from their role in continuing the species, we know little about the women represented by this figurine. The pre-historical record of the social meanings and statuses associated with their role as mothers remains inaccessible to our modern minds. The myths and folktales which have come forward in time tell of motherhood as a complex cultural phenomenon – surrounded by taboos, superstitions, and ancient associations not only with life and fecundity, but also death and barrenness (c.f. Von Franz 1993). In Jungian terms, child-bearing women symbolized the oppositional concepts of the Good Mother, full of nurturance, love and protection and the Bad Mother, destructive, vindictive and violent (Jung 1968). While these motifs are easily recognized in present-day depictions, they no longer tell the full story of motherhood in Western cultures.

Successive waves of feminism in the United States from the early 1900s to the millennium have led to women moving increasingly from the domestic sphere to the public realm of corporations, the military, elected office and the judiciary (Freedman 2003). Indeed during the recent economic recession (2008 – 2012) more women than men were employed in the US for the first time in that country's history (US Bureau of the Census 2011). The majority of these women are also *mothers* (US Bureau of the Census 2011) which means that their traditional roles as child-bearers and child caretakers are now supplemented by their responsibilities as wage earners, soldiers, office-holders, and judges. This transition has come about over a grinding, bumpy and occasionally brutal revision of the traditional women-in-the-home/men-in-the-world cultural structure that preceded it (Freedman 2003).

My purpose is to examine the representation of this societal evolution of motherhood in motion pictures from the outset of World War II to the present day. Nine films – noted for their commercial success and critical acclaim – are

Figure 2.1 Venus of Willendorf; image by Matthias Kabel (Own work) [CC-BY-2.5 (http://
creativecommons.org/licenses/by/2.5)], via Wikimedia Commons

examined as narrative cultural 'markers' over this time period. As I shall show, each film can be viewed as depicting the cultural struggle over the responsibilities of motherhood and the increasingly ardent desires of women to construct identities for themselves beyond the realm of home and childrearing.

The series of films begins at the outset of World War II, works through the conformity of the 1950s, to the civil rights eras of the 1960s and onward to the large scale entry of women into the professional workforce of the 1980s and 1990s. As will be documented, the films exhibit the shifting values of and social attitudes towards motherhood. By the 2000s the nature of the family, itself, became re-cast as gay men and lesbian women formed marriages and raised children, and the final film in the set, *The Kids are All Right* (2010), explores the challenges, both personal and familial, of this issue. The nine films covered by the analysis include *Mrs. Miniver* (1942), *Mildred Pierce* (1945), *Imitation of Life* (1959), *Mary Poppins* (1964), *Kramer vs. Kramer* (1979), *Mommie Dearest* (1981), *Terms of Endearment* (1983), *The Joy Luck Club* (1989) and *The Kids are All Right* (2010).

Begin the beguine

Mrs. Miniver (1942)

This film is an excellent initial grounding point for our discussion, as it provides an ideological snapshot of mothers' roles in Western cultures at the outset of World War II. The Second World War brought into sharp focus the moral structure of the 'democratic West' versus the tyrannical governments set in opposition. Motherhood – long a foundation of moral beliefs (Neumann 1963) – can serve as a desirable vantage point to view the 'good' versus 'evil' moral dichotomy. *Mrs. Miniver* was a commercial and critical success, winning six Academy Awards, including Best Picture and Best Actress. Starring Greer Garson and Walter Pidgeon, the narrative presents a highly-idealized vision of Wartime Britain and of the desired traits exhibited by its families, especially the mother.

Mrs. Miniver (Greer Garson) is presented as a pretty, proper, middle class housewife and mother of four children: two boys and two girls (note here her high fertility level and the perfect gender balance). She dresses attractively and appreciates roses (a national symbol of England). Her husband (Walter Pidgeon) is handsome, affectionate and successful enough to provide a well-appointed house and maid for his wife and family. The prevailing social norms represented include having a female (young unmarried) maid, cigar smoking by the husband (but no tobacco use by the wife), separate beds for the parents (indicating that sex is infrequent), and upwardly mobile consumption patterns (use of a silver tea service and white linen table cloth with fresh flowers). The household is acquisitive, with the husband purchasing a new car and the wife a new hat. This, in short, is the English ideal of family life. Before proceeding to the story-line, the reader should note two small, but telling, details.

First, the household includes a subservient (unmarried and childless) female who performs the less-desirable cleaning, cooking and maintenance labor of the household. Mrs. Miniver, the wife and mother, by virtue of marrying well, has advanced upward socially and now has leisure time to shop and consume. Second, consider the greatly discrepant purchasing patterns of the husband and wife. The husband – as the sole income producer – is entitled to purchase a car, while the wife, who produces no income, feels free to purchase a hat. We thus deduce a widespread – but usually unvoiced – principle in marriages, the person(s) who earn money are entitled to spend it; those who do not earn money must make do with whatever the dominant partner permits. This central principle will carry through the entire set of films and become critically important as mothers enter the public domain. As the narrative unfolds, we learn that the Miniver's college-aged son has a pretty, well-bred girlfriend, and the entire family attends Anglican Church services on Sunday. Midway through one sermon, the minister announces 'Britain is now at war', as air raid sirens blare. The son promptly enlists in the Royal Air Force.

Over the course of the film, Mrs. Miniver engages in the following behaviours typifying the 'ideal' English woman during wartime: first, she deals with a German paratrooper who has invaded her home by giving him food and then getting his gun (when he faints from injuries). She turns him over to the police, saying, 'You will be safe with the police; war is not forever'. She comforts her husband when he returns from participating in a rescue flotilla. She helps arrange the marriage of the eldest son to his girlfriend (who comes from an aristocratic family). She comforts her children and makes tea for her husband as they spend the night in an air raid shelter.

What we can distill from this pattern of behaviour is that the wife and mother of the time period was positioned firmly in the home, where her duties included caring for her children and husband, attending to aesthetic and social arrangements, including the next generation's upward mobility, instilling values of religious observance, moral integrity, compassion, and courage. She notably does not engage in manual labor, does not engage in combat, and relies on 'male authorities', e.g., police, army, doctors, to tend to any challenges outside her range of responsibilities. In essence, she serves as the domestic moral and social anchor for the family. The family members, themselves, are also shown to be performing their roles in a perfect and idealized manner and the services of unmarried females are required to obtain the desired level of leisure and comfort. The husband, as income producer, has dominant control of familial expenditures. Let us now take a look at a film which examines what happens when one or more of the familial ensemble fail in their responsibilities.

Mildred Pierce (1945)

Starring Joan Crawford (who won the Best Actress award) and nominated for five other Academy Awards, *Mildred Pierce* was a commercial and critical success. But for our purpose, it documents what happens to motherhood in the wake of divorce from a weak, unfaithful husband during the 1940s. Mildred Pierce (Joan Crawford) was 'married at 17' and 'felt like I'd been born in a kitchen'. She and her lower middle class husband, Burt, have two daughters, Veda and Kate. Mildred does all of the household labor including cooking, cleaning and washing; she additionally bakes and sells cakes and pies to earn money to give her children 'better things', such as pretty dresses and piano lessons. Early in the narrative, she learns her husband is having an affair and divorces him.

To support herself and the children, Mildred transfers her domestic skills to the public sector, opening up a seaside restaurant, 'Mildred's', that features her cooking. (As an aside here, it is significant to note that she uses her given name to label the restaurant, as her last name, Pierce, 'belongs' to her husband – again, this is a widely known, but rarely voiced indication of the identity lost by woman upon marrying). The restaurant becomes very successful; Mildred is hard-working and becomes skillful at managing both money and employees. However, she submerges her own needs and sexuality until meeting a handsome, wealthy, upper class man, Monty. They begin an affair. Unfortunately, he too mistreats her by 'borrowing' large sums of money and ultimately, by having an affair with her spoiled, vain, beautiful daughter Veda.

Notably, over the course of the narrative, Mildred's initial feminine/domestic persona becomes increasingly infused with masculine traits. She makes large-scale financial and managerial decisions, takes up cigarette smoking and dresses in suits and fur coats with massive shoulder pads – in short, she becomes *androgynous*. Yet she still places her children's welfare ahead of her own. Veda, always narcissistic and selfish, is disgusted by her mother's working status. Tricking a boy's parents into thinking their son got her pregnant, she gets a $10,000 sum and tells her mother, 'with this money I can get away from you. You smell of grease. You will never be anything but a common frump'. In voicing this attitude, Veda reveals the same essential standard employed in *Mrs. Miniver*, i.e., respectable women do not work outside the home and in particular, they do not do manual labor outside the home.

Ultimately, Veda and Monty drain Mildred of both her money and her happiness. The two of them (representing the anti-husband and the anti-daughter) suck her dry by manipulating her inability to deviate from role expectations regarding the self-sacrificing wife and mother. When we compare this narrative with that of Mrs. Miniver, described previously, we see the precarious nature of the husband-wife-child family ideological structure then prevailing. If anyone (and in this case, two) of the persons filling the familial roles fails to fulfil his/her responsibilities, the complete structure collapses.

Imitation of Life (1959)

With this film, we arrive at a cultural turning point in the United States. By the end of the 1950s, nascent glimmers of feminism were emerging (see Friedan 1963). Concurrently, Jim Crow (Hirschman 2012) laws restricting the rights of Blacks (then termed Negroes) were beginning to weaken, however slightly, throughout the South. *Imitation of Life* examines the dissolution of these gender and racial restrictions with probably as much 'liberalism' as was commercially possible for the time period. The film features two young widows, one white, one black (Lana Turner, Juanita Moore) and their daughters (Sandra Dee, Susan Kohner) who meet by chance at a Coney Island beach in 1947. The black mother and daughter are newly homeless due to financial problems, and the white mother and daughter invite them to share their small apartment in New York (this, in and of itself, would have been highly unlikely during the time period, as housing was very segregated – as were the beaches – so it is improbable that the two single mothers would have ever met).

As the story develops, we learn that Sara Jane, the daughter of Addie, the black mother, desires to 'pass' as white. She can do this successfully, as she is light-skinned with European features and hair. Addie is hurt by Sara Jane's rejection of their heritage. Lora (Lana Turner) and her daughter, Susie, both blonde, express no racial prejudice. However, as time goes by and Lora's career as a Broadway actress becomes very successful, Addie's role evolves into one of caretaker/maid/nanny for the two children. Essentially she becomes the 'stay-at-home' mom, who cooks, cleans and provides emotional support, while Lora earns a living. This, of course, places Lora in the traditional 'husband' role and provides her with the unspoken right to dominance in the family structure and expenditure choices. The inequality of their statuses becomes clear in the narrative through the gradual shift in terms of address: Addie calls Lora 'Miss Lora', while Lora calls her simply 'Addie'.

Lora's demanding stage career leaves her little time to nurture Susie, which creates stress throughout the narrative. The story provides her with the opportunity to wed a handsome and successful advertising executive, which would permit her to re-assume her wifely and motherly roles in an affluent setting (thus fulfilling the vision of the traditional middle class housewife/mother), at the cost, of course, of her career outside the home. Very significantly, she refuses this – choosing instead to pursue her out-of-home career as an excellent actress. As she gazes at the Manhattan skyline after a triumphant performance, she declares, 'I feel so complete and happy'. Thus, her motivation to pursue a career is not premised on 'providing nice things for my children' as in *Mildred Pierce*, nor simply to be a celebrity, but rather to fulfil her own creativity and personhood. This depiction of her motivation is, in and of itself, a very revolutionary notion for the time period.

Addie's career (she is playing the 'wife' role in the family) is shown to advance by the hiring of several more household servants (always 'persons of color') whom she oversees. Thus, both racial lines (she does not supervise white workers) and traditional middle-class values are preserved in her portrayal. The narrative also presents a cautionary tale for those who may be tempted to stray from the racial status order of white above black. Sara Jane, her now-grown daughter, has embarked on a demeaning career as a 'white' stripper and chorus girl, rejecting a possible marriage with an eligible young black man. The moral of the story here seems to be that if one tries to belie one's race and 'place', one ends up debased. Lora, while enjoying genuine creative success is also made to pay a price. She 'loses' her daughter, Susie, who tells her, 'you were never here for me; Addie is my real mother'. To which Lora retorts, 'I gave you a beautiful house, clothes, and a horse'. But Susie trumps her by declaring, 'You didn't give me yourself...'.

This, of course, raises the key conundrum of motherhood in modernity and post-modernity. Do mothers 'owe' their life's ambitions, efforts and self-identity to their children or should they be free (as most fathers are) to pursue their identities out-of-the home and beyond their children? Striking a comfortable balance between self-development and the development of one's children continues to be an illusive objective for many women.

Mary Poppins (1965)

In *Mary Poppins*, Julie Andrews plays the title character, a magical nanny who descends from the sky (literally heaven-sent) to assist a middle class English household during the 1910s. The time period is one of British capitalistic and imperialistic expansion, Victorian sexual mores, and the Suffragette movement, which sought to give women the vote. Thus, it is a time of emphasis on upward mobility – deepening the class separations already present in English society – and also one in which 'well-bred' women sought more than a life of domestic duty.

Ironically, they were enabled to pursue these out-of-home political and cultural activities by the presence of a household staff of servant women who were drawn from the classes who were not so fortunate.

The household that Mary Poppins enters represents just this structure. Mr Banks is in middle management at a prominent bank, the well-dressed Mrs Banks spends her time shopping and marching in Suffragette rallies, and their two children, a boy and a girl, are looked after by a series of stringent nannies against whom they rebel. Mary's physical appearance is worth comment. Though young, pretty and well-spoken, she wears 'frumpy/unrevealing' attire, indicating clearly her asexual status. She is nurturing, intelligent, and caring; she teaches the children imaginative games, takes them on outings to the park and introduces them to a working class chimney sweep, Burt, who represents the fun-loving nature of the lower classes − the middle class and above being much too consumed with formality and decorum to play, sing, or frolic about.

A crisis occurs when Mr. Banks takes the children (at Mary's suggestion) to work one day and the bank president tries to take away the boy's two-pence pieces (to invest for him). A struggle ensues and Mr. Banks is fired. However, upon returning home, Mr. Banks discovers he is happy to be rid of the strict regimentation of his existence; Mary's presence has helped him grasp the happiness of life.

Remarkable also is the simultaneous transformation of both the bank president and Mrs. Banks, who similarly realize that life should be fun. At the conclusion to the narrative, Mr. and Mrs. Banks take their children kite-flying in the park, Mary Poppins returns to the sky and Mr. Banks is re-hired as a full partner in the company. Notably, the financial status of the family has actually been improved (supporting the notion that having money is good), the mother has abandoned her suffragette folly, and the children now have the attentions of both their parents. On a class-based level, what the film seems to be doing is taking the best aspects of the working class and the middle class and 'gluing' them together in a 'best of both worlds' scenario (this is, of course, a fantasy film…).

Kramer vs. Kramer (1979)

After the historical idealism of *Mary Poppins*, the film *Kramer vs. Kramer* is a sharp return to the modern world. Set in New York City, it features two parents, Ted and Joanna, with a young son who live in a middle class urban apartment. Ted works at a very fast-paced and demanding job in advertising. He is completely committed to his job, frequently coming home late and then calling the office as soon as he does arrive home. His wife is left to attend to all the household duties of childcare, paying the bills, food shopping, cleaning, etc. Ted pays little attention to her or to their son, Billy.

One evening, Ted returns home (late) and finds Joanna packing her suitcases. She walks out the door, leaving him with Billy. Disbelieving, Ted expects her to return home and resume her household chores. Days pass and Joanna remains away. Ted finds himself unable to care for his son or for the apartment. Soon his boss is threatening him that he must be available '24/7' or lose his job. Ted flounders, flailing and failing at both sets of responsibilities, although ultimately deciding that caring for his son is of primary importance. He is fired. Desperate to find work to support himself and Billy, Ted takes a job on Christmas Eve at another advertising agency at a reduced salary.

After a 15 month's absence in California, Joanna returns. She now has a good career as a designer and wants Billy back. Ted – having now matured into a caring and capable parent – refuses to give up Billy. They go to court to determine custody of their son. At the custody hearing, Joanna testifies that she wanted to work when she married Ted, but he refused to permit her, wanting to be the family 'breadwinner'. Ted became consumed by his job, while Joanna withered into depression as a housewife: 'I was incapable of functioning in my own home; I could not take care of Billy. I had no identity, no self-esteem.' Ted acknowledges in the hearing that he was not a good parent or husband, but states that he now loves Billy deeply and is the best parent to care for him. The fact that Ted lost his job is used against him, as is the fact that Joanna now *earns more* than does Ted (he is therefore a failure as the male provider). The court awards custody to Joanna and orders Ted to pay child support.

On the appointed day, Ted has Billy packed and ready to go live with Joanna, telling him he will visit often. Joanna calls Ted down to the lobby and tells him she realizes that Billy is 'already home' with Ted; she will give Ted custody. What are we to make of this story? First, the narrative suggests that by leaving her child alone with an 'unfit' father in order to construct her own identity, Joanna has committed a damning act in terms of her own fitness for motherhood. Even though the court sided with 'the mother' (as they almost always did in the 1970s), she evidenced *to herself* a desire to place her own welfare above that of her child. She *left home*. Ted, by way of contrast, was a distant, ignorant and narcissistic parent, but – over the time Joanna was away – he *came home* and devoted the best part of himself to his child. At this point the narrative proposes, he is the fitter parent. An underlying condemnation, of course, is directed toward those women who choose to give themselves primarily to careers and self-development, e.g., just as with Lora in *Imitation of Life*. Likely flowing from our species' earliest images of motherhood, the mother is deemed to always owe her primary allegiance to her children and not to herself.

Mommie Dearest (1981)

As we turn now to the next film, we encounter perhaps the ultimate negative exemplar of a mother–child relationship: the child-as-career-accessory. *Mommie Dearest* features Faye Dunaway as Joan Crawford in an autobiographical narrative written by her adopted daughter, Christina Crawford. The autobiography, itself, was a bestseller due to its revelations that Joan Crawford (by then deceased) was abusive to her two adopted children, Christina and Christopher. Crawford was a Hollywood 'star' of great magnitude, ironically earning an Academy Award for her portrayal of self-sacrificing Mildred Pearce in the 1945 film. Divorced twice and having no children, Crawford adopted a daughter, Christina and then a son (Christopher) in the 1940s. This was highly unusual for the time period. Single women typically were not able to adopt children, because adoption agencies believed a traditional (i.e., husband-wife) home was the only suitable environment in which to raise a child. Likely because of her great fame, wealth and 'connections', Crawford was able to circumvent these regulations.

The film – and book – both depict her as a markedly ambitious, self-abusive, competitive career woman who demanded absolute cleanliness and perfection in her household and body, had an immense wardrobe, and functioned in a controlled and controlling manner. This stands in sharp contrast to the portrayal of Lora in *Imitation of Life*, who was depicted as creating a self-identity through her career as an actress. Crawford, conversely, is represented as an exemplar of the 'evil queen' archetype, ultimately self-destructive and destructive to her children.

The narrative suggests that her original motivation for adopting the children was genuine maternal longing. But quickly these feelings of motherhood seemed to be corrupted into using the children as 'props' to generate positive publicity to advance her career and to create a public facade of glamour and maternal perfection. Crawford dressed herself and Christina in the same clothes for birthday parties and insisted that gifts the child received be (publicly) re-distributed to charities. Their public life was essentially a movie set, whereas in private the children were beaten, humiliated, and punished for virtually any infraction of Crawford's 'rules'. A female nanny and service staff were assigned to keep both the children and the house in perfect form at all times – an indicator of Crawford's upper-class economic status. Christina, in particular, seemed to be singled out by her mother for abuse and humiliation centered upon her physical appearance, lack of athletic ability and perceived competition for Crawford's boyfriends' attentions.

In some aspects, *Mommie Dearest* resembles the classic Snow White fairy tale, complete with a virginal princess and evil, narcissistic stepmother (Birkhauser-Oeri 1988), yet it is more nuanced than the folk tale. As she ages, Crawford's essential inability/unwillingness to be 'motherly' is narratively tied to her physical and mental disintegration. She smokes heavily, becomes alcoholic, and alternately spends and hoards money. The film suggests that there is a linkage between destructive careerism and maternal deficiency; that is, one cannot be a good mother and famous celebrity simultaneously.

Terms of Endearment (1983)

This film won Best Picture, Best Actress (Shirley MacLaine), Best Supporting Actor (Jack Nicholson), Best Director and Best Screenplay, in addition to being the top grossing film of the year. Obviously, its narrative did something right. What 'worked', both with critics and audiences, is that motherhood was (finally) treated in a relatively realistic fashion, without idealization or demonization. The story featured no heroes or villains, no tragedies or triumphs, no epiphanies. In other words, it was pretty much like 'real life'. The story opens with a recently widowed mother and her young daughter. The mother is overly protective of the daughter, because she is 'all I have left'.

The daughter becomes a young woman, somewhat tomboyish, and marries a good-looking, but profoundly unambitious, young man who is embarked on a lacklustre career as an English professor. Her mother warns her against marrying him saying, 'If you marry him, you will be embarking on a life of mediocrity and regret, and you are not a strong enough person to find your way out of it.' Clearly, this is a classically middle-class ideological statement by the mother; one which neatly encapsulates the notion that it is the daughter's responsibility to 'marry well' (i.e., upward), and the husband's responsibility to earn a respectable living (preferably very respectable).

This damning prediction turns out to be accurate, because although Flap (the boy) and Emma (the girl) love each other and have great sex and are fertile (three children in five years), they are undirected, irresponsible and disorganized. They move to New Orleans where Flap teaches at a small college, while Emma tends to the children and the house. But soon Emma finds she must turn to her mother for money. As the mother, Aurora, tells her 'He can't even do the simple things, like fail locally.'

When Emma discovers Flap is having an affair with a graduate student at his college, she returns home to her mother (in Houston) with her three children in tow. The film now presents us with another issue to consider. Aurora has 'moved on' with her own life and is now dating a heavy-drinking, hell-raising, former astronaut (Jack Nicholson) and enjoying her life. She has also regained her sexuality, which is remarkable because in many narratives of motherhood, the presence of children, especially older children and most especially grandchildren, precludes the woman from having sexual relations (somehow older mothers are deemed sexually taboo in Western cultures). Thus, one of the submerged conflicts explored in the narrative is *how much* of a personal life a mother is permitted to have. Is motherhood the primary lifelong obligation of a woman or does she at some point earn the right to put her own needs and selfhood first?

Toward the close of the narrative, little is resolved, but tragedy strikes; Emma is diagnosed with terminal cancer. She, Flap and their children are living in Nebraska where he is head of the English Department and still having affairs with graduate students. Aurora travels to Nebraska to care for her daughter and grandchildren, leaving the astronaut back in Houston. Flap participates sporadically as a husband and father, and the astronaut shows up for a weekend to support Aurora. Consistent with the realism of the narrative thus far, there are no miracles. Emma dies, leaving behind people of varying competencies to look after her children. The 'take away' from this tale is that for most women, motherhood is not a heroic, triumphant endeavor, nor do most mothers wreck and cripple their children. Most often they muddle through, trying to do the 'right thing,' but often unsure of what that is or how to perform it.

The Joy Luck Club (1989)

This film presents narratives of interracial motherhood, but with markedly different outcomes than we saw in 1959's *Imitation of Life*. The Joy Luck Club is the name a group of four Chinese women friends give their weekly mahjong get-togethers. Upon arriving in the US, each of the women married a Chinese-American man and gave birth to a daughter. The narratives in the film recount their earlier lives in China and their daughters' lives as first generation Americans. At the outset, the narrator tells a parable of these immigrant mothers' hopes: 'I will have a daughter just like me…I will make her speak good American English…She will be too full to swallow any sorrows…She will carry all my good intentions.' Unfortunately, the narrative reveals that this parable brought its own sorrow, as the daughters found it difficult to fulfil their mothers' aspirations.

For example, one daughter recalls that her mother and one of the other mothers 'were best friends and biggest competitors. Each wanted her daughter to outdo the other.' The daughters were driven by their mothers to excel at piano and chess, respectively. Ultimately, both failed to live up to their mothers' expectations and felt like disappointments. The storyline traces the drive to have high-performing daughters back to the misogynistic, patriarchal culture of China, where men dominate the family and only sons are valued.

One of the mothers was a child bride sold to a wealthy family and beaten by her husband's grandmother when she does not bear a son. In another story, the mother in China was a young widow who is raped by a wealthy man and forced to become his concubine. The son resulting from the rape is taken from her and given to his favored wife. The woman commits suicide to enable her daughter to gain freedom and come to the US. In a third instance, a young woman marries a handsome entrepreneur who soon abuses her and brings whores to their home. To gain a divorce and freedom, she drowns their infant son in the bath. Finally, the fourth young Chinese woman is forced to abandon her two infant daughters in wartime China and make her way alone to the U.S.

In America, these damaged women turned to their US-born daughters to create better outcomes, while the daughters struggle with the burden of achieving their mothers' aspirations. Two of the young women marry Chinese men to please their mothers, with unhappy results. Both divorce and one begins dating a blonde American, but senses her mother's disapproval. In contrast, the second young woman is encouraged by her mother to divorce her demanding and self-centered Chinese husband. The mother asks her, 'What is this marriage based on?' 'Keeping Harold happy.' 'What do you want from him?' 'Respect and tenderness.' 'Then leave and don't come back until he gives you those things…Losing him does not matter…You will find yourself.'

The third daughter is engaged to the son of a socially prominent WASP family. The husband's parents are bigots and oppose the marriage ('everyone is still upset about Vietnam,' the boy's mother tells her). But they do love each other and marry. However, feeling unworthy of her new status, the young woman soon submerges her own identity beneath that of her husband. Ted, the husband, becomes bored by her docility and falls in love with another woman. Her mother tells her, 'You don't know what you are worth. You have *value.*' Once the young woman re-discovers her own voice, she and her husband re-build their marriage.

One very valuable lesson this narrative conveys about motherhood is that the scars of self-sacrifice borne by the mother can be carried forward to ultimately damage her children – especially daughters. Motherhood must focus on the *child's* happiness and potential, and not focus on compensating the mother for wrongs suffered. And once again we see the narrative encouraging women to choose men who appear likely to provide upward social and economic mobility. These immigrant women drove both themselves and their daughters to achieve wealth and recognition in their new environment, a motivation that proved to have both beneficial and destructive effects on the lives of the daughters who viewed themselves as the carriers of their mothers' dreams.

The Kids Are All Right (2010)

We have now come to the last movie in our set, *The Kids Are All Right*, travelling seven decades in the construction of motherhood from the idealized family of *Mrs. Miniver* (1942) to the present day. This film, like *Mrs. Miniver* and *Kramer vs. Kramer* before it, shows that the spouse who earns more outside the home is the partner who commands respect inside the home. The family in this narrative differs from all those we have discussed previously, however, consisting of two middle-aged lesbians, Nick and Julie (Annette Bening and Julianne Moore) and their two children (one born from each woman), Joanie and Laser, who were conceived using a sperm donor. This is the summer before Joanie is to go away to college, and she and her brother decide to locate their sperm donor Dad. After some initial hesitance, the man agrees to meet with them and turns out to be a laid-back, ruggedly handsome, organic restaurateur named Paul. Paul is unmarried, but has a casual relationship with a black woman working at his restaurant. He is genuine and caring and soon begins serving as a father-figure for both Joanie (who works in his organic garden) and Laser, with whom he 'hangs out' and plays basketball.

Unfortunately, Nick, the more dominant and financially successful (she is an MD, so once again we are told that monetary worth equals familial power) of the two women, feels threatened by Paul's 'masculine' entry into her family. She begins acting in a hostile, defensive manner toward everyone, and drinking more than usual. Her partner, Julie, complains that Nick has become angry, critical and difficult toward her and the children. Without 'intending to,' she and Paul begin an affair. Nick discovers Julie's unfaithfulness and issues an ultimatum that Julie and the children must choose between their relationships with her or with Paul.

Paul is the one not chosen and suddenly finds himself rejected by the two children who sought him out only a few weeks earlier. When he comes to their house to say goodbye to Joanie prior to her departure for college, Nick storms to the front door and tells Paul, 'This is not your family; you are an interloper.' The next morning, Nick, Julie and Laser drive Joanie to college and help her move into her dorm room. They have a tearful farewell. Driving back to their house, Laser tells Nick and Julie, 'I think you two should stay together; you're too old to start over.' Thus, the film is in the same anti-idealist narrative vein as *Terms of Endearment*; each of the characters is 'good,' but not perfect or noble. Their intentions toward one another are generally caring, but their behaviours are flawed by selfishness, narcissism, and irresponsibility.

The film was nominated for several Academy Awards, including Best Picture and Best Actress (for both Bening and Moore). But perhaps what is most satisfying about it is the recasting of the common familial 'mid-life crisis' found in so many films into a lesbian mothers and sperm donor dad context. We are challenged to consider the many and diverse ways in which 'motherhood' and 'fatherhood' can be carried out and families can be formed – and broken.

Perhaps the most difficult to reconcile aspect of the story is the manner in which Paul was 'discarded' by all four family members once he turned into a 'problem.' The children had sought *him* out, Julie had *initiated* the affair with him, and he had been doing a sound parenting effort with both the children. Ironically, given that he had just found his children, his loss of them was the most painful to watch.

Concluding thoughts

The carved image of the Venus of Willendorf at the outset of this chapter references the idealized vision of motherhood from the earliest epochs of conscious human history, the time period during which humans gained the ability to conceptualize images and beings that carried imagined or hoped-for characteristics (Mithen 2006). It was a time when self-awareness dawned and we were first able to look upon ourselves and create narratives not only of what was, but also what should be or might be. Myths and folktales came into being and were passed forward through succeeding generations of story-telling; each epoch of human history adding new possibilities, hopes and threats to the narrative.

But through much of this entire time, concepts of motherhood – both the fears and the hopes – remained tied to the notion that women and mothering were inseparable, that one required the other in order to exist, at least to exist in a 'good' way. Women were *always* the primary caretakers of children; it was inconceivable that it would be otherwise (except in the 'evil' versions of the mothering tale). Men were seen as not being able to care for children, nor did women have value or purpose without being mothers. The beginning of the twentieth century challenged these eons-old presumptions. Factories were founded and women began working in them (Freedman 2003). Affluence increased and permitted a large number of women who had 'married well' to separate themselves from the child-caring role they had always performed previously. Other women's labour could be purchased and used to care for the children; wives and mothers in the middle class and above could now venture outside the home and demand the right to vote, to travel, to cultivate other aspects of themselves (Freedman 2003).

Women with fewer resources had to make alternative arrangements for their children as they sought employment in factories and in the homes of the wealthy. The heretofore unbroken bond between mother and child was severed – at least for many women – and never re-forged. Thus, Mrs. Miniver, that representation of British middle class family life in the early 1940s, was not only idealized, she was mythical. Data indicate that many British women were employed outside the home by 1940 – a legacy of the Great Depression. Once World War II was underway, the shortage of employable men shrank to intolerable levels across the West and women entered out-of-the-home jobs in record numbers. Though stringent political and cultural efforts were made to get them back into the house after the war (Freedman

2003), by the late 1960s and certainly by the 1970s the battle to restrict mothers to the household with their children was lost irrevocably (Freedman 2003).

Mildred Pierce foreshadowed this shift as early as 1945. Over the following decades, motion pictures struggled to re-tell the narrative of motherhood in ways that would make sense to a rapidly evolving culture, resulting in a mixed set of signals to women and men about 'what is going on.' You can pursue a career, but your children will suffer and condemn you for it (*Imitation of Life, Mommie Dearest*); you had better pursue a career or your mother, who could not, will be disappointed with you (*Joy Luck Club*); your children need a mother and you'd better get back into the house (*Mary Poppins*), you can pursue a career, but your husband will hate you (*Kramer vs. Kramer*). Of course, countering this set of values were the narratives indicating that: you'd better be able to earn a living, because if your husband fails, you will be destitute (*Mildred Pierce, Terms of Endearment*). And, of course the moral lesson of *The Kids Are All Right*: one of the two mothers has to make a good living, because there are bills to pay, a child to send to college and the biological father has just been kicked out.

Underneath all of this back and forth ideological manoeuvring is a deeper structure. *Contemporary culture requires family financial capital for successful childrearing.* Someone has to earn it. As we have seen in virtually all of the films discussed, whoever brings home the higher level of financial resources, exerts control. This was found to be true whether the income bringers were two women and a man (*The Kids Are All Right*) or a husband/boyfriend and wife (*Kramer vs. Kramer, Mrs. Miniver, Mary Poppins*) or two women (*Imitation of Life*). Thus we end up with a final set of three propositions governing contemporary motherhood: firstly, that money is power in a family; secondly, that mothers with money have power, but they may still be condemned for seeking self-identity out of the home; and finally, that fathers with money have power; but unlike mothers, they are not condemned for seeking self-identity out of the home.

References

Birkhauser-Oeri, S. (1988) *The Mother: Archetypal Image in Fairy Tales*, Toronto: Inner City.

Freedman, E. (2003) *No Turning Back: The History of Feminism and the Future of Women*, New York: Ballantine Books.

Friedan, B. (1963) *The Feminine Mystique*, New York: W.W. Norton & Co.

Hirschman, E. (2011) 'A history of discrimination in the marketplace', in E. Howlett, J. Kozup, and J. Kees (eds.), *Marketing and Public Policy Conference*, Washington, DC: American Marketing Association.

Jung, C.G. (1968) *Man and His Symbols*, New York: Dell.

Mithen, S. (2006) *After the Ice: a Global Human History 20,000 – 5000 BCE*, Boston: Harvard University Press.

Neumann, E. (1963) *The Great Mother: an Analysis of the Archetype*, Princeton: Princeton University Press.

Prat, S., Péan SC, Crépin L, Drucker DG, Puaud SJ, Valladas, H., Lázničková-Galetová, M., van der Plicht, J. and Yanevich, A. (2011) 'The oldest anatomically modern humans from Far Southeast Europe', www.plosone.org, accessed 27 March 2012.

Von Franz, M. (1993) *The Feminine in Fairy Tales*, revised edn., Boston: Shambhala.

3   How to be a mother

Expert advice and the maternal subject

Mary Jane Kehily

Introduction

It is an assumption of modern life that pregnant women and new mothers must be in need of advice. Should this be true, the maternal subject doesn't have far to look. Expertise is widely available from a range of sources offering tips, techniques and instructions on every aspect of maternal experience. Hardyment (2007) identifies the proliferation of such advice literature as a phenomenon of Western societies to emerge in the last twenty years. Questions of how to be a mother and what a mother needs to know acquire significance in late pregnancy as women prepare for and think themselves into their new role. This chapter considers the expert advice available to new mothers-to-be and how they relate to this body of knowledge. As part of an ESRC-funded project on the experience of first-time motherhood (Thomson *et al.* 2011), we sought to find how expectant mothers engaged with expert advice in preparing for motherhood. Our initial questionnaire indicated that pregnant first-time mothers rely on people (doctors, family members and friends) rather than texts (magazines, books, websites or leaflets).[1] Yet when we met women and asked them to share with us their preparations for the baby, they often showed us a number of books and magazines that they had gathered in order to help themselves imagine their way into motherhood. In considering the status of expert advice for new mothers, we analyse the material that women signposted as significant for them, attempting to think about what this material represents as part of a wider picture of contemporary mothering, without overemphasising its significance in shaping expectations and practices. The chapter begins by placing contemporary advice literature in some historical context before going on to consider the key sources: pregnancy magazines and childcare manuals. We show that engaging with experts, collecting advice from different sources and building a personal knowledge-base can be seen as part of the *work* of motherhood that, as Miller (2004) and Clarke (2004) point out, has material effects. The selection and blending of advice literature that mothers engage in may appear as an accessorising activity at the fringes of mothering practices. Our study suggests that a competing body of expert advice is central to the maternal experience as a key resource in the construction of maternal types and practices that women variously identify with or define themselves against. The presence of different ways of *doing* motherhood has particular currency at the level of the local, having an impact upon approaches to parenting and decision making in matters such as childcare arrangements and use of local facilities.

The expert and the mother

In contemporary times, becoming well informed about your pregnancy involves navigating a mounting body of specialist knowledge, including the layers of moral injunction and pathologizing created by successive waves of expertise. In seeking this advice, mothers join a chain of mothers and experts that stretches back to the industrial revolution, with different models of babycare coming to represent competing forms of personhood – for both the woman and the child. In a comprehensive history of advice to women, Ehrenreich and English (1979) show how the manuals of the early twentieth century constructed the expectant mother as a 'domestic engineer' – the representative of the expert in the home, applying the rationality of the factory and the office to the project of producing the family: to time and on budget. In the second half of the twentieth century the gaze turns inwards with advice increasingly psychological in its focus. The expert now identifies with the 'permissive child', whose needs are assumed to guide the 'libidinal mother', 'the two happily matched consumers, consuming each other'.

Ehrenreich and English argue that as the end of the twentieth century approached, the 'romance between the expert and the mother' was effectively over, the former having lost much of their authority as advice proliferated becoming more a matter of choice and taste rather than diagnosis or science. Their prediction that wisdom would no longer be hoarded by experts has in many ways been realised. In the new millennium there is no cultural consensus about the right way to give birth or care for babies. Different perspectives co-exist, sometimes uncomfortably and often to comic effect. Standard texts are updated to incorporate new values and perspectives (Hardyment 2007), and readers can gain relief from retro-advice when overwhelmed by the demands of attachment parenting (Cusk 2001). What 'counts' as expert advice is also fluid. Hardyment's historical analysis of childcare advice *Dream Babies* can be found on a shelf alongside traditional parenting manuals and a proliferation of 'Mumoirs' which range from the literary (Cusk, Enright), to the celebrity (for example Mel Giedroyc *From Here to Maternity*, Jules Oliver's *Minus Nine to One* and Myleene Klass's *My Bump and Me*) and the comic, such as the 'laugh out loud' *Best Friend* guides to pregnancy and childbirth. In a review article of yet more 'Hen lit', critic Jenny Turner reveals her own omnivorous maternal reading habits as taking in the poetry of Sylvia Plath, the feminist classics of Dorothy Dinnerstein and Adrienne Rich, the child development theory of Donald Winnicott plus the full range of 'manically comic memoirs' that she 'binges on' in her local library (Turner 2009). Engaging with advice is not simply a matter of discovery, or fact-finding (although this plays an important part); it is more a case of working on the self, and attempting to position or recognize the self within 'maternal culture', however defined. This positioning goes beyond reading. Increasingly it is the medium of display rather than the advice itself that is the site of innovation and significance. Initially a new breed of pregnancy and mothering magazines intervened in order to both mediate and package the plethora of technical and consumer discourses. Internet-based social networking sites such as Mumsnet and Netmum are now the high-profile, influential forums in which motherhood is displayed and consumed, while reality TV shows such as *Supernanny, Wife Swap* and *House of Tiny Tearaways* provide public texts around which intense moral feelings about mothering circulate (Skeggs and Woods 2009; Tyler 2008).

Pregnancy magazines as purveyors of knowledge

Within the broader context of motherhood on display, pregnancy magazines exist as social texts in which advice is encoded within familiar cultures of femininity common to women's magazines as a genre.[2] Pregnancy magazines present themselves as sources of information and as conduits for other sources of information. Key information on pregnancy, labour and new motherhood is rehearsed in every issue. Most magazines include 'baby basics' features, introducing women to the rudiments of childcare such as bottle feeding, weaning and sleep routines. Additionally, books, cable television channels and websites on pregnancy, birth and childcare are frequently reviewed and profiled. Generally the approach to advice and information is instructional without being overly didactic. The emphasis is upon common sense, relying upon a post-Spock settlement that suggests to women – *if it feels right for you then it is right.*

Given that most pregnant women in our study reported that their family, friends and particularly mothers provide the richest source of information and guidance during pregnancy, it is perhaps surprising that the magazines do not comment more freely upon family communication and intergenerational conversations. While some features allude to pregnancy as a time to 'rediscover your mum' (*Prima Baby*, October 2005), there is little acknowledgement that new mothers form part of an extended family undergoing change and exchanging experientially-based knowledge. Mothers of new mothers are particularly noticeable by their absence, indicating that the magazines may be implicitly addressing the mobile couple of late modernity, living a version of the 'pure relationship' and geographically distant from the extended family. Additionally, there is little discussion of mother–daughter relationships despite their increased significance during this time. The lack of intergenerational conversation across the magazines as a whole suggests that a simple yet significant message may be at play – it's different for new mothers today, the experienced voice of grandmothers may no longer be relevant.

All pregnancy magazines have a stable panel of experts that commonly includes a GP, health visitor, midwife, couples therapist, consumer expert, childcare specialist, psychologist and obstetrician. Experts are often profiled in the opening pages of the magazine, suggesting that their presence offers readers comfort, reassurance and authority. Experts feature heavily within the problem page sections of the magazine, where readers are invited to request help for a particular difficulty they are experiencing. Many queries straight-forwardly ask for the opinion of a specialist – 'what can I do about morning sickness?' or 'why isn't my baby gaining weight?' In keeping with the genre, it is in the interactive features of the magazines that women's difficulties with childrearing emerge. Running counter to the generally uplifting tone of the magazines, a question and answer item invites a panel of experts to respond to the 'confessions' of 'brave mums' who admit to the otherwise contemporary taboo subjects of modern mothering such as 'I think my baby's ugly', 'I smack my child' and 'I don't like being a mum'. The unspeakable idea that some women may not like their children and that the experience of motherhood itself may be undesirable – is regarded as a temporary aberration, the regrettable effect of a depressive illness that can be overcome.

The extent to which other mothers drew upon pregnancy magazines for expert advice tended to depend on patterns of magazine readership prior to pregnancy. Women who enjoyed magazines related to pregnancy magazines in a similar way as a pleasurable leisure activity that blended positive thinking with humour. Fashion, gossip, celebrity news and problem pages could be enjoyed in what was usually a fleeting engagement with the form. Other first-time mothers were drawn to the idea of a magazine that was especially *for them*. Initially at least, pregnancy magazines contained valuable information, however, the format of the magazines follows a formula in which key features such as the step-to-step guide to pregnancy are repeated, making them less useful as time went by. Many women found magazines helpful as an initial guide to products, informing them of what was on the market. Some women, concerned with matters such as the provenance of advice, the status of expertise and the reliability of recommendations, expressed a preference for books, websites or research-based accounts for more detailed information.

Childcare manuals

The contradictory nature of advice available to new mothers is most evident in the best-selling guide books. That babies don't come with a manual remains a cliché of everyday discourse. Advice on how to be a mother is big business and an enduring site of struggle. Fashions, authors and practices ebb and flow. Indeed, in some cases it may be possible to guess the year a woman became a mother by asking her what books she read while pregnant. Whether it is *Breast is Best* or *The Fabulous Mum's Handbook*, the unfolding story is one of proliferating and diffuse voices of authority. The abundance of books aimed at pregnant women suggests an increasing diversity, fragmentation and the absence of consensus on the whole maternal project. Late modern perspectives may point to the struggle for meaning across texts as indicative of choice, reflecting the pluralism of new times. The incitement to discourse, in Foucaultian terms however, can be seen as regulatory, productive of new and creative forms of surveillance and control. Some women like Eleanor were particularly attuned to the disciplinary effects of advice literature though at other moments may invoke a knowing and agentic choice narrative:

You look for the sort of advice you feel comfortable with… I mean everyone that I know who has babies about the same age as me lies to their health visitor about something (laughs), sleeping in bed with them, weaning, you know, something.

(Eleanor, 26)

The most popular books among the women we surveyed were the information-heavy *What To Expect When You Are Expecting* and a series of guides written by Miriam Stoppard (*Conception, Pregnancy and Birth* 2005 and *The New Pregnancy and Birth* 2004). Yet women had relatively little to say about these texts, other than that they were useful and comprehensive. The two books that most featured in women's accounts were *The Baby Whisperer* and *The Contented Little Baby Book*. As polar opposites of different child development traditions, they acquired symbolic significance for women who read them. Gina Ford's *The Contented Little Baby Book*, first published in 1999, reinstates the importance of routine for babies. Following Truby King, Ford recommends that mothers settle babies into a sleeping and feeding schedule within weeks of birth. The aim is to establish a pattern of three–four hourly feeds ending at 10pm and beginning again at 6am the next morning. As Ford explains:

Routines teach you to recognise the difference between hunger and tiredness and how to listen to what your baby is really saying. They are all about providing your baby with security and comfort, giving him what he wants before he needs to cry and demand it, and the result is a contented little baby who is likely to sleep the longest spell at night at around six to ten weeks. You'll also be able to claim a little time back for yourself, which will help you enjoy the experience of parenthood much, much more. It has worked for hundreds of thousands of parents all over the world and it can work for you too – I promise.

(www.contentedbaby.com, accessed 17 August 2010)

In a move that runs counter to baby-centred, feed-on-demand practices embraced by feminists in the post-Spock era, Ford advocates structure that is determined by real time and instigated by mothers. The idea that mothers can 'claim a little time back' suggests a baby–me tug of war for individual space that challenges the selfless devotion of other methods, echoing the grandmotherly warning about the dangers of holding babies too much. Ford also advocates leaving babies to cry for up to an hour to train them out of expecting to be picked up. The contented baby idea outlined in Ford's first book has grown into a baby-care empire. There are more books, products, a website and an online community of followers. Critics of Ford are quick to point out that her baby-care credentials are slight; she has no formal qualifications and no children. Consolidating her status as 'easily the most popular baby care guru of the new century' (Hardyment 2007: 292), Ford's approach inevitably generates controversy, notably from members of the internet website Mumsnet and more recently from deputy Prime Minister Nick Clegg who described her routine as 'absolute nonsense'. After many critiques, parodies and a posting on Mumsnet amusingly suggesting that Ford 'strapped babies to rockets and fired them into south Lebanon', she took legal action to ban the site from discussing her methods.

Women we spoke to also expressed strong feelings about the contented baby approach, one respondent describing Ford as a 'baby Nazi' whose methods appear to invite pastiche:

> It's all timetabled [Ford's methods]. Oh it's horrible, horrible, like 6.51am you should get dressed in your heels and make-up ready to feed your baby at 6.52 and make sure your baby is awake at 6.52. It's just not me.
>
> (Debbie, 33)

The other book frequently referred to, *The Baby Whisperer*, appears to occupy less controversial territory. Written by midwife Tracey Hogg and first published in 1988, *The Baby Whisperer* encourages mothers to approach baby-care from the perspective of babies themselves. How to read your baby's signals becomes a starting point for the development of routines that respond to the needs of babies rather than seeking to impose a regime on them. Like Ford, Hogg describes her approach as simple and even brands it as the EASY routine, based on a common sense pattern of eating, activity, sleep and your time. Having read both books, Clara (40) comments:

> *The Baby Whisperer* is just interesting about how you can get different personalities of babies into some sort of semi-structure and be flexible given their type. But because it would help my partner because he LOVES routine, it would help him if he knew there was some sort of pattern to things. I would never be able to follow a '6.15 is when you feed' sort of thing … But it would be nice to know that maybe over time there's some sort of pattern of sleep or feeding or whatever… to ensure that he [partner] doesn't feel like the whole, everything about us, has been taken over by the baby.

Clara's reflections raise the question, who are routines for? Apart from the obvious need to make sense of postpartum chaos, mother-baby routines may be established to serve people and practices beyond the dyad. In this example, the desires and expectations of her partner become an important reference point, for other women, work schedules, childcare arrangements and financial resources may play a part in decisions relating to the early care of babies. Christina Hardyment observes that Ford and Hogg, the two best selling experts of the age, were both trained as maternity nurses. She suggests mischievously 'that women have fallen in droves for the seductive idea of being in themselves the maternity nurses they can't afford. Their methods also envisage baby adapting to a mother's absence easily because his or her routine can remain unaltered under a carer' (2007: 325). There is a sense in which these two texts exist in conversation for contemporary mothers – revealing the strains of working motherhood and contributing to a form of intensification that combines the lingering spectres of the rejecting and the over-protective mother. What is currently being called 'intensive mothering' is, as Hays (1998) indicates, a charge generally laid against absent (i.e. working) mothers who are acutely conscious of what their children may be missing – and thus seek to replace or compensate for this through professional input. It is a model that fits with Arlie Hochschild's understanding of the commercialization of the domestic that has followed women's transitions into the workforce, and which set new standards that are beyond what any stay-at-home mother could achieve. Within this logic then, it makes sense for women to imagine themselves as the maternity nurses that they cannot afford, consuming contradictory advice which echoes powerfully with their own experiences of being parented as well as fantasies of social mobility.

Mothers as 'organic experts'

Judy recognises how advice can change over time. Her own mother advised her to swaddle Debbie on her side to make her more comfortable. Yet six years later by the time she had her second daughter there was a greater fear of cot death which made her '*paranoid*' so she refrained from swaddling her and put her on her tummy to sleep which she now recognises is not seen as good for the baby. She has '*held back from*' giving Debbie advice because '*things have altered so much*' and '*there is nothing worse than giving old fashioned advice*'. Judy feels that she was influenced by the '*fashions*' when she was a mother and regrets not breastfeeding Debbie because at the time it was not the done thing. Judy's main source of advice was a booklet given to her by the hospital She did also have a book which gave advice on the timetabling of feeding, sleeping etc. She feels she has less of an 'enquiring mind' than her daughter although she has learnt so much from Debbie's research.

(The Pickards: Case history extract)

Grandmother Judy reflects on her maternal practice as formed in the confluence of time and place. Responding to intergenerational advice, changing medical opinion and current fashion, Judy recognizes that motherhood is reconfigured by successive generations of new mothers. Alongside dalliances with professional childcare experts, we found women building up their own local networks for advice and support. Invoking the idea of mothers as 'organic experts' gestures towards the everyday meaning making of 'organic intellectuals' (Gramsci 1971) whose experience is grounded in an understanding of local conditions that make change possible. Many women consumed the commercially available advice literature while establishing parental practices in relationships close to home. Making sense of neighbourhood networks and local knowledge in the development of a closely observed account of what works, new mothers generate a personally blended and contextually specific form of expertise organic to their experience and personal circumstances. For some women this involved a search for new contours of community, establishing connections with groups in the neighbourhood such as

tional Childbirth Trust and yoga classes for mothers-to-be, in the hope of
ng their network of fellow travellers. Crucially, women valued the advice of
family and friends who had children and commonly gathered together a coterie of
those they trusted emotionally. Many women cited their own mother as important
in the development of their maternal identity, even when the relationship was
troubled, distant or absent. For some women, their mother became an example
of how not to do it; they saw her as representing the residual trace of an older
generation whose advice was no longer relevant. Pregnancy for some women
produced powerful feelings of dis-identification with their own mother, though
they usually conceded that successfully reaching adulthood was testament to their
mother's good enough parenting. A more benign version of this acknowledges the
fragility and impermanence of human experience:

> Orla: I was talking to my mum, although it's quite interesting, you realise
> people forget pregnancy so quickly. It's a long time since my mum was
> pregnant and she's forgotten loads of things. I mentioned Braxton Hicks the
> other day and she said 'Oh are you supposed to be getting those so early?' so
> I had to explain and she said, 'Oh yes I remember that now but I don't think
> we called them that'.

Seemingly in parallel with the acts of memory and forgetting that shape the
evolution of the conception story, the experience of pregnancy and birth is also
selectively remembered. The temporary nature of pregnancy exists in harmony
with the temporary space it occupies in the memory as details and feelings
fade over time. Other women became closer to their mother during pregnancy,
identifying with her more closely as a source of knowledge that was entirely
dependable as an intergenerational legacy of biology and experience. For many
younger mothers, their mother was an important and ever-present source of
support and someone who provided a template for their own mothering. While
still living in the parental home, their mothers often made pregnancy and birth
possible through the provision of financial and emotional resources. In these
cases, new grandmothers became the uber-mummy of an expanding family that
absorbed the arrival of a new baby.

Impending motherhood invited women to evaluate their experience of being
mothered and to position themselves in relation to their own mothers. Many
women remained closely connected to their mother's style of mothering and
placed this experience at the centre of their approach to advice and expertise:

> Eleanor: Looking for this [advice] is definitely down to my mother ... We had
> conversations but I knew, I think I must have picked it up from a thousand
> comments and just her general attitude. And then she gave me this Penelope
> Leach book and she says, 'This is what I brought you up on' and she wanted
> me to have it. And it's a lovely book, it's very nice, she's very much 'follow
> your instincts, don't let anybody tell you you're failing at something' ...I
> would say that my mother is a far stronger influence than anything I've read.

I mean, I've developed the ideas further by reading ... but certainly the catalyst, the starting point was definitely the way I was mothered.

As someone who blends learning with experience to produce a unique form of praxis, Eleanor's mother achieves the status of organic childcare expert. She takes on her approach to motherhood and continues the tradition of generating organic knowledge by adding insights from her own reading. The Penelope Leach book passed on by her mother is likely to be *Your Baby and Child: From Birth to Age 5*, first published in 1977. Leach's academic background as a psychologist enabled her to interpret the Piagetian-style stages of child development for a broad audience of parents and non-academics. Her approach suggests that understanding the emotional and physical development of young children increases the confidence of parents and, in turn, the happiness of babies. Leach continues to contribute to debates on childcare, her comments acting as an anchor for child-centred, respectful and humanitarian practice. Leach is critical of the spread of contented baby-type methods, particularly controlled crying, saying that babies are too young to be 'naughty' and do not act with the intent that routines ascribe to them. In a new twist in the development of her ideas, Leach draws upon neuroscience to support her comments, claiming that unresponsive carers increase baby's cortisol levels, the hormone responsible for stress. The touchstone of Leach's comments rests on her disapproval of the me-me-ness of contemporary motherhood, hitting out against women who want a baby but do not want their lives to be disrupted. Leach bluntly points out that having a baby *will* change your life.[3]

Eleanor extends her mother's child-centred approach by adding attachment parenting methods to a framework shaped by Penelope Leach. Bill and Martha Sears popularized the idea of attachment parenting in the *Baby Book*, first published in 1993. Their philosophy drew inspiration from the work of anthropologist Jean Liedloff (1975) who documented the mothering practices of an Amazonian community of Yequana Indians who keep their babies strapped to them continuously during infancy until the child struggles to move away. The other reference point for attachment parenting lies in psychological studies of the 1950s. John Bowlby's attachment theory explored the emotional bond between parent and child and its impact upon the child. Emphasising the importance of the caregiver's physical presence and closeness to the baby, attachment theory was concerned with matters of secure attachment and particularly the relationship between maternal deprivation and childhood depression. The Sears' adapted these ideas in an approach that advocated the constant use of a sling to promote mother–child bonding through close physical contact. Attachment parenting involves total commitment to your baby, breastfeeding and sleeping together to enable mothers to become attuned to the needs of the child. Eleanor responds to the charge that attachment parenting is too demanding of mothers by describing how it worked for her in a home-based family business:

The important thing is to make sure your child is happy and cared for and knows you're there for them... This whole baby-wearing thing, it sounds very labour-intensive but in fact your baby doesn't need your attention if he's got your physical comfort, so you can put your baby on and do whatever you were going to do … I would work at the computer, I would do everything. Keeping to some kind of schedule seems more labour intensive to me than being able to bring him into the centre of your life and then carry on with it.

Attachment parenting has increased appeal for some new mothers as the idea of slow parenting gains currency among a sub-stratum of middle class parents. As a riposte to the accelerated speed of urban life and work-based practices, slow parenting advocates country living, home cooking, de-schooling, green everything and an unhurried approach to family life that values spending time together. Although Eleanor was the only mother in our study who put herself into this category, many others identified with aspects of slow parenting as a desirable ideal to be aspired to and possibly realised in a re-evaluation of priorities.

The situation

Our study aims to understand new motherhood as a situation that is constituted in different ways yet which also constitutes solidarities and commonalities. We have argued that age has become an organizing category through which normative notions of mothering are constituted, with a powerful discourse of efficient biographical planning incorporating social class, and mediating differences of sexuality, ethnicity and disability. Yet age is rarely spoken about explicitly within the texts of new motherhood. Instead a more subtle message is communicated in which becoming a mother is posed as the centre of a female choice biography, associated with the challenge of synchronizing the couple and career, and the capacity to enact parenthood through consumption. Those women in our study who constructed motherhood as part of an explicit project of self tended to have highly developed narratives about the kind of mother that they wanted to be, which included drawing (often ironically) on popular cultural resources. The 'choices' that women presented themselves as having appeared to focus on a series of binary divides between: natural and medical births (often associated with a commitment to either the National Childbirth Trust (NCT) or National Health Service antenatal classes); either child or adult-centred parenting (exemplified by the choice between '*Baby Whisperer*' and '*Contented Baby*' approaches). Although women of all ages and backgrounds drew strategically on the 'common culture' of mothering, it was women in the 26–35 age group who tended to position themselves in relation to these distinctions.

Viewing expert advice as part of the common culture of motherhood illustrates the significance of age and the fragmentation of generational cohorts based on shared life experiences. The abundance of advice across different media, available in a range of formats speaks most clearly to the 25–35 age group as experienced consumers, well rehearsed in the ways of the market and the significance of choice and taste. Keen to integrate motherhood into a biographical project of self, this group of women assimilated features of the common culture, creating a convergence between practices of consumption and maternal identities. By contrast, other age groups demonstrated less fluency in the common culture of motherhood, having less access to the fruits of it as younger mothers or feeling dislocated from it as older mothers.

Concluding comments

The post-war period has been marked by the proliferation of expert discourses on motherhood and childcare and the changing status of the expert in women's lives. Early twentieth century manuals spoke with authority and prioritized efficiency, telling women to run their homes like a small company. By the end of the century, advice manuals for women were more concerned with the psychological domain, paying attention to the unconscious world of desire and affect that assumes importance in mother–child relations. The shift in focus to matters of interiority runs parallel with other key developments – the declining authority of the expert and the breakdown of a cultural consensus on motherhood and childcare generally. The early care of children continues to be a publicly contested issue in which different models of baby-care come to represent competing forms of personhood for both mothers and babies.

Our study illustrates the many ways in which women use expert advice to imagine their way into motherhood. Drawing on a diverse range of expertise from bestselling books to local resources, new mothers negotiated a pathway through the common culture of motherhood in a quest to find their own place in the maternal project. The increased availability of advice through digital technology offers women more 'choice' but also potentially more pressure as domestic space is commercialized in ways that re-evaluate what mothers can achieve. Engaging with advice literature and different forms of expertise may entail encounters with class-coded and value-laden approaches requiring some affective manoeuvring. Blending and personalising advice become ways of managing information, containing contradiction and ascribing authority to the self as organic expert at the centre of a unique female choice biography. Intergenerational perspectives reveal the contingent nature of advice literature and maternal practice as subject to fashion in the constantly reconfiguring politics of motherhood. Finally, it is important to bear in mind the age-specific relationship to expertise as a cultural phenomenon that speaks to and resonates with the concerns of 25–35-year-old women as receptive late modern subjects in which motherhood is central to a female choice biography constituted through the synchronization of coupledom, career and consumption.

Notes

1 In the total questionnaire sample of 144 the most popular source of advice was from the doctor; 87.8 per cent sought advice from their doctor. 74.8 per cent took advice from their mother or family members, 52.7 per cent from friends, 39.7 per cent from pregnancy magazines and 42 per cent from internet websites. The least popular source was advice leaflets at 38.9 per cent. In the interview sample of 62 the most popular

source of advice was from the doctor (51 respondents); 36 took advice from their mother or family members, 35 from friends, 23 from their partner, 26 from pregnancy magazines and 27 from internet websites. The least popular source was advice leaflets (26).

2 This sector of the magazine market is well developed in the UK, supporting a range of titles, produced monthly with circulation figures of over 50,000 for the more popular magazines. This chapter draws upon the popular and commonly available magazines in this sector over an 18-month period from September 2004 – April 2006. In total, 28 magazines across eight titles were analysed: *Prima Baby and Pregnancy, Pregnancy, It's the Time of Your Life, Pregnancy and Birth, Junior Pregnancy and Baby, Mother and Baby, I'm Pregnant, Pregnancy, Baby and You* and *Practical Parenting*. Magazines were bought and analysed in parallel with the 18-month fieldwork period.

3 www.independent.co.uk/life-style, accessed 17 August 2010.

References

Clarke, A.J. (2004) 'Maternity and materiality: becoming a mother in consumer culture', in J.S. Taylor, L.L. Layne and D.F. Wozniak (eds) *Consuming Motherhood*, New Brunswick: Rutgers University Press, 55–71.

Cusk, R. (2001) *A Life's Work: On Becoming a Mother*, London: Faber and Faber.

Ehrenreich, B. and English, D. (1979) *For Her Own Good: 150 Years of the Experts' Advice to Women*, London: Pluto Press.

Enright, A. (2004) *Making Babies: Stumbling Into Motherhood*, London: Vintage.

Gramsci, A. (1971) *Selections from the Prison Notebooks*, London: Lawrence and Wishart.

Hardyment, C. (2007) *Dream Babies: Childcare Advice from John Locke to Gina Ford*, London: Francis Lincoln.

Hays, S. (1998) *The Cultural Contradictions of Motherhood*, New Haven: Yale University Press.

Hochschild, A. (2003) *The Commercialisation of Intimate Life: Notes From Home and Work*, San Francisco: University of California Press.

Liedloff, J. (1986) *The Continuum Concept*, Cambridge, MA: Da Capo Press.

Miller, D. (2004) 'How infants grow mothers in North London', in J.S. Taylor, L.L. Layne and D.F. Wozniak (eds) *Consuming Motherhood*, New Brunswick: Rutgers University Press, 31–54.

Skeggs, B. and Woods, H. (2009) 'The transformation of intimacy: classed identities in the moral economy of reality television', in M. Wetherell (ed.) *Identity in the 21st Century: New Trends and Changing Times*, Houndsmill: Palgrave.

Thomson, R., Kehily, M.J., Hadfield, L. and Sharpe, S. (2011) *Making Modern Mothers*, Bristol: Policy Press.

Turner, J. (2009) 'Yum yum! Delicious babies', *The Guardian*, Saturday 1 August.

Tyler, I. (2008) '"Chav mum, chav scum": class disgust in contemporary Britain', *Feminist Media Studies*, 8:4, 17–34.

4 Designing mothers and the market

Social class and material culture

Alison J. Clarke

Women's experiences and practices as mothers are inescapably bound to specific worlds of objects, brands and goods to the extent that critiques of mothers within popular culture increasingly focus on the social class relationships to consumption. This intertwining of the practice of mothering, with the cosmology of goods and taste knowledges, is encapsulated in media-generated labels such as 'yummy mummy' and 'slummy mummy': the former indicating a privileged, affluent middle-class mother for whom parenting is an extension of leisure and consumption, and the latter a woman with a slovenly attitude towards her appearance and her mothering (McRobbie 2006; Goodwin and Huppatz 2010a). The intertwined relationship between mothers, things and infants has become so normalized that reproduction, as a growing number of social scientists have observed, is identified as being as much a consumer, as a bodily, project (Clarke 2000, 2004, 2007; Goodwin and Huppatz 2010b; Layne 2000; Paxson 2004). Contemporary motherhood relies on the adroit articulation of 'choices' around consumption from birth plans, services and consumer brands, to style and aesthetic repertoires, all brought to bear on the 'making' of children (Taylor *et al.* 2004).

Archaeologist Joanna Derevenski, in a theoretical overview of the historical intertwining of material culture and children, has written that '[s]ocial life is not a pure construction of meaning, but mutually constructed from "heterogenous materials" including bodies, technology, material culture and minds each of which enrolls and orders the others in fluid and shifting combinations' (2000:9). Invoking contemporary sociologists of technology (Latour 1993) and childhood (James 2008) in exploring the potentials, and hazards, of material culture in the cross-cultural understanding of the 'child', from the archaeological perspective, Derevenski has little more than skeletal remains and burial artefacts with which to envisage the diversities of childhood and ensuing socio-material relations.

By way of contrast, the ranges and diversities of apparatus, technologies, images, and bodies available to us in examining contemporary and recent historical motherhood is so immense as to be daunting to social scientists as much as new mothers themselves. In this respect, the contemporary landscape of motherhood perfectly resembles the 'heterogenous materials' outlined in Derevenski's description of a 'mutually constructed' social life in which biologies, things, media and material cultures meld.

Over the last decade, a range of literature has dealt with the rise of 'the consumptive mother', and modes of mothering in which the market and its goods are actively valorized (Taylor *et al.* 2004). From an anthropological perspective, the everyday acts of women's provisioning have been understood as maternal acts of love and sacrifice (Miller 1997), and in geography and sociology an established literature has considered the exponential rise in consumption targeted at mothers and children (Crewe and Collins 2006; Cook 2008). Popular marketing publications (for example, *Trillion Dollar Moms,* Bailey 2005; *Marketing to Moms,* Bailey 2002; *Tuning into Mom*, Clements and Thompson 2011; *Marketing to the New Super Consumer: Mom & Kid* Coffey *et al.* 2006) and best-selling anti-consumerist polemics such as *Toxic Childhood* (Palmer 2006) and *Detoxing Childhood: How the Modern World is Damaging Our Children* (Palmer 2007), all identify contemporary motherhood as engaging, at a variety of levels, with a type of hyper consumptive activity.

More recently the pursuit of 'glamour' has emerged as a feature of mothering, affording new opportunities for the valorization of otherwise mundane tasks of child-care, but also exerting new forms of social pressure. Previously understood as being at odds with the 'real' issues and politics of mothering, both from the perspective of feminist *and* conservative notions of 'good' mothering, glamour now plays a central role (Goodwin and Huppatz 2010a). Nineteenth century glamour archetypes, such as the femme fatale, desirous, empowered, sexualized temptresses adroit at manipulating their appearances, stood as the antithesis to a model of homely, self-denying motherhood (Gundle 2007:391–2). The femme fatale's glamour emanated from a mysterious, internal capacity for seduction, rather than an affected appearance. This notion has waned in favour of a contemporary consumer-driven notion of glamour whereby 'glamour is not a natural attribute but a manufactured one' (Gundle 2007:390).

However, cultural historian Stephen Gundle (2007) has argued that the consumption of glamour, while operating in the nineteenth and twentieth centuries as a means of conveying distinction, has, in the twenty-first century, become radically democratized, with the potential to challenge social class and to destabilize cultural hierarchies. Furthermore, as a collective discourse, glamour and its associated objects and brands no longer belong to the elite taste-makers, but rather to those 'on the margins of society on account of their economic position, ethnicity or sexual orientation' (Gundle 2008:356). Taking a post-feminist stance, women's engagement with the 'trivia' of style change, celebrity gossip and its performative dimensions has been increasingly represented as one signalling empowerment. It is only in the last two decades, with the rise of print and online gossip media, that glamour has become associated with mothering; through the observation of the details of consumer items and the emergence of the 'super consumer' celebrity (Gundle 2007:394).

As the apotheosis of glamorized motherhood, *Sex in the City* (TV series and film) has been a frequently cited example (in both popular culture and academic scholarship) of the intertwining of motherhood, brands and fashion. Renowned for its orgiastic consumption of 'must-have' brand items, designer shoes and baby buggies are interwoven into the manners and mores of women's on-screen urban lives building on the historically intertwined relation of glamour and branded luxury goods, from Hollywood through to so-called 'fabloids'. [1]

In her article, 'Faking a Sonogram', an analysis of motherhood as represented in *Sex in the City*, Laura Tropp (2006) argues that this rarefied world of transient designer fashion brands is one ideally situated to explore the ideas of 'choice' around modern motherhood and reproduction; from the timing and the style of birth or the type of accessories associated with maternity and child rearing. While Tropp's media studies 'reading' of *Sex in the City* suggests an optimistic historical shift in acknowledging the paradoxical discourses around women's agency and 'choice' around motherhood, Heather Paxson's anthropological study *Making Modern Mothers* is more sceptical when she states 'women's maternal obligations are coming to be regarded as consumer projects' (Paxson 2004:65). Paxson's ethnographic work on mothers and the market considers the burdens, rather than the pleasures, of the contemporary notion of 'achieved motherhood' and its relation to the rise in consumption of brands, goods and reproductive technologies.

Achieving motherhood: technologies, brands and goods

Paxson's (2004) study of the shifting historical conventions of family planning in modern Greece considers the intricate interrelations of contemporary reproductive technologies, new middle class configurations and the rise of a sophisticated consumer culture in the process of the 'making of modern mothers'.

'The terms of what it takes', she observes, 'for a woman to be recognized as a good mother are changing as women's domestic responsibilities are compounded by extra-domestic responsibilities' – most notably those associated with children as 'consumer projects' (Paxson 2004:64). Even reproductive technologies such as IVF are incorporated into a culturally specific rendering of motherhood; whereas Marilyn Strathern (1992) observes that in Anglophone culture, reproductive technologies make explicit the social construction of nature and kinship, Paxson argues that in the Greek context it is 'accommodated by a prior, conscious understanding of nature as socially realised' (p. 215). The ethical questions raised by IVF, therefore, are less to do with a crisis around the symbolic order of nature and culture and women's reproductive rights, but more about the ethics of parenting and the *quality* of mothering; or what Paxson describes as the process of 'achieved motherhood'. The new ideal of achieved motherhood, she concludes, 'not only is underwritten by techniques of bio-medicine but is also facilitated more pervasively by the ideological power of consumer culture' (2004:217).

The making of children has become couched in the mutually reliant terms of consumer culture (the acquisition of goods, related services, etc.) and the biological realization of infants. Furthermore, a woman's 'reputation' is no longer solely dependent on the control of her sexuality and the 'having' of babies, it is also reliant on having the babies *one wants*, as much as reproductive technologies can facilitate this, as well as on goods and brands. Historically, family planning involved economic and biological concerns. Paxson argues that traditional practices of thrift (that also conveyed moral definitions of motherhood) have given way to expressive consumption; '[H]aving the will and purchasing power to obtain the right stroller can be viewed as analogous to saving and planning for a child' (p. 240). In a modernized Greek context, the proliferation of advertisements for maternal, infant and child-related goods is indicative of a shift from a traditional Greek dowry culture – in which the setting up of the new bride has sufficient preparation for 'having children' – to one where acquiring the accoutrements of mothering has become the key means of facilitating 'achieved motherhood' (p. 240).

What it takes to be a 'good mother' is being entirely re-made. Motherhood has become not about having children per se, but about the quality of a woman's mothering and the drive for 'self-fashioning' through consumer choice that underpins this re-definition (Paxson 2004; Goodwin and Huppatz 2010a). In the context of Greek middle classes it is seen that the dominance of material goods (the pressure to have the right Kicker shoes, video games or toys) that define being 'raised properly' results in the decline of the birth rate. The type of child a mother will have is now 'achieved', rather than given birth to and nurtured in any simple sense, thus transforming the meaning of the Greek term 'teknopiia' that describes the socially and morally appropriate way of bringing a child into the world (p. 38).

Women's 'consumptive work' as mothers, from the preparation of food (Finch and Groves 1983; Devault 1991) to the provisioning of clothing (Clarke 2000), is a well-established tenet of feminist studies into motherhood. A range of cross-cultural anthropological analyses have illuminated the culturally specific, localized renditions of mothering in relation to specific commodity cultures and the making of new social class positions. This trajectory builds on earlier anthropological studies around the household, most notably Ursula Sharma's (1986) detailed ethnography of women's work in the urban households of Shimla, North India, which established the shifting role of women as mothers engaging in an equivalent practice as that described as 'achieved motherhood' by Paxson. In Shimla, the more affluent mothers of the emerging urban middle classes invest in the latest kitchen consumables, from pop-up toasters to Western food-mixers, and spend their time designing children's clothing. 'The distinctions in style and taste which middle- and upper-class women reach for', argues Sharma, 'are not mere symptoms of an obsession with triviality. They should be seen as indications of a serious intention to invest in *status*, not just *display* it' (p. 83). Such details are the basis on which a household is judged, children reproduced and appropriate marriages brokered. 'Seen from this point of view', writes Sharma, ' the time [the mother] spends in choosing the precise shade of fabric for her table linen or the exact blend of spices for a new dish do not represent trivial preoccupations at all' (p. 88).

The anthropological insights above, from contemporary Greece and Australia to India, position consumption and women's engagement with specific forms of material culture at the forefront of understanding contemporary mothering in the last two decades (Taylor *et al.* 2004; Casey and Martens 2007). Extending the notion of the 'assertion of moral worth through consumerism' (Paxson 2004), this chapter uses an ethnographic example to explore how social class is engendered through the practice of mothering in Britain.

'Slummy mummy/yummy mummy': class, consumption and motherhood

In 'How infants grow mothers in North London' (1997) Daniel Miller's seminal article argued the way in which a distinctively middle class set of mothers articulate locally redolent commodities and styles (including Barbie dolls, 'folk' smock dresses, Day-Glo leggings and organic food products) is part of a mutually constitutive process through which mothers develop as 'mature' subjects. More broadly, the 'retrain[ing] of anthropology's analytical gaze away from an exclusive focus on the social, toward the materiality of the social life' (Henare *et al.* 2007:2) has been crucial in bringing to the fore 'things', and the aesthetic work that surrounds them, in the study of motherhood.

Attention to the social class renditions of mothering can most effectively be made, a growing body of scholarship asserts, through the scrutiny of material culture and related methodologies. Anthropological archaeologists Victor Buchli and Gavin Lucas (2000) offer a forensic examination of the material culture of an abandoned British State local authority flat vacated in urgency by the single mother avoiding her violent and drug-using partner. In the course of their formal material culture analysis, Buchli and Lucas identify key objects of mothering abandoned in the site (once cherished memento baby-memory books, high quality shoes, photographs and children's drawings) that signal the haste with which the mother abandoned the State housing. By fleeing the property and voluntarily 'giving up' her housing, this mother limits her chances of future State support. The rules and regulations inscribed in social housing provision, which by default also embody the State's notion of 'good mothering', mean that her act of abandonment signals a broader moral recklessness. It is in the minutiae of such material culture studies that the social class renditions of mothering reveal themselves as powerful and newly valiant facets of contemporary maternity. How might the newly enlivened scholarly debates and discourse around social class and consumption in Britain relate to the specificities of mothering?

Women and girls in general, a growing body of academic literature has argued, are increasingly identified through derogatory class terms (Hayward and Yar 2006; Thoburn 2007; Skeggs 2005; Hadfield, Rudoe and Sanderson-Mann 2007; Tyler 2008). Terminology such as 'Essex girl', 'teenage mother', and 'chav', belie a continuity with older pathologizing images of the working class as excessive, wasteful and culturally unskilled (Jones 2011; Thoburn 2007; Wilson and Huntington 2006). Hayward and Yar (2006) have argued that the concept of social marginality has been reconfigured under the widespread use in popular media of the term 'chav'. Whereas 'underclass', a term previously used across social science and media alike, centred on a perceived relation to production and socially productive labour, 'chav', to quote Hayward and Yar (2006:10) 'is in contrast oriented to purportedly pathological class dispositions in relation to the sphere of consumption'. It is not merely the excess of the socially marginalized that is embodied in the spectre of the 'chav', rather the focus revolves around 'the *excessive* participation in forms of market-oriented consumption' and a proclivity towards major brand consumption (p. 14). This, it is argued, marks a 'fundamental shift to consumerist aesthetics as the grounds of typification, denigration, and vilification' (p. 22). It is the lack of distinction, *the aesthetic impoverishment* rather than the inability to consume itself due to economic and social disenfranchisement, that comes to define a new notion of the subordinate classes.

While Hayward and Yar identify the 'celebrity chav' as the pinnacle of this phenomenon, Skeggs (2005) has explored how white working-class women in particular have become measured against a generalized populist public morality. Cast as 'chavs' and dysfunctional mothers [slummy mummies] they have come to represent national ideas of a new gendered underclass. In media discourse, it is working-class mothers 'incapable of *knowing how* to look after themselves and others' (2005:967) who are presented as culpable in reproducing unhealthy, irresponsible and unruly offspring. The threat to national propriety, seen in the media as a crisis of authority, is 'symbolically figured through the excess of the grotesque, weeping, leaking, excreting bodies of working-class women' (2005:968). Disgust, Skeggs reiterates, generates consensus and authorization of middle-class standards, 'maintaining the symbolic order' (p. 970). During the anti-paedophile protests in early 2000s Britain (Lawler 2002), immorality, irrationality and stupidity were 'condensed on to the body of the working-class mother' (Skeggs 2005:970). In the notorious trial of Karen Matthews, a working-class mother charged (and convicted) of kidnapping her own daughter Shannon in 2008, the testimony of the police officer included the observation that Matthews showed more interest in the support officer's mobile telephone ring-tone, and the possibilities of downloading a copy, than the safe recovery of her daughter. In the press, this guileless act seemingly betrayed the broader abject amorality of her actions as a working-class white mother (Jones 2011; Perrie 2008).

In her article 'Chav Mum, Chav Scum', Tyler (2008) similarly explores the vilification of young white working-class mothers as an embodiment of historically familiar anxieties about 'male sexuality, reproduction, fertility, and "racial mixing"'. Tyler argues that the underclass (associated with illegitimate birth, inadequate discipline and mis-socialization) was defined, in part, as having a pathological disposition towards key social responsibilities such as the obligation to provide a stable, nuclear family environment in which children can be raised. More recently, however, it is in the appropriation of consumption and 'choices' of mothering that this discourse resides. Significantly, moral discourses around certain objects and practices are incorporated into policy and social work practice as described in Whitmarsh's (2008) study, 'Mums, dummies and "dirty dids"', in which the pacifier [dummy] is held in bio-medical expert literature as an object redolent of compromised and sloppy working-class mothering.

Mothering, then, is awash with objects, styles and constellations of things and related practices that are not just carriers of *a priori* class disposition (as suggested, for example, in the bio-medical literature on the 'dirty did'). Branded objects and mothering-related goods should not just be understood as the passive, fetishized objects of a glamorized consumer motherhood. It is by 'thinking through things' (Henare *et al.* 2007) themselves that we might open up the interstices of cross-cultural perspectives on mothers and the market, and understand the broader externalized concepts such as class and how they are inculcated in the aesthetic management mothers engage with on a daily basis.

In the following empirical example of provisioning through online auctions in contemporary Britain, the significance of specific types of goods, in historical context, emerges; and the triangulated structure of mother, infant, good is further illuminated (see Clarke 2004).[2]

> You are bidding on my son's Maxi Cosi reclining car seat. He has grown out of it and as much as he loved to kip in it, it is now time to move on to a booster seat…We have never had a problem with this car seat and it has never been in an accident. It has come from a smoke free and pet free home. The fabric is black in colour with some dark grey. There are no stains and tears. There are a few marks on the belt strap, as shown in the photo, unavoidable with small children I feel!
>
> (http://popular.ebay.co.uk/baby/car-seats.htm, 15 July 2010)

Through the empirical evidence offered by the open forum of online auctions such as eBay, women decipher, compare and evaluate objects of mothering, and their temporal appropriateness, in relation to genres of toys and styles, as an integral part of forming aesthetic dispositions. In the process of bidding for an array of items (from car seats to toys) the temporality of childhood, and children as corporeal individuals, is melded with consumer goods; in this sense the goods act as normative, collective markers in the on-going process of mothering (unlike the face-to-face transactions of nearly new or retail spaces) are openly and constantly negotiated.

In their often cited theoretical overview of childhood and temporality, James *et al.* (1998) critique the treatment of children as occupying a space 'out of time' and childhood as enduring, timeless and universal; in which a type of 'cultural primitivism casts children as inhabiting "a timeless cultural space"' (p. 242). Conversely, children as 'adults in the making' are perpetually evoked as 'the future'.

Through eBay, described as the largest inventory and archive of contemporary life (Hillis 2006), the things and the potentialities of children are held in constant suspense. Through the trading and ridding of used goods in online auction we see how mothers in a productive process strive for an ongoing version of 'achieved motherhood' – juggling things, styles, temporalities, corporalities of their offspring captured in the temporality of things and styles. Through their interjection in this public, collectively negotiated forum, mothers actualize their mothering and their infants through things and their relations to other things.

Advertisements for private eBay users frequently incorporated 'mother to mother' advice for example, 'Label says size 4 but my child wore from age three – good value!' to 'my daughter looked stunning in this and got many compliments'. Mothers' testimonials to a garment's or product's success – or explanation that it is sold unworn due only to being a mis-sized gift and the use of superlatives, 'lovely', 'gorgeous', 'stunning', 'fabulous' heightens the excitement of a potential bargain but forges an aesthetic judgement mother to mother.

eBay branded goods can take on an inalienable status (they are cherished, protected and maintained – kept in the living collective brand-archive of online auction) to the point where their pre-emptive re-sale asserts a backward influence over the types of branded goods suited to the virtual second-hand market (Clarke 2010). In terms of genres of mothering, certain types of brands have emerged as normative aspects of online provisioning. But it is the materiality of these brands, as much as some value or culture applied to them, that has made them integral to this triangulated mother, child, thing relationship.

What the stigmatized dummy (or 'dirty did') is to some model of compromised working-class motherhood, the Bugaboo pram is to 'achieved middle class' motherhood. Bugaboo, a pram whose popularity has been tied to its media profile as the 'must-have' item of celebrity mothers (featured in the TV show *Sex in the City*), uses a self-consciously innovative design generated by a student from Eindhoven Design Academy in 1999 and manufactured by a Dutch company. Its radical design positioned it outside the mainstream, traditional mass market in infant goods, and as such it began as a relatively obscure product with niche market appeal. The consumer must self-fashion and customize the article – as its components are available in a range of colourways. At around £700 upwards for the basic model, the Bugaboo, despite having a shorter functional life span in comparison to other prams and strollers, boomed in line with the market growth of eBay which provided the ideal forum to re-sell at a measurable, calculated value. At first undermining the first-hand market, with the now established second-economy of online auction, the brand managers of Bugaboo incorporate the 'lease' economy approach into their design and pricing concepts. The corporality of infants, the temporality of the social relationships of mothering, are incorporated into the very design of the Bugaboo.

Caroline[3] bought her Bugaboo (with accessories) first hand at the cost of £800 two years ago, and along with a Danish STOKKE cot, Baby Bjorn bouncy chair and a Maxi Cosi car seat, she has carefully stored all the instruction manuals, guarantees and original packaging away so that when she comes to re-sell them on eBay, she will reassemble them as branded commodities. She also keeps the boxes from her branded children's toys (such as Playmobil, Lego, etc.) in the knowledge that she will be releasing them back onto the market. Pre-emptive brand re-sale, underpinned by the traceability and indexibility of online auction, thrives in the fluid baby and children's wares market.

The brand managers of child-related products such as Bugaboo pram and Maxi-Cosi have responded to what has emerged as a threat to the first-hand product market by generating increasingly diverse product lines and individuated, customized items. Child-related goods have emerged as a new luxury market in which once functional safety objects are now available in tiger pattern, paprika pink, primrose yellow – children's car seats have joined the 'It' accessories of the fashion world (with increased price tags to match) – their nuanced relation to changes in fashion and style generating a value beyond the prescription of age appropriateness.

While genres of branded commodities, such as cars, have long been understood in relation to their depreciation and second-hand brand appeal, the boom in the secondary product market of mothering is re-constituting the very categories mother-related branded commodities inhabit. Definitions of luxury, glamour and design, once tied to the materiality and skills of related industries from couture to leather goods, are now as relevant to functional baby goods as they are objects of high-end fashion. As brand managers try to engineer the temporalities of their goods, generating obsolescence through the introduction of ever-faster design changes, it is in the forum of the mass second-hand market that the processes, objects and negotiations of motherhood and its social class dimensions are made evident.

Conclusion

How is the understanding of the interrelation of mothers and markets furthered through analysis of the brands, goods, designs and concepts of glamour inculcated in this process? How might understandings of social class be enhanced by cross-cultural and inter-disciplinary inquiries that acknowledge commodities as integral agents, rather than passive reflections, of certain forms of mothering?

A wealth of established literature considers the role of mothers in generating social networks (Bell and Ribbens 1994; Di Leonardo 1987; Tivers 1985; Gullestad 1986; Hill 1989; McCannell 1988), the work of caring (Devault 1991; Finch and Groves 1983) and the project of education (Davis *et al.* 1993; David *et al.* 1994). More recently, the significance of material and visual cultures in inter-disciplinary studies of pregnancy and early maternity (Clarke 2004, 2008; Layne 2000, 1999; Kaplan 1994; Sharpe 1999; Taylor 1992, 1997, 2000; Kehily and Thomson 2011) has been established, but there remains enormous potential for a widening, cross-cultural understanding of the social class-based aesthetic practices of women as mothers, and the inseparability of objects and infants in the making of mothers.

There is an increasing call for the incorporation, through theoretical and empirical accounts, of children into consumption (Martens *et al.* 2004; Cook 2008). The invisibility of children in a new scholarship seeking to explore 'how consumption mediates social relations, … represents structural inequalities and … connects with, and acts to sustain, cultural ideologies' (Martens *et al.* 2004:162) is clearly problematic. As Martens *et al.* (2004) have highlighted, 'habitus', the theory of social class expounded by Bourdieu (1979), relies on the notion of socially reproduced, learned and internalized aspects of class dispositions premised on the socialization of children. As Derevenski (2000: 11) comments, Bourdieu himself talks of 'the mind born of objects'. Is it possible, though, to demarcate children as discrete entities and actors in consumption, outside the worlds of goods in which they are incorporated even before birth? As we build a greater and increasingly sophisticated web of inter-disciplinary inquiry into mothers and the market, it seems at least as valid to argue for the centrality of designed goods in this schema. If we accept the enormous significance of 'things' in the practice of mothering, we must also take into account the histories, trajectories and agencies of specific forms of material culture in the making of social class power relations.

Notes

1   Tina Brown, leading international fashion editor, identified 'fabloids' as a distinct genre of publication interweaving celebrity gossip, fashion and luxury brands which 'combines the tabloid hunger for sensation with the requirement to always look fabulous'. Tina Brown (2007) *The Diana Chronicles* (London: Century), p. 337, cited in Gundle (2008:347–87).
2   Research regarding informal and online provisioning was part of an ongoing study (2008–2010) related to the original AHRC Centre for the Study of Domestic Interior (Royal College of Art, Royal Holloway University and Victoria and Albert Museum 2003–2007) for which Alison Clarke was Principal Investigator leading the design and ethnography component.
3   This example also comes from the AHRC study referred to in the previous footnote.

References

Bailey, M. (2002) *Marketing to Moms: Getting Your Share of the Trillion-Dollar Market*, Ithaca, NY: Prima Lifestyles Publishing.

Bailey, M. and Ulman, B. (2005) *Trillion Dollar Moms: Marketing to a New Generation of Mothers*, London: Kaplan Publishing.

Bell, L. and Ribbens, J. (1994) 'Isolated housewives and complex maternal worlds – the significance of social contacts between women with young children in industrial societies', *Sociological Review* 42:2, 227–62.

Bourdieu, P. (1979) *Distinction: a Social Critique on the Judgement of Taste*, London: Routledge.

Buchli, V. and Lucas, G. (2000) 'Children, gender and the material culture of domestic abandonment in the late twentieth century', in J. Sofaer-Derevenski (ed.) *Children and Material Culture,* London: Routledge, 131–8.

Casey, E. and Martens, L. (eds) (2007). *Gender and Consumption: Domestic Cultures and the Commercialisaton of Everday Life.* Hampshire: Ashgate.

Clarke, A. (2000) '"Mother swapping": the trafficking of nearly new children's wear', in P. Jackson, M. Lowe, D. Milller and F. Mort (eds) *Commercial Cultures: Economies, Practices, Spaces*, Oxford: Berg, 85–100.

Clarke, A. (2004) 'Maternity and materiality: becoming a mother in consumer culture', in J.S. Taylor, L.L. Layne and D.F. Wozniak (eds) *Consuming Motherhood,* New Brunswick: Rutgers University Press, 55–71.

Clarke, A. (2007) 'Making sameness: mothering, commerce and the culture of children's birthday parties', in E. Casey and L. Martens (eds), *Gender and Consumption: Domestic Cultures and the Commercialization of Everyday Life,* London: Ashgate, 79–96.

Clarke, A. (2008) 'Coming of age in suburbia: gifting the consumer child', in M. Gutman and N. de Connick-Smith (eds) *Designing Modern Childhoods*, New Brunswick, NJ: Rutgers University Press, 79–96.

Clarke, A. (2010) 'The second-hand brand: liquid assets and borrowed goods', in D. Wengrow and A. Bevan (eds) *Cultures of Commodity Branding*, Walnut Creek, CA: Left Coast Press, 235–54.

Clements, M., and Thompson, T. L. (2011) *Tuning into Mom: Understanding America's Most Powerful Consumer*, West Lafayette, IN: Purdue University Press.

Coffey, T., Siegel, D. and Livingston, G. (2006) *Marketing to the New Super Consumer: Mom & Kid*, Ithaca, NY: Paramount Market Publishing, Inc.

Cook, D. (2008) 'The missing child in consumption theory', *Journal of Consumer Culture* 8:2, 219–43.

Crewe L. and Collins, P. (2006) 'Commodifying children: fashion, space, and the production of the profitable child', *Environment and Planning A* 38(1), 7–24.

David, M., West, A. and Ribbens, J. (1994) *Mothers' Intuition? Choosing Secondary Schools*, London: Taylor and Francis.

David, M., Edwards, R., Hughes, M. and Ribbens, J. (1993) *Mothers and Education: Inside Out? Exploring Family-education Policy and Experience*, Basingstoke: Macmillan.

Derevenski, J.S. (ed) (2000) *Children and Material Culture*, London: Routledge.

Devault, M. (1991) *Feeding the Family: the Social Organization of Caring as Gendered Work*, Chicago: Chicago University Press.

Di Leonardo, M. (1987) 'The female world of cards and holidays: women, families and the work of kinship', *Signs* 12, 440–58.

Finch, J. and Groves, D. (eds) (1983) *A Labour of Love: Women, Work and Caring*, London: Routledge & Kegan Paul.

Goodwin, S. and Huppatz, K. (2010) 'Mothers making class distinctions: the aesthetics of maternity', in S. Goodwin and K. Huppatz (eds) *The Good Mother: Contemporary Motherhoods in Australia*, Sydney: Sydney University Press, 69–88.

Goodwin, S. and Huppatz, K. (eds) (2010) *The Good Mother: Contemporary Motherhoods in Australia,* Sydney: Sydney University Press.

Gullestad, M. (1986) *Kitchen Table Society: a Case Study of Family Life and Friendships of Young Working-Class Mothers in Urban Norway*, Oslo: Universitetsforlaget.

Gundle, S. (2007) *Glamour: a History*, Oxford: Oxford University Press.

Hadfield, L., Rudoe, N. and Sanderson-Mann, G. (2007) 'Motherhood, choice and the British media: a time to reflect', *Gender Education* 19:2, 255–63.

Hayward, K. and Yar, M. (2006) 'The "chav" phenomenon: consumption, media and the construction of a new underclass', *Crime, Media, Culture* 2:1, 9–28.

Henare, A., Holbraad, M., and Wastell, S. (eds) (2007). *Thinking Through Things: Theorising Artefacts Ethnographically*, New York: Routledge.

Hill, M. (1989) 'The role of social networks in the care of young children', *Children and Society* 3:3, 195–211.

Hillis, K., Petit, M. and Epley, N.S. (2006) *Everyday eBay: Culture, Collecting and Desire*, London: Routledge.

James, A., with James, A. L. (2008) *Key Concepts in Childhood Studies*, London: Sage.

James, A., Jenks, C. and Prout, A. (1998) *Theorizing Childhood*, Cambridge: Polity Press.

Jones, O. (2011) *Chavs: the Demonization of the Working Class*, London: Verso.

Kaplan, A. (1994) 'Look who's talking, indeed: fetal images in recent North American visual culture', in E. Glenn, G. Chang and L.R. Forcey (eds) *Mothering: Ideology, Experience and Agency,* London: Routledge, 121–37.

Kehily, M. J., and Thomson, R. (2011). 'Figuring families: generation, situation and narrative in contemporary mothering', *Sociological Research Online*, 16(4) Article 16.

Latour, B. (1993) *We Have Never Been Modern*. Trans. by Catherine Porter. Cambridge, MA: Harvard University Press.

Lawler, S. (2002) 'Mobs and monsters: independent man meets Paulsgrove woman', *Feminist Theory* 3(1): 103–13.

Layne, L. (1999) '"I remember the day I shopped for your layette": consumer goods, fetuses, and feminism in the context of pregnancy loss', in L.M. Morgan and M.W. Michaels (eds) *Fetal Subjects: Feminist Positions,* Phildelphia: University of Pennsylvania Press, 251–79.

Layne, L. (2000) '"He was a real baby with real things": a material cultural analysis of personhood, parenthood and pregnancy loss', *Journal of Material Culture,* 5:3, 321–47.

Martens, L., Sutherton, D. and Scott, S. (2004) 'Bringing children (and parents) into the sociology of consumption: towards a theoretical and empirical agenda', *Journal of Consumer Culture* 4:2, 155–82.

McCannell, K. (1988) 'Social networks and the transition to motherhood', in R. Milardo (ed.) *Families and Social Networks*, Newbury Park: Sage, 83–106.

McRobbie, A. (2006) 'Yummy mummies leave a bad taste for young women. The cult of celebrity motherhood is deterring couples from having children early', *The Guardian*, 2 March. http://www.guardian.co.uk/world/2006/mar/02/gender.comment (accessed 3 July 2012).

Miller, D. (1997) 'How infants grow mothers in North London', *Theory, Culture & Society* 14:4, 67–88.

Palmer, S. (2006) *Toxic Childhood: How the Modern World Is Damaging Our Children and What We Can Do About It*, London: Orion.

Palmer, S. (2007) *Detoxing Childhood: What Parents Need to Know to Raise Happy Successful Children*, London: Orion.

Paxson, H. (2004) *Making Modern Mothers: Ethics and Family Planning in Urban Greece*, Berkeley: California University Press.

Perrie, R. (2008) 'The "fake" anguish', *The Sun*, 13 November. http://www.thesun.co.uk/sol/homepage/news/1925279/The-fake-anguish-of-Shannons-mum.html (accessed 3 July 2012).

Skeggs, B. (2005) 'The making of class and gender through visualizing moral subject formation', *Sociology* 39:5, 965–82.

Sharma, U. (1986) *Women's Work, Class and the Urban Household: a Study of Shimla, North India*, London: Tavistock.

Sharpe, S. (1999) 'Bodily speaking: spaces and experience of birth', in E.K. Teather (ed.) *Embodied Geographies: Space, Bodies and Rites of Passage*, London: Routledge, 91–104.

Strathern, M. (1992) *Reproducing the Future: Essays on Anthropology, Kinship and the New Reproductive Technologies*, Manchester: Manchester University Press.

Taylor, J. (1997) 'Image of contradiction: obstetrical ultrasound in American culture', in S. Franklin and H. Ragone (eds) *Reproducing Reproduction: Kinship, Power, and Technological Innovation*, Philadelphia, PA: University of Pennsylvania Press, 15–45.

Taylor, J. (2000) 'Of sonograms and baby prams: prenatal diagnosis, pregnancy, and consumption', *Feminist Studies* 26:2, 391–418.

Taylor, J.S. (1992) The Public fetus and the family car: from abortion politics to a Volvo advertisement, *Public Culture* 4:2, 67–80.

Taylor, J., Layne, L. and Wozniak, D. (eds) (2004) *Consuming Motherhood,* New Brunswick, NJ: Rutgers University Press.

Thoburn, N. (2007) 'Patterns of production: cultural studies after hegemony', *Theory Culture & Society* 24:3, 79–94.

Tivers, J. (1985) *Women Attached: the Daily Lives Of Women With Young Children*, London: Croom Helm.

Tivers, J. (1985) *Women Attached: the Daily Lives of Women With Young Children*, London: Croom Helm.

Tropp, L. (2006) '"Faking a sonogram": representations of motherhood on *Sex in the City*', *The Journal of Popular Culture*, 39, 861–77.

Tyler, I. (2008) '"Chav mum, chav scum": class disgust in contemporary Britain', *Feminist Media Studies* 8(1): 17–34.

Whitmarsh J. (2008) 'Mums, dummies and dirty "dids": the dummy as a symbolic representation of mothering?' *Children & Society* 22: 278–290.

Wilson, A. and Huntington, H. (2006) 'Deviant (m)others: the construction of teenage motherhood in contemporary discourse', *Journal of Social Policy*, 35, 59–76.

5 Negotiations of motherhood – between ideals and practice

Malene Gram and Helle D. Pedersen

Introduction

Today mothers are on average older than ever before when having their first child. For many women it is a challenge to get pregnant at all, and for the majority, in the Western world, having children is an active choice and a privilege. Expecting a child has always been entangled with some anxiety and uncertainty (Bourke 2005), which is probably why a number of rituals and superstition have long existed (cf. VOICE Group 2010). Whereas in earlier days the number of children (and mothers) dying during childbirth was much higher than today in the Western world, anxieties and uncertainties related to becoming a mother still persist. Mothers are exposed to a massive information flow about what could go wrong during pregnancy, during infancy, while children grow up and just in general. More knowledge about what to be anxious about can produce more anxiety (Mulgan 1996 in Kneafsey *et al.* 2004) in what has even been called an 'age of anxiety' (Wilkinson 2001; Jackson and Everts 2010).

At the same time, ideals and social norms related to what an expectant or new mother ought to do and, particularly, ought not to do, seem to have reached new dimensions (Schütze 1986; Badinter 2010; Fox *et al.* 2009) in shaping a normative identity for mothers. As Choia *et al.* (2005) discuss in an article tellingly called 'Supermum, superwife, supereverything', a strong belief in the myth of motherhood as natural and biological among participants in their empirical study caused these women to feel inadequate, because they were not able to live up to such standards. Similarly, Miller (2005) writes that essentialist ideas of women's natural capacity to nurture means that dealing with more difficult aspects of motherhood can be lonely work, as these concerns are often not discussed due to fears about not being perceived as a good enough mother.

Consumption is known to be strongly interlinked with the identification process of becoming and being a mother (Taylor 2004) and consumption is an important means of negotiating and displaying competency in entering the mother role (VOICE Group 2010). Consumption is one way to deal with both role transition (Hogg *et al.* 2004) and anxiety, not least as articulated in advertising discourse (e.g. Coutant *et al.* 2011).

This chapter explores, through qualitative methods, how some Danish expectant and first-time mothers deal with the high ideals of motherhood in an age of flourishing anxiety. It examines how consumption and modification of habitualized consumption were used in negotiating and performing motherhood.

Literature review

Motherhood

The implications of being a mother and the mythology of the good mother are all-encompassing in a way that has never been known till recent decades (Zelizer 1985; Schütze 1986; Badinter 2010). Choia *et al.* (2005) explore the gap between ideal motherhood and realities, which have been seen by some as leading to depression, with mothers as passive victims. Others argue that mothers resist the dominating ideals of motherhood and are active agents, choosing between available discourses according to particular contexts and situations to deal with the lack of coherence between ideals and practice. Still, these choices are seen to be within frames of what is socially acceptable and thereby not entirely voluntary; there are few alternatives to the role of dedicated mother (Choia *et al.* 2005). Miller (2005) finds that the fear of not fulfilling the expected mother role silences mothers on the difficulties of having and nurturing a child. At the same time, the pressure on women entering into motherhood is seen to be growing (Fox *et al.* 2009), and the level of demand for self-sacrifice is seen to have reached new heights (Badinter 2010).

Consumption in transition

Consumption is redefined in periods of transition, and new situations carry with them new challenges and demand new solutions. Consumers use consumption in relation to transition phases, and it can help in the articulation of a new life role (Schouten 1991). It can be used to fill the void amidst the anxiety experienced during a transition (Hogg *et al.* 2004; Noble and Walker 1997) and is thus a way for pregnant women and new mothers to find their feet in a period of transition, even though this consumption is not without ambivalence (VOICE Group 2010). The transition to parenthood can be anxiety-provoking as the individual needs to take on and fill a new role, and the mother role is particularly loaded with meaning and expectations. New practices need to be established, habitualized and carried out with competency.

Risk and anxiety

Contrary to earlier centuries when it was coupled with fate, risk has in recent decades been closely linked to responsibility, reflexivity and decision making (Lupton and Tulloch 2002). On the one hand, traditions are seen as dissolving and, on the other, a lack of trust in science and authorities has emerged. This led Beck (1992) to develop the concept of the risk society, in which the individual needs to make his or her own decisions and take responsibility for them, which is seen to be highly anxiety-provoking (Lupton and Tulloch 2002). Lash (1993), however, has criticized the rationalistic and individualistic views of the human actor presented by Beck, the generalizing character of these theories and their lack of acknowledgment of the significance of group membership (Lupton and Tulloch 2002). Warde (2005) also argues that the impact of reflexivity, independence and 'freedom' of choice for the individual is overestimated, and that the significance of the risk society in everyday life is overdramatized. He argues that social conventions and habit mean that individuals are not overanxious but can act within a relatively well-defined frame of action. Anxiety has both negative and positive sides; 'anxiety can be debilitating, but it can also be productive for those who respond with attempts to change themselves or their environments to counter their anxieties' (Kneafsey *et al.* 2004, p. 7).

In this chapter, anxiety is not seen as a source of deep psychological pain (Woodward 2006, p. 279) or a psychologically abnormal situation as in the clinical context (Woodward 2006), but as a state of uneasiness. The participants in this empirical study are not women in 'psychologically abnormal situations', but they do have anxieties.

Summing up, motherhood is constructed as a central life role with high expectations, the transition to which may seem overwhelming and anxiety-provoking. The high demands on women to take responsibility for motherhood in an 'age of anxiety' could mean that they experience this period as very difficult to handle. This chapter analyses the voices of some Danish women who are going through this transition, focusing on perceptions of anxiety, consumption and ideal motherhood.

Methodology

This chapter aims to explore women's negotiation of ideal motherhood in a Danish context, with a particular focus on anxiety and how they modify consumption of mundane products in the transition to motherhood. An interpretive approach was taken, with in-depth semi-structured interviews used to help unfold the meaning of these women's experiences and understand the world from their point of view (Kvale 1996). To address the complexity of motherhood, anxiety and consumption, it was found valuable to interview both pregnant women who were in the liminal phase of the transition, as well as first-time mothers who had gone through the transition and were in the process of internalizing their new life role. Interviews lasted from 45 minutes to two and a half hours and were conducted with four mothers and five pregnant women living around three Danish metropolitan regions. The interviewees were middle class in a broad sense, having various types of education and jobs. They ranged in age from 26 to 39 with a mean age of 29, and all were in relationships.

The women were recruited through postings on relevant internet fora that actively target pregnant women and mothers such as the social site mingraviditet. dk (mypregnancy.dk) and also by employing the snowballing principle (Bryman 2004). Some of the women knew each other through the fora. They were interviewed in their homes in February and March 2009, with an interview guide focusing on motherhood, anxiety and consumption. The interviews were conducted by the second author who was herself pregnant at the time. This helped establish an atmosphere of trust and understanding during the interviews, facilitating open-hearted talks about the issues at stake. The interviews were audiotaped with participants' permission and transcribed verbatim; names have been changed here to assure anonymity. The data was analysed through interview analysis (Kvale 1996) for patterns, tendencies and contrasts in the women's view of good motherhood, anxiety and consumption. The analysis draws on all interviews, with quotes presented to offer specific examples of how interviewees account for their negotiations of 'doing' motherhood.

Findings

Anxieties

The pregnant women in this study talk about a number of possible outcomes of the pregnancy that they fear, mainly related to the health of their child. These fears may inhibit looking forward to having the child, and the wealth of information to which these women have access is not just reassuring, as the following example shows:

> At some point I read that there is a 25 per cent probability that it [the pregnancy] ends in a miscarriage, and then I just thought: 'Don't write things like that'. I totally panicked! And then I became really overprotective towards myself, because I know that I would blame myself if…
>
> (Louise, pregnant, 29, trainee accountant)

'Panicking', 'being overprotective', and 'blaming oneself' indicate a situation of anxiety in contrast to the stereotypical picture of happiness when being pregnant, especially as all these women (except one) have chosen to become pregnant. Louise does not even finish her sentence, not wanting to articulate the worst case scenario.

The new mothers seem a little more relaxed, after having given birth safely and being able to see that the child is doing well. Still a number of concerns and fears are haunting them. There is a fear of invisible risks (Beck 1992), which is also found among the pregnant women, from chemicals and various harmful substances in food, pollution and clothes.

Breastfeeding is highly recommended in the Danish context to the point of stigmatization as bad mothering if some women choose not to breastfeed. This expectation brings with it a fear of not being able to breastfeed (see also VOICE Group 2010). The importance of breastfeeding is highlighted by one of the new mothers in the study:

> Then I could still feel when she was born that it [breastfeeding] actually meant quite a lot, even though a good mother isn't in her breasts. But still this is something you think: you have to be able to breastfeed your own child.
>
> (Majken, mother, 29, media student)

Rationally speaking, a good mother 'isn't in her breasts' but 'you have to be able to breastfeed your own child'. This is part of the social normativity and expectations of being a good mother in the Danish context, which can be anxiety-provoking for mothers-to-be and cause a feeling of failure and guilt in mothers who do not succeed in or do not wish to breastfeed. It is not questioned that Majken wants to be a good mother.

Another fear, which is not directly related to the child, regards the issue of losing one's identity.

The sudden attention to the expected child can be overwhelming, with friends and family being more interested in the unborn child or the new-born child than in the women. A fear is to become a mother who can only talk about diapers and care about children. 'Just' being a mother is not what these women want to be, no matter how much they want the child, as several informants express. For example:

> I am very aware of the fact that I don't want to be one of those who only talks about dirty diapers and baby vomit and faeces and things like that when I am with my friends. Then we have to talk about adult things.
>
> (Sanne, mother, 26, social work student)

This can no doubt be linked to the development of women's liberation in the Danish context, where girls are brought up to be in the labour market, and previous generations' work to jump out of the role of 'just' mothers, even if the mother role still takes up considerable space.

Practices of responsible motherhood

The women in this study range from those who hardly dare to believe they are pregnant to those with a young child needing attention and care. During this period they start performing motherhood and change their practices in a number of ways, but especially through consumption and modification of routinized consumption, as they face new needs, restrictions and suggestions that they feel they need to deal with. They do this in different ways, negotiating their own peace of mind and making their own interpretations of doing responsible motherhood through a process of bricolage. They seek to fill the mother role but negotiate the degree to which they give up their former identities and practices as young outgoing women. The practice of motherhood is to be responsible even if the concrete performance of motherhood is constantly negotiated in their everyday practices.

Consumption and consumption modification

As well as consuming baby-related goods, as is well-described elsewhere (e.g. VOICE Group 2010), being pregnant is very much about *not* consuming certain goods. Some products like alcohol, hair dye, perfume, lotion and shampoo with parabens are avoided completely by some women, whereas others find 'minimal' consumption of these goods acceptable. The women in the study negotiate the boundaries of for example alcohol consumption, and they do not accept all available advice, arguing that this is neither reasonable nor possible. They all set up a personal navigation map with rules concerning what cannot be consumed at all, what can be consumed in moderation, and what ought to be consumed in larger quantities. This personal navigation map is developed and modified through online research and through dialogue with midwives, friends, sisters, parents and colleagues. These women are about to take on or have just taken on what they perceive to be an extremely important role in line with how motherhood is perceived today. They want to demonstrate competency (Warde 2005). At the same time they problematize the boundaries of the demands imposed on them, and allow themselves to take things as they come, being pragmatic about what is doable and what is not, what advice must be adhered to at all costs and where one can be more indulgent.

The responsibilities associated with the transition to motherhood cause feelings of guilt, anxiety and of being constrained without really knowing whether one is doing all right. As one pregnant woman says:

> Sometimes I have wished that you got a piece of paper where it said: 'You can do this and this and this and this, or rather you can't do those things. These things can be directly dangerous. These things are up to you to decide [...] and these things you shouldn't worry about at all'.
>
> (Maj, pregnant, 28, English language student)

Just as women are confronted with various constructions of the 'good mother', they also have to juggle the different risks and sometimes even contradictory recommendations which must be taken into consideration. Thus the tensions which expectant and new mothers face when being in the transition to motherhood are many and complex. Although a considerable number of the participants trust information from experts and authorities to a large extent, several women rely on their common sense when making decisions. This means that they do not accept the information which experts produce unconditionally but instead develop strategies concerning which risks and recommendations they will pay attention to – often using the metaphor of taking recommendations 'with a grain of salt'. Being responsible is on the one hand about what others think:

> I: Do you think a lot about what others think about you for example when you do your shopping?
> A: Yes, because I will not buy cigarettes for [partner]. I won't. I don't want them to think that I smoke when I am pregnant.
>
> (Anna, pregnant, 26, postal worker)

Anna thus changes her behaviour as she would not run the risk of being stigmatized as a smoking pregnant woman, referring to 'them', the gaze of others. Anna has also chosen a specific pram because it makes her look responsible (cf. Thomsen and Sorensen 2006). Still, consumption modification is perhaps to an even greater extent related to peace of mind and dealing with fear and expectations. An important area of negotiation is alcohol consumption:

> I know some people think you should stay completely away from that [alcohol], but there I have chosen that I don't believe that…That is…of course I don't sit and drink wine while I breastfeed, […] I don't get drunk or anything like that.
>
> (Majken, mother)

In this excerpt, several claims are raised explaining why Majken does not resist consumption of alcohol. It is a choice – one of many Majken has made, indicating a level of reflexivity which is very outspoken among these informants – even if one could argue that 'choosing to believe' is a contradiction in terms – if she really believes, why then choose? Majken does not make explicit what it is she does not believe in. It can be interpreted that she does not believe in the harmful effects of a limited amount of wine. Here she refers to the recommendation from the Danish health authorities of not drinking at all, which she contests. She further argues that she does not drink while she breastfeeds. She implies it would be worse if she drank while breastfeeding, not elaborating on if it would be better for the child if she does not drink and breastfeed simultaneously or whether spectators would classify her as an irresponsible mother. Finally she argues that she does not get drunk. By limiting the intake and the situations of intake, she seeks to justify that she stays within the boundaries of good motherhood. As this example shows, a comprehensive work of justification follows consumption in this potential no-go area. She does not drink while she breastfeeds and does not get drunk, so on the one hand her account shows that she is not irresponsible. On the other hand, she is not 'fanatic' about advice and avoids being a perfectionist mother.

All participants claim that they take measures in relation to advice on changing consumption behaviour. Still there is some level of shrugging and accepting that not all dangers can be avoided where the interviewees choose to be pragmatic. The women in this study basically continue their consumption practices but modify according to what they assess as reasonable, in this process drawing particularly on friends, family, colleagues and (social) media.

The perfect, the normal and the irresponsible mother

Most women, in the study, realize that being 'the perfect mother' is neither possible nor desirable:

> The perfect mother… that is someone who does her best, because that is what you can do. I think that I don't necessarily become a more perfect mother from having cooked all food from scratch or something like that. I feel that I am the perfect mother to Maja. Maybe it happens that I talk too angrily to her, even though she doesn't understand it yet, or maybe I have let her stay in the pram crying two minutes longer than I should have. And I can also

get a bad conscience about it looking back, when I am suddenly in a good mood and have plenty of energy. But still, I think that that is part of being a human being, that you can't be perfect, and there is no reason to strive for perfection, because we are not robots who can do everything. And I think I am pretty good at focussing on that – on my good days. Ask me on the days when everything is just totally chaotic: 'No, I am just no good as a mum, I can't do anything'.

(Solveig, mother, 29, physiotherapist)

Solveig is very eloquent about these mechanisms of ideals versus practice, referring to good days and bad days, and using the metaphor of not being a 'robot'. She articulates the range of emotions involved from feeling competent to feeling guilty and shameful or even useless. Anxiety, bad conscience and guilt along with a wish to display and feel competency are inextricably linked with these women's experience of motherhood, even if they on their good days are able to disregard part of the overwhelming demands.

The women in the study sketch a number of ways of filling the mother roles which can be summed up as three main types, where one type is undesirable (the irresponsible mum), one type is partly undesirable but also to some extent worth striving for (the perfect mum) whereas the third type is the one all informants identify with (the normal or good mum).

The perfect mum, who switches into the perfectionist (and thereby undesirable mum) is described by the informants as someone who always remembers everything, picks up her child early (it is almost not an option to be a stay-at-home mum in Denmark), is always patient and cooks from scratch (cakes, jam, fruit purée), always has a clean house, and so on. This perfectionist mum is someone the informants do not identify with, e.g. described as 'totally holy' (Sanne, mother) and who is seen as someone who gives up her own life for her child.

On the other hand, the women have clear images of irresponsible mothers (who are for example seen to drink or smoke too much, or leave their child too long in the car seat), from whom they also distance themselves.

The women in this study position themselves as good and responsible mothers in a complex web of meanings of responsible/irresponsible, perfect/imperfect motherhood. They mostly articulate a pragmatic attitude to motherhood even if a touch of disappointment and guilt is part of the story of not living up to being the perfect mother:

And maybe I would have wished that I had had time and energy to [cook from scratch], but there I perhaps just think that I have accepted that I haven't got time to do everything, and I actually also prefer to use time playing with her [child], than being in the kitchen cooking while she has to play by herself.

(Sanne, mother)

Of course you want to be the all-embracing mother who succeeds in setting boundaries in the right places and has energy for everything, and those are some good ideals to have. But sometimes the energy is just not there, and then it is just not there.

(Majken, mother)

Rebellion against demands for perfectionism is seen in several interviews, particularly in relation to not cooking from scratch or providing homemade food, even if homemade food is seen as equalling devotional love (Miller 1998) and as providing certainty 'against dangers lurking in serialized market-made food' (Moisio *et al.* 2004, p. 368).

Sanne says: 'There is a greater focus [in recent years] on not being the perfect mother.' She notes that in books and TV programmes, some celebrities reveal that they are not perfect mothers; for example, Danish X-factor hostess Lisa Rønne has spoken in mainstream women's magazines about the less rosy side of motherhood. This offers alternative role models which were previously hard to find (Choi *et al.* 2005). Sanne continues:

I think that since there is this counter-reaction that you don't have to be a perfect mother, it must be because at some time there has been an image in society of perfect mothers: the ones who make all fruit puree themselves, bake and always have cleaned the house, pick up their child at 2.30 at the latest in the day care, etc, etc. And it is for that reason that some people have felt a need to make such programmes and write books like that, but I don't know. I have never thought that a mother or a pregnant woman should be in a certain way.

Discussion and conclusion

The transition to motherhood is complex for most of the women in this study, since the responsibilities associated with this transition cause feelings of guilt, anxiety and constraint. At the same time as the women are confronted with different constructions of the 'good mother' they also have to juggle the different risks and contradictory recommendations they need to take into consideration, and thus the tensions which they experience in the transition to motherhood are many. However, although a considerable number of the participants trust the information from experts and authorities, several rely on their common sense, meaning that they do not accept unconditionally the information provided by experts, but instead develop strategies concerning the risks and recommendations to which they will pay attention. These strategies draw on the discourse and practices they see among friends and family and what they find in online social fora. They are not free to choose just any coping strategy (Lash 1993; Lupton and Tulloch 2002; Warde 1994) but are anchored in overall ideas of responsible motherhood, such as whether or not to take one or two glasses of wine. The cultural practices around them thus frame their arena of choice and action.

The tensions that are experienced by the informants between how they would have thought life as a mother would be and how it turns out seems to be reconciled pragmatically with arguments regarding prioritization and realization of how low energy levels can sometimes be. Still – as exemplified in one account – the choice consists of whether they will spend time cooking from scratch or playing with the child, not if they will read the newspaper on the couch, thus staying within the realm of dedicated motherhood.

These women are not really resisting the normative identities of motherhood (child first, duties must be lived up to, a child is central to the good life, and so on). However, they oppose to some extent the overwhelming demands of motherhood. They resist giving up their previous identity and conforming to all of the proposals for appropriate pregnant living and mothering, where they take the freedom to negotiate the advice and improvise their own interpretation of reasonable motherhood practices in their own personal navigation maps. In spite of a wealth of information they need to deal with, they mainly keep calm, and seem to accept that nobody is perfect and that tensions and contradictions exist. They routinize their new practices where they have taken a stance on perceived risks (Kneafsey *et al.* 2004) and live with the inherent tensions.

Regarding the advice on alcohol, consumption of which everybody modifies, this becomes perceived as a question of ideology where each woman interprets and chooses what to 'believe' and how to deal with the advice all within a certain arena of acceptable behaviour. The women insist on hanging onto their previous identity as not 'just' mothers but active independent beings. Also the time-consuming ideal of cooking from scratch which is encountered is countered by the argument that time is better spent playing with the child, and several informants solve this dilemma through consumption, embracing the options of buying organic baby food, and buying cakes at the baker's and thereby resisting the ideal mother figure (in their accounts) who, with great dedication, bakes her bread herself and cooks everything.

Consumption and modification of consumption is thus used in a complex web of coping strategies, as symbolic props in search for peace of mind and identification as a responsible mother. The informants position themselves in comparison to other mothers and seem for the most part to be optimistic about their handling of responsibility.

As illustrated in Figure 5.1, informants see themselves as responsible and not completely perfect, who often strive to become better. These women are reflexive about the impossibility of being superwomen, but they still have a struggle between what the brain says and what the heart says as one woman expresses this dilemma. All interviewees identify other pregnant women/mothers as being either similar to their own position or, in a few examples, as either too perfectionist or too irresponsible.

The informants in this study situate themselves as mastering the new practices of responsible motherhood on the one hand, but on the other they refuse to accept all motherhood expectations, even if this brings some guilt and regret. Most importantly, through their personal navigation maps, which they develop in their transition to becoming mothers, they seem to accept their own performances and stay calm despite high demands and potential fields of anxiety.

These navigation maps are 'personal' but choices are kept within the relative narrow frames of acceptable motherhood within the cultural frames of which

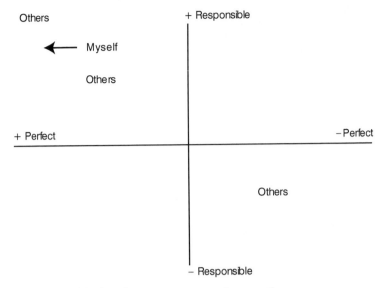

Figure 5.1 Self-positioning of pregnant women and new mothers

these women are part. Still decisions are not easy (to dye hair or not to dye hair, to drink alcohol or not), demanding significant discursive work of legitimization and their behaviour can provoke negative reactions from the surrounding world.

These women are Danish, for the most part well-educated, which no doubt plays a role in their enactment and articulation of motherhood. It would be interesting to reproduce this study in other social settings and other cultural contexts as issues related to motherhood, anxiety and consumption are known to be deeply culturally anchored. Moreover it would be interesting to explore the role of the father in relation to parenthood, consumption and anxiety.

References

Badinter, E. (2010) *Le Conflit: la femme et la mère*. Paris: Flammarion.

Beck, U. (1992) *Risk Society – Towards a New Modernity.* Originally published as *Risikogesellschaft: Auf dem Weg in eine Andere Moderne*. Frankfurt am Main: Suhrkamp Verlag, Sage Publications, (first published 1986).

Bourke, J. (2005) *Fear. A Cultural History*. London: Virago Press.

Bryman, A. (2004) *Social Research Methods*. 2nd edn. New York: Oxford University Press.

Choia, P., Henshaw, C., Baker, S. and Tree, J. (2005) 'Supermum, superwife, supereverything: performing femininity in the transition to motherhood', *Journal of Reproductive and Infant Psychology* 23, 167–80.

Coutant, A., de la Ville, I., Gram, M. and Boireau, N. (2011) 'Motherhood, advertising, and anxiety: a cross-cultural perspective on Danonino Commercials', *Advertising & Society Review*, 12:2, 1–19.

Fox, R., Nicolson, P. and Heffernan, K. (2009) 'Pregnancy police? Maternal bodies, surveillance and food', in P. Jackson (ed.) *Changing Families, Changing Food*. London: Palgrave.

Hogg, M.K., Folkman Curasi, C. and Maclaran, P. (2004) 'The (re-)configuration of production and consumption in empty nest households/families', *Consumption, Markets and Culture* 7, 239–59.

Jackson, P. and Everts, J (2010) 'Anxiety as social practice', *Environment and Planning A,* 42:11, 2791–806.

Kneafsey, M., Holloway, L., Venn, L., Cox, R., Dowler, E. and Tuomainen, H. (2004) 'Consumers and producers: coping with food anxieties through "reconnection"?', *Cultures of Consumption and ESRH-AHRB Research Programme*, Working paper 19.

Kvale, S. (1996) *Interviews*. London: Sage.

Lash, S. (1993) 'Reflexive modernization: the aesthetic dimension', *Theory, Culture and Society* 10, 1–23.

Lupton, D. and Tulloch, J. (2002) '"Risk is part of your life": risk epistemologies among a group of Australians', *Sociology* 36:2, 317–34.

Miller, D. (1998) *A Theory of Shopping*. Ithaca, NY: Cornell University Press.

Miller, T. (2005) *Making Sense of Motherhood: a Narrative Approach.* Cambridge: Cambridge University Press.

Moisio, R., Arnould, A. and Price, L. (2004) 'Between mothers and markets: constructing family identity through homemade food', *Journal of Consumer Culture* 4:3, 361–84.

Mulgan, G. (1996) 'High tech and high angst', in S. Dunant and R. Porter (eds) *The Age of Anxiety*. London: Virago, 1–19.

Noble, C.and Walker, B. (1997) 'Exploring the relationships among liminal transitions, symbolic consumption, and the extended self', *Psychology & Marketing* 14, 29–47.

Schouten, J. (1991) 'Selves in transition: symbolic consumption in personal rites of passage and identity reconstruction', *Journal of Consumer Research* 17 (March), 412–25.

Schütze, Y. (1986) *Die Gute Mutter: Zur Geschichte des Normativen Musters 'Mutterliebe'*. Hannover: Kleine.

Taylor, J.S., Layne, L.L. and Wozniak, D.F. (eds) (2004) *Consuming Motherhood*. New Brunswick: Rutgers University Press.

Thomsen, T. and Sorensen, E. (2006) 'The first four-wheeled status symbol: pram consumption as a vehicle for the construction of motherhood identity', *Journal of Marketing Management* 22, 907–27.

VOICE Group (2010) 'Buying into motherhood? Problematic consumption and ambivalence in transitional phases', *Consumption, Markets and Culture* 13:4, 373–97.

Warde, A. (1994) 'Consumption, identity-formation and uncertainty', *Sociology* 28:4, 877–98.

Warde, A. (2005) 'Consumption and theories of practice', *Journal of Consumer Culture* 5:2, 131–53.

Wilkinson, I. (2001) *Anxiety in a Risk Society*. London: Routledge.

Woodward, I. (2006) 'Investigating consumption anxiety thesis: aesthetic choice, narrativisation and social performance', *The Sociological Review*, 54:2, 263–82.

Zelizer, V. (1985) *Pricing the Priceless Child*. New York: Basic Books.

Part II
Feeding motherhood

6 'It won't do her any harm' they said, 'or they wouldn't put it on the market'

Infant weaning, markets and mothers' narratives of trust

Julia Keenan and Helen Stapleton

Introduction

Using participant-driven photo-elicitation (PDPE) from a broader longitudinal study,[1] this chapter employs a case study approach to explore tensions facing new mothers as they navigate the world of commodities and services associated with the weaning of infants. We focus on the trajectories of two first-time mothers with similar demographic backgrounds and ethical approaches to food and consumption practices, but with different health identities and journeys into motherhood, and living in different localities. We explore what these participants' narratives and photographs reveal about their evolving foodworlds,[2] with wider reference to how mothers more generally (re)present themselves, and their infant feeding relationships, through the provisioning of weaning goods (food and items supporting feeding) and services. We also consider how these items and facilities shape mothering practices, women's changing relationships with the market and embodied maternal and health identities. We question whether, and to what extent, women espouse ideals about weaning, how these ideals relate to (commoditized) modes of mothering, and whether ideals espoused prior to motherhood are subsequently enacted (or not) in mother-child-food relationships. We also reflect upon the contribution of PDPE in longitudinal research to our understanding of mothers' relations with the provisioning of food over a discrete, and often highly charged, period of early family life.

Photo-elicitation (and visual methods more broadly) have been strongly advocated by sociologists exploring identity (Harper 2002) and foodworlds (Power 2003). In late capitalist societies, and the era of 'intensive motherhood' (Hays 1996) characterized by constant reflexivity and attentiveness to reducing risk (Lupton 2012), we also consider the extent to which photographs may be regarded as self-conscious representations (Sharma and Chapman 2011) of an idealized version of the consuming maternal self. To facilitate a more critical and in-depth discussion, we purposely selected two mothers who *struggled to fulfil their ideals* with respect to infant feeding. Our analysis highlights trust as an important theme in commercial provision for weaning. We show how women's own food/health identities and social contexts (in terms of social and physical proximity to family and peers) relate to the different constructions of *trustworthiness* they ascribed to infant feeding products, actors (friends, family and professionals), and institutions (regulatory and biomedical) – perhaps as a means of mitigating the perceived *risks* posed (by commercial products) to both their infant's healthy development and their own emerging maternal identities.

Background: new mothers, markets and the provisioning of food

The arrival of a first baby is a time of upheaval when family processes, attitudes and expectations – including those underpinning food provisioning and consumption – are likely to be more closely scrutinized, and possibly revised (see also Devine 2005). In contemporary Western societies, the transition to motherhood, and from singleton/couple to family, is typically a 'total consumer experience' (Thompson *et al.* 2011: 198) involving immersion into a new world of products and everyday caring practices (Martens 2010). This market is highly fragmented, advertising an array of specialized goods and services (e.g. Martens 2009) allied to the feeding of infants. Women remain the primary targets of such marketing because, despite their increased participation in education and paid work, they remain broadly responsible for foodwork[3] within families, especially regarding infant feeding (Murphy 1998).

As noted by Sharma and Chapman (2011: 2), continuities and revisions in food-related consumption practices, whether undertaken consciously or otherwise, both *reflect* and *constitute* a complex interplay between identities (mother/child), ideals (motherhood/infancy), the material reality of local food environments (affordability, availability, 'choice', etc.) and structural inequalities (especially regarding the availability of [paid] maternity leave), as well as symbolic meanings associated with food/eating. We assert that the infant feeding market is deeply embroiled within this complex interplay, with mothers adopting various stances and taking pleasure and/or expressing anxiety in the consumer choices they make. However, the pervasiveness of the market influence is such that even a stance of non-engagement or anti-consumerism 'still entails modes of engagement with tropes of consumer culture' (Thompson *et al.* 2011: 198), as women frame what they don't (or refuse to) consume against what they could, or believe they 'should', consume.

The symbolic meanings surrounding infant feeding (as provisioning) are 'inseparable from the politics of mothering and the construction of mothers and babies as *social* beings' (Clarke 2004: 71, emphasis added). These meanings are arrived at through *relational* processes and discourses which typically constitute and polarize consumption and caring practices as 'good', 'right', healthy', 'natural' or 'appropriate'; or conversely as, 'bad', 'wrong', 'unhealthy', 'artificial', or 'inappropriate' for mothers and infants (as members of particular classed, ethnic groups, etc.). Symbolic meanings then form part of broader maternal 'repertoires' of skills, habits and styles that are drawn upon and enacted (Swidler 1986), and indeed displayed. Meanings are also ascribed and 'weighted' in relation to 'other' mothers:

...the stakes could not be higher – for every object and every style has attached to it some notion of a 'type' of mothering or an expression of a desired mother/infant relationship

(Clarke 2004: 61)

Empirical work on contemporary transitions to motherhood which examined (non-food) commodities, found age and social class as key elements in structuring such 'types' (above), and women's relationships with these markets (Thompson *et al.* 2011). Our data broadly support these findings as structuring mothers' relationships to weaning-related goods and services, but in this chapter we look specifically at food as a commodity, and the impact of mothers' health/food identities on their relationships with the increasingly commercialized world surrounding weaning.

Food, family, risk and trust

Food is no ordinary commodity (c.f. Warde 1997). While it is a necessity, sustaining life and nourishing healthy development, it also poses threats to it (choking, contamination). Food also generates meaning and fosters inter-personal relations as evidenced by DeVault (1991). Her work emphasized how, in considering different family members' needs, mothers actively produce family identity through food and meals (pp. 39–41) and has encouraged further inquiry into the thought and care put into such 'provisioning' (c.f. Power 2003, Cook 2009), illustrating how mothers 'are involved with intuiting, acknowledging and adjudicating children's desires on a daily, sometimes hourly, basis' (Cook 2009: 321–322). Within current infant feeding discourses, mothers are positioned as best placed to care for newborns who are portrayed in terms of their 'neediness' and 'vulnerability', with undeveloped immunity and 'innocent' desires/appetites (Murcott 1993; Everingham 1994; Murphy 2007, Lupton 2012), which require little adjudication as want/need are seemingly fused together (Cook 2009: 221). Young infants are not directly appealed to by advertisers, and carers are thus still largely in control of food offered/allowed. Nevertheless, constructions of infants' food-related desires are invoked by marketers, e.g. 'hungry baby' milk, and mothers are typically seen to ascribe agency to their infants within feeding relationships (see Murphy 2007 and Keenan and Stapleton 2009).

The relationship between food, motherhood and markets begins with pregnancy planning and is fundamental to the identity of a 'good' mother (see Lupton 1996; Murphy 1999; Kukla 2008). How women feed themselves and their babies is also a contested and moralized arena and a major issue for a range of agencies: governments, NGOs, volunteer support groups. Although mothers' foodworlds may reflect a variety of broader ethical and health commitments, biomedical risk discourses increasingly, and powerfully, govern the 'right' way to mother (Miller 2005). Current national and international public health policies strongly promote and protect breastfeeding, and guidelines recommend exclusive breastfeeding for at least the first six months of infant life, with supplemental breastfeeding continuing for two years and beyond (WHO and UNICEF 2003; DoH 2006). Such policies exhort breastfeeding mothers to eat well to ensure adequate supplies of nutritious breastmilk and to follow their infants' cues, feeding 'on demand' (i.e. allowing routine to emerge rather than imposing it). Furthermore, the introduction of solid food is to follow a 'staged' approach: first offering complementary foods, then increasing levels of complexity in flavour and texture, to avoid choking and enable the early identification of allergic reactions. What constitutes each stage is the subject of considerable debate amongst 'experts' and, like many areas of advice in the parenting arena, is typically presented as 'choice' between polarized options (see also Thompson *et al.* 2011), characterized here as 'carer-led' or 'baby-led'. The main difference concerning whether foods should be pureed and offered via a spoon, or to wait, skip this stage, and follow 'a path to family meals' (Rapley 2006: 275), by introducing finger foods and encouraging self-feeding. Proponents of both approaches claim to promote a healthier, safer option, although they also agree that introducing solids should not proceed until the infant demonstrates 'readiness' cues.

Weaning signals the end of the seemingly 'pure' feeding relationship between exclusive[4] breastfeeding mothers and their babies. As articulated by our participants, weaning (off the breast, and/or onto solid foods) signals a key moment in mothers' relationships with the market. Purportedly regulated, the infant feeding market also includes products and advice that remain untested and/or unsanctioned (Haigh and Schneider 2009). Particularly significant here are mothers' constructions of *risks* – especially as produced by rational, modern food technologies and diversified, globalized food chains, e.g. contamination of baby foods (Branigan 2008) – and *trustworthiness*, to mitigate the anxiety such weaning products create. Bildtgård's (2008) review of social theory regarding how trust in food is produced and maintained is particularly useful here. He explores three foundations for trust: emotional (unconditional), habitual and reflexive, in modern and late modern eras, further subdividing habitual trust: as an effect of community, modern rational organization (of food production), social policy and systems of knowledge.

Because nurturing is supposed to be 'uniquely free of the kind of calculating instrumentality associated with the consumption of objects' (Taylor 2004: 3) the weaning market poses further *risks to maternal identities*. As Warde (1997: 132) asserts, infant foods exemplify this intersection between the conflicting logics of the nurturing arena, (where 'care' is paramount) and the rationalizing global market economy (which promotes 'convenience'). Infant food manufacturers are aware of this, as evidenced by their attempts to, as Moisio *et al.* (2004: 363) note, 'imbue mass-produced, processed food with the character, tradition and meanings of homemade'. How do new mothers, therefore, perceive and negotiate the *risks* of the market (to both healthy infant development and maternal identities) in weaning their babies? And, in living with such risks, in whom or what do they invest *trust*, and what are the effects of this?

Words and pictures: participant-driven photo-elicitation

Visual research methods offer significant potential for the study of food and eating to capture context and evoke the sensory, non-rational, material aspects of life and the commercial world (Power 2003, Sharma and Chapman 2011 and O'Connell 2012). Previous work into food and family has also advocated the use of photo-elicitation to tackle such issues of 'linguistic incongruence' when describing the taken-for-granted practices and experiences related to feeding the family (DeVault 1991). Other recent studies have employed visual methods to look at food choices made by mothers for their children (Johnson *et al.* 2011); our research shifts the focus to infants.

Photo-elicitation – inserting photos into the interview process – can take a variety of forms. With participant-driven photo-elicitation (PDPE), participants have greater freedom in deciding *what* to photograph, potentially identifying new areas for enquiry; this has been shown to be particularly effective in exploring identities (Rose 2012, Harper 2002). Although photographs are taken at fixed points in time and hence are unlikely to capture the dynamic quality of participants' social lives, the use of PDPE in longitudinal research can address some of these shortcomings and act as an aid to empowerment by inviting participants to elaborate upon themes between interviews, augmenting researchers' understanding of their evolving lives. However, photographs are not neutral depictions of reality, but offer meaning through participants' interpretations, including (re)presentations of the self (see Sharma and Chapman 2011). Photographs also indicate an act of selectivity on the part of participants – presenting their selves and relationships to food within a frame, in ways they may not necessarily be aware. Meaning is also co-constructed through the social context in which the images are viewed and discussed; the 'positionality' of both researcher and participant is thus significant.

The study, methods and contexts

The empirical data presented in this chapter comes from a longitudinal cohort of thirty pregnant women anticipating first-time motherhood, one third of whom were 'average weight', one third 'very overweight/obese', and one third were managing diabetes. Women were interviewed on three occasions: during the final trimester of pregnancy, and when infants were approximately three and nine months; interviews explored the contested and processual nature of parenting, consumption practices including weaning decisions and related concerns. Women were provided with disposable cameras[5] and guidelines, and invited to take study-related photographs between interviews; approximately half obliged. Ethical approval was granted by the Local NHS Research Committee, and consent was re-negotiated and obtained prior to each data collection episode. Participants were assured that photographs would be digitally anonymized before use in publications or presentations.

Images were analysed by the researchers prior to individual interviews to develop participant-specific prompts (see Rose 2012). Photographs were then inserted into transcripts at relevant points and all data were analysed thematically

(Attride-Stirling 2001) and iteratively, in accordance with the method of cross-sectional, categorical indexing outlined by Mason (2002). The software package NVivo7 was used to manage data cataloguing and retrieval.

Narratives for both case-study participants, introduced below, are grounded in their past experiences whilst also evoking future aspirations (see also Backett-Milburn *et al.* 2010); and key stages in infant feeding relationships as they related to the prevailing market, are our primary focus. Rather than being representative, the accounts encourage the differences and overlaps in mothering styles to emerge, and hence illustrate how food provisioning, health/food identities and markets intermingle in everyday caring/feeding practices.

The case studies:

Natalie (White British) was 38 years old at recruitment and had professional qualifications in her specific commercial sector. She lived with her husband in a rural location on the outskirts of the city. Other family members, including young children, lived nearby although Natalie's parents, to whom she was particularly close, had now retired abroad. Natalie was recruited through the antenatal diabetes clinic and had been diagnosed with Type 2 diabetes a few years previously, following a miscarriage and (sub)fertility. She was aware of the need to maintain stable blood sugars and monitor her insulin requirements for 'optimal outcomes', reporting a few hypoglycaemic episodes in pregnancy (associated with low blood sugars).

Elsie (White Welsh), an arts graduate with a health professional qualification, was aged 31 years at recruitment and was known to the author (JK). In contrast to Natalie, her (planned) pregnancy was achieved with relative ease. Elsie and her partner lived in an inner city neighbourhood with good local amenities, including support groups for new mothers. Although other family lived further away, Elsie's sister (also expecting) lived around the corner. The couple had a wide circle of peers, having both stayed in the city after graduation.

Both (middle-class) women were cognisant of the ethics of food production and disliked wasting food; both households grew their own food and supported local suppliers – mixing organic and non-organic produce. Whilst Natalie also shopped in supermarkets, Elsie expressed strong political views about 'evil multi-national supermarkets', preferring her local 'Co-operative' ('Co-op') store. Both women reported histories of being what would be defined medically as 'overweight' (Natalie to a greater extent), and presented as comfortable in their body image (particularly Elsie), their relationships and lifestyles. Both reported enjoying food and eating, but having a functional relationship with day-to-day cooking, expressing little interest in the ritualized and/or social aspects associated with mealtimes. Unusually, in respect to our wider cohort, the male partners in both these households did more of the routine cooking.[6] Within the context of entitlement to maternity leave and financial packages commensurate with their full-time service records, however, both women anticipated taking prime responsibility for feeding their infants, and the family cooking.

Both women planned to exclusively breastfeed their infants for the much-publicized health benefits. Elsie also cited the *'convenience'* of breastfeeding in contrast to the 'faffing about' of formula feeding. Elsie planned to introduce solid foods at around four months and was planting vegetables 'to harvest' for future use. Perhaps understandably given her history, Natalie was not planning as far ahead. Indeed, both women were noticeably hesitant in articulating their feeding intentions with reference to weaning, telling researchers that they had not yet 'read up' on such matters. Both also expressed ambiguity about becoming mothers: excited at the prospect of a new baby/parenthood, but unsure of how they would cope with the change in role from professional to full-time mother.

The early postnatal period: the demands of breastfeeding 'on demand'

Elsie's labour and birth were uncomplicated; her son weighed 6lb 1oz (2.75kg) and she began exclusive breastfeeding. In contrast, Natalie's birth was more medicalized: her daughter (7lb 9oz , or 3.43kg) arrived three weeks prematurely by caesarean, and she stayed in the high dependency unit of the hospital for a week. Her daughter was given formula milk supplements (to stabilize her blood sugar levels) until breastfeeding was established.

Both women's narratives and photographs of the immediate postnatal period document a pressurized trade-off between finding time and energy to care for themselves (to eat) whilst also being available to distinguish and meet, 'on demand', the breastfeeding needs of their infants, which as Elsie noted, 'dictates everything'. Both reported how their foodworlds and relationships with the market altered as they sought to best accommodate this trade-off. Natalie's narrative related more to her concerns about (mis)managing her blood sugars/ diet in the context of breastfeeding, especially given that she was no longer regularly testing her blood sugars and she couldn't quantify the breastmilk her daughter consumed. She photographed her freezer (after a power cut ruined the frozen, home-cooked meals she'd pre-prepared for this period) and cereal and microwavable savoury packet foods (as the first convenient 'meals' she could eat). Elsie articulated (during interview) feeling overwhelmed, and struggling to cope with the all-consuming nature of feeding a newborn without any routine; she didn't take any photographs at this time. Supported by her family, she 'grazed' on cold foods, eating 'consciously' with regard to supporting breastfeeding, avoiding foods perceived to adversely affect it.

> ...you're so anxious all the time, thinking about getting the breastfeeding right and making sure the baby's getting enough milk.
>
> (Elsie, second son, five months old)

Elsie expressed frustration at the lack of support and specificity in the advice she received from professionals about what feeding 'on demand' actually meant, and entailed (Keenan and Stapleton 2009). Interestingly, neither participant

Figure 6.1 Weaning off the breast

produced any photographs of themselves breastfeeding, or struggling with this activity, and although not fully discussed, we surmised that juggling a camera and a baby without help may have presented insurmountable problems, at what was an already difficult time.

After ten weeks and two and a half weeks respectively, both Elsie and Natalie introduced formula, primarily because they had both been prescribed medication: Natalie received antibiotics for an infected caesarean wound whilst Elsie was prescribed anti-depressants. As breastfeeding was contraindicated in both instances, women were advised to offer their infants formula for the duration of treatment. In order to maintain supply they were advised to use a commercially available hand pump to express (and discard) their breast milk. Natalie documented her struggle to persevere with breastfeeding; the images of breast pads on which she drew happy and sad faces, vividly attest to her feelings about having been forced to stop prematurely.

> ...it's (breastfeeding) what I thought I wanted. Well I didn't just think, I wanted to do it. I did want to do it. I did want to breastfeed, and I was happy with the fact that I was breastfeeding […] it was just very stressful. […] It wasn't good for me. […] we tried to erm, to express [milk] and everything and it just wasn't happening. […] Sometimes it [expressing] would and other times it just wouldn't. […] I think that added to the pressure of how, yeah, it was pressure, but also it helped us make that decision just to, we're going to go with formula rather than carry on [trying to express].
>
> (Natalie, second daughter, three months old)

Natalie's interview excerpt illustrates her frustration with the inefficiency and unpredictability of hand-expressing milk. She rationalizes her switch to formula as the 'right' decision with respect to improving her diabetes management: 'it actually made it easier for me to eat as well. I seemed to have more time because she feeds a lot quicker on bottles'. Although supported in her decision to cease breastfeeding by her husband and health visitor, Natalie reported withholding this information from her parents (who visited intermittently):

I'm 38 years old but I was scared to tell my mum and dad […] but mum knew that it was the best thing for me to stop doing it I think, she could see how upset I was getting and how stressed I was getting about trying to do it.

(Natalie, second daughter, three months old)

This quotation illustrates the strength of the cultural pressure she feels to breastfeed – even strong and enduring relationships may be challenged by women's infant feeding decisions.

In this section we have highlighted how photo-elicitation may be employed to (re)present maternal identities. Natalie used photographs to illustrate the depth and extent of her struggles and her perseverance (as a 'good' mother) with the breastfeeding project, navigating threats to her own health and maternal identity. Although Elsie did not photograph her struggles, her interview narrative communicated her wariness of the advice of health professionals, and the fragility of her emergent maternal identity. We have also shown the differing levels of support provided by professionals and family members, and how food provisioning and women's relationship to the market changed over the postnatal period. We now turn our attention to their relationships with the formula feeding market.

Entering the formula feeding market: 'surely a bottle is a bottle?'

Natalie described how she and her husband searched the internet for information to help them decide on a brand of formula. Ultimately, they deferred to the opinions of a trusted family member (sister-in-law):

She's (niece) fine, so that's the one that we decided to go for. It's the most expensive one as well and I know that doesn't mean anything but […] it has these extra things in that are very similar to breastfeeding.

(Natalie, second daughter, three months old)

Natalie's comments reveal her choice of formula as an important marker, or signifier, of her maternal identity; that although product price does not necessarily reflect quality, it is important for her to know and tell that it has been 'tried and tested', to good effect, on her niece. It is also clear that she trusts in the marketing claims of this brand of formula – that the constituents are as close to breastmilk ('natural') as possible – hence justifying the higher price. Having decided on a brand of formula, another trusted family member (Natalie's mother – now supportive of her decision to formula feed), introduced the couple to the unfamiliar 'baby bottles and teats' market. In pre-selecting a range of samples for them to try, the potential anxiety associated with multiple choices and decision-making is removed:

…we never thought about different teats for bottles, […] we just thought bottles were bottles.

(Natalie, second daughter, three months old)

In Elsie's account of provisioning for formula feeding, we again see how participants have used photo-elicitation to represent their maternal identities to interviewers. Elsie took a (poor quality) photograph of a line-up of bottles, against the backdrop of a branded (SMA) packet of baby powdered formula, specifically – 'to symbolise the fact that I *had* to give up breastfeeding'. Elsie also related that, in a play on the brand name SMA, her friend referred to the formula as 'smack' – the highly addictive drug heroin, and a powerful denigration which serves to underline this option as the deviant choice for mothers in her (middle-class) social group. Elsie confirmed that introducing formula feeding inevitably involved the use of commercial products and re-organization within the domestic environment, but that formula feeding was also more amenable to establishing a routine, allowing her time to meet other maternal needs/wants.

Like Natalie, Elsie made reference to feeling obliged to defend her decision to switch to formula feeding to family members. Where Elsie's account differs significantly from Natalie's, however, is in the identity work she had to do to present herself as a 'good' bottle feeding mother to her peer group. Elsie considered withholding her 'decision' to cease breastfeeding from her local mothers' group; the following except clearly portrays her discomfort with what she perceived as their unsympathetic and moralizing attitude:

> ...there is that smug sense of, 'Oh you've gone on the bottle have you?' [...] It's are you a good mother you know, how much of yourself are you willing to sacrifice for your baby? [...] it's an element of people thinking that you're a bit selfish for going on to bottle-feeding. Or that yeah, you haven't got the moral fibre to stick with it when the going gets tough.
>
> (Elsie, second son, five months old)

Our findings here support previous research with women unable to breastfeed who articulate feelings of distress and frustration that they have failed to conform to the culturally dominant, middle-class ideal of a 'good' mother (Murphy 1999, 2000, 2003; Lee 2007; Knack 2010). Significantly, the use of photo-elicitation in our study revealed that giving up breastfeeding was presented to researchers almost entirely in relation to defending participants' maternal identities, and how women managed the perceived risks that the formula feeding market posed to the health of their infants. Natalie's account highlights the trust invested in family members to navigate these risks, whilst Elsie's account details the consequences of not conforming to the dominant discourse amongst her peer group.

Introducing 'proper' food: production systems, flavour combinations and storage

Like other participants, Elsie and Natalie used photographs to document their baby's 'firsts' in feeding relationships as markers of developmental progress. Elsie photographed the first time her son showed an interest in eating what was on his parents' plates, and his first time in his new (second hand, wooden) highchair. Natalie photographed her daughter's first meal of baby rice, with elicitation revealing its significance as a family occasion: 'we were all there, we did it first of January, and even my mum came round'. Both women framed their introduction of solids with reference to their perceived developmental 'readiness' of their infants, government guidelines and the advice they received from health professionals.[7] Elsie also made reference to the advice of infant feeding 'gurus' (books) in circulation amongst her peers.

Elsie and Natalie both voiced intentions to make their own baby food using organic ingredients where possible – with commercial products, specifically 'jars', for *'emergencies only'*. However, both mothers chose a commercially produced, albeit organic, product (baby rice) as their baby's first solid feed, which they gave 'early' (in the context of government guidelines) at five months. Elsie's account of this episode reveals her frustration with her health visitor, whom she perceived as undermining her maternal confidence in determining her son's readiness. Natalie also reported feeling confused by her health visitors who, although sanctioning her early weaning, subsequently told other mothers in her postnatal group not to use a commercial food (baby rice), as she had done. When Natalie told the group that she had already offered her daughter the baby rice, the health visitor promptly provided reassurance that no harm was done:

> ....last week the health visitors were saying try not to give them baby rice [...] just go straight into family foods, just pureed up vegetables and what have you. [...] But *it's all organic*, her food and her baby rice and what have you, *and it won't do her any harm they said*, so, or they wouldn't put it on the market would they?
>
> (Natalie, third daughter, six months old)

Natalie's comments (emphasis added) clearly demonstrate her deference to the authority of the health visitors, her belief in the superiority ('safety') of organic products and her trust in market regulators (policy) to protect her infant from possible harm. In mounting a robust defence of her decision to wean early, she also protects herself against being cast as a 'bad' mother. Natalie largely followed the advice of her health visitor to avoid commercially produced items in favour of a 'family foods' approach, combining elements of 'baby-led' weaning and supplementing this with pureed food from the family meal in response to 'readiness' cues. This photograph (Figure 6.2) illustrates her first attempt at blending the leftovers of a stew her husband cooked. The next stages of production involved transferring the prepared food into the plastic, portion-sized containers and freezing for her daughter's later consumption.

Natalie articulates a clear distinction between 'proper' and 'jarred' foods, and demonstrates how mothers employed standardized mass production techniques, redeploying familiar kitchen technologies to reduce effort and save time but perhaps most importantly, to ensure their infants have continuous access to high quality, home-produced foods. It is interesting that Natalie embraced a 'family foods' ideal for her daughter, given her (guilty) use of convenience food, dislike of cooking and

Figure 6.2 Blended leftovers

her dietary/health requirements to manage her diabetes. During our final interview, she rationalized her approach as a key element in a longer term ideal to improve her own diet/health 'because I've gone off the rails a bit lately' and to avoid the extra work involved with cooking separate meals for family members.

In keeping with many of our middle-class participants, Natalie emphasized her own non-expert status (see Miller 2005) in relation to weaning, and put considerable trust in the prescribed approach presented by health professionals. Elsie's account, however, documents power struggles in the feeding relationship which focused on her son's irregular eating habits, his bouts of illness and uneven weight gain. Interestingly, given she herself is a health professional, her trust in regard to health visitors, and the solutions provided by the market to such 'problems', is more complex. There are no photographs of her making or freezing batches of baby food, or preparing food they've grown for her son. Consciously rebelling against the prevailing model of 'intensive motherhood', Elsie deliberately avoided researching, choosing and defending a prescribed approach and went with her own (albeit still culturally informed) ideas. Interestingly, her relatively minor deviations from weaning norms did not escape the notice of her peer group, some of whom challenged the order in which she introduced foods:

> … And it was like, 'Oh, you're doing it differently then' I was like, 'Well, differently to what? Differently to Gina Ford? Differently to you know all these guru baby books that are out there?' There is a lot of kind of pressure I think just between new mums […] this little micro world of rules and regulations.
>
> (Elsie, third son, ten months old)

Elsie highlights the difficulty in developing a confident maternal identity in a culture which sanctions such commercialized advice, and where peer scrutiny operates to silence individuals and/or pressures them into conforming to the dominant model. Whilst avoiding the 'advice market', she did look to the baby weaning product market. Here again she faced dilemmas (articulated below), such as the actual suitability (for her son aged five to six months) of a chocolate pudding marketed for infants of four months plus:

> ...I was like *agonising* thinking, well obviously it's okay for babies because it's made by this well-known brand (pause) in the end I just couldn't do it. So I ate it.
>
> (Elsie, third son, ten months old)

This agonising highlights Elsie's reflexive disposition towards trust and food markets. The outcome of her questioning – and *dis*trust in market regulation – contrasts starkly to Natalie's earlier investments in infant formula and the regulation of baby rice.

Whereas Natalie had noted the novelty of some of the 'weird and wonderful' infant foods available before dismissing them (as contra to 'family foods'), Elsie's interest in an organic range of baby foods which offered novel flavour combinations, was aroused by a close friend (with twins roughly the same age as her son) who offered them when her son was recovering from a cold and not eating as usual.

> I thought there's no way he's ever gonna eat that. I don't think I'd even eat that. [He] Loves it. Absolutely wolfs it down. [...] So we've been (pause) going to Waitrose to get those 'cause they're like the emergency back-up if, if we haven't had time or we haven't got anything in that's really gonna do it then we've always got those.
>
> (Elsie, third son, ten months old)

Following her surprise that her son relished unusual flavour combinations, Elsie went on to describe how his acceptance of such foods allayed her maternal anxieties (about his development) and informed her future parenting when her son refused meals or certain parts of meals; offering alternatives from within the same nutritional food group as the item/meal refused, which when combined may not constitute a culturally recognizable 'meal', but which meant that, on balance, her son ate in accordance with nutritional science requirements – echoing her own functional approach to food. Also, Elsie reflected on how her son's ready acceptance of this product range – only available at certain (upmarket) food outlets – had seduced her back into supporting (profit making) supermarkets she had resisted.

In the final photograph (Figure 6.3), Elsie describes baby food items in her refrigerator, emphasizing the variety, her son's preferences and the importance of 'order' to ensure older items are eaten first. She also emphasized her customary

Figure 6.3 Storing food

practice of recycling; in this instance re-using commercial baby food jars as containers for her home-produced food instead of purchasing purpose-designed containers.

Women's accounts and photographs of provisioning for weaning in many ways exemplify Warde's (1997: 44) work on the antonyms of taste in consumer culture (care and convenience, novelty and tradition, and health and indulgence), which give meaning to food items and here shape mothers' practices and narratives. In focusing on weaning, we have also shown how 'naturalness' is evoked within each of these acronyms. By illustrating how norms associated with branded baby food products (quantities, textures, flavours, production, storage and date rotation) have penetrated homemade food production and consumption practices, our data further highlight Moisio *et al.*'s (2004) findings about the 'dynamic tensions' which exist between 'homemade' and 'market made' food.

Conclusion

In selecting our case studies and presenting their changing foodworlds and provisioning for weaning through their transitions to motherhood, we have demonstrated the ways in which women's food/health identities and social contexts intersect with the market and particular modes of mothering: where the 'good' mother is vigilant, responsive and risk averse and infants are portrayed as helpless and vulnerable. This is particularly evident in the differential levels of anxiety and constructions of trustworthiness in the accounts of these women in relation to actors and systems associated with the infant feeding market, in the compromises they ultimately make regarding their food/mothering ideals and the social consequences of these compromises on their maternal identities. Returning to BildtgÅrd's (2008) review of social theory regarding how trust in food is produced and maintained, we see how both our case studies cited the influence of *emotional* trust – Natalie in her sister-in-law and mother in helping her navigate formula feeding, and Elsie in the close friend who sanctioned a commercially produced, organic infant food range with unusual combinations. Natalie's successful, highly medicalized route into motherhood can be seen to have shaped the more *habitual* trusting disposition she exhibits towards the institutions and actors (health professionals) of biomedicine (as a system of knowledge). The 'distance' between Natalie and her peers, both because of her age and geographical remoteness, has also perhaps spared her from harsh peer judgements regarding her infant feeding/weaning practices. Elsie's response to the potential 'risks' inherent in the infant feeding market is (in line with the discourse of intensive motherhood) very much more *reflexive* – she consciously 'weighs different values and corresponding forms of knowledge against each other, while trying to determine which systems and actors to trust' (BildtgÅrd's 2008: 118). Able to see beyond her own situation, Elsie is concerned about the possible anxiety this heightened reflexivity may create for new mothers. Elsie, and to a lesser extent Natalie, therefore choose to invest trust in the social policies (national and international organizations) underpinning the regulation of infant feeding markets. Natalie uses her diabetic identity and the social mechanisms of her family to help alleviate any anxieties about expectations that she will indeed emulate the autonomous ideal of intensive motherhood whilst Elsie, who is integrated within a local peer group of mothers, is more socially stigmatized by a (mental) health problem. She is thus more exposed to, and less protected from, the social consequences of not conforming to the infant feeding/weaning ideals of her middle-class, educated peers.

Finally, although visual methods have been advocated for their potential to illuminate the more taken-for-granted aspects of food provisioning, we have shown that the transition to first-time motherhood is very much a conscious exercise, as the relational identity of the mother emerges and women acquire what Bourdieu (1977: 105) has termed an embodied 'feel for the game' of practical logic and skilful practice. Specifically, whilst PDPE allowed participants to (re)present controlled versions of themselves to the researcher (see Sharma and Chapman 2011), for Elsie and Natalie – struggling to live up to culturally informed ideals of motherhood allied to infant feeding – PDPE evoked 'deeper elements' (Harper 2002) of their identities and demonstrated the strength of dominant maternal discourses allied to infant feeding. PDPE also enabled a fuller insight into the wider material and social contexts of participants' worlds and the practical and organizational aspects of infant feeding. We found a strong degree of congruence between what was said and the photos taken, and elicitation prompted further reflections on how intentions, practices and feelings changed over time. Noting the 'absences' – in what wasn't photographed – alerted researchers to potential areas participants might be uncomfortable about sharing, although inevitably constraints within interviews meant some aspects were sometimes unfortunately missed.

Acknowledgements

We would like to thank the participants in this study and all of the members of the advisory panel for this research.

Notes

1 The 'Changing Habits?' study was one of seventeen individual projects which contributed to the *Changing Families Changing Food* programme funded by the Leverhulme Trust: http://www.shef.ac.uk/familiesandfood/
2 Foodworlds: where people obtain or buy food, how it is prepared, kept and eaten and what types of relationships they have with it (Sharma and Chapman 2011).
3 Foodwork requires 'material, mental and social labour' and is comprised largely of meal planning, grocery shopping and cooking (Bove and Sobal 2006).
4 Of course, breastmilk can be expressed and given to infants in a bottle by other people, which was something practised by other mothers in our study. Expressed breastmilk can also be banked and sold as a commodity for profit (aka Baby Gaga icecream), or donated altruistically. Neither practice was reported by any of the women in this study.
5 These data were collected in 2006–2008, just before digital cameras and mobile phone cameras became commonplace. This meant that women couldn't edit the photographs taken, and that the quality of photos was sometimes poor.
6 Elsie reported cooking 'more healthily' than her partner did, but eating 'more than she should', while Natalie tended to rely more on 'convenience' food when left to cook for herself.
7 Whereas Natalie was personally invited to attend a weaning 'workshop' run as part of a series of free (NHS) weekly post-natal groups she attended, Elsie was left to research this herself (similar local options were available in the public and private sector).

References

Attride-Stirling, J. (2001) 'Thematic networks: an analytic tool for qualitative research', Qualitative Research 1, 385–405.
Backett-Milburn, K., Wills, W.J., Roberts, M. and Lawton, J. (2010) 'Food, eating and taste: parents' perspectives on the making of the middle-class teenager', *Social Science and Medicine* 71, 1316–23.
BildtgÅrd, T. (2008)'Trust in food in modern and late-modern societies', *Social Science Information* 47:1, 99–128.
Bourdieu, P. (1977) *Outline of a Theory of Practice,* Cambridge: Cambridge University Press.
Bove, C. and Sobal, J. (2006) 'Foodwork in newly married couples. Making family meals', *Food, Culture and Society* 9:1, 69–89.
Branigan, T. (2008) 'Chinese figures show fivefold rise in babies sick from contaminated milk', *The Guardian*, 21 December. http://www.guardian.co.uk/world/2008/dec/02/china (accessed 4 June 2012).
Clarke, A. (2004) 'Maternity and materiality: becoming a mother in consumer culture', in J. Taylor, L. Layne and D. Wozniak (eds) *Consuming Motherhood*, New Brunswick: Rutgers University Press, 55–71.
Cook, D. (2009) 'Semantic provisioning of children's food: commerce, care and maternal practice', *Childhood* 16:3, 317–34.

DeVault, M. (1991) *Feeding the Family: the Social Organisation of Caring as Gendered Work*, Chicago: University of Chicago Press.

Devine, C. (2005) 'A life course perspective: understanding food choices in time, social location', *Journal of Nutrition Education and Behaviour* 37, 121.

Department of Health (2006) *Birth to Five*, London: Crown Copyright.

Everingham, C. (1994) *Motherhood and Modernity*, Buckingham: Open University Press.

Haigh, C. and Schneider, J. (2009) *Junk Food for Babies: an Investigation Into Foods Marketed for Babies and Young Children*, Children's Food Campaign, http://www.childrensfoodcampaign.net/CFC_Baby_food_report.pdf (accessed 5 May 2010).

Harper, D. (2002) 'Talking about pictures: a case for photo elicitation', *Visual Studies* 17:1, 13–26.

Hays, S. (1996) *The Cultural Contradictions of Motherhood*, New Haven and London: Yale University Press.

Johnson, C., Sharkey, J., Dean, W., McIntosh, W. and Kubena, K. (2011) '"It's who I am and what we eat": mothers' food-related identities in family food choice', *Appetite* 57, 220–28.

Keenan, J. and Stapleton, H. (2009) '"It depends what you mean by feeding on demand": mothers' interpreting of babies' agency in feeding relationships, routines and weaning decisions', in A. James, A. Kjørholt and V. Tingstad (eds) *Children, Food and Identity in Everyday Life*, New York: Palgrave Macmillan.

Knack, S. (2010) 'Contextualising risk, constructing choice: breastfeeding and good mothering in risk society', *Health, Risk & Society* 12:4, 343–55.

Kukla, R. (2008) 'Measuring mothering', *The International Journal of Feminist Approaches to Bioethics* 1:1, 67–91.

Lee, E. (2007) 'Health, morality and infant feeding: British mothers' experience of formula use in the early weeks', *Sociology of Health and Illness* 29:7, 1075–90.

Lupton, D. (1996) *Food, the Body and the Self*, London: Sage.

Lupton, D. (2012) '"The best thing for the baby": mothers' concepts and experiences related to promoting their infants' health and development', *Health, Risk & Society* 13:7–8, 637–51.

Martens, L. (2009) 'Creating the ethical parent–consumer subject: commerce, moralities and pedagogies in early parenthood', in J. Sandlin and P. Maclaren (eds) *Critical Pedagogies of Consumption: Living and Learning in the Shadow of the 'Shopocalypse'*, London: Routledge.

Martens, L. (2010) 'The cute, the spectacle and the practical: narratives of new parents and babies at The Baby Show', in V. Tingstad and D. Buckingham (eds) *Childhood and Consumer Culture*, New York: Palgrave Macmillan.

Mason, J. (2002) *Qualitative Researching*, 2nd edn., London: Sage.

Miller, T. (2005) *Making Sense of Motherhood: a Narrative Approach*, Cambridge: Cambridge University Press.

Moisio, R., Arnould, E.J. and Price, L. (2004) 'Between mothers and markets: constructing family identity through homemade food', *Journal of Consumer Culture* 4:3, 361–84.

Murcott, A. (1993) 'Purity and pollution: body management and the social place of infancy', in D. Morgan and S. Scott (eds) *Body Matters: Essays on the Sociology of the Body*, London: Falmer Press, 122–34.

Murphy, E. (1998) 'Food choices for babies', *in A. Murcott (ed.) The Nation's Diet: the Social Science of Food Choice*, Harlow: Addison Wesley Longman, 250–66.

Murphy, E. (1999) '"Breast is best": infant feeding and maternal deviance', *Sociology of Health and Illness* 21:2, 187–208.

Murphy, E. (2000) 'Risk, responsibility, and rhetoric in infant feeding', *Journal of Contemporary Ethnography* 29:3, 291–325.

Murphy, E. (2003) 'Expertise and forms of knowledge in the government of families', *The Sociological Review* 51:4, 433–62.

Murphy, E. (2007) 'Images of childhood in mothers' accounts of contemporary childrearing', *Childhood* 14:2, 105–27.

O'Connell, R. (2012) 'The use of visual methods with children in a mixed methods study of family food practices', *International Journal of Social Research Methodology* 16:1, 1–16.

Power, E.M. (2003) 'De-centering the text: exploring the potential for visual methods in the sociology of food', *Journal for the Study of Food and Society* 6:2, 9–20.

Rapley, G. (2006) 'Baby-led weaning: a developmental approach to the introduction of complementary', in V. Moran and F. Dykes (eds) *Maternal and Infant Nutrition and Nurture: Controversies and Challenges*, London: Quay Books, 275–98.

Rose, G., (2012) *Visual Methodologies: An Introduction to Researching with Visual Materials,* 3rd edn. London: Sage.

Sharma, S. and Chapman, G. (2011) 'Food, photographs and frames: photo elicitation in a Canadian qualitative food study', *Food Language and Identity* 3:1, 1–14.

Swidler, A. (1986) 'Culture in action: symbols and strategies', *American Sociological Review* 51, 273–286.

Taylor, J.S. (2004) 'Introduction', in J. Taylor, L. Layne and D. Wozniak (eds) *Consuming Motherhood*, New Brunswick: Rutgers University Press, 1–19.

Thompson, R., Kehily, M.J., Hadfield, L. and Sharpe, S. (2011) *Making Modern Mothers*, Bristol: The Policy Press.

Warde, A. (1997) *Consumption, Food and Taste*, London: Sage.

WHO/UNICEF (2003) *Infant and Young Child Nutrition: Global Strategy on Infant and Young Child Feeding*, Geneva: World Health Organisation.

7 Contesting food – contesting motherhood?

Bente Halkier

Media and contested food

Although food provisioning, cooking and eating are routinized, taken-for-granted activities in the daily lives of households, parts of these food activities are being questioned in society (Lang and Heasman 2004). Food consumption is debated in relation to a long line of societal issues such as climate, environment, health, nutrition, risk, quality, social justice, animal welfare, generational skills, learning abilities – and you name it! Media discourses and communication campaigns ascribe responsibility to individual ordinary food consumers for helping to solve such societal problems by changing their daily routines. Consumers are encouraged to eat less meat in order to help the environment, to eat more vegetables in order to prevent cancer, and to cut down on sugar for their kids in order to improve their learning abilities. This way, many patterns of ordinary food consumption become questioned and foods become contested.

The contestation of food potentially affects everyday food habits because contemporary societies are relatively mediatized (Hepp 2012; Krotz 2007). Media and media-texts are integrated in everyday life to such a degree that media and media-texts in general potentially influence form, content and organization of core activities in everyday life (Hjarvard, 2008). Thus, a majority of the population relate to and use many media discourses in their daily activities.

When societal consequences of food habits are debated in media and raised with consumers as part of behaviour change campaigns, the content and framing of such media discourses can add up to so called 'privileged representations of the world' (Bird 2010: 87) due to their high circulation across social contexts of such discourses. Otherwise unnoticed food routines may become noticed when consumers relate to such media discourses, and habits of provisioning, cooking and eating potentially become objects of reflection, negotiation and explicit moral regulation among consumers (Halkier 2010: 1–5). Hence, media discourses on 'healthier eating' or 'climate-friendly cooking' for example form part of the unfoldings and negotiations of what is considered appropriate food conduct in everyday life.

However, a high degree of citizen attention to specific public media discourses cannot be presumed, even in relatively mediatized societies (Couldry *et al.* 2010). Rather, one consequence of mediatization seems to be that many people come into contact with a large number of different mediated discourses, narratives and imagery, leaving them with the major task of sorting, negotiating and relating to such multiplicities of mediated representations. One such consistent representation is the contesting of ordinary food habits and the ascription of individual responsibility for societal issues such as health, environment and food quality. Due to factors including media competition (Walgrave and Aelst 2006: 93–94), the manifold media food genres (Roussau 2012), and the difficulties of distinguishing media use from other everyday activities (Couldry 2004: 125), we should expect a variety of citizen relations with and appropriations of media discourses that contest food consumption in everyday life.

Food contestation and mothering

Food is central to family life (De Vault 1994). Food is an element of the practical necessities, social organization, identification processes, forming of relations and the moral regulation of conduct in families. Much research has shown how food practices form an important part of processes of motherhood (e.g., Anving and Thorsted 2010; Blake *et al.* 2009; Bugge and Almås 2006; Cook 2009; De Vault 1994; Ekström 1990; Jabs and Devine 2006; James and Curtis 2010; Moisio *et al.* 2004; Molander 2011; Ristovski-Sliepcevic *et al.* 2010). Feeding the family and managing food consumption in the household has traditionally been seen as women's responsibility. Thus, when food consumption becomes contested through media discourses, processes of carrying out motherhood may also become entangled in this. Indeed, it is pointed out in the literature on parents and consumption that parents face normative dilemmas in relation to their children's consumption (Martens *et al.* 2004: 170). Such dilemmas have been succinctly exemplified in the research on food and families in a Swedish mother's comment that '*I give them what they love, not what would be good for them*' (Ekström 1990: 160).

By using the term 'mothering', I place my argumentation in the part of the literature on food, family and gender that underlines the importance of the performative character of 'doing' motherhood (e.g., Clarke 2004; Cook 2009; Mitchell and Green 2002; Molander 2011). Motherhood is not a social category with fixed content, pre-formed by structures or values. Rather, motherhood is a social category which is being constructed while being performed among everyday social actors. The process term of mothering refers to these performances, and mothering is thus something that is done, re-done and differently done, and how motherhood is done is enacted, re-enacted, adapted and experimented with in everyday life. Motherhood as social category is at the same time being constructed through mediated institutional discourses, both in commercial formats, public regulation and policy-making formats, and expert formats. The mediatized character of everyday life potentially brings institutional and mundane constructions together in performing mothering.

The term mothering also dovetails with intersectionality approaches to gender (Butler 1990; Moloney and Fenstermaker 2002; Skeggs 1997; West and Zimmerman 1987) where social categories such as motherhood are seen as contextual relational activities, not essential attributes. This way, mothering is something that is accomplished in interaction with other social actors and in relation with representations (often mediated) of the category.

When performing motherhood is a continuous negotiation of socially expected and acceptable conduct, mothering becomes a normative as well as a social category. I use the terms normative and normativity rather than moral and morality, because social norms are more specific, practical and flexible ways of regulating human conduct than moral values, which are often more general, abstract and treated as more rule-bound (Mortensen 1992). But in a sense, normativity means practical morality. Contested food as social category in media texts often becomes represented as a normative category relational to categories of family and mothering conduct such as feeding, provisioning, cooking and eating (Cook 2009; Coveney 2000; Johansson and Ossiansson 2012; Thomson *et al.* 2012). What does it mean to 'feed the children appropriately', 'serve healthier meals', 'cook properly' and 'eat green'? When mothering is connected intimately with family food conduct, the handling of contested food in daily food practices also becomes connected with mothering. Thus, different everyday life normativities become entangled in the intimate social regulation of family life practices.

In order to analyse performances of mothering in relation to contested food practices, I draw on a practice theoretical approach, which in many ways implies the performative character of everyday life, intersected by many different kinds of activities and normativities.

A practice theoretical approach is a particular reading of an assembly of theoretical elements from, among others, Pierre Bourdieu's (1990) early concepts of habitus and field, Judith Butler's (1990) understanding of performance, Anthony Giddens' (1984) early structuration theory, and Michel Foucault's (1978) later thinking about social regulation of bodies through discourses. These theoreticians' shared assumptions about how social action is carried out and carried through are central in practice theory. Although there are different versions of practice theories (Halkier *et al.* 2011), they all revolve around the concept of social practices. It is the details and conditions in how ordinary activities – such as mothering through the provision of food – are socially done that a practice theoretical approach is intended to conceptualize.

Recent conceptual systematization (Reckwitz 2002; Schatzki 2002; Warde 2005) offers a distinct analytical approach to the performativity of social life – how social life is carried out in different micro-contexts. Mundane performativity in everyday life is organized through different collectively shared routinized practices, such as cooking, cycling, parenting and working. The individual is a carrier of practices and a place for the intersection of this multiplicity of different practice processes, including food provisioning and mothering. Thus, the unit of analysis is not the individual parent or cook, but rather the different ways in which practices such as mothering or cooking are performed.

Food practicing in two Danish contested food contexts

The analysis of performances of mothering in relation to contested food practices draws upon two research projects in Denmark, where food in families was contested in different ways, in terms of 'homemade food' and 'healthier food' respectively. Homemade and healthier food issues have featured prominently in different genres of Danish media coverage of food, from lifestyle magazines and television programmes, blogs and other social media, to behavioural change campaigns and advice on public institutions' websites.

The first research project, *'Cooking in medialised society'*, was a qualitative study of cooking practices among female Danish readers of a lifestyle magazine called *Isabellas, Enthusiastic about Everyday*, a typical coffee-table magazine targeting women aged 25–50 that deals mainly with cooking, gardening and home decorating. The general tendency of its discourses and visual representations of food is a celebration of everyday activities traditionally associated with domestic femininity (Hollows 2007), such as cooking homemade meals from scratch, baking and preserving.

The 17 women in the sample varied in terms of age, education level, family status (with and without children) and place of living. The qualitative data material was produced by individual in-depth interviewing, auto-photography and focus groups. Individual interviewing and re-interviewing was undertaken to produce the participating women's enactments of cooking in their life-story and everyday life, cooking in relation to other people in their network, and cooking in relation to the representations of cooking in *Isabellas*. These interviews were ethnographic (Spradley 1979), biographic (Atkinson 1998) and active (Holstein and Gubrium 2003). Ethnographic interviewing helped produce enactments characterized by descriptions of everyday cooking practices and understandings, procedures and engagements. Biographic interviewing helped produce enactments about trajectories of practices and engagements in cooking. Active interviewing helped produce enactments characterized by positioning and change of perspective, for example in relation to engagement in food practices.

Auto-photography (Heisley and Levy 1991; Hurdley 2007) involved participants taking photos of their own cooking on one or two everyday evenings (ingredients, food stuff, tools, places, activities and the cooked food or meal). These photos were used as part of the second individual interview to help embody and materialize stories about cooking activities and procedures, and the pictures also served as data in themselves. Focus groups (Barbour 2007; Puchta and Potter 2005) were undertaken with the individually interviewed women together with women from their particular social networks; one focus group for each age group (20s, 30s and 40s) was conducted, producing negotiations and normative positionings between the women about cooking practices and representations of cooking in *Isabellas*.

The second research project, *'Network communication and changes in food practices'*,[1] was a qualitative study examining food habits among ethnic Pakistani Danes and how they handled official communication on healthier food. Pakistani Danes have been targeted with public food health initiatives because this ethnic group has a comparatively high risk of contracting Type 2 diabetes and coronary heart disease (Mellin-Olsen and Wandel 2005; Ristovski-Slijepcevic *et al.* 2008). Official discourses of public food health communication targeting this group tend to be based on a deficit model, where citizens are seen as lacking correct or sufficient knowledge on healthier food (Eden 2009).

The 19 Pakistani Danes in the sample varied according to gender, age (15–65), education, country of birth (Denmark or Pakistan), whether a family member had Type 2 diabetes, and whether participants worked in the health sector. The qualitative data material was produced by several methods. Individual in-depth interviews were undertaken with the main cooking practitioner in the family about provisioning, cooking and eating in their everyday life and social network, and in relation to constructions of healthier food. The study also included auto-photography (Heisley and Levy 1991) of food and drinks consumed during weekdays and the weekend. The photos were used as data in themselves and as input in family interviews and group interviews (Frey and Fontana 1993). During all the interviews, held in the family home, participant observation (Hammersley and Atkinson 1995) was also used.

For both research projects, the working up of the data involved ordinary qualitative coding and categorizing (Coffey and Atkinson 1996) and visual data analysis techniques (Hurdley 2007), drawing on concepts from practice theory (Warde 2005) and positioning theory (Harré and Langenhove 1999).

Variations of mothering through food

In this section, the different ways of performing mothering through food that could be analysed across the two datasets are presented. The different ways of performing mothering through food are related to practices and not to individuals. Thus, each way of performing mothering is performed by multiple participants in the research project. Likewise, every participant conducts mothering by shifting and gliding between several ways of food provisioning, cooking and eating in different contexts or relations, and each participant enacts several ways of doing mothering in one context. Thus, in methodological terms, these variations of mothering are not based on methodological individualism (Jepperson and Meyer 2011).

The constructions of mothering in the two datasets concern the women's own performing of motherhood, the performing of motherhood of the women's mothers and the performing of other women's mothering. The different ways of performing mothering through food that are presented here are only the ones that were shared between the two studies.

Mothering as loving

This is the kind of performing mothering where food is used for building and maintaining family relationships (Holm and Kildevang 1996; Warin *et al.* 2008) and where cooking labour turns food into homemade gifts of love (Bove and Sobal 2006: 80–1; Moisio *et al.* 2004: 374; Ristovski-Slijepcevic *et al.* 2010: 476). Ellen,[2] one of the lifestyle magazine readers, expresses the experience of giving food as love in the following manner:

> You know, if I have baked bread or something, that's lovely tangible compared to what I do in my job...and then some meal came out of it, and often the children go yum-yum, and you can see they shove it in, and that is some kind of satisfaction.
>
> (Ellen)

This is a positive version of the cooking for the children as giving love, but especially the data from *Isabellas* readers also contained negative versions where the cooking or the meal served for children was not considered sufficiently loving. Below, Thea explains about an episode relating to a Christmas meal in her parents' home, where the gift of love aspect of food is particularly important due to the highly ritualized character of meals.

> We were over there for Christmas, and she [Thea's mother] had, yes she had bought ready-made rice porridge in one of those plastic bags, right, to make the ris a la mande,[3] and it was really like this, when I opened the fridge, they were just lying there, and I was just like, okay we are going to have a good Christmas, I am not going to make a scene, and then I just went out to Emil and said, do you know what's in the fridge (laughs)...she obviously doesn't bother to make the porridge...it didn't taste too good either, that was really a bit of a miss, not stirred with love!
>
> (Thea)

The lack of loving in this example is due to the lack of time sacrificed by the mother to prepare this traditional Christmas dessert. Sacrificing time as an expression of love in family food relations has also been identified in other international literature (e.g., Moisio *et al.* 2004: 370–1; Molander 2011: 85).

In both studies, the women with children cook meals they know the children like and serve them food items or meals different from what the rest of the family is having. Shahel, who is a teenage daughter in one of the Pakistani Danish families explains about her mother's caring cooking like this:

> You know, all of us are a bit spoiled, right. You know, a lot of times when my brother comes home from work, or maybe just suddenly at 11 o'clock in the evening, then he just feels like eating French fries or something like that, right. So sometimes he makes it himself, but he also says, mum, I need to have something now at eleven o'clock, and then she has to make it.
>
> (Shahel)

So the mothering as loving is enacted from the daughter's perspective here. One of the Pakistani Danish mothers expresses the engagement of serving what the children like quite clearly: 'If we have friends of the children over, of course we make a bit more out of it. If the children like pizza, they get pizza, if they like schawarma, they get schawarma' (Shabana).

Serving other kinds of food for the children than the rest of the family is eating is clearly a normative issue; some women claim they never cook different food for their children and others negotiate from situation to situation. Some plan for and organize alternative servings for the children, like Zabel, one of the Pakistani Danish women, who fills her freezer with food items especially for the children:

> I like vegetables, but my children don't...[...]so if I make vegetables, I usually have this frozen meat in the freezer, like for example these meatballs or you know something like the Turkish long shishkebab. You just roast them on the pan and then the children are happy.
>
> (Zabel)

One of the other Pakistani Danish women gives her children chicken nuggets when the parents want to eat something the children don't like, '...but they cannot have it every day' (Solejma). The addition that the children cannot have it every day indicates the normative unease at serving something different and serving convenience food. A Swedish study on family meals shows the same normative ambivalence on mothering as loving. A main part of the regulation of eating in the families is to not have parallel dishes (Anving and Sellerberg 2010: 206–8). On the other hand, mothers explain that feeding their children something can be more important than living up to expectations about no parallel dishes or feeding their children healthily (Anving and Thorsted 2010: 41).

Mothering as protecting

In the existing literature on food, families and gender, enacting protection of children through provisioning of food and cooking is often seen as part of managing or regulating children's eating (Coveney 2000). Mothers see themselves as 'default family food managers' (Blake *et al.* 2009: 6), mothers in several generations prefer to cook meals from scratch to defend their families against the dangers of processed food (Moisio *et al.* 2004: 368), and mothers argue that they do the lions' share of foodwork in their families because otherwise their families would eat 'junk' (Beagan *et al.* 2008: 661–2). Mothering as protecting is closely related to enhancing healthier eating with the children.

One of the Pakistani Danish women explains in detail her concrete procedures of cooking which are employed to protect her children from too much fat at dinner:

> Ehm, not so much oil, I don't do that either. You know regarding the procedure, I think a lot about how to do it...ehm, for example our Pakistani rice, the way I make it for my children, I boil them first. And then I mix the other things into it. But if I do it the Pakistani way, then it's over-greasy.
>
> (Solejma)[4]

In a similar vein, one of the *Isabellas* readers explains about protecting her daughter from eating too much sugar or artificial ingredients:

> It's always been like this with me that if I just looked at a cream puff, then I've put on weight, and unfortunately Paula has inherited this, so I'm very conscious about…what and how she eats, and we have a very conscious candy-policy in our family…[…]if I'm having something, it has to be a pure piece of chocolate or cake and none of all that synthetic stuff…argh, I can't have it. And then it's, you don't know what it does to the children, both in relation to sugar and chemicals and such, right.
>
> (Dorte)

Current studies from Canada and Sweden also report upon mothering through food as protection via control and regulation of the children's eating habits. The Canadian study labels these processes 'dietary governmentality' (Ristovski-Slijepcevic *et al.* 2010) and describes how the mothers in the study adapt complicated, shifting scientific evidence and public advice into concrete food provisioning and cooking for their families (ibid: 473–4). Three Swedish studies exemplify different protective performances of mothering through food, such as controlling the shopping lists for food, storing food and food items placed in front of the children (Anving and Thorsted 2010: 38; Johansson and Ossiansson 2012) and cooking meals from scratch (Molander 2011: 85).

For the women in these two Danish studies, cooking from scratch is clearly an important element in performing mothering through food as protecting. One of the magazine readers, Pia, explains how cooking from scratch is not just intended to protect her daughters while they are young but also to teach them how to protect themselves with food as adults: 'I thought they had to learn how to cook food, because I did not want us to have children who could only get by with fast food.' But cooking from scratch in itself is not necessarily understood as sufficiently protective; the protective element of the performing is enacted in little adaptations of cooking procedures for example. One of the Pakistani Danish mothers, Rushy, explained how she had shifted from cooking particular traditional dishes from scratch in pans and pots to cooking them in the oven instead:

> Kebab for example, you make that too, right, when I make kebab, I make it in the oven as a way of avoiding it, it's also because I have some children who are very healthy, you know, they are a bit big, so you have to constantly think about how to save, right.
>
> (Rushy)

Protecting the children through food is a distinct way of performing mothering, but mothering as protecting also has overlaps, adaptations and ambivalences with mothering as loving. The example with Solejma serving chicken nuggets, 'but not every day', shows the normative negotiations between the different ways of 'doing good mothering'.

Mothering as identifying

The social scientific debates on motherhood mostly relate the performing of motherhood to female identification processes, although in complicated ways (e.g., Mitchel and Green 2002), and in ways which intersect with other elements of identification such as class and ethnicity (Skeggs 1997; West and Zimmerman 1987). Food is part of these identification processes in mothering (e.g., Warin *et al.* 2008), but at the same time, food and eating itself is considered a major element of social and personal identification in the social and cultural scientific literature on food (e.g., Ashley *et al.* 2004; Bourdieu 1984; de Certeau 1984; Fischler 1988; Lupton 1996; Murcott 1983; Warde 1997).

There are two main ways that performing mothering through food is enacted as identifying among the women in the two Danish studies. The first is when mothering is connected with belonging to a family. This is of course expressed in many little ways when the women use the term 'we' about how they themselves provide their current families with food which they consider tasty, good quality, 'real Pakistani', cooked from scratch, healthier, and so on. Sada, a Pakistani Dane, talks about a typical family meal in the following manner:

> My elder brother always makes fun of us, 'oh, are you having your Saturday chicken',[5] right. [laughs]. But it's usually that chicken in the oven.[...] Because the only thing is just to peel off the skin of the chicken. Some people make it with the skin, but as I've told you, I prefer not to because of all that fat. So, you know, off with the skin, and it also becomes better marinated. It gives more taste of the spices instead of the skin just getting it.
>
> (Sada)

Sada creates this particular kind of chicken, which even has a nick-name in the wider family network, so her cooking of this chicken demonstrates her belonging with her family through the provisioning of food.

Mothering through food as belonging is also enacted as expressions of childhood memories about the mothers of the now grown–up women who themselves are mothers. Rushy, another Pakistani Dane, recalls weekend breakfasts from her childhood, linking her mothers' breakfast cooking closely with her own belonging to her family:

> My mother for example, when I think about childhood I often think Sunday, ah, I really crave the chickpea bread she makes, and it's chickpea flour with all sorts of green and chilli and everything she puts in. And then lots of Lurpak butter on top of it and then you eat it together with a drink made of natural yogurt. It's just...then I go straight back into childhood. That's not something I do myself.
>
> (Rushy)

Likewise, Ellen, an *Isabellas* reader, remembers how practical learning of cooking was part of being together with her own mother as a child:

I sat on the kitchen table or heard her talk about how her mother used to make particular things and…I think, I have sort of seen how to do some things without actually doing them myself, but I can see that I know…[…]…And I think, not because I have baked much bread as a child, but I have seen the movements, how to do it, and if it feels too greasy then you pour more flour into it and such.

(Ellen)

The other main way in which mothering through food is enacted as identifying is when mothering is connected with social status and distinction (Vincent and Ball 2007). An example among the Pakistani Danes is when Solejma explains where she gets her understandings about healthier food from, and she positions 'sisters-in-law'[6] as a social group less knowledgeable:

… and if we search on the internet, you know, we get to know from many different places, also from the media, yes, …ehm, in contrast to us, our sisters-in-law and the others who are not so much into this, they have to learn – they have to be taught a bit…

(Solejma)

In the example, Solejma differentiates herself and her social status as a mother who is capable, knowing how to cook healthier food for her family, from a social group whom she distinguishes as not so capable. There are also examples where the women position themselves in a more ironic manner in a particular social status group:

Right, yes, I thought it was really funny when coming down to Anders' school, and you knew that you had got this vegetable box from Årstiderne,[7] very nice with recipes, and you had got those turnips, and then when we put all the food on a common table at the school, you could see that there were at least three of us who had made the same salad with vinaigrette and the turnips from the Årstidernes box, and it's just…oh no (laughs)…it just becomes so politically correct and predictable.

(Ellen)

Ellen expresses that she knows she probably can be identified as a middle-class mother with tendencies to buy organic food and wanting to display this way of doing mothering to other mothers. A British study also showed women constructing their families and what family meant to them through displaying to others what they understood as proper family meals (James and Curtis 2010).

Inappropriate mothering

The three former ways of performing mothering through food have exemplified conducts of mothering considered socially expectable and acceptable among the participants in the two Danish studies. However, the quotes from the participating women have also expressed ambivalences and hints about less normatively acceptable food conduct. It seems that the contestation of food through media discourses on quality food as cooked from scratch and healthier food might be strengthening the normative negotiations already taking place in everyday life about how to do appropriate mothering. In this sub-section, two concrete examples are given where inappropriate mothering through food is negotiated and concluded upon in groups of the participating women. Parallel examples of analyses of inappropriate mothering through food can be found in a qualitative Norwegian study of women's cooking practices and what is constructed as a proper domestic dinner (Bugge and Almås 2006), and in an American study on how three generations construct their family identity through homemade food (Moisio *et al.* 2004).

Among a group of *Isabelles* readers, the women negotiate inappropriate mothering from the daughters' perspective, and the character of the interaction in the following sequence from one of the focus groups is characterized by expressions of agreement with what is constructed as improper cooking – overcooked frozen vegetables:

Dorte: When you say bad cooking, it brings something to my mind, and I'm sorry mum, but the worst she can do when I visit them, and she knows I like to eat vegetables, right, and then she's taken you know one of these 500 grams, usually green peas, cauliflower and carrots, and she has… boiled [Birgit: Oh, that…]…them for much too long.
Sonja: Argh…
Birgit: Oh, no.
Karen: Ha, ha!
Dorte: And to me, it is simply the worst…and yes, here you are, you really wanted some vegetables – yes. [sighs loudly]

In the first example, it is the mothering through food of somebody's own mother that is being positioned as inappropriate. In the following example from a family interview with two Pakistani Danes, it is the mothering through food of a sister that is being constructed as inappropriate. The socially less acceptable element here is that the taste of the meal is seen as being dispensed with to signal that the meal is healthier.

Maria: My sister, do you know what she does? She only uses two teaspoons [of oil], and then when the onions have coloured, she takes the oil out and throws it away. And then she finishes the dish, that's why her food tastes to bad.[…]
Sada: That's not good. That definitely doesn't taste nice.
Maria: No, it doesn't taste good, but then she feels she has done a good deed, right…NOW we're eating healthy!

This last example shows that to practice 'good' mothering through food can be quite a difficult task, with competing and intersecting normative engagements to live up to.

Concluding remarks

This chapter is written with a starting point in a practice theoretical perspective where the performative and normative character of motherhood and food is underlined. In the chapter, four different ways of performing mothering through food are presented and exemplified on the basis of two Danish case studies about food practices in families and the handling of contested food issues: mothering as loving, as protecting, as identifying, and inappropriate mothering. In both studies, much more variation around mothering through food was of course analysed, but this chapter only presents what was shared across them. It shows how mothering through food and notions of normatively expected and acceptable mothering are enacted in connection with contested food issues such as homemade food and healthier food and related everyday activities.

The question is whether these processes lead to the contesting of mothering and a risk of blaming the individual mother, just like media discourses and change behaviour campaigns blame the individual consumer. The quick answer to this is that blaming individual mothers for not feeding their families properly is not news (see Coveney 2000). It may be, however, that some tendencies in contemporary media help sustain or exacerbate the moralization of mothering in relation to food. One such tendency is for contested food issues to appear across traditional media food genre boarders, for example when healthier food campaigning is integrated in culinary entertainment television programmes (Hollows and Jones 2010) or when contested food issues are mentioned in social media and made visible to all network members (Rousseau 2012).

Notes

1 The research project was funded by the National Danish Social Science Research Council (FSE), 2008–10, and was carried out in collaboration with associate professor Iben Jensen, Roskilde University.
2 Participants in both studies have been given pseudonyms.
3 Ris a la mande is the most traditional Christmas dessert in Denmark, made from cold rice porridge mixed with blanched chopped almonds, whipped cream and vanilla and served with warm cherry sauce.
4 This is called biryani rice, where the rice is steamed and oil-roasted vegetables and spices are made separately and mixed into the rice just before serving. For pilao rice, the rice is roasted together with vegetables and spices, requiring more oil so the rice does not stick to the pot.
5 To use the expression 'Saturday chicken' is to make an ironic reference to the first type of ready-made meals available in Denmark in the 1980s: pre-roasted chicken pieces dripping with oil and packed in aluminium foil trays.
6 Sisters-in-law to women born in Denmark are often born in Pakistan.
7 Årstiderne is an organic box delivery programme in Denmark.

References

Anving, T. and Sellerberg, A. (2010) 'Family, meals and parents' challenges', *Food, Culture and Society*, 13: 201–14.

Anving, T. and Thorsted, S. (2010) 'Feeding ideals and the work of feeding in Swedish families: interactions between mothers and children around the dinner table', *Food, Culture and Society*, 13: 29–45.

Ashley, B., Hollows, J., Jones, S. and Taylor, B. (2004) *Food and Cultural Studies*, London: Routledge.

Atkinson, R. (1998) *The Life Story Interview*. London: Sage.

Barbour, R. (2007) *Doing Focus Groups*. London: Sage.

Beagan, B., Chapman, G.E., D'Sylvia, A. and Bassett, B.R. (2008) '"It's just easier for me to do it": rationalizing the family division of foodwork', *Sociology*, 42: 653–71.

Bell, D. and Hollows, J. (2005) *Ordinary Lifestyles: Popular Media, Consumption and Taste*, Maidenhead: Open University Press.

Bird, S.E. (2010) 'From fan practice to mediated moments: the value of practice theory in the understanding of media audiences', in B. Bräucher and J. Postill (eds) *Theorising Media and Practice*, New York: Berghahn.

Blake, C.E., Devine, C.M., Wethinton, E., Jastran, M., Farrell, T.J. and Bisogni, C.A. (2009) 'Employed parents' satisfaction with food-choice coping strategies: influence of gender and structure', *Appetite*, 52: 711–9.

Bourdieu, P. (1984) *Distinction. Social Critique of the Judgement of Taste*, London: Routledge and Kegan Paul.

Bourdieu, P. (1990) *The Logic of Practice*, Cambridge: Polity.

Bove, C.F. and Sobal, J. (2006) 'Foodwork in newly married couples: making family meals', *Food, Culture and Society*, 9: 69–89.

Bugge, A.B. and Almås, R. (2006) 'Domestic dinner: representations and practices of a proper meal among suburban mothers', *Journal of Consumer Culture*, 6: 203–28.

Butler, J. (1990) *Gender Trouble: Feminism and the Subversion of Identity*, New York: Routledge.

Clarke, A.J. (2004) 'Maternity and materiality: becoming a mother in consumer culture', in J.S. Taylor, L. Layne and D.F. Wosniak (eds) *Consuming Motherhood*, London: Rutgers University Press.

Coffey, A. and Atkinson, P. (1996) *Making Sense of Qualitative Data*, London: Sage.

Cook, D.T. (2009) 'Semantic provisioning of children's food: commerce, care and maternal practice', *Childhood*, 16: 317–34.

Couldry, N. (2004) 'Theorising media as practice', *Social Semiotics*, 14: 115–32.

Couldry, N., Livingstone, S. and Markham, T. (2010) *Media Consumption and Public Engagement: Beyond the Presumption of Attention*, Basingstoke: Palgrave Macmillan.

Coveney, J. (2000) *Food, Morals and Meaning: the Pleasure and Anxiety of Eating*, London: Routledge.

De Certeau, M. (1984) *The Practice of Everyday Life*, Berkeley: University of California Press.

DeVault, M. (1994) *Feeding the Family: the Social Organization of Caring as Gendered Work*, Chicago: The University of Chicago Press.

Eden, S. (2009) 'Food labels as boundary objects: how consumers make sense of organic and functional foods', *Public Understanding of Science*, 18: 1–16.

Ekström, M. (1990) *Kost, Klass och Kön* [Food, Class and Gender], Umeå: Umeå Universitet.

Fischler, C. (1988) 'Food, self and identity', *Social Science Information*, 27: 275–92.

Foucault, M. (1978) *The History of Sexuality, Vol. 1*, Harmondsworth: Penguin.

Frey, J.H. and Fontana, A. (1993) 'The group interview in social research', in D.L. Morgan (ed.) *Successful Focus Groups*, London: Sage.

Giddens, A. (1984) *The Constitution of Society*, Cambridge: Polity.

Halkier, B. (2010) *Consumption Challenged: Food in Medialised Everyday Lives*, Farnham: Ashgate.

Halkier, B., Katz-Gerro, T. and Martens, L. (2011) 'Applying practice theory to the study of consumption: theoretical and methodological considerations', *Journal of Consumer Culture*, 11: 3–13.

Hammersley, M. and Atkinson, P. (1995) *Ethnography: Principles in Practice*, London: Routledge.

Harré, R. and van Langenhove, L. (1999) *Positioning Theory*, Oxford: Blackwell.

Heisley, D.D. and Levy, S.J. (1991) 'Autodriving: photoelicitation technique', *Journal of Consumer Research*, 18: 257–72.

Hepp, A. (2012) *Cultures of Mediatization*, Cambridge: Polity.

Hollows, J. (2007) 'The feminist and the cook: Julia Child, Betty Friedan and domestic femininity', in E. Casey and L. Martens (eds) *Gender and Consumption: Domestic Cultures and the Commercialisation of Everyday Life*, Aldershot: Ashgate.

Hollows, J. and Jones, S. (2010) '"At least he's doing something": moral entrepreneurship and individual responsibility in Jamie's Ministry of Food', *European Journal of Cultural Studies*, 13: 307–22.

Holm, L. and H. Kildevang (1996) 'Consumers' views on food quality: a qualitative interview study', *Appetite*, 27: 1–14.

Holstein, J.A. and Gubrium, J.F. (2003) 'Active interviewing', in J.F. Gubrium and J.A. Holstein (eds) *Postmodern Interviewing*, London: Sage.

Hurdley, R. (2007) 'Focal points: framing material culture and visual data', *Qualitative Research*, 7: 355–74.

Jabs, J. and Devine, C.M. (2006) 'Time scarcity and food choices: an overview', *Appetite*, 47: 196–204.

James, A. and Curtis P. (2010) 'Family displays and personal lives', *Sociology*, 44: 1163–80.

Jepperson, R. and Meyers, J.W. (2011) 'Multiple levels of analysis and the limitations of methodological individualism', *Sociological Theory*, 29: 54–73.

Johansson, B. and Ossiansson, E. (2012) 'Managing the everyday health puzzle in Swedish families with children', *Food and Foodways*, 20: 123–45.

Krotz, F. (2007) 'The meta-process of "mediatisation" as a conceptual frame', *Global Media and Communication*, 3: 256–60.

Lang, T. and Heasman, M. (2004) *Food Wars: the Global Battle for Mouths, Minds and Markets*, London: Earthscan.

Lupton, D. (1996) *Food, Body and the Self*, London: Sage.

Martens, L., Sourtherton, D. and Scott, S. (2004) 'Bringing children (and parents) into sociology of consumption: towards a theoretical and empirical agenda', *Journal of Consumer Culture*, 4: 155–82.

Mellin-Olsen, T. and Wandel, M. (2005) 'Changes in food habits among Pakistani immigrant women in Oslo, Norway', *Ethnicity and Health*, 10: 311–39.

Mitchell, W. and Green, E. (2002) '"I don't know what I'd do without our mam": motherhood, identity and support networks', *The Sociological Review*, 50: 1–22.

Moisio, R., Arnould, E.J. and Price, L.L. (2004) 'Between mothers and markets: constructing family identity through homemade food', *Journal of Consumer Culture*, 4: 361–84.

Molander, S. (2011) 'Food, love and meta-practices: a study of everyday dinner consumption among single mothers', in R.W. Belk, K. Grayson, A.M. Muniz and H.J. Schau (eds) *Research in Consumer Behaviour*, Emerald Group Publishing.

Moloney, M. and Fenstermaker, S. (2002) 'Performance and accomplishment: reconciling feminist conceptions of gender', in S. Fenstermaker and C. West (eds) *Doing Gender, Doing Difference: Inequality, Power and Institutional Change*, New York: Routledge.

Mortensen, N. (1992) 'Future norms', in P. Gundelach and K. Siune (eds) *From Voters to Participants*, Aarhus: Politica.

Murcott, A. (1983) '"It's a pleasure to cook for him": food, mealtimes and gender in some South Wales households', in E. Garmanikow, D. Morgan, J. Purvis and D. Taylorson (eds) *The Public and the Private*, London: Heinemann.

Puchta, C. and Potter, J. (2005) *Focus Group Practice*, London: Sage.

Reckwitz, A. (2002) 'Toward a theory of social practices: a development in culturalist theorizing', *European Journal of Social Theory*, 5: 243–63.

Ristovski-Sliepevic, S., Chapman G.E. and Beagan, B.L. (2008) 'Engaging with healthy eating discourse(s): ways of knowing about food and health in three ethnocultural groups in Canada, *Appetite*, 50: 167–78.

Ristovski-Sliepevic, S., Chapman G.E. and Beagan, B.L. (2010) 'Being a "good mother": dietary governmentality in the family food practices of three ethnocultural groups in Canada', *Health*, 14: 467–83.

Rousseau, S. (2012) *Food and Social Media: You Are What You Tweet*, Plymouth: Altamira Press.

Schatzki, T. (2002) *The Site of the Social: a Philosophical Account of the Constitution of Social Life and Change*, Pennsylvania: Pennsylvania State University Press.

Short, F. (2006) *Kitchen Secrets: the Meaning of Cooking in Everyday Life*, Oxford: Berg.

Shove, E., Pantzar, M. and Watson, M. (2012) *The Dynamics of Social Practices: Everyday Life and How It Changes*, London: Sage.

Silverman, D. (2006) *Interpreting Qualitative Data*, London: Sage.

Skeggs, B. (1997) *Formations of Class & Gender*, London: Sage.

Spradley, J.P. (1979) *The Ethnographic Interview*, Fort Worth: Holt, Rinehart and Winston.

Thomson, R., Hadfield, L., Kehily, M.J. and Sharpe, S. (2012) 'Acting up and acting out: encountering children in a longitudinal study of mothering', *Qualitative Research*, 12: 186–201.

Vincent, C. and Ball, S.J. (2007) '"Making up" the middle-class child: families, activities and class dispositions', *Sociology*, 41: 1061–77.

Walgrave, S. and Aelst, P.V. (2006) 'The contingency of the mass media's political agenda setting power: toward a preliminary theory', *Journal of Communication*, 56: 88–109.

Warde, A. (1997) *Consumption, Food and Taste*, London: Sage.

Warde, A. (2005) 'Consumption and theories of practice', *Journal of Consumer Culture*, 5: 131–53.

Warin, M., Turner, K., Moore, V. and Davies, M. (2008) 'Bodies, mothers, and identities: rethinking obesity and the BMI', *Sociology of Health & Illness*, 30: 97–111.

West, C. and Zimmerman, D.H. (1987) 'Doing gender', *Gender and Society*, 1: 125–51.

8 Food, cooking and motherhood amongst Bosnian refugees in Sweden

Helene Brembeck

Introduction

Motherhood and consumption shape and constitute each other in contemporary Western society. Mothers provide for their children by purchasing food, clothing, toys, and an ever-increasing range of other commodities (Taylor 2004; Seiter 1993; Miller 1998; Clarke 2007). This is true not least for mothers moving to a new country, as we shall see in this chapter, particularly focusing on food. Feeding motherhood can be conceived of as emerging out of a special relationship between a woman, her child/children and food in a situated cultural context where the feeding mother is produced in culturally specific ways. In this chapter, the ambition is to show the specificity of this process in the case of migration to another country and the very explicit role of food consumption, women's skills as food makers and children's position as gatekeepers between home and market in this context.

The special case is the forced migration from Bosnia-Herzegovina during the 1990s, where about four million had to leave their homes and, of those, two million took refuge in other European countries. Sweden received about 60,000 refugees from Bosnia, of whom 20,000 came to Gothenburg, Sweden's second largest city, and the site of the ethnographic study forming the background to this chapter. Most of the women in this study were from the Banja Luka area in what is now the Serbian-controlled part of Bosnia, Republica Srbska. They were Muslim, but highly secularized after 50 years of socialism in the former Yugoslavia. At the time of the study, they had lived in Sweden for more than ten years (most of them arriving between 1992 and 1994) and had adult children (and usually grandchildren) in Sweden. They had all been granted Swedish citizenship.

The women had all arrived in Sweden with babies and young children, with or without their husbands. Like other refugee families, they had left their home country to be able to live in peace and freedom and give their children a better future (see for example Bryceson and Vuorela 2002). This accords also with Povrzanovic Frykman's (2002) findings of Croatian refugees from Bosnia-Herzegovina in Sweden. Children's wellbeing and a cluster of values connected to the family were recurrent themes in the narrations she recorded. 'We came to Sweden offering ourselves at the altar of the children', as one of her respondents put it (2002:129). The women in our study tried really hard, from the very start, to enhance the children's chances of being happy and leading a good life in their new country. Their lives should not become the same as their parents, but something different, requiring a new set of competences, desires and objectives, which were hard for the parents to decide on. The responsibility for this process mainly fell on the mothers' shoulders.

Studies of motherhood and food have often tried to highlight other relations between women and food than the traditional role of feeding the family. In the migration context, traditional roles and skills were what was required and what made life go on, although many of these women had had professional roles in their home countries as white- or blue-collar workers. Rather it was this traditional gendered role that empowered women and enabled a new women's role and a new motherhood. This process was, however, not one-sided, but relational, and it was rather the whole cluster women–child/ren–food that moved out of the ordinary context and became something else.

Methods and materials

The chapter draws primarily on personal interviews which were an integral part of a micro-ethnographic research study carried out in autumn 2005 among 24 Bosnian refugee families as represented by women in Gothenburg. Several kinds of data were collected by the members of the project group.[1] We started out doing life history interviews, generally in groups of two or three women with an interpreter present. At this instance we also gave the women food diaries to complete and disposable cameras with which to photograph their cupboards, cooking, and dining. We interviewed them a second time with reference to the contents of their diaries and snapshots, individually and sometimes with an interpreter present. Finally, we met them a third time to discuss the future. They made collages, invented key words, and were engaged in group discussions about the future/old age of their dreams, as well as in a more realistic sense. During the six-month fieldwork period, we also made frequent informal visits to the meeting point, where we had initially contacted the women, and took advice from the staff on how to interpret our findings or just on some words we did not understand. This multi-dimensional method offered us insight into the women's lives and dreams for the future, despite language and cultural differences.

Food and migration

Since the inception of the discipline, anthropologists have demonstrated how food is a profound medium of reciprocity that marks and distinguishes persons and relations through acts of sharing, giving and receiving (Malinowski 1922; Mauss 1925), and also how this food work is basically mothers' duty (Murcott 1982, 1983; Charles and Kerr 1988; DeVault 1991). Today there is a broad consensus that food is about commensality, and that it is the capacity of food to make connections that is its most essential function (Lien 2004). It thus comes as no surprise that the relation-building potential of eating together is pronounced in what Bryceson and Vuorela (2002) have termed frontiering families; frontiering referring to agency at the interface of two (or more) contrasting ways of life, resonating with the lives of European migrants at the Western frontier in America a century ago. Eating together is part of what Bryceson and Vuorela call relativizing, referring to the variety of ways individuals establish, maintain or curtail relational ties with family members. Relativizing refers to modes of materializing the family as an imagined community with shared feelings of mutual obligations and is intended to stress the sense of relativity, of being related, that occurs in transnational families (Bryceson and Vuorela 2002). In this chapter, the issue is how this process of relativizing happens through food in the close circle of mother–child relationships. The analysis is inspired by Bryceson and Vuorela's thesis of frontiering families, and also draws from anthropological studies of motherhood and food (for example Miller 2004; Clarke 2004, 2007). Another inspiration is the contributions by Rick Dolphijn (2004) about foodscapes as relational spaces where eaters are generated and matter becomes food (see also Brembeck 2009; Brembeck and Johansson 2010; Brembeck *et al.* 2013).

The importance of cooking

It is obvious that food and cooking, particularly for the women, had been a way not only to survive physically, but also socially and culturally during the long months in refugee camps and during the exile years in Sweden. Food preparation had filled the days with content and meaning and well-known roles and identities, creating a sense of normality in a mixed-up world. This had been a way of keeping the family together and adapting to the new homeland. Many of the women had had professional employment in Bosnia and many had wished to go on working in Sweden, although not many had had the possibility. Yet it was obvious that the women had kept their self-esteem and trust in themselves due to their involvement in and responsibility for cooking and other household chores. As has been shown in other studies (for example Avakian 1997), housework and, above all, cooking, comprise a last resort when life is changing and becoming unpredictable and difficult.

Among the things making cooking so pleasurable was that it was something at which the women excelled, a skill in which they felt competent and clever. As has been shown, for example by Avakian (1997) and Short (2006), to be able to create something others enjoy with your own hands and the tactile meeting with the foodstuff evokes feelings of great satisfaction; this was evident in our study. The women often reminded us that some of the Bosnian specialties were very complicated, requiring special skills that took a long time to learn. And that this really was nothing that men could manage was often pointed out to us. The Bosnian pie, with its layers of very thin filo dough was, for example, described as very complex and difficult to learn: 'It is a lot of work; the dough must rest and you have to roll it. It takes time.'

Food as embodied practice

Recreating lifestyles and identities through food does not, however, come easy. We not only 'are what we eat,' but we certainly also 'are what we ate,' Sutton (2001:7) argues. For the women in this study, food and cooking was very much an embodied part of female identity. 'Bosnianness' for them was, first of all, something they carried in their bodies: in movements and gestures when chopping vegetables or stirring ingredients in pots and pans, in their fingertips ensuring that the filo dough was thin enough for Bosnian pie, and on their palates checking the seasoning. It is also, as shown by Sutton (2001) and others, embedded in materiality in terms of the landscape, the good and fertile soil and the warm and generous sun. Not even the Bosnian pepper (a long, slim, sweet pepper), that can be grown in Sweden, tastes the same. The Swedish earth is not the same; the sun is different – not as healthy, warm and streaming, the women argued. Cooking in Sweden always included bands of missing.

Cooking was something the women had learned as little girls by watching their mothers. All of the women, irrespective of social status, told the same story: how as very young girls they were together with their mothers in the kitchen, interested in what she was doing, watching her, and finally trying things out on their own.

As mothers it had been very important for them to transfer this knowledge to their children. Obviously, in first order, it was the girls the women expected to help out, but also young boys could take part in housework and cooking. Teenagers were certainly not as easy to attract to cooking and the sons were almost invisible in the narratives at this point. But neither were the girls as easy to interest anymore. One woman said that she really did not know what to do about her teenage daughter who was hardly interested in cooking Bosnian specialties. 'Come and watch me,' she told her daughter. 'Sometime she watches me but sometimes no, then it is just the computer that will do.' 'What shall I do?' the mother sighed. She felt that it was important that her daughter learned how to cook, including the more complex Bosnian pies and dishes, now that she was about to turn 18. The frustration of the women was due to their expectations that their children (daughters) would show a spontaneous interest in their mothers' work in the kitchen and watch and learn the same way they themselves had done.

From our study it became apparent that learning how to cook was not a pedagogic project, even if there were exceptions; rather it was part of an unproblematized female identity. When the daughters did not show a natural interest, the mothers did not know what to do. An important part of Bosnianness and Bosnian female identity would disappear with the skills. And forcing the children seemed out of the question and contradicted the spirit of community and the joy which food and cooking was supposed to mediate. That was why they enjoyed it so much when small grandchildren showed an interest in grandmother's food and liked to be with her in the kitchen. 'My son married a Swedish girl and they have a daughter two years of age and she likes Bosnian pie. Every time she comes to my house she only wants pie. She says "Grandma, I want pie." "Just pie and nothing else."'

Food in the new country

In Gothenburg, food existed in a seemingly endless assortment in the grocery shops and the necessity of food every day was forcing the women (and the men) to shop and browse among the new and the well-known. It became obvious that the children from the very first days in Sweden played a vital role in meeting with the market. They quickly picked up information. They learned the language and were able to read the text on the packages of the supermarket shelves and help their mothers decipher the content. They went to school and watched other children, had school lunches and Home Economics classes where they learned to cook new food. They acquired new tastes and new food favorites that they wanted to try at home. In short: they soon got acquainted with their new foodscape and learned to navigate it (Brembeck 2009). The mothers were proud of their progress and relied on them and saw this decision-making by children as the fulfillment of their dreams for their children in the new country.

Children's influences over food seemed to have been most prominent from around the age of six to 11-12. These represent the first years of school, when the children learn to read and spend time outside the home, and parents also expect them to begin to cope on their own, without constant supervision. Younger children generally spent their days with mother and siblings and, since all of the women with small children were housewives, they had little firsthand knowledge of the foodscape outside home. The mothers also told us that they had been able to influence their children's eating when they were small, for example, when they were spoon-feeding them, but not so much anymore when they were older.

'*I always have extra food at home*'

The women obviously planned their purchases and did their shopping with family and friends in mind. It was highly important to always have something extra at home to treat them. 'When I buy food and when I cook I always try to combine things and have extra food at home. I don't buy just one banana; I buy four or five. If my daughter and her husband and children come to visit I want to be able to ask, "What do you want to eat?" and always have some extra food at home.' And, 'Sometimes the children come to visit... my daughter calls me from work and asks if she can come. I always have food at home. Or pie in the fridge.' It was also obvious from the interviews that catering for adult children and grandchildren was a traditional duty for Bosnian women, especially if the daughter or daughter-in-law was working. This was a given role for older women, which they had brought with them to Sweden.

Women's cooking and household duties are often interpreted as a work of love in order to establish connections to family members, especially children. From this point of view cooking could be seen as a sacrifice in order to obtain love from family members (Miller 1998). This type of relational work was certainly going on in these families. Nonetheless, rather than an individual project between a mother and her children, food and cooking in our study proved to be more of a collective project aimed at family and friends. Here the women were acting not so much on their own behalf, but more like spiders in a web connecting family members, as well as the new country to the old. Food and meals were essential opportunities for meeting, talking, and relaxing, and then everybody should feel fine, eat tasty food, be content, and have a good time together. This was how to create relations and how to become a family. To see to this was the women's duty, and they were prepared to make considerable concessions, above all to the demands of their children, in order to obtain the right atmosphere. We will now see examples of such concessions in the case of children's likes and dislikes.

'If the children want it, you have to cook it'

> She decides lots, lots. I don't really like it, but I ask her and… if we don't eat, what shall I do? If it is only me eating and not her? I can't tell her: 'You must eat!' When she was little, I tried to, when I spoonfed her. But now I have to like what my daughter likes.

Food is a special commodity. It is necessary for survival, and it is perishable. You cannot save it for very long, or bring it in large quantities from your home country when you leave. Instead, you have to go to the local shops, and pick something from their local assortment, bring it home and transform it into dishes that give nourishment and delight to the family. Food and eating is, therefore, a very practical and mundane way to get to know a new culture and, as Aviakan (1997) has maintained, downplaying the importance of their own food and adopting the foodways of the new country is one of the ways that immigrants opt for integration. Already, in the initial interviews, it became obvious that it was largely the children (and grandchildren) who were the leading and most knowledgeable actors in this process. Although the women often remarked that they were the ones who eventually decided what to cook, they did this taking the children's opinions into account. It was important for them to cook food their children liked in order for them to eat it and be full and contented, they argued.

The women were, for example, not very happy about semi-manufactured or deep-frozen foods, like French fries, fish croquettes or pizzas. However, they felt that they had to buy them anyway, because their children wanted them. 'We have to,' the women argued. It was also common that the children had Coca Cola at weekends and on holidays, even though the women did not really want to buy it. But they still did buy Coca Cola because their children enjoyed it. They got it 'with meat,' when the family was having something special for dinner; 'they decide,' one of the women remarked. Her children were also allowed to have chips at weekends. They liked it and she bought them large bags.

Another woman was deeply concerned that her daughter had too many sweets. 'I tell her not to eat sweets; it is not good for your teeth, but she likes sweets a lot.' Her daughter did not eat any fruit at all, and she spent all her pocket money on sweets, loads of sweets. The mother also, reluctantly, bought pizza to take home now and then, since this was another one of her daughter's favorites. She got really sad thinking about this, she told us, but she felt that there was not much that she could do about it. Her daughter also liked deep frozen fish croquettes and meatballs with boiled potatoes, so she made this, even though she herself preferred traditional Bosnian foods, which she considered to be healthier. She also bought deep frozen hamburgers and readymade hamburger rolls, although she really did not want to. It was just because her daughter fancied that kind of food.

'*I cook everything, Swedish, Bosnian, it doesn't matter*'

> My daughter makes Swedish food. And Bosnian pie, for example. I have shown her how to make various sorts of pie. It is important to learn both Bosnian and Swedish cooking. Maybe half Swedish and half Bosnian foods. It can be any kind of food, just any kind.

The children's delight in Swedish food was not presented as a problem by the mothers. With little trouble, the women were able to find compromises that were accepted by the family. One woman told us that her children did not like the soup that is often part of a Bosnian meal, but wanted a sandwich instead. For her it was no problem to put both soup and water, and bread and butter with milk on the table. The children also liked milk shakes and they preferred meat or sausage on the table every day, which she did not consider healthy. But this was not a problem, she said. Although the family could not afford meat on the table every day, they had it now and then to please their children.

Hybrid cooking was thus another dimension of the capacity to 'relativize' that the experiences as frontier families made clear; a little bit of this and a little bit of that in different combinations in different situations. Indeed, this was a marker of a frontier lifestyle (Bryceson and Vuorela 2002) and in our interviews there were several examples of the women creating their own dishes, combining Swedish and Bosnian food to please both the children and themselves, such as Bosnian pie with Swedish shrimps, or soup with bread with Swedish hard cheese on top and milk to drink.

The children had Swedish food favorites not least from school. One of the women told us about her son: '"Oh, mother, today it is spaghetti day in school!" Then he is really pleased.' Other women told how their children wanted potatoes with their food, which they had learned to appreciate in school. By contrast, in Bosnia potatoes were only eaten as an ingredient in soup or a pie. The children also learned to cook dishes in the Home Economics classes, which they wanted to try at home. That the boys also attended these classes was appreciated by the women. In Bosnia men rarely cooked, and such Swedish equality was felt by them to be much better. One woman said: 'Yesterday my daughter made dinner for the whole family; potatoes, onions, spices and cheese in a pan that she put in the oven. She had learned this in school, and it was very good.'

The most prominent feature found in the interview data is that it really did not matter, for the women, if the food was Bosnian or Swedish. Their main concern was that the children liked it and wanted to eat it. Most of them remarked that they made all kinds of food at home and that mixing Swedish food with Bosnian was no trouble for them: 'We eat Swedish food, Bosnian, sometimes we have pizza. It is not Swedish but we eat it. First time I had pizza was in Italy, but we make food from various countries. I like Swedish food, it is easy to make and good for your stomach.'

Relativizing and synchronizing tastes

As shown in the narratives above, the children and their desires were the antennas in the relativizing process, and the mothers tried their best to accommodate their children's feelings and tastes in their decisions. Even if this meant accepting food on the table that they themselves did not like or thought was unhealthy, they succumbed to their wishes and even tried to like the same food themselves.

In contrast to this, the family meal is generally considered a main site for socialization. The children have to learn 'food rules' (Counihan 1999), not only with regard to manners at the table, but they also have to learn to restrict their own food tastes and desires. They have to learn 'family tastes' and what are considered to be the normal food choices. This process is what Swedish sociologist Sellerberg (2008) calls the synchronization of tastes. To be able to talk of yourself as a 'soup family,' or to be able to say 'in our family we always have steak on Sundays,' is very important, she argues. This is (primarily still) mother's work in all families, but the process is of special significance in migrant families, Sellerberg maintains, because there is such a huge difference between the food of the old country and the food in the new country that the children like. In her own study of mothers with young children from countries like Lebanon, Iraq and Afghanistan, the 'cognitive engineering' the women engaged in to continually maintain proper eating, while also being flexible to the individual projects and preferences of the household members, is highlighted.

From our study it was obvious that the synchronization of tastes was very much what feeding motherhood in these frontiering families was about. Where it is normally considered that the children are the ones who are supposed to change – to restrict childish or egoistic tastes and mature to appreciate a broader range of healthy foods that are considered socially acceptable and 'normal' – in frontier families this synchronization is to a large extent happening in the close relationship between mother, child/ren and food. The whole family has to like what the children like. Families have to synchronize tastes to go on being families since synchronizing tastes is a concrete way of materializing their unity as a family in new circumstances, and mother is the spider in the web in this process.

Normalizing Swedish food

Much of the food that was considered by the mothers as Swedish had very little to do with what is 'originally Swedish.' Instead, 'Swedish food' was the everyday cooking for families with children today and was what was considered children's food, probably not only in Sweden but in many other parts of the world (Roos

2002, Johansson *et al.* 2009, Vallianatos and Raine 2008). In this sense, it was Swedishness or normality as viewed by the children and performed by the mothers. In Sweden 'children's foods' – foods children generally like – are pizza, hamburgers, hot dogs, tacos, and pasta. This was the kind of food the children wanted at home, together with crisps and sodas. In Sweden parents offer their children this kind of food to please them or to make sure they get full, but it is not considered very healthy food (Johansson and Ossiansson 2012). Rather it is regarded as exactly the kind of food that children should restrict themselves from liking too much, in order to learn to eat a broader variety of healthier, more grown-up food.

The children in our study also liked traditional Swedish foods, usually served in the school canteen, such as potatoes, brown sauce, meatballs, lingonberry preserve, rye bread, and milk. They sometimes also wanted the privilege to take chips, candy and soft drinks to their rooms to eat by themselves on weekends, and not in the company of their families. This was something they were generally allowed to do, much to their parents' displeasure, since this was considered the Swedish way. For the parents (like for Swedish parents), food was about sitting and talking together while having a tasty and nourishing common meal, and should not be consumed in solitude.

As data from other European countries demonstrates, it is a common experience for mothers to adhere to their children's demands for food from the new country, and adapt their cooking (see Ruud 1998 for a Norwegian example, and Vallianatos and Raine 2008 for a Canadian one). The argument of this chapter is that processes like normalization and synchronization, and hybrid dishes such as Bosnian shrimp pie or Bosnian soup with Swedish hard cheese on top are generated in the relation, or cluster 'mother–child/ren–food'; children's desires and knowledge of the local foodscapes, mother's skills as cook, the traditions she carries and her dreams and ambitions for her children. This unique position of mothers and children between home and market and between two cultures renders agency and generates responsibility and self-confidence among both children and mothers, with mothers as the spiders in the web.

Feeding motherhood

As refugees in a new country, food took on new meanings for the women in this study, most importantly as a means of keeping the family together (both the one in Sweden and the one in Bosnia), and of linking the family members to Swedish society. Food worked as a mediator between old and new, the habituated and unfamiliar. Food was about sitting and talking together while having a tasty, nourishing, common meal, and most often the preferences of children and grandchildren had a great impact on what was being served. The women took a great interest in Swedish food and mixed Swedish and Bosnian dishes without any trouble. Still they were eager to preserve Bosnian specialties, like the pie, which were very much connected to Bosnia and the role of a skilled housewife and cook. Their hope was that their children (especially daughters) and grandchildren would learn to appreciate and prepare these dishes; their fear was that they would not be able to pass this on because of their children's lack of time and interest. This way a vital link to the home country and to the traditional women's role and skills would be lost.

At first glance, the food work these women do might seem very traditional and backward; a retreat to an old-style gendered role in times of crisis. In this chapter, I have argued that this would be a reduced way of comprehending what is going on. The feeding motherhood of these women is not about subordination, but about power and status. The same way as 'Las madres', the mothers of Plaza de Mayo in Buenos Aires, used the special position in Catholicism as Mater Dolorosa, the grieving Virgin Mary, as a political action against a repressive state power (Elshtain 1994), these women use skills and knowledge as cooks that they have learned from their mothers as empowerment. Reviving these skills and knowledge reinforces motherhood and renders mothers the agency to move freely in shops, mix products and dishes, grant their children a special role as guides to the new country, and themselves assume the role of mediator between family members, the old and new, well-known and unknown. This should not be mistaken for a service-motherhood, but rather be seen as a spider-in-the-web position, generated by the new circumstances, the new foods, tastes and wishes of their most precious possession and the main reason for leaving their home country: their children. Feeding motherhood emerged in the balancing between the ambition to be responsive to their children, their desires to opt for integration and a good life for them, and the women's own feelings, identities, background, dreams and traditions that they wanted to convey to their children, and especially to their daughters.

Note

1 The researchers for this project include Eva Ossiansson (Business Administration), MariAnne Karlsson, and Pontus Engelbrektsson (both representing Human Factors Engineering), and Helena Shanahan, Lena Jonsson, and Kerstin Bergström (all three representing Home Economics). I myself am an ethnologist as well as the project leader. It goes without saying that I am deeply indebted to my fellow researchers, all contributing to the results of the project, in writing this article. The full material is presented (in Swedish) in the CFK-report 'Maten och det nya landet' (Food and the new country), available from www.cfk.gu.se/publications/CFKreports.

References

Aviakan, A. V. (1997) *Through the Kitchen Window: Women Explore the Intimate Meanings of Food and Cooking*, Boston: Beacon Press.
Brembeck, H. (2009) 'Children's "becoming" in frontiering foodscapes', in A. James, A. T. Kjorholt, and V. Tingstad (eds) *Children, Food and Identity in Everyday Life*, Palgrave: Macmillan.
Brembeck, H. and Johansson, B. (2010) 'Foodscapes and children's bodies', *Cultural Unbound: Journal of Current Cultural Research*, 2, 797–818.
Brembeck, H., Johansson, B., Bergström, K., Engelbrektsson, P., Hillén, S., Jonsson, L., Karlsson, M., Ossiansson, E., and Shanahan, H. (2013) 'Exploring children's foodscapes', *Children's Geographies*, 1, 74–8.8

Bryceson, D. and Vuorela, U. (2002) 'Transnational families in the twenty-first century', in D. Bryceson and U. Vuorela (eds) *The Transnational Family: New European Frontiers and Global Networks*, Oxford: Berg.

Charles, N. and Kerr, M. (1988) *Women, Food and Families*. Manchester: Manchester University Press.

Clarke, A. (2004) 'Maternity and materiality: becoming a mother in consumer culture', in J. S. Taylor, L. L. Layne, and D. Wozniak (eds) *Consuming Motherhood*, New Brunswick: Rutgers University Press.

Clarke, A. (2007) 'Making sameness: mothering, commerce and the culture of children's birthday parties', in E. Casey and L. Martens (eds) *Gender and Consumption: Domestic Cultures and the Commercialisation of Everyday Life*, Aldershot: Ashgate.

Counihan, C. M. (1999) 'The social and cultural uses of food', in K. F. Kiple and C. K. Ornelas-Kiple (eds) *The Cambridge World History of Food and Nutrition*, New York and Cambridge: Cambridge University Press.

DeVault, M. L. (1991) *Feeding the Family: the Social Organization of Caring as Gendered Work*, Chicago: The University of Chicago Press.

Dolphijn, R. (2004) *Foodscapes: Toward a Deleuzian Ethics of Consumption*, Delft: Eburon Press.

Elshtain, J. B. (1994) 'The mothers of the disappeared: passion and protest in maternal action', in D. Bassin, M. Honey, and M. Kaplan (eds) *Representations of Motherhood*, New Haven and New York: Yale University Press.

Johansson, B. and Ossiansson, E. (2012) 'Managing the everyday health puzzle in Swedish families with children', *Food and Foodways: Explorations in the History and Culture of Human Nourishment*, 20: 2, 123–45.

Johansson, Mäkelä, J., Roos, G., Hillén, S., Hansen, G.L., Jensen, T.M. and Huotilainen, A. (2009) 'Nordic children's foodscapes: images and reflections', *Food, Culture and Society: An International Journal of Multidisciplinary Research*, 12:1, 25–51.

Lien, M. E. (2004) 'The politics of food: an introduction', in M. E. Lien and B. Nerlich (eds) *The Politics of Food*, Oxford: Berg.

Malinowski, B. (1922) *Argonauts of the Western Pacific: an Account of Native Enterprise and Adventure in the Archipelagos of Melanesian New Guinea*, London: Routledge.

Mauss, M. (1925) *The Gift: the Form and Reason of Exchange in Archaic Societies*, London: Penguin.

Miller, D. (1998) *A Theory of Shopping*, Cambridge: Polity Press.

Miller, D. (2004) 'How infants grow mothers in North London', in J. S. Taylor, L.L. Layne, and D. Wozniak (eds) *Consuming Motherhood*, New Brunswick: Rutgers University Press.

Murcott, A. (1982) 'On the social significance of the cooked dinner in South Wales', *Social Science Information*, 21: 4–5, 667–96.

Murcott, A. (1983) '"It is a pleasure to cook for him": food, mealtimes and gender in some South Wales households', in E. Garmanikow, D. Morgan, J. Purvis, and D. Taylorson (eds) *The Public and the Private*, London: Heineman Educational Books.

Povrzanovic Frykman, M. (2002) 'Homeland lost and gained: Croatian diaspora and refugees in Sweden', in N. Al-Ali and K. Koser (eds) *New Approaches to Migration?: Transnational Communities and the Transformation of Home*, London: Routledge.

Roos, G. (2002) 'Our bodies are made of pizza – food and embodiment among children in Kentucky', *Ecology of Food and Nutrition*, 41, 1–19.

Ruud, E. M. (1998) 'Matlagning på schemat', *Invandrare & Minoriteter*, nr. 3: 37–9.

Sellerberg, A. (2008) 'En het potatis: om mat och måltid i barn- och tonårsfamiljer', *Research Reports in Sociology* 2008:03, Department of Sociology: Lund University.

Short, F. (2006) *Kitchen Secrets: The Meaning of Cooking in Everyday Life*, New York: Berg.

Seiter, E. (1993) *Sold Separately: Parents and Children in Consumer Culture*, New Brunswick: Rutgers University Press.

Sutton, D. (2001) *Remembrances of Repasts: an Anthropology of Food and Memory*, Oxford: Berg.

Taylor, J. S. (2004) 'Introduction', in J. S. Taylor, L. L. Layne, and D. F. Wozniak (eds) *Consuming Motherhood*, New Brunswick: Rutgers University Press.

Vallianatos, H. and Raine, K. (2008) 'Consuming food and constructing identities among Arabic and South Asian immigrant women', *Food, Culture & Society*, 11, 3, 335–53.

9 Images of motherhood

Food advertising in *Good Housekeeping* magazine 1950–2010

David Marshall, Margaret Hogg,
Teresa Davis, Tanja Schneider and
Alan Petersen

Introduction

This chapter takes a slightly different perspective from most others in this collection, in two respects. First, rather than explaining mothers' accounts of markets and consumption, it examines media and marketers' accounts of mothers and women; and second, it adopts an historical perspective, examining how motherhood has been presented over time in the pages of *Good Housekeeping*, a popular UK monthly magazine. While we do not promise any illumination on the actual practices of mothering, we do reflect on the ways in which *Good Housekeeping* has contributed to the construction of 'good mothers' and 'good mothering'. We are particularly interested in how *Good Housekeeping* equips its predominantly female readers with advice on mothering and housekeeping over a sixty-year period (1950–2010). We examine how *Good Housekeeping*'s advertisers position, depict and portray mothers in their advertising features. Based on the analysis of family and food advertising, we focus in this chapter on one key theme that emerged in our analysis, namely the link between motherhood and domesticity. This link, despite significant changes in women's contributions to labours outside the home, particularly from the 60s, has endured, notwithstanding the tensions involved in balancing work and family life. We examine how motherhood and domesticity are closely interlinked in all decades and shed light on how this interdependence is renegotiated over time.

We first review the literature on motherhood, domesticity and the media. Much of this literature, although insightful as regards the techniques of representing motherhood, presents a rather static ('snapshot') portrayal. Second, we outline the research project and the rationale for examining media portrayals of families based on representations across a number of decades. In the third section we consider how mothering and consumption activities – with a focus on cooking and eating – are depicted in more detail. Finally, we consider how food consumption and mothering activities are intertwined in the pages of *Good Housekeeping*[1] and how these change over time.

Motherhood, domesticity and the media

The dominant view of motherhood places women in the home with responsibility for childcare (Keller 1994; Chambers 2001; Johnston and Swanson 2003; Odland 2009). Despite a number of challenges to this 'traditional' idea of motherhood, reflecting changes in the nature of women's work, the responsibility for children's well-being remains with the mother (Woodward 1997, 2003; Sullivan 2000; Prothero 2002; O'Donohoe 2006; Hogg *et al.* 2011; Slaughter 2012). While these maternal responsibilities include child-rearing, education, nursing and household maintenance, a large part of this duty of care centres on domestic food provisioning. Accounts of family meals, for example, detail the roles and responsibilities of women in domestic care and food provisioning for children and partners, highlighting the gendered nature of this task and affirming where the burden of the task lies (Murcott 1983; DeVault 1991; Charles and Kerr 1988; Bugge and Almas 2006; Beagan *et al.* 2008; Cook 2011). Families are constructed through food, and women and mothers[2] are defined in and through the activities and tasks associated with feeding the family (DeVault 1991). This involves physical and emotional work, although this is largely invisible and unacknowledged; Hochschild and Machung (1989) highlighted the 'second shift' that working mothers do as they carry responsibility for these tasks and show they are 'good mothers'. Emotional work can be seen in what Garey (2011) calls 'maternal visibility' whereby mothers in full-time employment 'work hard to make their performance of motherhood visible, particularly in contexts that involve their children' (2011: 172). Thus motherhood is constructed and communicated through the practices of preparing food for the family. It is also increasingly mediatized as motherhood is represented, reflected, recreated and reconstructed through media images, not least in the context of food provisioning.

Mediated motherhood

Odland (2009) examines the role of the media in the construction of gender identity in post-war America, noting 'that the range of meanings a text offers is not infinite; there is a preferred reading or meaning that is encoded in the production process' (2009: 65). She makes an important distinction between motherhood and domesticity:

> In disentangling motherhood from domesticity, I define motherhood as it relates to activities involving the care of children—both physical and emotional—and I define domesticity as it relates to the physical location of women within the home, tending to the daily chores of managing a household, excluding the care of children (p. 67).

As she notes, it is possible to be a mother without being domestic and vice versa. In her analysis, the US *Ladies' Home Journal* falls firmly on the side of domesticity, as the woman's responsibility regarding any form of employment outside the home is portrayed as incompatible with this domestic role; albeit mildly 'tolerated' prior to having children. The dominant theme remains that of the white middle-class women in the home engaging in maternal self-sacrifice and child rearing.

It is clear that advertising has a role to play in (re)creating 'motherhood roles, identities and relationships in media representations' (Hogg *et al.* 2011).

Coutant *et al.* (2011) examine the ways in which advertising for the French yogurt *Danonino* evokes the 'tensive rhetoric' (Hetzel 2002, in Coutant *et al.* 2011) whereby advertisers enact a 'paradoxical injunction' of being a good mother and having a professional career, that is manifest in a series of anxieties for mothers around food in terms of providing sufficient nutrients, avoiding family conflict, ensuring social inclusion of children, and actually being present as part of their duty of care. As they note,

> ...mother is the main figure in most commercials where adults appear (a few men appear in more playful situations with the children). Mothers appear mostly in kitchens, smiling, well-dressed and energetic, where they often are seen to offer the product to children.
>
> (Coutant *et al.* 2011: online)

In targeting mothers, the company understands the nature of these anxieties across different cultures and the ways in which their products offer commercial 'solutions' to resolve these issues for modern (working) mothers in contemporary societies (Cook 2009; Carrigan and Szmigin 2007). Health has become a major anxiety for many and with increasing public discourse around issues like childhood obesity, food marketing has been scrutinized from a number of quarters (Kline 2011).

Cook (2011) unpacks the ways in which a mother's relationship with her children is presented in popular media, examining how advertising is used to convey care and love for offspring through maternal consumption. For Cook, mother and child cannot be seen as separate, but co-exist in and as a part of the family. Reflecting on the broader construction of mothers as devoted carers, he suggests that

> ...(t)he near-ubiquitous fear of being an incomplete, inadequate, or "bad" mother undoubtedly presents marketers and advertisers with opportunities to offer not simply goods and services to assist women in being the kinds of mothers they envision, but also to make available the semantic-visual materials from which such visions are assembled. Thus, publicity images made for the maternal market offer some reassurance that the products promoted assist in accomplishing a "good" motherhood.
>
> (Cook 2011: online)

Mother and child are seen as an important unit of consumption – a 'super-consumer' entity (Coffey et. al. 2006) – each with their own identity in a form of consumption co-existence. It is the commercial environment that provides solutions, such as dining out and ready meals, to partly resolve the conflict between paid and domestic labour that some mothers experience as part of the broader social changes in relation to 'women's work' (Cook 2011; O'Donohoe 2006).

Cook's analysis of US magazines revealed a variety of 'motherhoods' but relatively few visual representations of mothers in magazine advertising. Motherhood was more likely to be depicted through images of children in the print adverts. As he notes, these 'commercial personae' are the outcome of a series of interpretations by commercial actors in the form of advertisers, magazine editors and companies who approve the campaigns. The outcome arises from 'an amalgam of characteristics—characteristics derived from research as well as from ideology, from systematic study, and from cultural presumption' (Cook 2011: online). 'Women' in these adverts can be read as: a) the mother 'as mother', b) the mother 'as worker', and c) the mother 'as woman'. The first cares for children; the second has a career outside the domestic sphere; and the third is presented as an individual 'self' with identities independent of motherhood. Moreover, mothers and children are more likely to be engaged in a 'loving gaze' when depicted in advertising. This 'matriocular' view – presenting children as though through the mother's eyes – allows the viewer-mother-audience-consumer to write herself into the script.

The study

A number of studies have used women's magazines to examine how motherhood has been represented and interpreted by advertisers and editors at a particular point in time (Reiger 1985; Winship 1987; Greenfield and Reid 1998). Some have looked specifically at *Good Housekeeping* magazine, the focus of this study (White 1970; Warde 1997; Horwood 1997; Martens and Scott 2005). This research forms part of a larger study[3] designed to look at the role of media in shaping consumer culture, and particularly the role of marketing in promoting particular consumer subjectivities around the family and food (Schneider and Davis 2010a,b; Burridge 2009; Burridge and Barker 2009). It aimed to address a number of research questions around the representation of the family (including motherhood) in relation to branding, advertising and marketing (Cronin 2004).

Adopting an historical perspective allowed us to look at the ways in which the family and motherhood has been represented in advertising for food products in UK *Good Housekeeping*[4] spanning the second half of the twentieth century. We used an historical slicing method, sampling the first year of each decade (1950, 1960, 1970, 1980, 1990, 2000 and 2010[5]) and selecting each of the monthly issues for that year (following Martens and Scott 2005; Schneider and Davis 2010a,b). Within each issue, any material referencing the 'family' was selected, and included both visual images and textual references in advertising material, editorials, articles, special features or supplements. The data set comprised a mixture of advertisements (*n* = 777), articles (*n* = 538) and other material including front covers, contents pages and editorials. The data were coded[6] according to the type of material (advertising, an article or some other material that referenced family);

which family members featured, including mothers, and mothers and children, apart from the nuclear family. For each item we composed a summary of the specific theme or issue in the visual and textual content.

This chapter focuses on the advertising material that featured mothers, or mothers and children, and those promoting food products. Drawing on visual discourse analysis, we identify the ways in which motherhood is represented in this body of advertisements (Schroeder and Borgerson 1998; Schneider and Davis 2010b; Rose 2012). Following Rose (2012: 190) we refer to discourse as a 'particular knowledge about the world which shapes how the world is understood and how things are done in it'. We use both visual and textual references to motherhood in the advertising as a means of examining how motherhood is constructed by advertisers in this magazine. This meaning is carried across images, in what Rose refers to as intertextuality, as subjects are made visible through these representations. Our analysis centres on pictures of mothers and children used in the advertisements either alone or as part of a family scene where these images dominate the visual, or where there is a textual reference to mothers or motherhood or related terms. In addition, referencing Cook's (2011) idea of 'matriocularity', we examined material where the messages were directed towards the mother as reader; in a number of these advertisements only products are shown. During our analysis we asked the following questions: how are mothers portrayed through the use of visual imagery and rhetorical devices? How are they positioned in relation to others? What spaces do they inhabit?

Visual and textual references to mother and children, taken here as a proxy measure of discourse around motherhood, were evident across a range of family-orientated advertising in *Good Housekeeping* between 1950 and 2010. Just over a quarter of the advertisements make reference to mothers and children, ranging from around 45 per cent in the early period, dropping to around a fifth in the middle period and increasing to around one third by 2010. In the following sections we focus on how motherhood has been represented over this sixty-year period in food advertising, which accounts for just over one sixth of the advertisements examined.

Mothering, cooking and consuming in *Good Housekeeping*

So how is motherhood represented in the pages of *Good Housekeeping*? In the next section we reflect on the representation[7] of mothers and children in family orientated print advertising for food products, as distinct from other health and care products (Martens and Scott 2005). We are interested in the nature of that communication and the implications for how motherhood is displayed in one of the most popular UK women's magazines.

Mother as nurturer

Motherhood is often closely aligned with domesticity and the duty to look after home and family (Beagan *et al.* 2008). In line with this we found that food advertising in *Good Housekeeping* in the 1950s rarely depicts mothers on their own and nearly always in the company of their spouses and children. The Colman's Semolina advertisement in June, for example, shows a mother presenting a plate of homemade biscuits to her family with the copy 'Crisp, rich, Shortbread biscuit. How delicious! And how *easy* to make with Coleman's Semolina!' The illustration shows two young children seated at a table with a sibling standing by as their father, also seated, looks on approvingly. The advertisement provides shortbread recipes and the opportunity for other mothers to delight their family. Continuing with the family theme, the Crosse and Blackwell tomato soup advert in October 1950 (Figure 9.1) shows a mother placing a bowl of hot soup on the table as she looks out through the window at her daughter who looks back at her mother. The mother and child are at the centre of the illustration but we see the rest of the family outside in the garden. The copy reads 'Children love C&B the soups that nourish'. In both these advertisements the emphasis is on being a good mother and providing for the family. Mothers are very clearly located in the domestic space of home and in the kitchen, busy feeding the family, fulfilling the role of mother as mother (Cook 2011). This representation of motherhood is much less evident in food advertising in later editions of the magazine.

Figure 9.1 Crosse & Blackwell soup advertisement, *Good Housekeeping,* October 1950, p. 134, reprinted by permission

Mother knows best

While mothers feature in a range of family adverts, there are relatively few food advertisements that show only mothers and their children together. The August 1950 advert for McVities and Price biscuits has an illustration of a cherubic young girl, hands clasped under her chin, claiming 'mummy knows what's good'. The girl is smiling and looking up longingly – the loving gaze – at someone, presumably her mother, who is about to give her some McVities and Price biscuits. The copy reads 'Digestive Sweet Meal Biscuits by McVitie and Price' and under this in smaller copy 'Makers of Finest Quality Biscuits'. Compared to many other adverts in this period there is relatively little text and the only other image is of the product. The execution is an early example of Cook's 'matriocularity' where only the child is shown and the mother, as reader, can read herself into the script.

There is relatively little family food advertising in the 1960s sample of advertisements. The Spam advertisement featured in the November issue includes an illustration of a young mother, wearing an apron and holding a can of spam up in the air. Her son, dressed as a cowboy, sits to her left astride a chair waving his toy guns and proclaiming 'I want the REAL spam mam'. At the same time as he talks directly to his mother, the advertiser talks directly to the reader about the value and versatility of Spam: '*All* children delight in *real* SPAM – especially the mouth-watering *hot* meals you can make!' At the bottom right is the *Good Housekeeping* Institute seal of approval. This idea of food as an expression of care and love can also be seen in a July 1970 advertisement for butter depicting a small boy with long blonde hair sitting in his school uniform (cap, shirt, tie, blazer buttoned up) looking up – the loving gaze – at his mother who is buttering toast for him. The strapline reads: 'if you love your children, butter them up'. In this execution we see only the mother's arm as she spreads the butter on the bread. A humorous full page advertisement for the Cheese Bureau (March 1970) shows a mother standing in the background, arms folded looking sideways at her son and thinking 'we must have more cheese'. The copy extols the benefits of cheese as a body-building food containing protein and calcium to help develop the body and brain. Her son, in the foreground of the picture, is looking down, somewhat pensively, thinking 'when do I start going out with girls?'. The copy talks to the mother about the body-building properties of cheese and how much calcium children need compared to adults, and how much boys need compared to their fathers. There are several recipes for cheese dishes, with an offer for a free recipe book for another 100 'body-building meals'. This is cleverly executed, with the use of thought bubbles to convey the 'private' thoughts of both mother and son, emphasizing their different perspectives. The mother's stance with folded arms is more authoritarian, suggesting that she is in control of her son's needs, nutritional and otherwise. These two 1970 campaigns (for butter and cheese) are industry-sponsored and designed to promote dairy products rather than specific brands. Both address mothers as responsible and concerned with the care and well-being of their families and children.

Mother as guardian of health

From the 1980s onwards we begin to see more advertisements[8] with children eating on their own or visuals of the product. This is increasingly evident in a number of the advertisements from the 1990s, for example the National Peanut Council (June) advertisement has the tag line 'who says kids aren't into healthy eating?' It lists the benefits of the protein, calcium and vitamins in peanut butter and warns parents (mothers) not to tell children about these benefits, otherwise they will go and eat something that is not as good for them. The advertiser acts as expert, siding with parents to overcome children's alleged aversion to healthy, but not tasty, foods. Framing the messages in this way allows mothers to show 'love' and 'care' by providing healthy products that taste good and reconcile the health-taste dilemma (see Burridge 2009: 203–4). In offering solutions, these food advertisements reflect underlying anxieties that some mothers have over trying to balance work and family life and look after their children's health and well-being in the process (Coutant *et al.* 2011).

In the 2000 sample we see more advertisements selling the benefits of the products. Health features in several advertisements but so does fun; for example, McCain's low-fat oven chips in the March issue has the tag line 'you (mother) can't tell us off for playing with our food'. This product is low fat and, by implication, healthier. The Walls ice cream advertisement in July shows a mother spraying her children and their friends with a water hose as they stand in a water tub in the garden on a sunny day. The informality of the occasion is reflected in the treat of a family fun pack of Walls ice cream, with the 'family' extended to include friends. In this advertisement, the mother is having fun playing with her children as opposed to cooking or baking for them in the kitchen. Despite the relaxed and informal tone, she remains responsible for controlling the situation and her detachment is also reflected in the fact that there are eight children and eight ice creams; none for mum. In this era we also see more advertising featuring older children, for example in the advertisements for Kingsmill Rolls (August) or Juice Up (December), but again the advertisements speak to mothers about their 'duty' to ensure that their children have a healthy diet.

The Alpro Soya advertisement (Figure 9.2) shows a young mother and her child jumping up in the air with the headline, 'Together we've got a lot of living to do'. At the bottom, it reads 'recommended by kids for grown-ups'. Here, while the emphasis is still on care, the product is targeted at both the mother and child, and is endorsed by the child. This is about mothers caring for children but also children caring for mothers. This co-existence between mothers and children (Cook 2011) can be seen in the marketing of products designed to appeal to both children and mothers, while still allowing mothers to fulfil their duty of care by providing products that taste good. The health indulgence antinomy (Warde 1997) is resolved through the marketplace. This idea of care also extends to mothers caring for their own health as a means of allowing them to care for the health of other family members (Beagan *et al.* 2008). This emphasis on care can be seen in this advertisement which is directly positioned as healthy.

Figure 9.2 Alpro Soya advertisement, *Good Housekeeping*, March 2010, p. 129, reprinted by permission

Discussion and conclusion

This review of advertisements in a popular women's magazine illustrates how one British magazine both represents and recreates motherhood through the discourse created by advertising images for food products. As Cook (2011) argues, mothers, as readers, are clearly engaged in this world of advertising and commerce. This analysis shows how mothers are 'made' via these portrayals and the ways in which relationships are established through the food that they 'make' for their families. Advertisers (along with editors and creatives) not only contribute to the construction of motherhood and the 'good mother' through the images they chose to present, but also reflect the broader familial, social and economic changes that women experienced over this period.

In providing products that are tasty and healthy, as well as convenient, advertisers have tapped into some of the anxieties felt by women trying to balance careers with the demands of being a mother. The white middle-class women featuring in Odland's (2009) analysis of the *Women's Journal* in 1940s America also adorn the pages of *Good Housekeeping*, but we detect a shift away from the ethic of maternal self-sacrifice and child-rearing that dominated the pages of the post-war editions. Through engaging with the marketplace, women are presented as having opportunities to create and shift time in ways that allows them to be 'good mothers', not simply through providing care with healthy, fresh, natural foods, but by spending time, maintaining and strengthening social bonds with others (Carrigan and Smigzin 2007; Warde 1997). We can see this in the later advertising images that challenge the notion that care and convenience, or health and indulgence, are mutually exclusive when feeding the family (Burridge 2009). This raises questions about the intricately intertwined relationship between care, health and convenience that working mothers are asked to resolve for the sake of their children and families. Moreover, with an increased emphasis on health and wellbeing we see a new emphasis on caring for oneself as well as caring for others (Schneider and Davis 2010b).

This review of the discourse around motherhood contained within the pages of *Good Housekeeping* over a sixty-year period allows us to look at the stories that emerge in relation to mothers from the 1950s onwards. Our analysis reveals a shift away from more traditional depictions of 'mothers who care for children' (and partners) and are predominately depicted in domestic settings, towards mothers who leave the house for work and are encouraged to look after themselves, but in a way that remains closely aligned with responsibilities towards children and less so towards spouses and partners. There is no evidence here of a fundamental shift regarding who is responsible for family food as others have shown (James *et al.* 2009) but even as the emphasis shifts from 'mother as mother' to 'mother as worker' and 'mother as woman', the centrality of care endures in constructions of motherhood. 'Mother as mother' is much less explicit in later advertising campaigns and we see fewer depictions of mothers in the kitchen (Coutant *et al.* 2011) as the focus shifts towards professional women located (visually) outside the home. However, it could be argued that the portrayals of motherhood present an idealized vision of mothers' lives, as effective managers of work and family life, and that in so doing fail to acknowledge the tensions and complexities involved in balancing both. Foodwork still remains women's work.

Acknowledgement

This paper is based on data collected from a 2011 Leverhulme International Research Network Project, 'Discursive families: a comparison of magazine advertising across two countries' (F/00158/CS); see http://www.business-school.ed.ac.uk/discursive-families/ for further details.

Notes

1 We acknowledge that *Good Housekeeping* is largely read by a white, middle-class, female readership and recognize the largely class-based nature of consumption activities depicted in the magazine.
2 In contrast, fathers and children are noticeable by their absence in many accounts of family food provisioning. Although, to some extent this may reflect their relative (lack of) involvement in these practices and the fact that despite expressing egalitarian

concerns, men have not effectively been socialized into these domestic roles (Warde 1997; Gershuny *et al.* 1994; Curtis *et al.* 2009; Metcalfe *et al.* 2009).

3 This study forms part of a longitudinal and comparative study of UK and Australian advertising in popular magazines to systematically analyse advertisements, editorials, advertorials and advisory columns, focusing on family and food over the past fifty years, using discourse analysis (Hall 1997; Rose 2003). We examined the representations of food, eating and family in one popular Australian magazine, *The Australian Women's Weekly*, and the UK *Good Housekeeping* spanning the second half of the twentieth century.

4 *Good Housekeeping* has a readership of just under 1.5 million, predominantly ABC1, and a combined print and digital circulation of 411,724 (NRS/Hearst magazines) http://www.hearst.co.uk/magazines/Good+Housekeeping/5-magazine.htm (accessed 15 February 2013).

5 This was not part of the original proposal but included during the data collection.

6 All members of the research team coded the 1950s data independently in order to identify the key themes and this served as the basis of the coding for the remainder of the data. Several months from each year were double coded to check and verify the coding process and check for inter-coder reliability.

7 While readers may not necessarily agree with the depictions of motherhood and will have their own interpretations they are subjected to these by virtue, or not, of being readers.

8 None of the advertisements in our 1980's sample showed mothers and children together.

References

Beagan, B., Chapman, G., D'Sylva, A. and Bassett, B. (2008) '"It's just easier for me to do it": rationalizing the family division of foodwork', *Sociology*, 42, 4, 653–71.

Bugge, A. and Almas, R. (2006) 'Domestic dinner representations and practices of a proper meal among young suburban mothers, *Journal of Consumer Culture*, 6, 2, 203–28.

Burridge, J. (2009) '"I don't care if it does me good, I like it": childhood health and enjoyment in British women's magazine food advertising', in A. James, A. Kjørholt and V. Tingstad (eds), *Children, Food and Identity in Everyday Life*, Basingstoke: Palgrave Macmillan, 192–212.

Burridge, J. and Barker, M. (2009) 'Food as a medium for emotional management of the family: avoiding complaint and producing love', in P. Jackson (ed.) *Changing Food, Changing Families*, Basingstoke: Palgrave Macmillan, 146–64.

Carrigan, M. and Szmigin, I. (2007) '"*Mothers of invention*": maternal empowerment and convenience consumption', *European Journal of Marketing*, 40, 9/10, 1122–42.

Charles, N. and Kerr, M. (1988) *Women, Food and Families*, Manchester: Manchester University Press.

Chambers, D. (2001) *Representing the Family*, London: Sage.

Coffey,T., Siegel, D. and Livingston, G. (2006) *Marketing to the New Super Consumer: Mom & Kid*, Ithaca, NY: Paramount Market Publishers.

Cook, D. (2009) 'Semantic provisioning of children's food: commerce, care and maternal practice, *Childhood*, 16:3, 317–34.

Cook, D. (2011) 'Advertising through mother's eyes: ideology, the "child" and multiple mothers in US American mothering magazines , *Advertising and Society Review*, 12, 2, http://muse.jhu.edu/journals/advertising_and_society_review/v012/12.2.cook.html. Accessed 21/05/2013.

Coutant, A., de la Ville, V., Gram, M. and Boireau, M. (2011) 'Motherhood, advertising and anxiety: a cross-cultural perspective on Danonino commercials', *Advertising and*

Society Review, 12, 2, http://muse.jhu.edu/journals/advertising_and_society_review/vol2/12.2.coutant.html. Accessed 21/05/2013.

Cronin, A.M. (2004) 'Regimes of mediation: advertising practitioners as cultural intermediaries, *Consumption, Markets and Culture*, 7, 349–69.

Curtis, P., James, A. and Ellis, K. (2009) 'Fathering through food: children's perceptions of fathers contributions to family food practices', in A. James, A.T. Kjørholt and V. Tingstad (eds), *Children, Food and Everyday Life*, Basingstoke: Palgrave Macmillan.

De Vault, M. (1991) *Feeding the Family: The Social Organisation of Caring as Gendered Work*, Chicago: University of Chicago Press.

Garey, A. (2011) 'Maternally yours: the emotional work of "maternal visibility"', in A. Garey and K. Hansen (eds), *At the Heart of Work and Family: Engaging the Ideas of Arlie Hochschild*, New Brunswick: Rutgers University Press.

Gershuny, J., Godwin, M. and Jones, S. (1994) 'The domestic labour revolution: a process of lagged adaptation?', in M. Anderson, F. Bechhofer and J. Gershuny (eds), *The Social and Political Economy of the Household*, Oxford: Oxford University Press, 151–97.

Greenfield, J. and Reid, C. (1998) 'Women's magazines and the commercial orchestration of femininity in the 1930s: evidence from *Woman's Own*', *Media History*, 4, 2, 161–74.

Hall, S. (1997) *The Work of Representation in Representations: Cultural Representation and Signifying Practices*, ed. by S. Hall, London: Sage, 16–61.

Hogg, M., MacLaren, P., Martens, L., O'Donohoe, S. and Stevens, L. (2011) 'Recreating cultural modes of motherhood in contemporary advertising', *Advertising and Society Review*, 12, 2, http://muse.jhu.edu/journals/advertising_and_society_review/vol2/12.2.hogg.html. Accessed 21/05/2013.

Horwood, C. (1997) 'Housewives' choice + launching of the British version of *Good Housekeeping*, March 1922 – women as consumers between the wars', *History Today*, 47, 3, 23–8.

Hochschild, A.R. and Machung, A. (1989) *The Second Shift: Working Parents and the Revolution at Home*, New York: Viking.

James, A., Curtis, P. and Ellis, K. (2009) 'Negotiating family, negotiating food: children as family participants', in A. James, A. Kjørholt and V. Tingstad (eds), *Children, Food and Identity in Everyday Life*, Basingstoke: Palgrave Macmillan, 35–51.

Johnston, D. and Swanson, D.H. (2003) 'Invisible mothers: a content analysis of motherhood ideologies and myths in magazines, *Sex Roles*, 49, 1–2, 21–33.

Keller, K. (1994) *Mothers and Work in Popular American Magazines*, Westport: Greenwood.

Kline, S. (2011) *Globesity, Food Marketing and Family Lifestyles*, Basingstoke: Palgrave Macmillan.

Martens, L. and Scott, S. (2005) '"The unbearable lightness of cleaning": representations of domestic practice and products in *Good Housekeeping* magazine (UK), 1951–2001', *Consumption, Markets and Culture*, 8, 4, 379–401.

Metcalfe, A., Dryden, C., Johnson, M., Owen, J. and Shipton, G. (2009) 'Fathers, food and family life', in P. Jackson (ed.), *Changing Food, Changing Families*, Basingstoke: Palgrave Macmillan, 93–117.

Murcott, A (1983) 'Cooking and the cooked: a note on the domestic preparation of meals', in A. Murcott (ed.), *The Sociology of Food and Eating*, Aldershot: Gower.

National Readership Survey (2011) *Readership and Circulation Trends*, http://www.nrs.co.uk/choosetrends.html. Accessed 21/05/2013.

O'Donohoe, S. (2006) 'Yummy mummies: the clamour of glamour in advertising to mothers', *Advertising & Society Review*, 7, 3, http://muse.jhu.edu/journals/advertising_and_society_review/v007/7.3odonohoe.html. Accessed 21/05/2013.

Odland, S. (2009) 'Unassailable motherhood, ambivalent domesticity: the construction of maternal identity in *Ladies' Home Journal* in 1946', *Journal of Communication Inquiry*, 34, 1, 61–84.

Prothero, A. (2002) 'Consuming motherhood: an introspective journey on consuming to be a good mother', *Proceedings of the 6th Association of Consumer Research on Gender, Marketing and Consumer Behaviour*, Dublin, June, 211–25.

Reiger, K. (1985) *The Disenchantment of the Home: Modernizing the Australian Family, 1880–1940*, Melbourne: Oxford University Press.

Rose, G. (2003) *Visual Methodologies: An Introduction to the Interpretation of Visual Materials*, London: Sage.

Rose, G. (2012) *Visual Methodologies: An Introduction to Researching with Visual Materials*, 3rd edn, London: Sage.

Schneider, T. and Davis, T. (2010a) 'Advertising food in Australia: between antinomies and gastro-anomy', *Consumption Markets & Culture*, 13, 1, 31–41.

Schneider, T. and Davis, T. (2010b) 'Fostering a hunger for health: food and the self in *The Australian Women's Weekly*', *Health Sociology Review*, 19,3, 285–303.

Schroeder, J. and Borgerson, J. (1998) 'Marketing images of gender: a visual analysis', *Consumption, Markets & Culture*, 2, 161–201.

Slaughter, A. (2012) 'Why women still can't have it all', *Atlantic Magazine*, http://www.theatlantic.com/magazine/archive/2012/07/why-women-still-can-8217-t-have-it-all/9020/ Accessed 21/05/2013.

Sullivan, O. (2000) 'The division of domestic labour: twenty years of change?', *Sociology*, 34, 3, 437–56.

Warde, A. (1997) *Consumption, Food and Taste: Culinary Antinomies and Commodity Culture*, London: Sage.

White, C. (1970) *Women's Magazines: 1693–1968*, London: Michael Joseph.

Winship, J. (1987) *Inside Women's Magazines*, London: Pandora.

Woodward, K. (1997) 'Motherhood: identities, meanings and myths', in K. Woodward (ed.), *Identity and Difference*, London: Sage, 239–98.

Woodward, K. (2003) 'Representations of motherhood', in S. Earle and G. Letherby (eds), *Gender, Identity and Reproduction: Social Perspectives*, Basingstoke: Palgrave Macmillan.

Part III

Motherhood, consumption and transitions

10 Bouncing back

Reclaiming the body from pregnancy

Maurice Patterson and Lisa O'Malley

Introduction

Pregnant bodies are sites of extraordinary flux. The most obvious changes are corporeal as bodies leak, flow, ooze, and are transfigured. In this way, pregnant bodies exhibit an 'indifference to limits' (Shildrick 2002) which dissolves the boundaries between self and other and, ultimately, problematizes established notions of subjectivity (Young 2005). Indeed, Warren and Brewis (2004: 228) contend that 'the pregnant body is a particular source of anxiety because it clearly represents the co-existence of nature and culture, the way in which the body can wilfully "deform" itself from the inside'. Further, for women who are accustomed to treating their bodies as malleable and plastic, this 'bursting in' of the body often brings with it a sense of losing control.

However, pregnancy also bears witness to transformations in the 'imaginary body' (Gatens 1999); a socially and historically specific body that impacts upon a body's orientation in space and relationship to other bodies (Mullin 2005). Pregnant bodies thus become sites of contestation as women shift from being seducers to producers (Price 1988), from ornamental to functional (Charles and Kerr 1986), from sexual to maternal (Stearns 1999). This shift traditionally positioned the non-pregnant body as an object for public consumption while the pregnant body was subjected to a period of 'confinement'. As a consequence, pregnancy opened up a space where women could enjoy relative freedom from the demands of idealized femininity.

Nevertheless, the institutions of consumer culture increasingly encroach upon the space of pregnancy. They demand that women engage in body work in order that they may better manage their pregnancies, produce healthy offspring, avoid many of the deleterious 'symptoms' of gestation, and reclaim their pre-pregnancy bodies (Dworkin and Wachs 2004). Indeed, it is possible to frame pregnancy as consumption given that 'for many women, a change in patterns of consuming food, drink and drugs both precedes pregnancy and in some cases "causes" it. The daily ritual of swallowing oral contraceptives, for example, gives way to the swallowing of special vitamins high in folic acid, special foods full of nutrients, and special waters labelled and sold as free of contaminants' (Taylor 2000: 43).

As such, pregnancy is not just a biological fact, it is an event performed within the limits set down by the institutions of motherhood within consumer culture.

It is against this backdrop that images such as those of a naked and heavily pregnant Demi Moore on the cover of Vanity Fair in August 1991 may be seen to have liberated the pregnant body from confinement and propelled it into a very public arena (O'Malley 2006). However, such liberation brings with it certain challenges and responsibilities. Images such as those of Moore depict the pregnant body as highly sexualized, eroding pregnancy as a period of grace as women are compelled to maintain their grooming routines. Further, celebrities now routinely demonstrate that the idealized body can be reclaimed postpartum, losing their 'baby weight' in a matter of weeks (O'Donohoe 2006). These reclaimed bodies are almost masculinized in the sense that they are 'unencumbered by biology' (Cunningham 2002: 430).

Women experiencing their first pregnancies tend to rely rather heavily on external sources of information and evaluate their own experiences as 'normal' or 'deviant' in so far as their experiences align with idealized portrayals. Indeed, the rupture 'between ideologies and lived experience can appear bewildering, large and difficult to reconcile and voice' (Miller 2005: 45). Women thus come under pressure to resist the asexualization of the body brought about by pregnancy and buy into the expectation for the postpartum body to 'bounce back'. In this way they can demonstrate that they are left unchanged by pregnancy (Earle 2003). To this end, this study accesses women's embodied experiences during and after pregnancy in an effort to understand the role of marketing and consumption in encouraging and supporting their attempts to temper the boundaries of their bodies and once more affirm a sealed, controlled selfhood reflective of idealized femininity. The chapter continues with informants' initial experiences of losing control over their bodies during pregnancy. Next, experiences focus on the need to re-establish control achieved primarily through consumption. We then continue with experiences that recount efforts to bounce back postpartum.

Methodology

Many of the extant studies on motherhood have been criticized for failing to explore the lived experience of becoming a mother (Smith 1999), and there have been calls for the adoption of methodologies capable of generating more complete pictures of the experiential world of women (Crawford and Marecek 1989). Here, phenomenological-type interviews (Mick and Buhl 1992) were undertaken, thus privileging the experiences of our informants over any a priori conceptual beliefs that we may have had (Thompson *et al.* 1989). Thompson *et al.* (1990) contend that the phenomenological research process involves dialogue set by the informant rather than by the researcher and, because it is not guided by pre-determined questions, it provides a view of the informant's behaviour as seen through her own eyes. This method of enquiry lends itself to an understanding of how our informants make sense of their world and thereby provides an insight into their perceptual process.

Table 10.1 List of participants

Name	Details	Name	Details
Grace	Age 31, project manager, first baby	Kate	Age 28, self-employed, first baby 1 month old
Catherine	Age 35, teacher, first baby	Debbie	Age 31, IT specialist, just given birth to her first baby
Margaret	Age 31, decided to become a full-time mum following the birth of her second baby	Jayne	Age 43, professional woman, Single, first baby conceived by IVF, age 5 months
AnnMarie	Age 28, married, first baby	Carolina	Age 28, second baby is 1 month old, first baby now 18 months old
Michelle	Age 23, was a retail assistant, now staying home to look after first baby. She does not live with a partner	Issy	Age 32, is a married mid-wife, first baby

As is common when adopting a phenomenological approach, sampling was determined by the lived experience under investigation (Goulding 1999). In total 10 interviews were conducted with women who had recently given birth. The majority of informants had just had one baby but we also included women who had been through a second pregnancy. Six of the interviews were carried out during the summer of 2006 and the remaining four were conducted during the summer of 2010. Consistent with pure phenomenology (Thompson *et al.* 1994), each interview started with the question 'tell me about your experience of pregnancy'. All other questions emerged spontaneously from the ensuing dialogue.

An initial round of interviews was organized with each informant, each lasting between 80 and 110 minutes and took place in their homes. Analysis followed a hermeneutical style, where the authors immersed themselves in the data, and embarked on an iterative and interactive back-and-forth process, relating parts of the text to the whole (Thompson *et al.* 1990). Subsequent rounds of interviews were organized to tease out relevant issues in line with the emergent themes. These lasted between 30 minutes to an hour. The informants are listed in Table 1.

Losing control

Prior to pregnancy, many women regard their bodies as malleable and subject to their control. However, during pregnancy the body 'becomes "present" in new, surprising and sometimes double-edged ways' (Warren and Brewis 2004: 226). The pregnant body experiences a host of physiological changes including morning sickness, tiredness, food cravings, backache, heartburn, high blood pressure, insomnia and mood swings (Stoppard 2000).

I puked for nine months and was exhausted. It's so much harder; the vomiting started two weeks into my pregnancy. I think I was only four weeks pregnant, two weeks after I found out and I threw up several times a day, every day for, let's see, five and a half months; in and out of hospital on drips until June.

(Kate)

As other informants explain, 'morning' sickness can occur at any time of the day or night, and at any time during the pregnancy. For Jayne, heartburn was problematic throughout her pregnancy:

You get it [heartburn] when you don't eat, you get it when you do eat, and no matter what you eat it's just there.

(Jayne)

The body is also more susceptible to infection, and many women find it difficult to deal with their fluctuating emotions.

I was quite sick. I used to get kidney infections, migraines... felt sick all the time... and like I was all over the place emotionally.

(Michelle)

For other informants, it wasn't just that the body made itself known; it was the feeling that they no longer had control over their bodies.

I was just going through the motions of pregnancy. My body was performing this act. I wasn't really emotionally in touch with the whole thing. I felt fat. I felt fat, heavy and my body wasn't my own. I wasn't able to do with my body what I wanted to do with it.

(Grace)

For Grace, pregnancy serves to create a distance between her and her body. For women like Grace, not only is the baby separate and alien, but through the process of pregnancy, the body itself becomes alien. 'The blood system and the body appear as entities unto their own, exhibiting an agency, knowledge and willfulness' that are distinct from the body's owner (Root and Browner 2001: 204). Control is also important for Catherine:

For me pregnancy is the process that you have to go through to get to the end result. For me, there's nothing enjoyable about being pregnant. It's the whole process of losing control – I'm a bit of a control freak so it's the whole loss of control thing, oh, and not being able to drink and eat what you want.

(Catherine)

Because many women are more accustomed to 'mobilising their bodies as a "resource" to be managed', (Warren and Brewis 2004: 227) women are often surprised by how their bodies 'burst in' during pregnancy:

So you're uncomfortable all the time. You don't sleep, headaches, and oh yes I got really bad skin in the first two months. And I had never had spots [before] and I just started breaking out all over my chin. Just the tiredness and the hugeness. Oh the hugeness. Like I was huge, huge. It was actually just so shocking.

(Kate)

For other informants, it was the lack of knowledge about what was happening to their bodies and what would happen as the pregnancy progressed that caused some distress.

I didn't know what was happening month by month, I was nervous about the whole thing and everything was strange.

(Margaret)

The loss of control associated with pregnancy is problematic for many women because 'failure at the menial task of maintaining control over one's body throws into question one's capacity to accomplish the brainwork of controlling capital,' (Han and Upton 2003). Thus, professional women may encounter more problems as a result of their pregnancies because they occupy working bodies. Indeed, women like Catherine and Grace find pregnancy more challenging because of the ways in which their experiences upset the mind-body hierarchy, with pregnancy a biological experience under the control of the body, not the mind. 'Pregnancy perforce entails a violation of the conceptual boundary separating ... personal and professional realms of life. Sexuality and children are plainly part of the personal domain; they do not belong at work. But pregnant women visibly and obviously not only take their children into the workplace, but also to even the most important meetings' (Davis-Floyd 1994: 206).

So, I was trying to keep a low profile at work. Dark clothes meant that I didn't look pregnant, that I didn't stand out...[later] I was very conscious that I didn't want to be out [of work] because of the pregnancy, because I was unwell. Because I knew that would be like, you know, a pregnant woman!

(Grace)

Pregnancy impacts upon women's relationships with their bodies, as it provides a very public display of sexuality and fertility (Bailey 1999). For some women, the masculinized ideal of the autonomous self dominates how they regard their pregnant bodies, with the experience representing 'a distressing loss of control over their bodies and of the identity they had established before pregnancy' (Schmeid and Lupton 2001: 38).

I don't think there is ANYTHING sexy about being pregnant. No, not sexy. If there is something maybe homely and maybe womanly, but sexy, No! I think pregnant women are gross and not sexy and I was never so gross as when I was pregnant.

(Kate)

Re-establishing control

Women often deal with the lack of control by seeking information about the biological and emotional aspects of pregnancy.

> You expect to feel a certain way and if you don't feel that way you think 'oh God' maybe I don't want this [baby] as much as I thought I wanted it – because I'm not as emotional about it or whatever. Because you think you should feel a certain way about everything… I suppose the media makes you feel that way.
>
> (Kate)

Because it is culturally unacceptable to share news of the pregnancy until the middle of the second trimester, many women turn to the medical profession (Gammeltoft 2007), books (O'Malley *et al.* 2006) and magazines to understand if their experience is 'normal'.

> I bought a magazine…it showed that you weren't abnormal you know when you were flying off the handle or when you were emotional. It just showed that everyone can go through that and it's normal to be a lunatic (laughs). I suppose the way it explained every week was good too 'cause you felt you knew what was going on and you could imagine how the baby is growing and developing inside of you.
>
> (Michelle)

This 'imagining' of the baby growing inside is nothing compared to the 'knowing' that the foetus is truly a baby that will one day be part of their lives. In this sense, technology, primarily in the form of the ultrasound scan, is used to provide clear evidence. Indeed, the ultrasound is deployed to bypass their own felt experience as women in an effort to provide certainty and control (Taylor 2000).

> When we had the scan, I think it was around 20 weeks or something like that, we found out that it was a little girl. We were delighted to know that, we decided on a name and then she had an identity. It also made it easier to start shopping because you could imagine what she will be like and how she might look in the little baby clothes.
>
> (Michelle)

This knowledge allowed Michelle to recognize the baby's separate identity and to acknowledge that identity with a name, and to initiate consumption on the baby's behalf. As such, similar to other studies, our informants made significant changes to their lifestyles, abstaining from or consuming certain foods or medicines in order to ensure the production of a healthy baby (Harris *et al.* 2004). Indeed, 'consumption constitutes the chief avenue of control for middle-class women, who are just beginning to conceptualize themselves as mothers, and also the chief performative arena where they may exemplify their mothering skills for others' (Taylor 2000: 402).

As such, buying things for the foetus demonstrates that it has been recognized as a baby, a person, an individual consumer, and provides opportunities to bond with the baby (Thomson 2011). When and how women grant that recognition depends upon whether they wish to embrace their pregnancy or distance themselves from it, as well as how far their pregnancy has progressed (Taylor 2000).

In making the transition from individual consumer to 'mother-as-consumer' (Taylor 2000: 403), new, more highly disciplined regimes of consumption often emerge. Many women discipline their desires in order to ensure the well-being of their unborn child. As such, women are compelled not to smoke, drink or take drugs (Betterton 2006) and must prioritize the foetus' nutritional needs above their own (Root and Browner 2001).

> I tried to eat more nutritious food for her. I cut down on coffee obviously and I might have had a cup, not even a mug, every two or three days. I would save my coffee allowance to have a nice cup of coffee after dinner or something like that… I loved Coke when I was pregnant but I tried not to drink that kind of stuff, you know fizzy drinks, just water and diluted juices and stuff like that.
>
> (Debbie)

Other informants believe that they can control the side effects of pregnancy through consumption. Interestingly, Jayne understands her consumption of vitamins etc. as feeding her body so that it is capable of nurturing her baby. She explains the absence of cravings in this way.

> I got no cravings though. Now I kept taking my Pregni-care, you buy these tablets, these Pregni-care tablets, and am, Folic acid. They say though that you don't get cravings if your body is fine, if your body has got what it needs.
>
> (Jayne)

While Jayne believes that her consumption of vitamins ensured that her body was strong enough to nurture the baby, Kate rationalizes her experience in a very different way.

> They say the sicker the mother – the healthier the baby. Yes, because all your nutrients are being drained from you to go to him. So, that is why I was so sick all the time.
>
> (Kate)

This narrative of wanting to eat more healthily is echoed in all of the informants' stories. However, efforts to re-establish control were not always successful and this created some dissonance:

> As soon as I found out I was pregnant I went on de-caffeinated drinks, I gave up alcohol and I tried to eat healthily. And I did for the first three months. But then Christmas came and I think I went AWOL – then I never got back

to eating properly. So it was probably February… Christmas lasted right through to then. I was a bloody pig. I was eating all the good food but I was eating all the bad food as well. I did intend to be good. Like I didn't want to be an obese pregnant person.

(Jayne)

Thus, consumption becomes a means of controlling pregnant bodies, as well as influencing the outcome of pregnancy in terms of a healthy baby.

Bouncing back

One of the great things about giving birth was getting my body back.

(Catherine)

For Catherine, then, giving birth meant she no longer had to share her body with her baby, she had liberated it. However, it appears that it is insufficient for women to just get their bodies back, but they must get their old bodies back.

You expect to be like 'oh I'll be pregnant and then [after the baby is born] I'll be back to my normal self in like a month'. And it just doesn't happen like that at all.

(Carolina)

For informants like Issy, who did not attempt to control their weight gain during pregnancy, there was a realization that while they had enjoyed the apparent freedom of pregnancy, the day of reckoning would still arrive.

It was great. It was the only time in my life that I've been able to eat whatever I wanted and not have to worry. I put on three stone and I've still got one and a half stone to lose – so you've got to pay sometime.

(Issy)

Issy celebrates the fact that pregnancy afforded her a time when she didn't have to control herself, when she could eat what she wanted. This 'letting go' is consistent with arguments that pregnancy allows women to shift from 'seducers' to 'producers' (Price 1988) and from 'ornamental' to 'functional' (Charles and Kerr 1886). That is, if the purpose of pregnancy is entirely functional and productive, women are freed (or indeed, free themselves) from imperatives to be ornamental as is consistent with idealized femininity.

However, for many women the ideal of a healthy, toned body is incongruent with the postpartum body. For example, AnnMarie recognizes that her postpartum body, un-toned and brandishing stretch marks is unacceptable and must be subjected to control.

Floppy. Everything became floppy. My tummy is floppy, my bum, and even my breasts. The big breasts didn't last. I have some stretch marks but I'm using bio oil, which is really good and has helped a lot. I do really need to get back to the gym though and get toned. And I'm going to start walking now when the weather improves.

(AnnMarie)

AnnMarie is very aware that she needs to bounce back and has made plans to start walking and get back to the gym. Michelle is also acutely aware that following the birth of her daughter she needs to reclaim her pre-pregnant body.

There's a lot of pressure on normal people to lose weight and look perfect. When you look at pregnant celebrities, when they have their child they are usually skinnier than they were before within a week, and they always look perfect, and, well, never tired or fat.

(Michelle)

Michelle implicitly understands that representations of celebrities with tiny postpartum bodies are unrealistic but also regards these images as putting pressure on 'normal' people. However, she lives in a culture in which these celebrities attempt to control the postpartum body either through early elective caesareans or through a host of keep-fit gurus. 'The fantasy that one can cheat the postpartum body and that the biological processes of pregnancy and postpartum can be dispensed with, is a consequence of the compelling cultural narrative that fat is bad and that it behoves a woman in whatever stage of her life to manage her body, her appetite, and her size' (Orbach 2006: 68). Indeed, it is increasingly difficult to distinguish between the desire to get your body back postpartum, and the demand to manage your pregnant body. Margaret also refers to how celebrities 'bounce back' and echoes Michelle's assertion that it is different for 'normal' people.

Jordan, the bitch, looks brilliant again after having her baby, she's smaller now I'd say. But she doesn't eat at all anymore. Only water. And I'd die if I tried that.

(Margaret)

Implicit in this is that it is not possible for normal women to achieve this pre-pregnancy body and certainly not so quickly. Normal women have to eat. And, yet, there is also recognition of the pressure this places as evidenced by reference to 'Jordan, the bitch'. 'Increasingly, celebrity moms are depicted as women who anticipate and even preempt the challenges of the postpartum period in the management of their pregnant bodies. Hence, it has become almost impossible to separate the desire to get your body back from how you manage your pregnant body' (Cunningham 2002: 438).

I had a resolve that I was going to go back to work and that it would be like I hadn't left at all. That I'd look the same. It was very important that I didn't have... you know look like I was a Mommy... cuddly and all that. That was because of the women at work. Because of their attitude, very much that because you're a mother now you're pretty much written off because your focus is not your job any more, it can't be your priority now.

(Grace)

Cunningham (2002: 449) argues that 'un-recovered postpartum bodies are bothersome to the working world because they link women to the world of family and therefore signal a more long-term disruption of capitalist routines'. For Grace then, looking like she'd never been pregnant or had a baby would create a perception that she hadn't left the working world at all. For her, 'cuddly' implied a maternal body while thin and toned represented a working body. Grace felt that her maternal body would allow her to be dismissed by her colleagues as making her baby rather than her job a priority, what Cunningham (2002: 449) refers to as 'deadbeat workers'. As such, bouncing back demonstrates an ongoing commitment to the working world, and limited opportunities for colleagues to question her priorities.

The lady managers said, oh, you look so well. You've lost so much weight. And the way they were talking to you, and I wanted to say, well I was pregnant – I wasn't fat. But that was the way I had felt too. I viewed myself as fat and it was only after my daughter was born that I realized I had been pregnant.

(Grace)

It is interesting that Grace didn't really recognize that she had been pregnant (rather than fat) until long after the baby was born. This demonstrates the apparent disconnect between working bodies and maternal bodies for some women. For many informants, choosing to breastfeed also appears to be as much about getting their bodies back as it is about nurturing their babies.

To be honest it was selfish as well. Because most people were saying 'oh you will get your weight back quicker' so I was like 'SOLD' ... I came out of hospital and I still felt six or seven months pregnant and three months later I was still really heavy. I was wearing size 14 and I have always been a size 12. That was a real stickler for me because I couldn't fit into any of my pre-pregnancy stuff. And everyone was like, 'oh it will just melt off you when you breast feed'.... But it didn't. So that really stressed me out because I had been so body conscious beforehand.

(Carolina)

Because 'pregnancy presents one of the few periods in a woman's life during which it is acceptable to be fat' (Earle 2003: 245), women who are naturally larger seem to embrace changes to their bodies during pregnancy and are more relaxed about getting their bodies back postpartum.

If you were a nice slim girl and you got pregnant and put on the weight you'd probably feel bad but I'm a nice big girl and being pregnant in that sense didn't really bother me... No I'm just a natural mother [laughs].

(Margaret)

Debbie was not a larger woman but also seemed relaxed about her body postpartum.

Well I never loved my body anyway. So I don't feel any different. I only have a few small stretch marks but they don't bother me.

(Debbie)

Kate is also realistic about her expectations of her postpartum body, although she recognizes the exhortations in the media to bounce back. Referring to model Heidi Klum on the Victoria's Secret runway three weeks after giving birth, she rationalizes as follows:

You see she has her career. And she probably exercised the whole time she was pregnant. And she got pregnant with that body. You know I didn't have Heidi Klum's body before I got pregnant, so why would I expect it afterwards?

(Kate)

Conclusions

Pregnancy is an embodied experience that forces many women to suddenly (and for some, shockingly) acknowledge the agency of their bodies as they become susceptible to physiological forces over which they have little control. Because of the physiological and emotional demands of pregnancy, it was traditionally understood as a period during which women could enjoy relative freedom from the demands of idealized femininity. More recently, pregnant bodies are no longer required to be hidden and have thus been subjected to more public consumption. Originally conceived as a 'liberation', a number of commentators suggest that this subjects the pregnant body to additional demands, requiring it to be actively managed (Cunningham 2002; O'Donohoe 2006).

In this chapter we demonstrate how women experience the initial loss of control, and subsequently attempt to re-assert control through 'managing' their attendant consumption. Our informants demonstrate that they undergo significant lifestyle changes including: abstaining from unhealthy consumption (cigarettes, alcohol, coffee, fizzy drinks, etc.); increasing consumption of healthy 'natural' products (organic fruit, vegetables, water), and; bolstering their ability to provide nutrients to their unborn child through consumption of specialized vitamins and minerals. These changes in consumption evidence the shift from seducer to producer experienced by pregnant women (Price 1988) which requires them to acknowledge the primacy of their body's functional role (Charles and Kerr 1986). Thus, women are compelled to 'manage' their bodies in order to maintain a healthy environment for their growing foetus and in order to 'produce' a healthy baby. However, while individual bodies take on productive, functional and maternal characteristics (growing bump, enlarged breasts, increased weight), societal expectations prevent women from fully 'letting go' of their seductive, ornamental and sexual characteristics. This disconnect appears to be particularly problematic for corporate women, where it appears that the 'maternal' signifies a disengagement from the world of work (Cunningham 2002). Thus, women are required to maintain an appropriate aesthetic throughout their pregnancy (how they look, how they dress, etc.), and return to their pre-pregnant bodies as quickly as possible postpartum (Earle 2003).

Thus, far from being a period of grace, during which pregnant women can retire from the usual demands of their lives, in contemporary society, there is a strong imperative for them to manage their bodies, so that they (i) provide the optimal environment for their growing foetus; (ii) maintain an appropriate aesthetic throughout the pregnancy; and (iii) ensure that their bodies bounce back as quickly as possible. Thus, demands to 'manage' pregnant bodies are driven by two distinct and sometimes mutually exclusive ideologies. Demands to create the optimal environment to produce a healthy baby are driven by the medicalization of pregnancy and, to a greater or lesser degree, influence the behaviours and experiences of all of our informants. The aesthetic demands and imperatives to quickly 'bounce back' appear to be fuelled by celebrity culture and the media, and while recognized as 'not normal' by many informants, it still places significant pressure on women during their pregnancies and postpartum. This is particularly true of women who accept the compelling cultural narrative that 'fat is bad' (Orbach 2006: 68), many of whom are in corporate positions (Cunningham 2002). Indeed, a number of informants experienced a great deal of anxiety regarding changes in their bodies (Schmeid and Lupton 2001; Warren and Brewis 2004), particularly increases in size. Thus, contrary to Earle's (2003) suggestion, for many women, it is not acceptable to be fat, even during pregnancy. The apparent exceptions to this are women who did not actively manage their pre-pregnant bodies, and for these women, it does appear that pregnancy liberates them from societal pressures to be thin and toned (Earle 2003).

Pregnancy seems to offer an opportunity for change or 'time out' for those who want it – a departure from an old narrative of self. For these women, the foetus represents a substantial and harmonious part of themselves. For others, being pregnant represents a threat to their body boundaries and routines. They embrace the cultural imperative to affirm a masculinized, autonomous, closed self. Thus, for many women, pregnancy imposes a new set of rules and requirements to behave in particular ways. Of these, imperatives to control their consumption and to manage their bodies appear to be particularly strong, and are fuelled by both medical and media discourses. However, because the body is itself more wilful during pregnancy, it is not easily subjected to control (Stoppard 2000). Thus, while changes to the body are themselves a source of anxiety for many women (Warren and Brewis 2004), failure to control these bodies exacerbates such feelings (Han and Upton 2003). While the body is pregnant, it must be managed in order to produce a healthy baby (Taylor 2000); as soon as that function has been performed, it must bounce back as quickly and as seamlessly as possible (Dworkin and Wachs 2004). Thus, we conclude that pregnancy no longer represents a period of grace for women, nor is there a clear shift for women from seducer to producer (Price 1988; Stearns 1999), or ornamental to functional (Charles and Kerr 1986). Rather in contemporary society, women are compelled to manage their bodies during pregnancy, to perform the necessary function of producing a healthy baby, without undermining the aesthetics demanded by a more sexual/ornamental role. Thus, it is not a choice between an ornamental *or* a functional body, but rather, in contemporary society bodies have to be managed to display both (often simultaneously).

References

Bailey, L. (1999) 'Refracted selves? A study of changes in self-identity in the transition to motherhood', *Sociology*, 33:2, 335–52.

Bailey, L. (2001) 'Gender shows: first-time mothers and embodied selves', *Gender and Society*, 1:1, 110–29.

Betterton, R. (2006) 'Promising monsters: pregnant bodies, artistic subjectivity and maternal imagination', *Hypatia*, 21:1, 80–100.

Charles, N. and Kerr, M. (1986) 'Food for feminist thought', *The Sociological Review*, 34, 537–72.

Crawford, M. and Marecek, J. (1989) 'Psychology reconstructs the female: 1968–1988', *Psychology of Women Quarterly*, 13:2, 147–66.

Cunningham, H. (2002) 'Prodigal bodies: pop culture and post-pregnancy', *Michigan Quarterly Review*, 41:3, 428–54.

Davis-Floyd, R. (1994) 'The technocratic body: American childbirth as cultural expression', *Social Science and Medicine*, 38:8, 1125–40. Online. Available http://davis-floyd.com/the-technocratic-body-american-childbirth-as-cultural-expression/ (accessed 21 July 2012).

Dworkin, S. L. and Wachs F. L. (2004) '"Getting your body back": postindustrial fit motherhood in *Shape Fit Pregnancy* magazine', *Gender & Society*, 18:5, 610–24.

Earle, S. (2003) 'Bumps and boobs: fatness and women's experiences of pregnancy', *Women's Studies International Forum*, 26:3, 245–52.

Gammeltoft, T. (2007) 'Sonography and sociality: obstetrical ultrasound imaging in urban Vietnam', *Medical Anthropology Quarterly*, 21:2, 133–53.

Gatens, M. (1999) *Imaginary Bodies: Ethics, Power and Corporeality*, London: Routledge.

Goulding, C. (1999) 'Consumer research, interpretive paradigms and methodological ambiguities', *European Journal of Marketing*, 33:9/10, 859–73.

Han, S. and Upton, R. (2003) 'Maternity and its discontents: getting the body back after pregnancy', *Journal of Contemporary Ethnography*, 32, 670–92.

Harris, G., Connor, L., Bisits, A. and Higginbotham, N. (2004) 'Seeing the baby: pleasures and dilemmas of ultrasound technologies for primiparous Australian women', *Medical Anthropology Quarterly*, 18:1, 23–47.

Mick, D. G. and Buhl C. (1992) 'A meaning-based model of advertising experience', *Journal of Consumer Research*, 19 (December): 317–38.

Miller, T. (2005) *Making Sense of Motherhood: a Narrative Approach*, Cambridge: Cambridge University Press.

Mullin, A. (2005) *Reconceiving Pregnancy and Childcare: Ethics, Experience and Reproductive Labor*, New York: Cambridge University Press.

O'Donohoe, S. (2006) 'Yummy Mummies: the clamor of glamour in advertising to mothers', *Advertising & Society Review*, 7(3). Online. Available http://muse.jhu.edu/journals/advertising_and_society_review/ (accessed 4 February 2013).

O'Malley, L. (2006) 'Does my bump look big in this?', *Advertising & Society Review*, 7(3). Online. Available http://muse.jhu.edu/journals/advertising_and_society_review/ (accessed 4 February 2013).

O'Malley, L., Patterson, M. and Ní Bheacháin, C. (2006) 'Paperback mother', in S. Brown (ed.) *Consuming Books: the Marketing and Consumption of Literature*, London: Routledge, 83–95.

Orbach, S. (2006) 'There is a public health crisis: it's not fat on the body but fat in the mind and the fat of profits,' *International Journal of Epidemiology*, 35, 67–9.

Price J. (1988) *Motherhood: What It Does to Your Mind*, London: Pandora.

Root, R. and Browner C. H. (2001) 'Practices of the pregnant self: compliance with and resistance to prenatal norms', *Culture, Medicine & Psychiatry*, 25, 195–223.

Schmeid, V. and Lupton, D. (2001) 'The externality of the inside: body images of pregnancy', *Nursing Inquiry*, 8:1, 32–40.

Shildrick, M. (2002) *Embodying the Monster: Encounters With the Vulnerable Self*, London: Sage.

Smith, J. (1999) 'Towards a relational self: social engagement during pregnancy and psychological preparation for motherhood', *British Journal of Psychology*, 38, 409–26.

Stearns, C. (1999) 'Breastfeeding and the good maternal body', *Gender and Society*, 13:3, 308–25.

Stoppard, M. (2000) *Conception, Pregnancy and Birth: the Childbirth Bible for Today's Parents*, London: Dorling Kindersley.

Taylor, J. (2000) 'Of sonograms and baby prams: prenatal diagnosis, pregnancy and consumption', *Feminist Studies*, 26:2, 391–418.

Thompson, C. J., Locander, W. B. and Pollio, H. R. (1989) 'Putting consumer experience back into consumer research: the philosophy and method of existential-phenomenology', *Journal of Consumer Research*, 16 (September), 133-44.

Thompson, C. J., Locander, W. B. and Pollio, H. R. (1990) 'The lived meaning of free choice: an existential-phenomenological description of everyday consumer experiences of contemporary married women', *Journal of Consumer Research*, 17 (December), 346–61.

Thompson, C. J., Pollio, H. R. and Locander, W. B. (1994) 'The spoken and the unspoken: a hermeneutic approach to understanding the cultural viewpoints that underlie consumers' expressed meanings', *Journal of Consumer Research*, 21(December), 432–52.

Thomson, R. (2011) 'Making motherhood work', *Studies in the Maternal*, 3:2. Online. Available www.mamsie.bbk.ac.uk (accessed 12 July 2012).

Warren, S. and Brewis, J. (2004) 'Matter over mind? Examining the experience of pregnancy', *Sociology*, 38:2, 219–36.

Young, I. M. (2005) *On Female Body Experience: 'Throwing like a girl' and Other Essays*, Oxford: Oxford University Press.

11 Managing pregnancy work

Consumption, emotion and embeddedness

Caroline J. Gatrell

Introduction

In this chapter I discuss the consumption and emotion work required of pregnant women as they attempt to meet the standards set for 'good' expectant mothers in terms of their health. Focusing on the maternal consumption of health advice available on the internet, I highlight the disparity between the idea of pregnancy as a 'project' for mothers to manage (Brewis and Warren 2001), and cultural narratives which present the work of mothering as a 'natural' or instinctive female attribute (Miller 2005). In so doing, I argue that pregnant women's consumption of health advice, and their consequent management of their pregnant bodies, is a form of work. Drawing upon Miriam Glucksmann's Total Social Organization of Labour (TSOL), I suggest that the maternal work involved in managing pregnancy is discounted, or 'embedded', within these notions of the maternal instinct.

Pregnancy and the consumption of health advice

For over thirty years, feminist writers on pregnancy have acknowledged the pressures on women to be 'good' expectant mothers (Oakley 1981; Pollock 1999; Kitzinger 2005; Miller 2005; Young 2005). However, within the last fifteen years the notion of pregnancy as a 'project' that women are supposed to 'manage' to a given standard has been proposed (Brewis and Warren; Longhurst 2001). Pregnancy has subsequently been described as a form of maternal body 'work' (Gatrell 2008). The definition of pregnancy as a 'project', requiring 'work' on the part of expectant mothers, reflects contemporary Euro-American assumptions that women have both the responsibility and the resources to control embodied and lifestyle behaviours during pregnancy (Brewis and Warren, 2001; Longhurst 2001). This assumption is based upon the belief that consumption of, and compliance with, health advice and medical guidelines will positively influence pregnancy outcomes, reducing infant morbidity and resulting in improved health among populations overall (Miles 1992; Nettleton 2006; Gatrell 2008).

The presumption that pregnant women should consume and follow health advice, and accede to medical routines and procedures in their own and their babies' best interests, is fundamental to ideologies of pregnancy as a 'project' which women are encouraged to manage pro-actively (Brewis and Warren 2001). Within Euro-American health contexts, pregnancy is presented to women as an endeavour which they are expected to manage to a specific set of standards while under close surveillance from health and other professionals, as well as family and friends (Longhurst 2001).

While pregnant women have been encouraged to consume, digest and follow research-based health advice for many decades (Miles 1992), the past decade has seen a burgeoning of 'expert' advice on the internet as both 'official' medical and commercial pregnancy websites proliferate, with increasing numbers of women drawn to these sites as a source of information and support (Lagan *et al.* 2006). As noted by the commercial pregnancy and baby care advice site BabyCentre (2012), rapidly increasing numbers of pregnant women consume the guidance posted on such sites. Women are exhorted to regulate their dietary and social behaviours, measuring themselves (and being measured by others) in relation to complex and demanding standards and goals (Miles 1992; Brewis and Warren 2001; Longhurst 2001, 2008; Warren and Brewis 2004; Young 2005; Gatrell 2008).

As a minimum, pregnant consumers of health advice are recommended to follow special diets, abstain from drinking alcohol and smoking cigarettes, monitor their weight, get plenty of rest and take pregnancy-specific exercises (Gatrell 2011c). Additionally, however, pregnant women, living in what feminist philosopher Young describes as 'technologically sophisticated Western societies' (2005:47), are often expected to accommodate and to consume a level of health surveillance usually associated only with serious illness. As Young observes, pregnancy is treated by health experts 'as a condition that deviates from normal health' (2005:47). Pregnant women are expected to attend regular ante-natal screening appointments, which means that their pregnant bodies and developing babies fall under the surveillance of health professionals in circumstances where weight, diet and lifestyle are scrutinized. Women will be expected to undergo regular medical tests such as ultra-sound scans. These usually take place at 12 weeks, 18–20 weeks and sometimes at 36 weeks – and more often if recommended by clinicians (NHS Direct 2012; Web MD 2009).

Ultra-sound scans are unlikely to cause physical pain, though they may be a source of anxiety for pregnant women and uncomfortable if mothers are obliged to drink a lot of fluid beforehand. In order to be consumers of ultra-sound scans, however, pregnant women are required to undertake the work of travelling to an appropriate clinical centre, waiting for the procedure to take place and then experiencing the procedure itself. NHS (2012) advice describes ultra-sound scanning as follows:

> You'll probably be asked to drink a lot of fluid before you have the scan. A full bladder pushes your womb up and this gives a better picture. You then lie on your back and some jelly is put on your abdomen. An instrument is passed backwards and forwards over your skin, and high-frequency sound is beamed through your abdomen into the womb. The sound is reflected back and creates a picture, which is shown on a TV screen.

Some clinical ante-natal tests may be more invasive, more uncomfortable and more painful than ultra-sound. For example, amniocentesis testing is often recommended for women over 35. This involves the insertion of a needle into the uterus in order to draw off amniotic fluid so that checks may be made for chromosomal irregularities. This test may be difficult for women to resist, even if they are uncertain about its benefits, if health professionals consider it necessary (Pollock 1999). Women undergoing amniocentesis may be required to have bed rest following this procedure because it carries a risk of miscarriage. They may experience cramping following the procedure, and may have to wait for up to three weeks before they learn the results of this test (Gatrell 2011a).

Health advice on diet and lifestyle

As well as submitting to clinical procedures and regular ante-natal appointments, pregnant women are required to invest time and intellect consuming, and implementing, health advice on diet and lifestyle, managing their pregnancies and their pregnant bodies in accordance with such guidance. As Brewis and Warren (2001) and Warren and Brewis (2004), Longhurst (2001) and Gatrell (2011a) all note, it is anticipated by health 'experts' – both clinical and commercial – that pregnant women will carefully consume, digest and internalize what may be complex health advice so as to comply with exacting health standards. In relation to the consumption of health advice and compliance with medical guidelines, while under the close scrutiny of health professionals, the pregnancy 'project' could be seen as requiring a very precise type of work, or maternal labour. As health sociologist Miles (1992:192) has observed,

> ...from the day a woman's pregnancy is announced until after delivery, what she eats and drinks and [everything she does] becomes the concern of health professionals. In the name of health, not only her own, but with even greater emphasis on that of the fetus, the activities of the pregnant woman are controlled ... [and monitored].

In relation to pregnant women's consumption of, and compliance with, health advice, I seek to make two points in this chapter. First, such consumption and compliance involves pregnant women in a form of unpaid work which requires careful management of pregnancy and the pregnant body, in line with given health standards. The second point relates to the obfuscation of this maternal labour within the discourse of maternal instinct as a natural outcome of pregnancy – the implication being that if mothering skills are an inherent component of motherhood, then women should be able to manage the project of pregnancy without much effort. In other words, the 'work' required of women to manage the project of pregnancy is discounted. The challenge of understanding women's work in relation to pregnancy specifically has been highlighted by Martin (1989), Brewis and Warren (2001), Gatrell (2008) and Longhurst (2008), who note social expectations that pregnant women should strive to attain given health standards with the anticipated reward of a 'healthy baby' (Brewis and Warren 2001:385) but with little acknowledgement of the pregnancy work involved in consuming, and complying with, health advice.

It is acknowledged, at this point, that delineating what counts as 'work' or 'maternal labour', in relation to pregnancy, is complex. As management sociologist Keith Grint (2005) has observed, definitions of 'work' are ambiguous and contested: 'work' as a concept is 'unstable' due to its dependence upon the 'temporal, spatial and cultural conditions in existence' (2005:6). Nevertheless, the need to pursue sociological understandings of women's work has been identified by sociologist Miriam Glucksmann (2005) who argues that, despite a feminist focus on women's work during the 1980s (Hochschild 1983; Beechey 1987; Pringle 1989), women's work remains under-theorized and the question 'what is [women's] work' has never been answered satisfactorily (Glucksmann 1995, 2005).

Consumption work, emotion work and women's embedded labour

In what follows, drawing particularly upon the work of Miriam Glucksmann (1995, 2005), this chapter attempts to articulate pregnancy work in relation to maternal consumption of health advice by drawing upon Glucksmann's theoretical concept Total Social Organization of Labour (TSOL). TSOL offers a framework for theorizing women's 'work' activities which are neither recorded nor remunerated, and which may not previously have been recognized as 'work' (Glucksmann and Nolan 2007:97). Here, TSOL is helpful in defining the unrecorded work of pregnancy because it facilitates exploration of those women's work activities which are often discounted, focusing on the 'relational organization of all [women's] labour, however and wherever it [was] undertaken' (Glucksmann 1995:63).

In its totality, TSOL comprises four dimensions: (1) *relationships between social practices*; (2) *economics;* (3) *articulation of work activities* and (4) *temporality*. Each of these four dimensions is explained fully by Glucksmann in her (2005) description of TSOL as a framework for enhancing understanding of women's work. For the purposes of this chapter however, only the *articulation of work activities* dimension is utilized, as it is the most relevant to articulating the work involved in managing pregnancy as a project. This dimension offers a three-point framework for reflecting the multi-dimensionality of work activities in terms of consumption work, emotion work and embeddedness. These three research areas are outlined below in detail in Framework 1, then drawn upon in the chapter to interpret research findings and to articulate pregnancy work within the context of health advice.

Framework 1: Consumption work, emotion work and embeddedness

1   Consumption work: by 'consumption work' Glucksmann refers to the demands of understanding domestic technologies (e.g. washing machines),

and the intellectual and operational skills required of women who buy and use such technologies. In this chapter, the notion 'consumption work' is applied to pregnant women's researching, understanding and implementing of health advice, as described by Bernhardt and Felter (2004) as women attempt to understand and comply with social and cultural constructions about how to be a good mother (Hogg *et al.* 2011).

2   Emotion work: Glucksmann describes 'emotion work' as a key topic within feminist scholarship (see also Hochschild 1983; Adkins 1995; Bolton 2001). Emotion work is often defined as work which demands that women workers provide emotional support to others (for example flight attendants, Hochschild 1983). In this chapter, the concept of emotion work is adapted and applied to highlight the emotional energy expended by pregnant women in trying to manage the levels of anxiety which they experience in relation to their consumption of knowledge about the recommended management of pregnancy. Bernhardt and Felter (2004) describe how pregnant women cling to the internet as a source of reassurance, facilitating the emotion work of attempting to allay their anxieties about pregnancy and its management. As one of Bernhardt and Felter's (2004:1) respondents states: '…I was so scared and I would go to this web site every day and just look at it (for) like ten minutes straight and I just found so much helpful information on it (about) being scared and not knowing what to expect'.

3   Embeddedness: Glucksmann defines 'embeddedness' as work activities which are taken for granted and/or discounted. For example, housework often falls to women, but tends to be discounted due to social expectations about women's domestic roles. Here, 'embeddedness' is applied to the work involved in managing pregnancy as a project (Brewis and Warren 2001); such work may be discounted because motherhood is assumed to come instinctively, or 'naturally', to women (Miller 2005).

Methods

For over six years, I have investigated women's experiences of pregnancy and maternity through netnographic (or internet) research. The internet is an important resource for understanding how women manage and understand pregnancy because growing numbers of women consume health advice from a rapidly proliferating range of pregnancy and baby care websites (both clinical and commercial) which base their counsel on medical guidelines. Pregnant women are known to be consumers of such websites not only as recipients of advice, but also because they can join website chat communities drawing upon other mothers' views as a source of collective support and information (Lagan *et al.* 2006). The notion of pregnant women as consumers not only of commercial products, but also of advice and information as detailed in Framework 1 above, is established within health literature (Bernhardt and Felter 2004) as well as within research on motherhood and consumption (Hogg *et al.* 2011). As Bernhardt and Felter (2004:1) observe:

> Pregnant women and mothers of young children are active consumers of health information about themselves and their children, and there are countless ... resources on childbirth, parenting, and pediatrics from which mothers and mothers-to-be can choose...[in particular] the World Wide Web, has grown into a popular destination for women seeking health information.

As noted by Bernhardt and Felter 2004, popular websites such as BabyCentre and WebMD are accessed worldwide. BabyCentre (2012) for example, claims up to 25 million consumers per month, hosting annually almost three quarters of a million discussions, 4.3 million comments from consumers and 123,000 photo uploads.

In collecting data for this chapter, I have explored both 'official' clinical sites such as the NHS and also commercial sites such as Babyworld, verybestbaby and whattoexpect, all of which offer community facilities. In addition, I have also drawn upon smaller sites, which I do not identify for purposes of anonymity. The data has been interpreted thematically, and classified electronically which is time-consuming but enables closeness to the data.

Although the health advice and community discussions considered here were openly available on the internet, I have had no personal contact with individual internet correspondents and thus no knowledge of how they might feel about being a research subject. In order to address this issue (even though most users adopt fictitious internet identifiers to preserve anonymity, Lagan *et al.* 2006), I have further anonymized all those quoted below, replacing chosen internet identifiers with pseudonyms (as advised by Eriksson and Kovalainen 2008:106). I have omitted all personal details and do not refer to specific jobs or geographic locations.

The consumption work of pregnancy

An exploration of the health advice offered on pregnancy and baby care websites demonstrates that notions of consumption are implied on two levels – first, in respect of the intellectual effort required to research, understand and consume the wealth of health advice offered (as indicated in Framework 1 above); and second, in respect of implementing such guidance on diet and ante-natal care. This chapter is concerned with both levels of consumption, in relation to the intellectual digestion, compliance with, and implementation of health advice which is demanding to the point where it may be articulated as a form of 'work'. Findings from this research demonstrate how consumption of such advice necessitates intense emotion work in terms of coping with anxiety. It is observed how both the consumption and emotion work of pregnancy may be discounted, or 'embedded', due to social assumptions that pregnant women should cope instinctively with maternal responsibilities, which are presumed to come naturally to them.

Managing diet and lifestyle

In keeping with the idea of consumption as work, advice offered to pregnant consumers on pregnancy and baby care websites sets tough challenges, demanding that women make decisions about changes to diet and lifestyles based upon information which may be at the same time complex and ambiguous. On an everyday basis, the expectation that pregnant women should consume, interpret and implement advice on diet and lifestyle to the most detailed level suggests that an intensity of intellectual focus is required to meet the criteria for healthy behaviours (and 'good mothering') during pregnancy (Hogg *et al.* 2011; Miller 2005). Thus, most pregnancy websites present women with long lists of food and beverages that should (or conversely must not) be consumed during pregnancy. This advice is often lengthy and may also be difficult to interpret. Consider, for example, the somewhat confusing advice offered by the popular website BabyCentre regarding the benefits and risks of eating fish while pregnant:

> ...fish is a major source of omega-3 fatty acids (specifically DHA and EPA), which are important for your baby's brain and eye development. It's also low in saturated fat and high in protein, vitamin D, and other nutrients that are crucial for a developing baby and a healthy pregnancy. On the other hand, you've probably also heard that some types of fish contain contaminants such as mercury. In high doses, this metal is harmful to a baby's developing brain and nervous system. Most experts agree that pregnant women should eat some fish. But it can be hard to figure out which ones are safe and how much to eat.

Similarly perplexing is recent advice from the NHS on whether or not pregnant women should eat nuts:

> You may have heard that some women have, in the past, chosen not to eat peanuts when they were pregnant. This is because the [UK] government previously advised women that they may wish to avoid eating peanuts if there was a history of allergy (such as asthma, eczema, hay fever, food allergy or other types of allergy) in their child's immediate family. This advice has now been changed because the latest research has shown that there is no clear evidence to say if eating or not eating peanuts during pregnancy affects the chances of your baby developing a peanut allergy.

The management 'project' of pregnancy thus appears to require of women serious intellectual consumption work in relation to following (and interpreting) advice such as this aimed at rendering their bodies 'healthy' for the benefit of the growing baby. Data gathered from internet discussions among mothers demonstrates (in accordance with the findings of Brewis and Warren (2001) and Gatrell (2011a)) that pregnant consumers invest time and energy in researching and trying to understand information about diet and lifestyle behaviours. For example Belinda, having read up on what she should (or should not) be eating during pregnancy, cannot find information on safe levels of salmon consumption. She thus writes in to seek more information from the 'expert' advisor on a health information site:

I am 10 weeks pregnant and I have a craving for salmon sandwiches. There is no guidance on how much tinned salmon is safe to eat – it says two portions of salmon per week, but what counts as a portion and does this refer to fresh salmon?

Similarly Julie (writing on a general message board on a different site) requests advice from other users regarding levels of fish oil supplements she should be taking. She explains how she has presently been taking only one capsule per day, instead of the dosage of four tablets which is recommended on the bottle. Worried that either her chosen dose is insufficient, or the recommended dose is too high, Julie asks other correspondents their views:

hi I'm now 13 weeks pregnant and i took nature made fish oil with EPA and DHA 273mg for almost 40 days with 1 tablet per day. Bottle prescribed to take 4 tablets per day – but will it harm my baby? please help.

Emotion work

The consumption work undertaken by Julie, Belinda and countless other pregnant women, supplementing their apparently extensive web research by seeking the counsel of others, is characterized by the emotion work of anxiety and worry about their own and their babies' health. In keeping with the findings of Bernhardt and Felter (2004), many posts demonstrate how pregnant women cling to the web as a source of information and reassurance. The more anxious mothers become, the more information they appear to seek, in the hopes of allaying anxieties. This is particularly noticeable when circumstances prevent mothers from putting into practice the health advice they have consumed from 'experts' on optimum modes of diet and lifestyle during pregnancy. For example some women, such as Susan, are both short of money, and simply too weary to shop or cook, and then worry that their supposedly sub-optimal diets will be damaging to the baby:

Livin on my own and no money, just soo tired and eating bread and cereals at nite no energy to cook soooo worried tho' … will it harm baby?

Others – Jen, for example – write of fears about harming their babies because morning sickness prevents them from eating those foods they understand to be healthy. Jen thus seeks reassurance from other mothers:

With this morning sickness flaring up and being difficult, I have had to eat things that aren't exactly the healthiest, I try to still get in some good fruits, but I haven't eaten that many vegatables … i'm just worried … about all these things like gestational diabetes and etc … do most of you just eat whatever agrees with your stomach in moderation? Is it ok to be a bit off the mark the first trimester? I don't want to hurt the baby, but I can't force myself to eat massive amounts of vegetables and etc.

Similarly Bella, also experiencing morning sickness, seeks advice from fellow sufferers about how much she should be worrying and explains how she is taking supplements to try and replace lost nutrition:

> i am currently 16 weeks pg. For the past whole week, I am having trouble eating. I don't feel like eating anything, even if I force myself to eat something, I feel sick and throw up. I've only been eating fruits, 2 glasses of milk, just 1 small meal. I do feel hungry but can't stand any type of food. Am I harming my baby??? I am taking pregnacare's one (17 vitamin + folic acid included) tablet everyday.
>
> Do/did any of u have/had this problem :?: I am quite worried abt it :(

Both Jen and Bella have evidently undertaken the consumption work of learning about optimum nutrition, and are now caught up in the emotion work of trying to manage their anxieties about foetal health in a situation where the consumption of supposedly 'good' foods in appropriate quantities is problematic. Like many other women in the same situation, both express guilt at not managing their diet in accordance with health advice:

> …I guess i'm just worried, should I feel guilty? Should I force down foods that make me sick, just to make sure i'm not hurting the baby?
>
> (Bella)

In addition to worries about nutrition, mothers corresponding on pregnancy and baby care websites were also anxious that they might be judged by health professionals as performing the work of pregnancy poorly if, having consumed and understood advice about the most appropriate diet and lifestyles, they were deemed to be purposefully contravening this. Jo, in particular, worried that health professionals would label her as overweight at her forthcoming ante-natal appointment:

> Feeling like crap so not eating good and worried they will ask what i have been eating i've always been big and i just worried what they will say about my weight.

Mothers' fears about being censured for failing to manage the project of pregnancy extended beyond worries about the views of midwives and doctors to include family and friends. These anxieties are not unreasonable because 'other people' often consider it appropriate to scrutinize the performance of pregnant women (Kitzinger 2003, 2005). The imposition of such social surveillance is rationalized on the grounds that women's bodily adherence to health advice is in the public interest (Davidson 2001; Kitzinger 2003, 2005; Longhurst 2001, 2008; Murphy 2003). As Robyn Longhurst (2001:55) argues: 'the fetus is often treated as if it were a public concern'.

Conflict thus arises for pregnant women who do not comply with social expectations about the maternal body work required to manage the pregnancy project. Pregnant women whose embodied behaviour is judged by others to be inappropriate (for example smoking cigarettes) may be treated with opprobrium (Kitzinger 2003). Thus Pat, responding to a query from another pregnant correspondent about smoking in pregnancy, observes her own anxieties both about her inability to quit smoking, and the disapproving treatment she receives from others. Pat's post illustrates the emotion work involved in managing her own anxieties, as she attempts to stop smoking, as well as the emotion required to cope with the disapproval of others who treat her like a 'leper' as she attempts to cut down on cigarettes, in keeping with medical advice:

> [Smoking] is something I am totally embarrassed about and makes me feel horrible... Don't be surprised if you get a lot of sh*t [about smoking in pregnancy]... I have ... felt attacked. I personally feel a lot of it is a social acceptability issue. If you smoke nowadays... You are a "leper." I want my baby to be healthy and happy... so I am trying to quit smoking b/c I truly want what is best for my child ...I am NOT trying to justify smoking OR smoking while pregnant, [but] as I have been a smoker for 17 years... It is a difficult habit and addiction to break. Some people (especially those that have never smoked) have NO idea what it is like...

Consumption and emotion work and clinical treatment of pregnancy

As well as their anxieties about diet and lifestyles, pregnant women engage in intense consumption and emotion work regarding the clinical treatment of pregnancy. As observed by Young (2005) above, pregnant women are expected, by health professionals, to be consumers in a range of clinical situations. Pregnant bodies are regularly assessed and screened in line with clinical guidelines and procedures, and women who resist or query these screening requirements may be treated as irresponsible or seen as performing the project of pregnancy to an inadequate standard (Pollock 1999; Gatrell 2008). As observed earlier, pregnant consumers of ante-natal screening may find themselves engaged in the consumption work of travelling to clinics, waiting for treatment, digesting health advice, and undergoing tests such as scans and amniocentesis. The nature of this consumption work may be demanding. For example, employers and colleagues may be impatient with employed women who are unavailable for work while attending ante-natal appointments (Gatrell 2011b) and women themselves might be obliged to manage the emotion work of coping with feelings of anxiety experienced while undergoing such tests. For example Marla, having undergone a clinical procedure during the early stages of her pregnancy, expressed her concerns about worrying too much, as she sought the advice of other mothers on a pregnancy website:

> All I can think about is things that can go wrong. I'm so worried about miscarrying...my boobs were sorer yesterday than today and I did the stupid thing and googled it to find stories of women who noticed this and then

miscarried. L. I feel like I'm being ridiculous but I just can't get it out of my head and [my next scan] seems so far away. Keep worrying I'll have missed a miscarriage and go to my scan for them to tell me my baby died weeks ago.

Women undergoing the invasive test of amniocentesis express, similarly, a high level of consumption work involved in gathering information about this test, and in undergoing it. In particular, women who undergo amniocentesis engage in emotion work in terms of coping with high levels of anxiety over sustained periods. As Julie and Marie recall, respectively:

> it was the most traumatic time of my life because … we didn't have a child together, he was 40, I was 36 – so my pregnancy was very precious. To be told that there was a risk that i could miscarry for up to three weeks after the amnio was too much, i didn't cope very well at all, even after i'd had the results . I wouldn't do it again.
>
> (Julie)

> I look back now and wonder why i had that test … it was the emotional disruption to my life that affected me the most – terribly. The reason why i had the test was because we were older parents with three older children. But had the test shown any abnormalities I'd have kept my baby anyway. Thankfully my little girl was born at 37 weeks by elective section and is now 5 years old.
>
> (Marie)

The embedded work of managing pregnancy as project

Thus far, this chapter has observed how the work of managing the pregnancy 'project' may be complex and demanding. The consumption and emotion work described by Julie and Marie above illustrates the intellectual, emotional and physical labour invested by both in undergoing amniocentesis tests on the basis of clinical recommendation. Yet such forms of women's work are often unrecorded. It is assumed that expectant mothers should be able to 'manage' the work of consuming and implementing pregnancy advice and screening, coping with emotions and anxieties without complaint and without query. Social assumptions tend to construct women's management of pregnancy and of their pregnant bodies as a skill which should come 'naturally' to them (Miller 2005). It is presumed that the supposed maternal instinct will be sufficient to support pregnant women in these endeavours. They should thus be prepared to deal, easily and/or stoically, with what are described by the 'What to Expect' web-site as 'temporary discomforts' (What to Expect 2012), specifically:

> [during the first trimester of pregnancy] you might be less than thrilled with some of the stuff you'll be coping with (did we mention heartburn and constipation?), but remember that these temporary discomforts are part of the incredible process that's happening inside: You're growing a child!

The consequence of assumptions that mothers may manage instinctively the exacting work of pregnancy (i.e. maternity should come naturally to you, so don't complain), is that the work involved in managing pregnancy as a project is discounted and is thus unlikely to be articulated as 'work'. The irony of managing the project of pregnancy in accordance with demanding levels of health surveillance and screening is that, while mothers who fail to achieve (or prefer to resist) such goals face disapproval, the work involved in maternal compliance is unlikely to be acknowledged. This chapter indicates how maternal management of the project of pregnancy (Brewis and Warren 2001) may be taken for granted and discounted. In accordance with Glucksmann's observations about the 'embedded' nature of women's work, pregnancy work is subsumed within the discourse of 'good mothering' which, as Miller (2005) observes, is assumed to come naturally to women and is thus not recorded as 'work'.

As Hogg *et al.* (2011) observe, 'myths endure around ideal motherhood archetypes that imply certain behaviors, norms, and indeed, taboos. These social and cultural constructions about how to be a good mother proliferate through numerous intersecting discourses'. Findings in this chapter suggest that such cultural and market forces continue to support ideologies of 'good' mothering and combine to perpetuate the situation where pregnant women are measured against the standards expected of supposedly 'good' mothers.

Yet the consumption and emotion work required in these maternal activities may not be articulated as 'work'. The importance of attempting to address the embedded nature of maternal labour, and to reconceptualize this within specific social contexts, has been highlighted by Gatrell (2008), Morgan *et al.* (2005) and Wolkowitz (2006), all of whom focus on the diversity of unrecorded body work undertaken by women as nurturers and carers. In this chapter, the examination of pregnancy in the context of consumption and emotion work, and the embedded nature of this maternal labour, has highlighted how the work of pregnancy goes unrecognized. Pregnancy work tends to be classified as natural, instinctive – at best, a 'temporary discomfort'. This finding suggests the need for further and continued reflection on how maternal responsibilities and identities might be articulated and, most particularly, for the labour of maternity to be recognized as 'work'.

References

Adkins, L. (1995) *Gendered Work: Sexuality, Family and the Labour Market*, Buckingham: Open University Press.

BabyCentre (2012) 'About BabyCentre', http://www.babycentre.co.uk/press-centre/about-babycentre/ Accessed 16 May 2013.

Beechey, V. (1987) *Unequal Work*, London: Verso.

Bernhardt, J. and Felter, E. (2004) 'Online pediatric information seeking among mothers of young children: results from a qualitative study using focus groups', *Medical Internet Research* Jan–Mar, 6(1): e7. Published online 1 March 2004. DOI: 10.2196/jmir.6.1.e7

Bolton, S. (2001) 'Changing faces: nurses as emotional jugglers', *Sociology of Health and Illness*, 23, 85–100.

Brewis, J. and Warren, S. (2001) 'Pregnancy as project: organising reproduction', *Administrative Theory and Praxis*, 23, 383–406.

Davidson, J. (2001) 'Pregnant pauses: agoraphobic embodiment and the limits of (im)pregnability', *Gender, Place and Culture*, 1, 283–97.

Eriksson, P. and Kovalainen, A. (2008) *Qualitative Methods in Business Research*, Thousand Oaks: Sage.

Gatrell, C. (2008) *Embodying Women's Work*, Maidenhead: Open University Press.

Gatrell, C. (2011a) 'Policy and the pregnant body at work, strategies of silence, secrecy and supra-performance', *Gender, Work and Organization*, 18:2, 158–81.

Gatrell, C. (2011b) 'Managing the maternal body', *International Journal of Management Reviews*, 13, 97–112.

Gatrell, C. (2011c) 'Putting pregnancy in its place: conceiving pregnancy as carework in the workplace', *Health and Place*, 17:2, 395–402.

Glucksmann, M. (1995) 'Why "work"? Gender and the "Total Social Organization of Labour"', *Gender, Work and Organization*, 2:2, 63–75.

Glucksmann, M. (2005) 'Shifting boundaries and interconnections: extending the "total social organisation of labour"', *Sociological Review*, 53, supplement, 19–36.

Glucksmann, M. and Nolan, J. (2007) 'New technologies and the transformation of women's labour at home and work', *Equal Opportunities International*, 26, 96–112.

Grint, K. (2005) *The Sociology of Work*, Cambridge: Polity Press.

Hochschild, A. (1983) *The Managed Heart: the Commercialization of Human Feeling*, Berkeley, CA: University of California Press.

Hogg, M., Maclaran, P., Martens, L., O'Donohoe, S. and Stevens, L. (2011) '(Re)creating cultural models of motherhoods' in contemporary advertising, *Advertising & Society Review*, 12:2,

Kitzinger, S. (2003) *The New Pregnancy and Childbirth: Choices and Challenges*, London: Dorling Kindersley.

Kitzinger, S. (2005) *The Politics of Birth*, London: Elsevier Butterworth Heinemann.

Lagan, B. M., Sinclair, M., and Kernohan, W. G. (2006) 'Pregnant women's use of the internet: a review of published and unpublished evidence', *Evidence Based Midwifery*, 4:1, 17–23.

Longhurst, R. (2001) *Bodies: Exploring Fluid Boundaries*, London: Routledge.

Longhurst, R. (2008) *Maternities: Gender, Bodies and Space*, New York: Routledge.

Martin, E. (1989) *The Woman in the Body: A Cultural Analysis of Reproduction*, Boston: Beacon Press.

Miles, A. (1992) *Women, Health and Medicine*, Buckingham: Open University Press.

Miller, T. (2005) *Making Sense of Motherhood: A Narrative Approach*, Cambridge: Cambridge University Press.

Morgan, D., Brandth, B. and Kvande, E. (eds) (2005) *Gender, Bodies and Work*, Aldershot: Ashgate.

Murphy, E. (2003) 'Expertise and forms of knowledge in the government of families', *Sociological Review*, 51, 433–62.

Nettleton, S. (2006) *The Sociology of Health and Illness*, 2nd edn, Cambridge: Polity Press.

NHS (2012) 'What foods should I avoid during pregnancy', http://www.nhs.uk/conditions/pregnancy-and-baby/pages/foods-to-avoid-pregnant.aspx#close. Accessed 16 May 2013.

Oakley, A. (1981) *From Here to Maternity: Becoming a Mother*, Harmondsworth: Pelican Books.

Pollock, D. (1999) *Telling Bodies: Performing Birth*, New York: Columbia University Press.

158   *Caroline J. Gatrell*

Pringle, R. (1989) *Secretaries Talk: Sexuality, Power and Work (Questions for Feminism)*, London: Verso.

Warren, S. and Brewis, J. (2004) 'Matter over mind? Examining the experience of pregnancy', *Sociology*, 38, 219–36.

Web MD (2009) 'Health and pregnancy, eating right when pregnant', http://www.webmd.com/baby/guide/eating-right-when-pregnant. Accessed 16 May 2013.

What to Expect (2012) 'What to expect in the first trimester of pregnancy', http://www.whattoexpect.com/first-trimester-of-pregnancy.aspx. Accessed 16 May 2013.

Wolkowitz, C. (2006) *Bodies at Work*, London: Sage.

Young, I.M. (2005) *On Female Body Experience: 'Throwing Like a Girl' and Other Essays*, Oxford: Oxford University Press.

12 Engaging with the maternal

Tentative mothering acts, props and discourses

Tina Miller

Introduction

Becoming a mother for the first time is a tricky undertaking for many women. It involves significant personal transition experienced in a context of assumed natural capacities that women know how to mother, together with practices and performances of mothering which are (often) undertaken in the public sphere and subject to scrutiny. This mismatch between women's expectations and experiences of mothering has been a focus of academic research over many years and the 'moral minefield' in which mothering displays occur has been consistently noted (Murphy 1999; Miller 2005). More recently the commodification of motherhood and the ways in which patterns of consumption contribute to, and reinforce, motherhood ideals has also been noted (Thomson *et al.* 2011; Nash 2009; Kehily and Thomson 2011; Baraitser 2008). This chapter will contribute to debates in these areas by drawing on the findings from a UK-based qualitative longitudinal study on women's experiences of transition to first-time motherhood (Miller 2005, 2007). This study collected data before the birth and during the first year following the birth and focuses upon the ways in which women prepare for and then perform and narrate[1] early, tentative maternal acts as 'appropriate' forms of preparation and consumption are narrated. Acquiring the physical properties – 'props' – the right pram, cot and other baby equipment required to facilitate early acts of caring and mothering form a dominant thread running through the women's accounts in which socially recognizable and acceptable elements of 'good mother' discourses provide a potent and gendered context. Over time, the longitudinal focus reveals just how 'risky' early performances of new mothering can feel for the women becoming mothers. Whilst the props of motherhood are perceived to signal maternal competency – a pram and a baby provide uncomplicated signifiers of motherhood in Western societies – these can be at odds with how the women feel about their own competencies as they become mothers for the first time. These themes of preparation, props and performances provide the focus for this chapter.

Motherhood, props and discourses

Transition to first-time motherhood is experienced in most Western societies against a fluid backdrop of change and continuity. For example the obduracy of societal expectations in relation to who is assumed to be the primary carer for a child and how 'good' mothering should be performed are recurring findings in research, whilst small changes in relation to men and their emotional involvement in a child's life are also now more discernible (Dermott 2008; Miller 2011). A further change evident in contemporary society is the extent to which consumer culture and consumerism has moved into the reproductive arena, occupying space once the preserve of the family or medicine (Thomson *et al.* 2011). In all sorts of ways women becoming mothers are prime targets for commercial endeavours in relation to demonstrating appropriate preparation and presentation of self as a 'good' mother-to-be and mother: this is just the beginning of a long child- and family-orientated consumer relationship (Carrigan and Szmigin 2004). Thomson *et al.* and others have noted this commodification of motherhood and the ways in which 'the commercial world is omnipresent in the lives of new mothers, inviting them to buy their way into this new identity' (2011:197). Yet whilst buying a way into the new identity of mother is on the one hand straightforward and predominantly economic,[2] performances of this new identity – first-time, embodied mothering – can be experienced as complex, challenging and problematic. Whilst performing a new self as mother is in part envisaged antenatally through having the props which will convey appropriate symbolic meaning (the pram, changing bag and other baby accoutrements), following the birth unpractised performances of mothering can leave the women feeling exposed (at risk) and encumbered by the very same props as they are felt to convey contradictory meanings.

Pregnancy, motherhood and consumer behaviour have become 'inherently linked' and it is clear that consumption can provide 'a vital key to a new life role' which can be examined in numerous ways across the trajectory of the pregnancy and beyond (Carrigan and Szmigin 2004: 771; Thomsen and Sorensen 2006: 908). As noted earlier, consumption patterns through pregnancy can project and signal both appropriate preparation and desired presentation of self as good mother-to-be. The links between presentation of selves, interaction with others, and props which can help to convey or sustain a particular performance has been explored in the work of sociologist Erving Goffman (1969) who reveals the ways in which we are able to present a particular self in particular settings using 'impression management' to accentuate certain facts and conceal others. He uses the language of drama and back and front stage performances, props and audience interaction/reaction to explore the 'all-too-human task' of staging a convincing performance of self (Goffman 1969; Branaman 1997; Miller 2005; Collett 2005). Although Goffman's theory of selves has been critiqued for saying 'little about the emotional or psychosocial dynamics of personal life and social relationships' (Elliott 2001: 35–36) and lacking concern with the moral and visceral dimensions of gendered bodies and performances (Jackson and Scott 2001; Miller 2005), it provides a useful conceptual lens through which to consider experiences of transition to first-time motherhood. Here the contours of successful motherhood can be seen as a socially constructed performance, which is increasingly managed and 'read' through the consumer goods and consumption patterns which signal and facilitate its successful accomplishment. In the context of motherhood, impression management 'helps women to convey competence to both self and audience in a situation where they want nothing more than to be successful' (Collett 2005: 329). The moral minefield in which (especially first-time) mothering is performed makes this a particularly challenging context and when 'impression management' fails to convince the audience, the performance – and self – may feel/be discredited or 'spoiled' (Goffman 1969). So whilst props and 'objects can support identity construction' (Thomsen and Sorensen 2006: 907) this chapter will argue that they can also unexpectedly confuse, encumber and jeopardize intended presentations of self as new mother.

Preparations for motherhood through the antenatal period are informed by powerful, dominant discourses which shape societal expectations of behaviours and practices during this period. These include normative assumptions that women attend antenatal clinic appointments for monitoring, alter their diet, dress and behaviours, engage with appropriate baby books and other 'expert' information, attend scans (and purchase the resulting image and perhaps even a special frame in which to display the image) and prepare the house for the baby's arrival. These activities all engage material aspects of maternal consumption and confirm the commodification of motherhood. Research also points to significant gendered differences in patterns of parental consumption and demonstrations of appropriate preparation for motherhood and fatherhood involvement (Miller 2011). In the following sections of this chapter, data from the transition to first-time motherhood study will be used to illuminate how consumption practices are drawn upon to initially demonstrate appropriate antenatal preparation. However, data collected in later interviews reveals how even having the appropriate props may not be sufficient to signal accomplished – and so convincing – forms of impression management as new mothering is enacted in the public sphere. The complexities of real, fleshy sensate maternal bodies which must be managed, discourses about 'instincts' and expert information which turn out not to be 'truthful' and props which are experienced as providing only a fake veneer of competent mothering can leave new mothers feeling confused and misled.

The research study

This chapter draws upon data from a qualitative longitudinal study carried out in the UK which focused on women's experiences of transition to first-time motherhood (Miller 2005, 2007). The study explored women's unfolding experiences of transition through in-depth interviews conducted across a year in the women's lives as they became mothers for the first time. The iterative research process involved interviewing the women on three separate occasions, followed by an end-of-study postal questionnaire used to collect demographic data and feedback on their experiences of participating in the study. Semi-structured interview schedules were designed for each of the three interviews. The schedules covered areas around expectations, birth, mothering experiences, information seeking, perceptions of self and others, and work intentions. The first interview was timed to take place antenatally, between seven and eight months, once the pregnancy was well established. The second interview took place between six and eight weeks postnatally and the final interview was carried out between eight and nine months postnatally. In the first interview, participants were asked to begin by describing how they had felt when they found out they were pregnant. In the subsequent interviews, participants were asked to begin by describing what had happened since our last meeting. This open-ended and reflexive approach gave the women the opportunity to produce their accounts of anticipating and later experiencing mothering and motherhood in the ways they wished. Participants were accessed using snowballing, which involved asking mothers at my own children's school to act as potential gatekeepers. One consequence of using my own social networks to initiate access to a sample was that most of the women who finally participated in the study described themselves as 'middle class', with socio-economic circumstances similar to my own.

The participants were all white, heterosexual women, and the mean age was 30 years at the time of the first (antenatal) interview. This was slightly older than the national average age for first birth in the United Kingdom but typical of the trend among professional women to delay decisions about reproduction. In many ways, this sample conforms to normative ideas held in wider society about those who are positioned as good mothers. These women were predominately middle class, white, and either married or in cohabiting partnerships and becoming mothers at a societally approved age. Yet the emerging data revealed how diverse and complex early mothering experiences can be even amongst an apparently homogeneous group (Miller 2005, 2007).

Interviews took place in the home of the participant or a location of their choosing. The longitudinal design of the research mirrored the period of transition, giving the data collection period fluidity not achieved in one-off, 'snapshot' interviews. Emerging concepts were explored across the data collection periods. The interviews were all tape-recorded with the participants' permission and at the end of the study, following verbatim transcription, the tapes were returned to those participants who wanted them.[3] All names and any other identifying features have been changed in the data. For all the women, transition to motherhood was different to how they had envisaged it – often harder and lonelier.

Findings

Anticipating mothering: preparing appropriately in the antenatal period

Across the antenatal data it is clear that discourses have informed behaviours associated with preparing for motherhood as tentative maternal selves are narrated and performed. Optimistic accounts of preparation are presented and these involve doing the right thing, following the right – expert – advice and purchasing the necessary (and desired) baby goods, whilst rejecting others. Even though these can only be tentative accounts, narrated without having the subjective experience of birth and motherhood, the maternal sphere is well marked out in terms of expected behaviours and consumption activities, much more so than the paternal sphere (Miller 2011). Clinic appointments and other classes are attended, books and DVDs are purchased and consumed, and items necessary to care for the baby are gradually purchased as houses are prepared for the new arrival at which point *'the sort of nesting thing'* is allowed to *'take over'*. Engagement in these various activities has the 'potential to provide the consumer with a certain *experience* of self' as here first-time motherhood is anticipated (Thomsen and Sorensen 2006: 909, italics in the original). In the following extract Rebecca, in ways similar to other participants in the study, talks of prioritizing 'expert' information sources:

I don't like getting information from other people because it's always so subjective and they always want to harp on about their little story and so I have actually avoided other people....those are the most unhelpful, personal experiences that I've steered away from. But I think the books, and the midwives and my doctor, my doctor's been good.

(Rebecca)

Wendy too is pleased that the health professionals 'just tell you everything':

I'm going for the breast first to see how I get on. I did actually say to the midwife that I wanted to do both, I wanted the bottle and...but she said you can't actually do that....(but) it has been good. They just tell you everything.

(Wendy)

Preparing for motherhood involves the women in acquiring the right information and purchasing goods, but the timing of these activities is important too. As Carrigan and Szmigin note 'in the case of first-time mothers, time and the experience of time are also inextricably linked to their behaviour' (2004: 772). Examples of there being a right time for various pregnancy-related activities was found across the data and is evident in the following extract in which Felicity implies both the right time (12 weeks) and behaviour perceived by others to be too late (38 weeks):

I went out and bought (pregnancy book) after 12 weeks once you know sort of the danger periods that you hear about were over...we didn't do anything until after 12 weeks, we didn't tell anybody until after 12 weeks, we've only just bought baby clothes (38 weeks pregnant). People said 'you must have everything by now' – No!

(Felicity)

Cultural expectations about how women prepare for the impending arrival of a new baby were evident across the antenatal interviews in relation to what to purchase and when. On occasions this was invoked to show how appropriately 'prepared' or not, the women were. For example, in the following extract Gillian compares her preparations to another expectant mother she has met at the parent-craft classes she has attended:

> There's just one…she's very practical. She has got her baby's room absolutely ready. She's not due (until) a couple of weeks after me (participant is 33 weeks pregnant) but the cot's there, the pram's ordered, but you see she is great for advice and says 'go to [shop] because he's really impartial there and get your (cot) mattress there….nip round to [shop] and you can buy all the bits… and get your blankets and quilt'….I never thought of all these things, whereas when it comes to 'what's a Braxton Hicks' she's not sure about what that is….so she doesn't know quite as much as I do on the physical side (but) she's so much more organised than me on the practical bits.
>
> (Gillian)

Several things are illustrated through this extract, that Gillian admires her friend's consumer skills and seeking out of the best ('impartial') places in which to purchase baby goods, but at the same time she also regards these activities and getting the *'baby's room absolutely ready'* as being premature when her friend is (only) approximately 30 weeks pregnant. At the same time Gillian still positions herself as preparing for motherhood appropriately through emphasizing her concentration on the *'physical side'* of preparation, implicitly still having enough time at 33 weeks into her pregnancy to purchase the necessary baby goods. Importantly both approaches to preparation – practical and physical – convey individual responsibility and acting in ways which signal the good mother (to be). However, if Gillian does not also purchase – in time – the practical goods now deemed necessary for the baby's arrival, she will risk being judged as unprepared and not behaving in ways deemed societally appropriate of a good mother-to-be.

The importance of signalling intentions to conform to normative ideals of good motherhood – even before the birth – is well recognized. For example, types of pram consumption convey symbolic meaning and influence consumer behaviour so that mothers can feel that 'only the best pram makes the best mother' (Thomsen and Sorensen 2006: 917). They can feel drawn in to engaging in consumer practices which reinforce and perpetuate such beliefs (Thomsen and Sorensen 2006: 917). And whilst evidence of the commodification of motherhood is found across the data, there is some evidence that fatherhood is being drawn into this arena too. In a later companion study[4] on transition to first-time fatherhood, it was found that men too are increasingly engaging in particular acts of consumption (the purchase of 'large items' and DIY) as a way to signal their involvement in preparing appropriately for new fatherhood (Miller 2011). However, these activities are largely mediated by wives – partners and fathers-to-be are much more able to narrate ignorance and indifference in regard to these matters than would be acceptable for women becoming mothers. The men are most centrally involved in physical and structural aspects of consumption, for example 'painting', 'building' and 'buying the big stuff'. The gendered differences both in patterns of consumption and assumed knowledge in the antenatal period are evident in the following extract taken from the fatherhood study:

> We've had to prepare the house and erect prams and cots and things and I guess financially we've directed money to this rather than other things… That's definitely been (wife's) lead really and she's decided, well I suppose *I've had a hand in the big stuff like which pram will we go for*, what does a cot look like and stuff and that was by virtue of a fact of two trips to John Lewis so I haven't really invested a lot of kind of effort in to it or knowledge really. I think (wife) has done all the talking to other people who've had kids, she's found out *what's required, what the list of newborn stuff is that we need* and I haven't really got involved in that….I could have made up a list which would have been so not comprehensive. It would have been such a partial list you know, *obvious stuff like a pram and a cot I would have got…* but muslin cloths would have passed me by. How do I know about muslin cloths?
>
> (William)

Gendered responsibilities associated with particular consumer activities and specific objects are clear in this extract as well as the implied mystery surrounding some items on 'the list of newborn stuff', which it is assumed women will (naturally) know about. The ability of objects to signal change (Thomsen and Sorensen 2006) is evident in the data from both studies. In the extract below from the fatherhood study, the addition of a cot to a room is described in transformative terms as a room changes into a 'nursery'.

> It probably took a couple of months to really sink in…I was thrilled because I'd wanted kids for ages and I was desperate to start planning and telling people and buying things. Yes. The cot arrived today and I've just put the cot up in the nursery and now the nursery has got everything whereas up to yesterday it was a room with lots of stuff in it, it's now got everything in it.
>
> (Nick)

The home as a 'transformative site of consumption' is demonstrated here as the 'domestic space is rearranged to accommodate the new baby' (Thomson *et al.* 2011: 227). But as noted earlier, the data also shows that women are more likely to trigger and mediate practices of consumption as father-to-be Joe makes clear in the following extract:

> But I think most men are just literally the ones who carry the shopping to the car you know they go out to buy the buggy but are generally not the ones doing the research.
>
> (Joe)

The data from both studies also shows that women are more attuned to ideas of there being a right time to make particular purchases and the detail of what those purchases should include. Goods become a proxy measure of good motherhood and provide a (potentially false) sense of security of being prepared and ready and things being under control: but the birth changes everything.

The early postnatal period: tentative mothering performances

For all the mothers, the birth is different to what had been expected and/or planned for. Birth provides a 'narrative turning point' as the imaginings and preparations across the previous months turn into reality and the identity of new mother is gradually practised and made sense of (Miller 2005). The ultimate prop – the baby – is now physically present and instantly conveys new meaning to everyone else that a woman has become a mother, regardless of how the individual woman and new mother may feel. The majority of the new mothers find the early weeks of caring to be challenging ('no one prepares you for how tired you will be'), with some talking of feeling their lives are 'out of control'. Whilst they sit surrounded by all the paraphernalia associated with new mothering in these early weeks, they can feel baffled: they have followed the expert advice provided through their pregnancy, they have made decisions about types of product to purchase – the type of pram or pushchair, the car seat, the cot, the changing table and portable baby changing bag and prepared the house – and yet they (mostly) don't yet *feel* like a mother. This particularly manifests itself when they are required to undertake their early mothering in the public sphere outside the home. Leaving the house is described as akin to a 'military operation' which in the early weeks involves 'taking all day to pack the baby bag' – but also experienced as potentially 'risky' even with, or perhaps as a consequence of, having all the props which imply competency in a role.

Whilst Thomson *et al.* (2011) discuss the confidence which can be provided by having an expensive (or the right) buggy/pram for young mothers and envisage the potential of the 'mother, baby and buggy' as 'intrepid adventurers, able to handle anything and everything they encounter' (2011: 224) this was not the experience of the new mothers in the very early days and weeks (and sometimes months) in the transition to motherhood study. Amongst this group of older mothers, it is only with the passage of time and learning from early public mothering performances which are felt not to have been successful, that the pram or buggy actually facilitates confident practices of mothering. In early, tentative outings with the new baby the pram as prop was experienced as projecting a confident, knowledgeable maternal self, which the individual did not yet feel and so the pram encumbered and confused early performances of mothering, signalling maternal competency when the women felt they were not yet competent in relation to 'controlling' their new baby. For these mothers, expectations of being able to confidently do mothering assisted by all the necessary maternal objects were abruptly challenged in early forays into the public sphere following the birth. In the extracts below, Philippa and Gillian describe their early experiences of going out with their new baby and the responses of others to what they felt were their unconvincing attempts at 'impression management' and maternal performance.

> So I didn't go out very much which made it hard…I don't think I went out, literally set foot outside the door for 3 or 4 weeks or something which is quite…it was a long time, and that was too long actually, because I didn't… but I just felt …I didn't feel very confident taking her out because I just thought she was going to cry the whole time and I felt a bit sort of self conscious about it….I mean even now I feel, if I take her out shopping and she started crying….this woman in a shopping queue said to me 'they hate shopping', and they're so sort of accusing and I felt like saying 'well, I have to eat'….
>
> (Philippa)

> I know I'm a mother…but I don't quite feel like a mother yet…I went to [shop] once and she screamed the whole way round, then I did feel like a mother because all these old ladies were there and they were going 'that baby shouldn't be out', 'it's too hot for that baby to be out'. I could hear them rabbiting on behind me. So then I did feel very much like a mother…a dreadful mother
>
> (Gillian)

Feeling scrutinized and sanctioned on account of their early maternal caring acts was a theme across much of the motherhood study data.[5] A sense of feeling that others were judging their performance as new mothers was further complicated by the women themselves feeling that mothering had not come 'naturally'. They now had all the components required to undertake good mothering – including the baby – but many felt confused because they didn't actually feel like a mother. This led several participants to speak of their concern that other people would think they had 'pinched', 'kidnapped' or 'borrowed' their baby. In the following extract, Felicity describes an early outing with her new baby.

> We had to go to the doctor's and both of us went, Robert and I went with the baby and then I got a prescription. Robert went to get the prescription. I said I'll come home because the estimators were coming for the removals. And I'd *done…you know I'd got one of the changing bags like you're supposed to*, taken a bottle of milk with us in case he got horrible, and he had in the doctor's, and Robert had started to feed him and then we'd left and he was quite happy. But I was coming home and he started to get hungry again and Robert had the bottle in his pocket and had gone off to the shop to get the prescription, so I had this screaming child in the middle of town…it was hot…and I felt like shit and I couldn't walk very fast, and I had to virtually run from the middle of town to here…and you could hear everyone was (saying) 'poor child', 'what's that woman doing with that child'. And I thought, I was convinced somebody was going to like stop me and say 'you've pinched that

child, that's not your child, you aren't a mother, you don't look like you can cope with him, this baby, you should be doing something to stop it crying'.

(Felicity)

In this profound account it become clear that whilst material props associated with motherhood can antenatally engender a sense of preparedness, and postnatally signal maternal competency ('*I'd got one of the changing bags like you're supposed to*') early public performances of mothering leave the women confused. Drawing on an idea of 'the wrong properties on the stage of motherhood' put forward by Thomsen and Sorensen (2006: 915) the women in the transition to motherhood study share a sense that the props they have to facilitate their mothering performances do not correspond to how they actually feel in this very early phase of new mothering. In contrast and because men have not been so closely associated with assumed instincts and capacities to care, new fathers going out with their baby do not experience the same sense of risk or being 'found out' in some way. For men who are new fathers (almost) *any* performance of fathering is publicly positively received (Miller 2011). And yet because women are assumed to instinctively know how to mother, the public stage is a risky one and as Abigail confides, 'it has taken 8 weeks to be confident to walk along with a pram with a screaming child'.

Discussion

This chapter's focus on women's transition to first-time motherhood provides an opportunity to see how the modern props associated with motherhood are consumed in various ways by women, and how appropriate choices signal 'good' motherhood. But the longitudinal approach taken also shows the complexity of a transitional event which involves the acquisition of a new identity and one that is importantly morally circumscribed: purchases of baby objects provide one dimension of this new identity but alone are never sufficient. Whilst ideas of impression management being facilitated and successfully achieved by the acquisition of the appropriate props are compelling in a range of social settings, early first-time mothering presents a more complicated case. This is because it is infused with normative essentialist assumptions about women's instinctive maternal capacities. The gendered dimensions of impression management – and abilities to accentuate certain facts and conceal others – in relation to the acquisition of new parental identities are also apparent in how early motherhood and fatherhood are performed and crucially appraised by the audience. Performances of new mothering which fail to convince (or to conceal early confusion) are ultimately experienced as risky and so limit the new mother's forays into the public sphere. But this is a temporary – if heightened – phase of transition: once the women have become more practised at mothering and getting to know their baby's changing needs (achieved through practise in the safety of the home), accomplished performances of (good-enough) mothering are possible and any perceived negative comments from onlookers can be rebuffed.

The commodification of motherhood invites women becoming mothers 'to buy their way into this new identity' (Thomson *et al.* 2011: 197) and demonstrating appropriate preparation through the purchase of the right props featured prominently in the women's displays of preparation. Acts of consumption were seen to provide evidence of doing the right thing and also gave the women a sense of being in control of the impending event of motherhood. Following the birth of the baby, having a sense of being in control was not how the new mothers felt and the props now provided mixed messages: on the one hand maternal competency was publicly signalled and symbolized through the props, whilst the new mothers personally experienced feelings of incompetence and fear that they might be revealed as not being a mother ('you aren't a mother', Felicity) or as being a 'dreadful mother' (Gillian). It is the passage of time which allows a mother–baby relationship to develop alongside maternal competency, so that it no longer takes 'all day to pack the baby bag'. However, the birth also marks the beginning of an enduring consumer relationship through which women as mothers will continue to be expected to demonstrate good mothering (and be judged) in part through their consumerist practices in relation to their growing child and family (Collett 2005).

Conclusion

Transitional life events and 'transitional consumers represent a valuable "site" for exploring issues of identity creation' (Hogg *et al.* 2003). Through focusing on transition to first-time motherhood, an opportunity *par excellence* is provided in which to see both personal 'mother' identity creation and public manifestations of appropriate preparation through consumption acts. Taking a qualitative and longitudinal approach to researching transitions also enables both change and the more nuanced and complex aspects of behaviours to be illuminated in ways one-off interviews cannot achieve. Adopting this approach in the study discussed in this chapter has confirmed the commodification of motherhood but also revealed the confusion which can be experienced when the right props feel wrong in particular transitional contexts. The morally underpinned context of motherhood can mean that even the right props might not be enough to convey societally expected performances of mothering and may confuse or jeopardize early attempts at impression management as a new mother. Optimistically the uncertainty is usually short lived and whilst props help symbolize imaginings of first-time motherhood during the transitional antenatal phase, it is everyday mothering which in time and with practise takes centre stage.

Notes

1 For further information on the narrative approach taken in the study described in this chapter see chapter 1 'The storied human life: a narrative approach' in Miller, T. (2005) *Making Sense of Motherhood: A Narrative Approach.* Cambridge: Cambridge University Press.

170 *Tina Miller*

2 It is important to note that material circumstances and the availability of capital resources pattern individual lives and 'choices' in significant and unequal ways.
3 For further details on data analysis see Miller, T. (2005) *Making Sense of Motherhood: A Narrative Approach*. Cambridge: Cambridge University Press.
4 This study used the same research design as the Transition to Motherhood study and explored men's experiences of transition to fatherhood across a two year period.
5 Interestingly in the fatherhood study the new fathers were much more likely to report highly positive public reactions to their early solo outings pushing their new babies in a pram (see chapter 4, Miller 2011).

References

Baraitser, L. (2008) *Maternal Encounters: the Ethics of Interruption*, London: Routledge.
Branaman, A. (1997) 'Goffman's social theory', in C. Lemert and A. Branaman (eds) *The Goffman Reader*, Oxford: Basil Blackwell Publishers.
Carrigan, M. and Szmigin, I. (2004) 'Time, uncertainty and the expectancy experience: an interpretive exploration of consumption and impending motherhood', *Journal of Marketing Management*, 20, 771–98.
Collett, J.L. (2005) '"What kind of mother am I?": impression management and the social construction of motherhood', *Symbolic Interactionism*, 28(3): 327–47.
Elliott, A. (2001) *Concepts of the Self*. Cambridge: Polity Press.
Dermott, E. (2008) *Intimate Fatherhood*, London: Routledge.
Goffman, E. (1969) *The Presentation of Self in Everyday Life*, Harmondsworth: Penguin.
Hogg, M., Maclaran, P. and Curasi, C.F. (2003) 'Consumption, role transitions and the reconstruction of the self: an exploratory study of social capital within the context of transitional consumers', *European Advances in Consumer Research*, 6, 258–62.
Jackson, S. and Scott, S. (2001) 'Putting the body's feet on the ground', in K. Backett-Milburn and L. Mckie (eds) *Gendering the Body*, London: Macmillan.
Kehily, M.J. and Thomson, R. (2011) 'Displaying motherhood: representations, visual methods and the materiality of maternal practice,' in E. Dermott and J. Seymour (eds) *Displaying Families*, Basingstoke: Palgrave.
Miller, T. (2005) *Making Sense of Motherhood: a Narrative Approach*, Cambridge: Cambridge University Press.
Miller, T. (2007) '"Is this what motherhood is all about?": weaving experiences and discourse through transition to first-time motherhood', *Gender & Society*, 21: 337–58.
Miller, T. (2011) *Making Sense of Fatherhood: Gender, Caring and Work*, Cambridge: Cambridge University Press.
Murphy, E. (1999) '"Breast is best": infant feeding decisions and maternal deviance', *Sociology of Health & Illness*, 21(2): 187–208.
Nash, M. (2009) 'Yummy mummies, baby bumps and body image: shaping "postmodern" pregnancy in Melbourne, Australia', unpublished thesis, University of Melbourne, Australia.
Thomsen, T.U. and Sorensen, E.B. (2006) 'The first four-wheeled status symbol: pram consumption as a vehicle for the construction of motherhood identity', *Journal of Marketing Management*, 22, 907–27.
Thomson, R., Kehily, M.J., Hadfield, L. and Sharpe, S. (2011) *Making Modern Mothers*, Bristol: The Policy Press.

13 Mothers and their empty nests

Employing consumption practices to negotiate a major life transition

Carolyn F. Curasi, Pauline Maclaran
and Margaret Hogg

Introduction

In this chapter we explore women's changing experience of mothering as their children leave home and as family life becomes diffused across time and space. During this important life stage transition, women use consumption practices as they seek to re-configure family relationships, routines and rituals, and thereby sustain a sense of family life. We demonstrate how both material and symbolic resources are central to the process of family (re)formation, and the associated lifelong project of mothering. We pay particular attention to mothers' emotional labour in managing the re-negotiation of family relationships. In conclusion we show how mothers' consumption practices at this lifestage can be understood in terms of Worden's (1991) four tasks of grief and mourning as women learn to accept the reality of their children leaving the nest.

Transitions

Transitions can be emotionally turbulent because, by definition, they are accompanied by a liminal phase in which the individual holds an ambiguous non-status, liminal position and is in-between two different statuses, and is not firmly grounded in either. Turner (1974) explains that culturally prescribed rituals or rites of passage can provide individuals with an experience of communitas, or a sense of a shared psychological support system throughout major status passages that can help to relieve some of the tension and uncertainty that accompany major life status changes. In the modern secular world, however, people typically experience liminoid states (c.f. Turner 1974) devoid of such supportive formal rites of passage (Schouten 1991:49). Without some type of societal support system firmly in place, consumers attempt to cope with difficult transitions and their resulting ambiguous self-concepts in a myriad of ways. Our goal is to examine how women navigate the life status transition represented by the empty nest, and specifically how they use consumption and material objects to negotiate this transition in family life.

Research study

This research project employs an interpretive, mixed method research design, and is based on two data sets, both containing women informants from diverse geographic areas. Our first data set is comprised of twenty-two first round in-person interviews conducted with mothers in Ireland, England, and the United States, and second round follow-up interviews with ten of these original participants. Our informants were obtained from our interpersonal networks, or through subsequent snowball sampling. The interviews lasted between 45 minutes and 2 hours. All interviews were audio-recorded, transcribed verbatim, and analyzed using an iterative hermeneutic process. The second data set was collected by participating in online bulletin boards over the course of a year, resulting in over 500 postings in English to the bulletin boards. In terms of research ethics, we announced our presence on the bulletin board. Data were collected by participant observation to develop a better understanding of the experiences and feelings of women whose children were leaving home and to allow us to understand how they negotiate this transition as expressed via respondents' repeated postings to cyber-space bulletin boards.

Findings

In the analysis of our data sets, four main themes emerged. First, our data suggest that distress often accompanies this life stage transition, and that the distress can sometimes be severe, not unlike the experiences of those going through the stages of grief and mourning. Second, we found that our informants typically engaged in a process of self-evaluation of their mothering role as their children move away from the family home. Progressing from this self-evaluation, our informants re-negotiated their approaches to mothering in order to recognize the changing power balances in their relationships with their children. Third, possessions figure prominently in accommodating this liminal life stage. And, fourth, our informants' enactment of the mothering role typically changed during this life stage transition from doing family work largely within the home to a new focus on different consumption practices in order to maintain ties between family members after the children had moved out of the home. In the next section of the chapter we will discuss these four themes, allowing our informants to illustrate each theme in greater depth with their representative remarks.

Managing distress in this life stage transition

The empty nest stage represents a liminal state (Van Gennep 1960) in women's mothering identities. Our investigation found that many of our informants experienced distress and their adjustments were complex, idiosyncratic and affected by many factors, including: their relationships with other family members, especially their children; activities outside the home, including employment, and involvement in church or other organizations; and the length of time the women have spent adjusting to this life stage transition. In a few cases our informants spoke only of minor difficulty adjusting to their empty nests. However, many more of our interviewees and all online community participants described the difficult time they had dealing with this transition in family life. Melissa below illustrates the distress communicated by informants.

> Hello to all, Melissa here, one daughter, Becky, age 19. Becky married on July 7 and moved to England to live. Needless to say—I crashed and burned. It has been 4 months and I am happy to say, I am having some good days, more good days than bad. Between seeing a great doctor and some assistance from Prozac, Wellbutrin, and Ambien, I am making my way back. I am hoping to be drug free soon.
>
> (Empty Nest Online Site)

Many of our informants complained that the distress surrounding their experience of entering the empty nest stage was rarely discussed, so that they felt isolated. Until these women found the empty nest website with other women talking about feelings and experiences similar to theirs, many had felt their problems adjusting to this change in their lives was abnormal. Established participants freely offered support to the newer posters to the site, as the following two vignettes illustrate:

> Thanks for your response. …Thanks for listening and yes, it's great having this board to just pour out our feelings to people who can understand.
>
> (Empty Nest Online Site)

> Thanks for your support. It's great to know that there are others out there who feel the same way I do. I am doing some better. …This has meant so much to me, and I hope it will help you, too. Please feel free to email me if you would like. Thanks again.
>
> (Empty Nest Online Site)

Contributors to the empty nest websites expressed powerful and raw emotions especially during the early stages of the transition to the empty nest. The websites' anonymity granted these women greater freedom to discuss their feelings, and provided a much needed outlet for shared psychological support in the transition. These sites provided their participants with the experience of 'communitas,' or the feeling of being part of a community; serving an important function and one otherwise not typically afforded to many progressing through this transition. The Internet allowed empty nest women to find population segments of others going through this transition, providing them with an outlet to help them cope with this often distressing change (Schouten 1991; Turner 1974).

Women contacted for in-person interviews often also had their own form of 'communitas,' or informal shared psychological support groups (Schouten 1991) that helped them, too, to negotiate this role status change. Informants' distress can be understood in terms of loss and the consequences of suffering a loss. Many informants went through stages similar to the feelings of loss, grief, and mourning that accompany the death of a loved one (Kübler-Ross 1997). The following woman also illustrates this:

> This year hasn't been bad. It's the second year. The first year was... The first year started about Christmas time of her senior year and her graduation from high school and it was just devastating for me. ...I mean, I stopped eating, I stopped sleeping. By the time she graduated from high school my parents were looking at my husband and going (laughs), 'Feed her, make her sleep,' (laughs) because I looked horrible in the graduation pictures. Then, we took her to school and I thought I was going to die. I cried all the way home.
>
> (In-person interview)

Some also experience anticipatory grief:

> I still have a 17 yr. old daughter at home, so the nest is not completely empty. I do think about how it is going to be when my baby goes off to college and it just tears me apart. I know I'll get over all of this eventually, but it is really hard to just shift gears.
>
> (Empty Nest Online Site)

Simple acts of 'mothering' are often missed when children leave home, even when women initially don't think they will miss those mundane duties. Whilst their children are still at home, chores such as cleaning, cooking, and doing laundry allow mothers to express their love for their families. After their children leave home, the reduction of the household work that needs to be done accentuates the void resulting from the children's departure. Many informants discussed how they missed doing household chores (Miller 1998; Oakley 1974) and other tasks (e.g. taxiing their children around for different activities) that provided an outlet to express their feelings for their children.

Re-evaluation of the mothering self

The realization that their days of raising their children had come to an end seemed to initiate a self-evaluation of how well they felt they had done as a mother. Many women asked what their identity was now, feeling that their child-rearing role was behind them. Often this appraisal was bittersweet:

> My nest has been empty for about one and a half years. Our daughter is married and lives 90 miles away. Our sons are in the army and will be for nearly another 3 years. So far empty-nesting is kind'a like limbo. Putting up the Christmas tree was a bittersweet task. So many pieces of my life that now are a part of the past. I am not the me I understood myself to be. I love being a Gramma but I miss being the mom I was.
>
> (Empty Nest Online Site)

This self-assessment mode usually started with mothers asking what they would do now that their children had grown up and moved away from home. Informants question what their new selves should be:

> Our youngest son is about to finish his sophomore year in college. When he first left all I noticed was how much I loved giving up the mommy duties (food, clothing, worry), so I thought I had escaped the dreaded syndrome. Now, I'm not sure. If I'm no longer a nurturer---my most satisfying role thus far in life---what am I? Has anyone been through this? Any suggestions?
>
> (Empty Nest Online Site)

Commonly, the 'test' of their mothering achievements was linked to their children's successful departure from the nest. They reviewed how well their children were doing, or how well they thought their children would do when they were out on their own. Typically there was a hint of anxiety associated with this 'test,' since our informants' identity was so closely tied to how well they felt they had done in parenting their children. Their children's entry into the adult world served as the ultimate test of their mothering ability. This launch was repeatedly met with feelings of uncertainty and some trepidation.

> It was time for the children to leave and I was ready. I knew they needed it as well as I needed it. It is just a fact of life. It was going to happen...*It was just a good way of knowing that I was somehow close to being a good parent if they could stand on their own. If they could become productive individuals in society, then I have done what I was supposed to do as a parent.* The other thing was just loving them to the point that they could become this individual that could function in society.
>
> (In-person Interview; italics added)

Notice the pleasure and a hint of relief in the following vignette as this woman mentions how satisfying it is for her to see her children doing well on their own:

> One day you're a mommy who your children depend on for everything and the next day they are all grown up and are doing things on their own. *It's great to see them doing so well and making their own decisions.* I am so very proud of my girls and love them sooooo much.
>
> (Empty Nest Online Site; italics added)

Changing power balances emerged in the parent–child relationships in empty nest families. Adjustment to becoming a successful empty nester seems to include a transformation of the mother–child relationship. Many of our informants suggested that mothering changes from being a 'top-sergeant' to becoming a friend and a good listener.

> I look at her as more of an adult now, definitely... I feel on a par with her more as a friend.
>
> (In-person Interview)

Many of our informants discussed how difficult it was to not have knowledge of how their children were doing, or what they were doing, for that matter. However, most were well aware that with this new parental role, they had to treat their child as more of an adult and not as a child. Their grown-up children could now come and go as they pleased in their own homes, without parental control. As many informants talked about this, they sounded like they were talking about a loss of control, as well as a loss of information. The women knew that they had to transition from mother as nurturing parent to that of mother/friend.

Information about their children's friends, classes, where their children were going and when they'd be home was no longer readily available. Mothers had to ask a lot of questions to learn about their children's lives, and the line of questioning required was sometimes resented by their newly independent children.

> It's so hard, yes, things have changed (laughs). And, I'm trying to back off and not ask a million questions on the computer (via email) but, you know, as I've told her many times, give me time. It's a weaning process and you sort of have to try to sit back and take what they tell you. You know, I've been there asking a billion questions. She'll finally go, "Quit Mom." It's real hard.
>
> (In-person Interview)

Informants suggested that once grown children leave the home, parents lose their right to make judgmental statements as they were able to do previously. Not all parents are able to accommodate this transition effectively as the mother here illustrates.

> Today I talked to a friend of my daughter's whom I ran into while I was shopping and she is making plans to move out but her mom doesn't know yet. She is moving because she said at this time in her life she needs a mom who can be her friend, but her mom can't seem to make the transition from mother to friend. She always has to get critical about any situation her daughter shares with her. I try not to do that and my daughter shares many things with me.
>
> (Empty Nest Online Site)

At the onset of this empty nest phase, informants engaged in a process of self-evaluation, often tinged with anxiety, assessing how well they had carried out their mothering role, and a redefinition of self ultimately resulted from negotiating this empty nest status change.

The role of possessions in this life stage transition

Objects in the informants' homes play a major role in this transition. Initially, possessions left behind serve as mnemonic devices with the ability to initiate strong bittersweet emotions. The child's bedroom, specifically, has the ability to stimulate memories and feelings that could be a painful reminder for the empty nest mother. The strength of the emotions that could be generated from the child's bedroom and the things in it resulted in some mothers being cautioned to stay away from the child's bedroom initially:

> People said to me don't go into her bedroom. You know, do not go in her room for a while. And so actually I didn't go into her room for about 5 or 6 days. But then I was able to go in her room and it didn't upset me, so that was alright.
>
> (In-person Interview)

Later, these objects, through their strong evocative ability, could be sources of comfort.

> Basically, as strange as it may seem, when you walk into their rooms, their rooms smell like them, even this one. When you just pick up something, even the odor smells like whichever boy it is. That's a strange thing when you walk into there, you think (sniffs) that's them alright.
>
> (In-person Interview)

The items left behind can allow the mother to emotionally reconnect with her child:

> His flight bag is laying up against the door...and I look at it and think, boy, I'm glad he did that and it was so hard. Because we had to really push him to finish it.
>
> (In-person Interview)

This vignette is especially telling, because it demonstrates how this mother has developed a narrative providing evidence that she is a good parent. Every time she looks at the flight bag, that is 'laying up against the door' in clear view, she is reminded that she and her husband had to 'really push' her son to complete his flight lessons and earn his pilot's license. While many other items have been moved or put away out of sight, this possession has been left out in clear view. Thus, mnemonic devices selectively arranged in the home have the ability to help individuals adjust to their modified mothering role. While possessions initially may have been painful reminders of their children's absence, over time these same items can become a source of comfort as they elicit positive memories and reassure empty nest mothers that they are good mothers. Strategically placed evidence reminds and reassures mothers of the positive impact they had on their children.

Possessions encoded with meaning figure prominently in the reconstruction of self. There were many examples in our data of women who found comfort in objects left behind by their children. Similar to the ability of a blanket to provide security to babies as they start the 'separation phase,' adults, too, in our samples were able to find comfort from particularly meaningful possessions (Belk 1988, 1990; McAlexander *et al.* 1993; Price *et al.* 2000; Silver 1996). Clearly the following informant is comforted by the warm memories encoded into her sons' t-shirts:

> So, I might sleep in them (sons' t-shirts) or work in the yard in them, and little favorites of theirs, old school team t-shirts from where they won something, a championship or something. So that's been fun. …Every time I put it back on again I can remember them racing in that t-shirt in a special road race, I can remember them wearing it, getting it dirty, washing it for them, and most of these are smaller shirts now. They probably couldn't even wear them, but I've kept them around and I had to go down [into the basement] and find them in their drawers and there's something warm and comforting about sleeping in them.
>
> (In-person Interview)

The following informant used music her son left behind to raise her spirits in the early stages of her transition to the empty nest stage:

> I've kept myself busy. But I consciously made the effort to get this table done. That's when I hark back to him when he went away—cuz it was really sunny and I was playing some of his tapes.
>
> (In-person Interview)

Just as 'transitional objects' remind people who are displaced of their personal and collective origins, acting as 'mementoes of sentiment and cultural knowledge' (Parkin 1999, p. 317), so too do children's possessions help mothers during a time when they also experience feelings of dislocation. Thus, these simple, but cherished objects, not only evoke the physicality of their children (the t-shirt), but also reinforce their mothering role and provide a sense of continuity in a changing home environment (the tapes).

Enactment of mothering via gift-giving

Our data illustrate a shift in how the informants in this project moved from an emphasis of expressing love through doing everyday maintenance tasks for their family (e.g. cooking, cleaning, laundry) to a focus on expressing love through a series of different consumption practices, largely focused on giving (e.g. phone calls, cards, email messages, texting, care packages, and purchases for their child's apartment or dorm). Although the detail of their mothering responsibilities changed, they continued to undertake the caring work and emotional labor characteristic of mothering, as informants took comfort in continuing to take care of their kids even after they left the nest. Informants discussed the 'care packages' they sent to their children:

> Did you all send your "kids" Halloween boxes? Daddy sent Jenny tons of M&M's, or m-em's as she always called them. We sent her four boxes in the past three weeks. ...I sent her a food box, then she got very sick and I sent her a medicine box! Then daddy sent her a dehumidifier. Then the candy. And I know daddy has sent her $$'s in there, also!
>
> (Empty Nest Online Site)

Purchasing technology for children was commonly discussed, allowing mothers to communicate with their relocated children:

> We also bought her a mobile phone. ...But we got her a mobile phone because there were so few phones in the hall and it was one that had one free phone number which was to home, so that we could have conversations without her paying.
>
> (In-person Interview)

This gift-giving served to incorporate or emplace the mother symbolically into the lives and homes of their launched children. This mother, trying to traverse this liminal period, talks about the things she has purchased for her daughter, now in her second year away at school:

> I bought a new rug for her apartment, because we only bought one set and I figure she needed more....And I send her care packages. I sent her a card, like once a week and in between I think I've sent her two or three care packages, no two. But I have some other things I like to buy for her when I see them, like last time I sent her a care package I sent her a CD and a magnet for her fridge and some jiffy pops....They're like a kool-aidy stuff, just fun stuff. ...She loves getting mail! She says e-mail is great fun and she hears from everybody, but, my mom will send her a card occasionally, sometimes with cash involved—she likes those. ...And it's fun for me, too.
>
> (In-person Interview)

Gift-giving was employed as a tool to continue the enactment of the mothering role. As an outlet for expressing love and continuing the mothering role, albeit via long distance, mothers seemed to find comfort in helping their adult children adjust to their new homes. Mothers were able to use the consumption practice of gift-giving to symbolically place themselves in their children's new homes through their purchases they located within their children's homes:

> They still need clothing, food, and shelter. And again, with the younger one, still being in college, still has those same needs. The other one (pauses), he's on his own. But we still help him out when we can, too.
>
> (In-Person Interview)

The later (second round) interviews with participants suggest that with time, empty nest women go through a metamorphosis of the self, as the adult parent has time to identify who she is and reconstruct her identity into a self more consistent with her present circumstances and with who she would like to be (a possible self, Markus and Nurius 1986).

Discussion and conclusion

Without some type of societal support system firmly in place, consumers attempt to cope with this difficult transition and their ambiguous self concepts in a myriad of ways. Consumers create symbolic acts of disposition and acquisition of consumer goods, allowing them to utilize products in their status transitions and in the transformation of their new self. Empty nest consumers made use of informal rituals, symbolically encoded possessions, reassuring possession narratives, gift-giving; and various other coping strategies to aid in the reconstruction of their identity during this liminal life stage.

We found that distress often accompanies this role transition and can sometimes be severe. This distress can be understood in terms of loss and the consequences of suffering a loss. Many informants went through stages similar to the loss, grief, and mourning that accompany the death of a loved one. The stages that accompany loss, grief, and mourning were consistent with the stages individuals progress through when traversing a liminal life stage (See Table 13.1.)

Women's experience of their children leaving home and its associated impact on their identities and sense of self can be understood within the wider literature about grief, loss, and mourning (Rosenblatt *et al.* 1976; Worden 1991). For most of these women their children's departure potentially represented a double loss: first, the loss of the child, his/her physical and emotional presence and that relationship; and second, the loss of tasks central to the motherhood role: daily maintenance and the production of sociability. The themes of separation, transition, and incorporation are interwoven throughout our informants' stories about the losses they experienced as their children leave home. Worden's (1991) four tasks of mourning are clearly evident as well as the importance of completing these tasks in order to work through this difficult life transition, i.e. first, accepting the reality of the loss; second, working through the pain of grief and dealing with the feelings; third, adjusting to an environment in which the departed is missing; and fourth, emotionally relocating the departed and moving on with life (Worden 1991:10–14) (see Table 13.1). We can trace themes which relate to the four tasks of mourning and grief (Bowlby and Parkes 1970; Worden 1991) in these women's stories of their experiences of the empty nest household. Worden (1991:10–14) further argued that in order to complete the tasks of grief and mourning successfully, it is necessary to actualize the loss; identify and express feelings such as anger, guilt, anxiety, helplessness, and sadness; adjust to living without the departed; facilitate emotional relocation of the departed; and provide time to grieve.

Table 13.1 Loss, transitions and empty nest women

Van Gennep 1960: Life Stage Transitions	Worden 1991: Loss, Grief and Mourning	Empty nest women
1 Separation	1 Accepting the reality of the loss	Women described it as 'a death of sorts' (Empty nest bulletin board) as they worked to accept the reality of the loss of their day-to-day mothering role as children leave the empty nest household
2 Transition	2 Working through the pain of grief and dealing with the resulting feelings	Women described feelings of pain, sadness and helplessness in the initial stages as they adapted the tasks of 'caring for' and 'caring about' in order to re-constitute their identities as 'loving, caring, responsible adults' (Worden 1991)
	3 Adjusting to the environment in which the departed is missing	Women described coming to terms with the absence of children from their daily lives as they adjusted to the decoupling of their daily lives from their children's new lives
3 Incorporation	4 Emotionally relocating the departed and moving on	Women described how they found new consumptionscapes and adapted consumption practices in order to do family work as they learnt to mother from a distance

We interviewed informants from at least three countries and found that the grief, mourning, and the associated consumption behaviors were consistent across the data, regardless of the informants' country of residence. We therefore suggest that this emotional upheaval appears to be a phenomenon commonly experienced by mothers new to the empty nest stage in developed countries, although the context will be unique and nuanced for each individual.

Within feminist sociology, McMahon (1995) argued that it is important to understand 'what kind of identities' are produced by the processes of separation, independence, and autonomy (McMahon 1995:268). She highlights how motherhood facilitates women in creating a feminine identity 'as a loving, caring, responsible person.' What was vested in the women's commitment to motherhood was not simply the social identity of being a mother, but also the character of being a caring, patient, responsible adult person; a positively valued character that may be symbolically expressed for many women through motherhood (McMahon 1995). We have started to explore here the subsequent stages of women's re-socialization as they learn how to mother 'at a distance'; and importantly, how they use consumption to negotiate this transition, and the resulting impact of this transition and their accompanying feelings of grief and loss on their market place behavior.

References

Belk, R.W. (1988) 'Possessions and the extended self', *Journal of Consumer Research*, 15 (September), 139–68.

Belk, R.W. (1990) 'The role of possession in constructing and maintaining a sense of past', *Advances in Consumer Research*, 17, 669–76.

Bowlby, J. and Parkes, C. M. (1970) 'Separation and loss within the family,' in E. J. Anthony and C. M. Koupermil (eds), *The Child in this Family*, New York: Wiley.

Kübler-Ross, E. (1997) *On Children and Death: How Children and Their Parents Can and Do Cope With Death*, New York: Touchstone/Simon & Schuster.

Markus, H. and Nurius, P. (1986) 'Possible selves', *American Psychologist*, 41:9, 954–69.

McAlexander, J. H., Schouten, J. W., and Roberts, S. (1993) 'Consumer behavior and divorce', in J. A. Costa and R. W. Belk (eds), *Research in Consumer Behavior*, Greenwich, CT: JAI, 6, 153–84.

McMahon, M. (1995) *Engendering Motherhood: Identity and Self-Transformation in Women's Lives*, New York: The Guilford Press.

Miller, D. (1998) *A Theory of Shopping*, Ithaca, New York: Cornell University Press.

Oakley, A. (1974) *The Sociology of Housework*, London: Martin Robertson.

Parkin, D. J. (1999) 'Mementoes as transitional objects in human development', *Journal of Material Culture*, 4:3, 303–20.

Price, L., Arnould, E. J., and Curasi, C. F. (2000) 'Older consumers' disposition of special possessions', *Journal of Consumer Research*, 27 (September), 179–201.

Rosenblatt, P., Walsh P., and Jackson, D. (1976) *Grief and Mourning in Cross Cultural Perspective*, Minnesota: HRAF Press.

Schouten, J. W. (1991) 'Personal rites of passage and the reconstruction of self', *Advances in Consumer Research*, Provo, Utah: Association of Consumer Research, 18, 49–51.

Silver, I. (1996) 'Role transitions, objects, and identity', *Symbolic Interaction*, 19:1, 1–20.

Turner, V. (1974) *Dramas, Fields, and Metaphors*, Ithaca, NY: Cornell University Press.

Van Gennep, A. (1960) *The Rites of Passage*, trans. M. B. Vizedom and G. L. Caffee, Chicago: University of Chicago Press.

Worden, J. W. (1991) *Grief Counselling and Grief Therapy: a Handbook For the Mental Health Practitioner*, 2nd edn., London: Routledge.

14 Whose work is it anyway?

The shifting dynamics of 'doing mothering'

Benedetta Cappellini and
Elizabeth Parsons

Introduction

The inspiration for this chapter came from a discussion with one of our participants from a previous research project. A few years ago we looked at the processes and practices of mothering in the household. Drawing from sociological, anthropological and consumer research literature, we wrote a couple of pieces showing how the restless work of feeding the family has analogies with the process of sacrifice (Cappellini and Parsons 2012a, 2012b). We sent a draft of one paper to Tracey (one of our participants) for her comments and reflections. A few days later she responded:

> Hi Benedetta,
> An interesting paper. It's not something I'd really thought about. I don't tend to put myself in such a virtuous light – for me I'm just being practical – I have to be organised if I want to live the way I do (i.e., not always tied to the kitchen sink). I feel bad though as Mark [husband] is cooking the tea whilst I'm here reading your paper (and he's done the shopping – but I still planned the weekly menus and wrote him his shopping list). In fact things have changed a bit since your observations – I've now got the kids cooking (Albert on one night and John on another). Mark and I share the other meals depending on who is home first. But it is still me that organises the menu (with the others piping up with the particular meals they want) and I have to create the shopping list (sometimes I shop, at other times Mark). As I was saying to Liz, I think a lot of it is down to me being a control freak!!

There are a lot of things to say about this email. It undoubtedly reflects the guilt and anxiety that Tracey experiences in trying to juggle her working life and home life while trying to match up to the norms of mothering which seem to constantly stalk her in her everyday life. The work of feeding the family is particularly demanding and, as Tracey's comments show, this work is routinely underestimated by women themselves, they tend to consider it as part of their own identity ('being practical[…] being a control freak') and an inescapable and integral part of their everyday life, something that they themselves are responsible for and therefore have to manage ('I have to be organised if I want to live the way

I do'). Thus Tracey's email satisfied us in a way, as it shows that our paper on motherly sacrifice at mealtimes successfully captured our participants' everyday experiences, and that our analysis did at least some justice to their lives. However, Tracey's email also illustrates how households change over time, as Tracey puts it: 'things have changed a bit since your observations'. Benedetta observed a mealtime at Tracey's house in 2008. In the intervening four years, her children have grown up and both she and her husband have changed modes of employment. As we discuss below, these changes have impacted quite dramatically on the division of labour in Tracey's household. Reflecting on our earlier interpretations, we became acutely aware that the picture of family life we had presented was rather static; in this respect we could be accused of reproducing the norm of the 'stable family' which has been problematized in the literature (Doucet 1996). We started questioning how the organization of labour in the household changes over time in relation to events like children growing up or moving out, people finding or losing jobs, getting divorced. Turning to the literature, our curiosity was not entirely satisfied. While some studies do focus on families during liminal stages such as children moving into their teens (Cody and Lawlor 2011), or children leaving home (Hogg *et al.* 2004), very few studies have adopted a longitudinal perspective on these issues. With a few exceptions (see for example Lindridge *et al.* 2004), longitudinal studies seem at present to be unpopular. This lack is problematic because, as Doucet (1996) observes, it results in an 'outstanding stability' of gender divisions in the domestic sphere.

Tracey's email therefore inspired us to go back to the families we visited in 2008 and see what had changed (and indeed what had not changed) in their households. This chapter is based on an analysis of this in-depth interview and is informed by our early studies of household mealtimes which explore issues of sacrifice (Cappellini and Parsons, 2012a), sharing and gifting (Cappellini and Parsons, 2012b). The theme of sacrifice came through quite strongly again in this second interview with Tracey, but here we are more concerned with the division of labour in the home and Tracey's view of her role within the home. As we worked with the data, we quickly realized that task division within the household cannot be separated from both an understanding of individual and collective family identities, and the power struggles between these. In teasing out these twin themes we have turned to feminist literatures on the doing of gender and the doing of mothering. The chapter therefore starts with an overview of the literature on doing gender and doing mothering and the ways in which these identities are intertwined with entitlement and accountability in the context of the home. In the analysis we begin by exploring the changes to Tracey's household that have taken place over time and how these changes have impacted on the division of task performance in the home as well as Tracey's identity as mother. The second part of the analysis uses the concepts of accountability and entitlement to gain a deeper interpretive insight into what is really 'going on' in relation to these same two issues. In the conclusion we make a series of contributions to our understanding of the shifting dynamics of doing mothering.

Doing mothering and doing gender: accountability and entitlement in the household

We have drawn on theorizations surrounding doing gender and doing mothering to understand the everyday reproduction of Tracey's identity in the household. The concept of doing gender is much used (and abused) in feminist literature (Deutsch 2007). Coined in the eighties by West and Zimmerman (1987), 'doing gender' refers to the assumption that gender is a practice constantly re-enacted in everyday social interactions and is not a monolithic, stable and unchangeable ontological individual property (West and Zimmerman 1987, 2009). As West and Zimmerman note, gender is a 'routine accomplishment embedded in everyday interaction' (1987: 125), and hence studying gender implies looking at 'the interactional work involved in "being" a gendered person in society' (p. 127). The vast body of study influenced by West and Zimmerman's idea of doing gender in the household shows how social and cultural meanings associated with the distribution of domestic labour serve to perpetuate inequality in gender relations. For example, work on 'doing mothering' explores the ways in which mothering reproduces gender identity, seeing mothering not only as a biological destiny but as a social institution (Chodorow 1978). In her seminal work *Feeding the Family*, Marjorie DeVault (1991) explores how women's work of providing food for the family is a restless work of care, love and responsibility as 'the food provided for a family cannot just be any food, but must be food that will satisfy them' (1991: 40). Similarly others show how shopping (Miller 1998), cleaning (Carrigan and Szmigin 2006), providing homemade food (Moisio *et al.* 2004) as well as dealing with leftovers (Cappellini and Parsons 2012a) are practices that perpetuate women's self-sacrifice for the greater good of the family. In these studies it is evident how cooking, and all the other work that makes cooking possible, operates as a form of doing gender in which 'a woman conducts herself as recognizably womanly' (DeVault 1991: 118). In many cases women adhere to, and perpetuate, the existing and prevailing social and cultural norms and practices associated with being (doing) a wife and a mother. Despite the emergence of the popular image of the male cook through the success of international celebrity chefs (Brownlie and Hewer 2007), behind closed doors women continue to undertake much of the mundane private work of feeding their families (DeVault 1991; Hook 2010). In addition, recent work on mothering observes the intensification of the investment required in mothering both financially and emotionally (Hays 1996; Warner 2006) as well as the tensions between individual and intersubjective identities often felt by mothers as they struggle with competing family versus personal needs (Hollway 2006).

Studies inspired by the doing of gender have been criticized recently for not taking into consideration the social and cultural changes in gendered interactions and work divisions in the home (Moloney and Fenstermaker 2002; Sullivan 2004; Risman 2009). Although we partly agree with these criticisms, we think that the original formulation of doing gender looks at changes in interactions using the concept of accountability. Following West and Zimmerman (1987, 2009), gender is done through enactments accountable to an existing and prevailing gender order, norms and conventions. As they recently point out, such prevailing gender order, norms and conventions are not '"free floating" and changes in these involve both changes in persons' orientation to these norms and changes in social relations that reflexively support changes in orientation' (West and Zimmerman 2009: 118). Therefore, doing gender and being accountable to an existing gender order are dynamic concepts as they describe how 'gender is not undone so much as redone' (p. 118) in situated gender enactments involving social relations and personal orientations. Recent work looking at personal orientations, as well as gendered interactions and practices, reveals that the labour distribution in the household is changing (Bianchi *et al.* 2000; Sullivan 2004). These are not dramatic changes, but 'a slow dripping of change that is perhaps unnoticeable from year to year but that in the end is persistent enough to lead to the slow dissolution of previously existing structures' (Sullivan 2004: 209–10). Sullivan (2004) proposes a way of looking at the division of domestic labour by examining the gender consciousness of all parties involved, their interactions, and the accompanying practices involved in doing gender in the household. We do not quite achieve this multi-perspective or holistic view of the household here because our analysis is based on the views and experiences of Tracey alone. However we can get some sense of how she constructs herself as mother and gain some purchase on the way in which household members relate to one another in her accounts of everyday household interactions.

We take inspiration from the idea of doing and redoing gender and accountability in specific situations, as we examine Tracey's understandings of 'doing mum and doing wife' in managing the household labour. We look not simply at the performance of household labour (the doing) but also at the management of, and responsibility for, household tasks (Sullivan 2004). We also explore the feelings of entitlement and gratitude surrounding domestic work (i.e., who is entitled to, and accountable for, the doing and the management). In looking at the operation of these wider norms and expectations both at household level and wider societal level, we have attempted to account for the transformative aspects of doing gender, and not simply the conservative aspects of it. We look at how Tracey reflects upon and understands her role in relation to her family members' expectations and sense of entitlement. We have explored the materiality of the practices surrounding the work of feeding Tracey's family elsewhere (Cappellini and Parsons 2012a, 2012b) and hence in this case we focussed on the changes of the distribution of labour in household over time and Tracey's feelings and understandings of such changes in relation to other family members.

The shifting responsibilities of motherhood: examining Tracey's household over time

The distribution of work in Tracey's household changed significantly over the time period we studied (see Table 14.1). When we first met Tracey in 2008, she was a PhD student working from home most of the time. Prior to this she worked long

Table 14.1 Distribution of labour in Tracey's household over time

Before 2008	2008	2011
Tracey has a managerial role in a large company and is the main breadwinner	Tracey is full-time MBA and then PhD student at a local university	Tracey is a full-time lecturer at a local university
Tracey is at home late at night and weekends, she travels a lot with work	Tracey is at home most of the time	Tracey is at home at 3.30 most days
Mark took redundancy to take care of the children. He is at home full time	Mark is at home full time	Mark starts his own business
The children (Albert and John) are both under 11	Albert and John are 11 and 13	Albert and John are 14 and 16
Task performance (Mark)	Task performance (Mark and occasionally Tracey)	Task performance (Mark/Tracey but children have to perform some tasks during the week)
Task management (Tracey) using kitchen paper diary/planner	Task management (Tracey) using kitchen laptop	Task management (Tracey) using kitchen laptop

hours in a managerial role for a big firm. As the main household breadwinner she was away much of the time, while her husband (Mark) had taken redundancy from his lower paying role to look after the children full time. During this period, while Tracey was not at home much of the time, she appeared to remain in charge of the task management of the household by introducing a diary planner which she placed in the kitchen. She used the planner to record tasks to be completed on a daily basis, including the menu for the dinner, the shopping and the cleaning tasks. Mark was responsible for accomplishing these tasks, while Tracey was at work.

> When the children came along he [Mark] took redundancy. I was on a better wage at that point. He stayed home and looked after the kids. [...] I was in charge of everything, but I gently started to put in routine with the diary [...] he was running everything but I was doing the input, there was always the element of me organising. Things changed when I was doing the MBA. Part of me felt that... I realised that I hadn't been to any sports days. I felt a bit sad... I thought 'now I am going to be a mum'.

Here we see the impact of Tracey's ideas of 'good mothering' on her decisions. Despite being in charge of the household routine, she felt that simply managing tasks was not 'enough', she felt that she had to be much more hands on in her role as 'mum'. Here, her presence both at home and in public was important. In terms of her presence at home elsewhere in the interview, she mentioned 'doing family' through activities such as making Christmas decorations and writing Christmas cards, as well as more mundane tasks like cooking, shopping, cleaning and ironing. Her presence at public events like sports days was also central to her ideal of 'doing family' outside home and hence 'displaying family' and 'displaying mothering'.

The striking thing about Table 14.1 is that despite significant changes to both Tracey and Mark's paid employment and therefore time spent at home, Tracey maintained sole control over task management. This control extended beyond household routines to planning holidays:

> Mainly I make the decisions, or we will talk about them but I'll be the instigator of the decisions. Sometimes he'll [Mark] put his foot down and say no we're not doing something, it's not very often, at certain times I know I'm not going to get anywhere... Most of the time we talk it through but very often it's me saying, 'shall we think about going on holiday, I want to do this with the house'... I tend to be the instigator of change.

This control (and as we argue later, conferred responsibility) of both ordinary and extraordinary household decisions is not always perceived in a positive light by Tracey. At points in our interview, she reflected on a desire to share some of this responsibility with the other members of the family.

> Most of the time I'm happy, sometimes I just think 'why can't somebody else take over and get on with stuff' you know 'what would happen if I'm not there' sort of thing. Most of the time its just routine anyway, just used to doing it, but you know, somebody's got to make the decisions and sometimes I think 'why can't somebody else make a decision' but you get used to it I suppose.

While Tracey feels that in her enactment of mothering she cannot delegate her task management role, task performance does shift between family members. When studying for her MBA and PhD in 2008, Tracey had more time at home and hence she reclaimed some of the tasks from Mark. When she re-enters the workplace in 2011, Tracey redistributes the tasks once more. Some of the tasks are allocated to Mark but now the two sons (Albert and John) are old enough to begin to play their part in the everyday work of the household. At present, Tracey delegates specific tasks to her sons including making dinner (that she has planned in advance), doing some cleaning and putting away the weekly shopping. In 2008 Tracey replaced the paper diary with a laptop which is again located in the kitchen, the hub of household activity. The computer software extends Tracey's control, facilitating an even more detailed breakdown of tasks along with their exact timings. The planned tasks extend from the daily feeding of the dog to the weekly shopping and washing but also less frequent tasks such as defrosting the freezer. Tracey manages the laptop schedule and carefully records the variety of tasks to be completed along with the family member responsible for each task. This system of task management is time-consuming and requires lot of effort from Tracey, but she observes that in doing so she is making sure 'everybody does their own bit'. For example, as the boys have grown up, Tracey tries to encourage them to take more responsibility for themselves and contribute to the household:

> When I take the shopping home I expect them to put it away, I try to, I make sure I do not get home before school is finished[...] We encourage them to take over a bit more. They know that they have to help themselves and feed themselves.

This redistribution of tasks is not necessarily only about sharing out the work more equitably but rather socialising and educating her children to be more independent and to take care of themselves. Therefore, while clearly the organization of tasks in Tracey's household is intimately linked to her own ideals of motherhood, it is also shaped by her understanding of 'sonhood' and also 'husbandhood' as she requires other members of the family to be accountable as sons and husband. However, this more equitable distribution not only takes time in the planning and inputting into the computer but also in the reorganization of family time around tasks and the setting up of some of these tasks. For example, in order for her sons to put away the shopping, Tracey has to make sure she arrives home with it while the children are there, and for her sons to cook a meal she needs to plan and shop for something simple. Thus Tracey's mothering practices go beyond feeding the family (DeVault 1991) since she also educates the children to contribute to the family meal. As such she is keen to create and maintain a cohesive family identity. Here Tracey's doing of gender is not simply related to her own performance of motherhood, but also her interactions with other members of the family and her expectations towards them (West and Zimmerman 2009).

The tensions and contradictions of motherhood: exploring the question of accountability

As we have explored above, the organization of tasks in Tracey's household is intimately linked to Tracey's identity as mother. However, this identity is not static; it changed as her family matured and as she moved in and out of the workplace. In addition, this identity was full of tensions and contradictions. The quotation below illustrates some of the internal struggles Tracey experiences over the amount of time and energy she devotes to her family (in particular her children) versus her working life outside the home. She is also aware that this is a particularly gendered dilemma, as she reflects on the fact that she does not place the same expectations on her husband, Mark, as she does on herself. She is aware that she takes on the lion's share of responsibility for parenting and puts pressure on herself to meet these responsibilities. The situation is complicated by a lack of time to meet these responsibilities as she also works full-time and a feeling that, as the children are growing up, she ought to have more time for herself; as she observes 'I have got to live my life as well'. Thus feelings of entitlement mix with those of guilt and responsibility.

You put pressure on yourself 'I should be doing it, I should be doing it' but I never think that Mark should be doing it [...]Should I force myself to do more? [...] I can't fit it in. Not being nasty but the total focus of my life can't be my kids. I have always said that, my friends would think 'what a horrible parent' but at the end of the day I have got to live my life as well. You always think that you have to do more, it is part of being a mum, of being a woman.

Feeding the family is a particular source of guilt for Tracey. When she was at home full-time while studying for her PhD and MBA degrees she was able to spend time cooking family meals from scratch. When she returned to the workplace in 2011, as she observes, 'jars start to sneak in'. This image of jars of pre-prepared sauce starting to sneak in nicely captures Tracey's sense of guilt in not preparing them herself anymore:

T: I feel as if I am getting more selfish. I can't be there for everybody, you can stop and do things for yourself.[...] I will use pasta sauces now whereas before I used to make everything from scratch, I use curry sauces now whereas I always used to make my own, marinade my own stuff, now jars sneak in there, it means having to do less preparation.

E: How do you feel about that?

T: It suits for the moment.

E: Is it temporary?

T: I don't know, everyone seems happy so, well perhaps it's just a phase that I went through when I'd got the time, because I'd gone away from the crazy working. Ok I was doing the PhD and the studying and things like that but it isn't as crazy as doing full time work. Again now, work seeps into everything again, I always find that if I have got spare time perhaps I don't want to spend it cooking and things like that. You do tend to think 'oh well I've got all this marking' or spending two hours creating something, you're gonna do the marking. I think it's just priorities...you can't do everything and I learnt a long time ago that you can juggle so many things and some things you leave. Everyone seems happy so...

Tracey is clearly far from being selfish since we discover elsewhere in the interview that one reason for using the pre-prepared sauces is so that she can satisfy the tastes of individual family members, often cooking two different dishes to keep everyone happy. The way in which she describes this change as 'just a phase, ... ready sauces sneaking in' also reveals the conflicting feelings Tracey has about her juggling between her work (doing some marking) and her role as mother in keeping everyone happy at mealtimes. Others (Carrigan and Szmigin 2006; Moisio *et al.* 2004) have illustrated the complex compromises women make on an everyday basis and the guilt they feel over these decisions. Here Tracey has compromised (in her opinion) by feeding the family with a form of convenience food in order to find time to engage in activities outside the home (i.e., working and having a social life).

Tracey's feelings of guilt are also often compounded by the actions of other family members, in particular her two sons who often require her to perform according to their particular views of motherhood. Despite Tracey encouraging her sons to be independent and feed themselves, they still feel entitled to ask her to provide food for them:

> He [Albert] comes to the kitchen and 'Feed me' [Tracey motions pointing her finger into her open mouth]. He thinks that is what Mum should be there for. I try to teach him otherwise.

In observing that she 'tries to teach him otherwise' Tracey is not only referring to her attempts to instil a sense of independence in her sons as they grow up but also a more balanced and equitable view of gender roles in the household, as she observes below:

> It is interesting because they still come to Mum. I say 'Ask your Dad, your Dad is cooking tonight', 'Yes but what are having? You know what we are having' […] Last week Mark did the shopping and I put roast on the list without specifying which roast. I thought he would remember that John doesn't eat beef, he bought beef. John came around 'what are we having?' I said 'beef' he said 'what am *I* having?' I said 'you have to have beef' he said 'but I don't like beef' and I said 'you have to ask your Dad, he has done the shopping'. But he comes to me, he never brought it up with his Dad. They always come to me, it is always my fault.

This beef incident shows how her children's feeling of entitlement towards Tracey can create tensions. Her children do not recognize their father as an 'instigator' who has to 'make everybody happy', but view him as the executor of tasks planned by Tracey. Therefore when something goes wrong (i.e., they feel their needs are not being adequately met for whatever reason) they feel entitled to call Tracey to account for these events. Despite the fact that Tracy's husband performed the tasks of shopping and cooking for the Sunday roast, the children do not consider him accountable for the overall management of the Sunday lunch, which in their eyes, remains entirely Tracey's responsibility. In doing so, her children place demands on Tracey to perform a version of motherhood which is concerned with keeping everybody happy, and thus providing an alternative meal for her son. What could also be going on here is Tracey attempting to put some pressure on Mark to learn the boys' food preferences. She mentioned later in the interview that Mark really ought to know by now that John didn't like beef. By deliberately not specifying the type of meat on the shopping list, in a small way she is trying to share some of her task management and decision-making responsibility with him.

Tracey's mother also requires a specific enactment of motherhood, which seems more focused on 'doing' rather than managing.

My mum makes it worse you know because if she sees Mark doing the housework she says 'What's he oooh...' you know 'Oh he's doing all the housework again, what are you doing?' 'Oh I'm actually doing some work you know'. Like when I was doing the PhD, I was doing quite a bit of sessional teaching but that 'wasn't a job, I should be there to be a homemaker' so little bits of that stick with you.

Tracey's mother measures Tracey's behaviour against her own received ideals of mothering which stem in part from her own experiences. Elsewhere in the interview Tracey notes that her father rarely completed any tasks in the household, leaving housework entirely to her mother. Tracey's mother is holding her accountable to these same ideals of mothering. While Tracey is clearly rather cynical about her mother's criticism, observing her mother's view that working as an academic 'wasn't a job', she still retains a burden of guilt from these views observing that 'little bits...stick with you'. Tracey's feeling that she should be taking on responsibility for household tasks is apparent from her following observation:

Sometimes I get annoyed because he [Mark] does it, and I should be doing it [...] I think it should be my job, other times I think that it's great. Again with the meals sometimes I think it's I that should be doing this, it should be my role [...] We almost compete on getting the job done. I don't know why but we compete on sort of 'I am going to do this', 'I am going to do that', 'I am going to be the martyr'.

The above comments contrast significantly with Tracey's earlier observation that 'the total focus of my life can't be my kids'. In the above observation Tracey seems to be at pains to reclaim some of the task performance in the home. Here she seems to take on board her mother's ideals of the stay-at-home mother performing all of the tasks in the home and sacrificing her own needs for the wider good of the family. However, at other times Tracey clearly resisted these norms and claimed a distance from them. In the course of our interview Tracey frequently contradicted herself revealing a pendulum swing between the desire to adhere to a prevailing existing gender order, and the norms and conventions of being a mum and a wife, and her desire to maintain a certain distance from this order by making time and space to live her own life and pursue her independent desires. Tracey's contrasting understating of her enactment of mothering shows how feeling of entitlement and gratitude are not static, but change over time in relation to the age of the children, the time spent at home and work commitments. They also change in relation to Tracey's interpretation of the expectations of different members of the family (i.e., her children, her mother). When it comes to the division of household tasks and feelings of entitlement in the home, Sullivan (2004) observes a very slow but nonetheless positive shift towards greater gender equality in the home. However, we find it extremely difficult to interpret Tracey's experiences in this manner. Our findings demonstrate how painful it is for Tracey to juggle between work and family commitments (see also Thompson 1996), trying to pursue her own career (which she describes as work for herself rather than work for her family!) and at the same time accomplishing the doing and displaying of mothering that others demand from her.

Discussion and conclusion

In returning to our initial assertion that there is a dearth of research which explores the dynamics of labour division in households over time, we have found a series of changes that impact on task performance in the home. We have explored the changing employment statuses of the parents and the children growing up as influencing the management and organization of task performance. The time spent at home by parents impacts on the volume of tasks they perform, however the management of (and responsibility for) these tasks remained the preserve of Tracey throughout the period studied. Tracey's observation in her email to us that she must be a 'control freak' is certainly borne out by our subsequent interview with her. However we think that this is not, as Tracey is probably alluding to, merely a personality trait, but a response to wider structural changes in society. Examining mothering in America, Warner (2006) observes the tendency of contemporary mothers to micro-manage the household, in particular the children in the household. In a chapter entitled 'A generation of control freaks' she describes the tendency of mothers to 'privatise problems' (p. 163) within the household and take on increasing responsibility for their children. Warner views this as symptomatic of the rise of individualism and a decline in opportunities to share the burden of raising a family more widely beyond the home. In Tracy's case, as the boys grew up they took on a slightly increased share of task performance in the home, but this seemed to be largely a reaction to Tracey's attempts to socialize them in preparation for when they would leave the family home. As such their task performance did not seem to reduce the workload for Tracey and Mark very significantly. Often the tasks they did perform were learning opportunities and therefore required extra planning and some instruction and help in executing them (in particular cooking). We also think that Tracey's attempts here are about making sure that the boys felt that they were contributing constructively to the family unit. These attempts to create and maintain a cohesive family identity and sense of togetherness is in turn central to Tracey's own identity as 'mother'.

We also have a series of observations to make about accountability and entitlement in the home which both impact on the division of household labour but also enable household members to require labour from others. In this case we have focused largely on the way in which other household members require certain enactments, and their associated implications for task performance and management from Tracey. Tracey was consistently required to account for her actions to others; both her sons and her mother called her to account if she wasn't delivering on their own received ideas about appropriate mothering. Her mother directly questions Tracey about the household division of labour (i.e., Tracey working in her study while her husband Mark does the housework). In a similar

194 Benedetta Cappellini and Elizabeth Parsons

way her son John is also drawing on a specific convention of mothering when he asks her why his meal has not been tailored to his tastes even though his Dad cooked it. While these examples may seem disparate, in both cases Tracey is called by other family members to account for her actions. Underlying these requests to account are highly normative ideas of mothering as sacrificing self (career, own tastes in food) for the wider benefit of the family (see also Cappellini and Parsons 2012a). While Tracey is often required to live up to the norms and standards of mothering held by others she is also clearly subject to wider norms of mothering. However, viewing Tracey as entirely subject to these requirements misses out on her own agency in the process. Many of Tracey's actions, her attempts to retain control over task management, as well as much of the actual performance of tasks, are undoubtedly efforts on her own part to both socialize her children and maintain her own narrative of family togetherness (Gillis 1996). Interestingly we also observed an instance of Tracey and her husband Mark as competing to perform tasks as a form of self sacrifice. Each wanted the other to acknowledge their input into the household. The politics of recognition are vital to understanding the dynamics of the household. Indeed, the division of labour in the household and the allocation of tasks to household members are not without their tensions. Time and again in the interview we saw Tracey struggling with the requirements of home versus workplace. In terms of her identity she often framed her work commitments based outside the home as her more selfish activities, as contributing to her own career as an individual, rather than as benefiting the family collective. Hollway (2006) explores these tensions between individuality and intersubjectivity in motherhood. While pressures on family time have increased with changing participation in the workforce as well as changes and fracturing of traditional family structures, norms and conventions surrounding the family have remained rather static (Daly 2001; Cinotto 2006). This mismatch results in a 'structural contradiction' (Daly 2001: 293) between the lived experience of family time and the powerful ideology which continues to govern it. As Gillis (1996: xvii) observes 'There has always been tension between the families people live with and the families they live by.'

There are also a series of power struggles constantly in operation between family members, as they bring their own needs and expectations to their everyday household interactions. These needs and expectations are moderated by a sense of the greater good of the family. However the nature of this shared sense of family, and the extent to which it impacts on willingness to sacrifice individual needs, differs between family members. Tensions between individual and collective needs are typically at the heart of power struggles in the household. These struggles were most prominent between the children and their mother. As they grow up they tend to challenge Tracey more often as they seek to access as much resource as possible for their individual needs whilst also asserting an increasing degree of independence from the family unit. This happens at the same time as Tracey attempts to instil in them a sense of responsibility for their role within the family. As they enter their teens, thinking ahead to a time when she thinks they will have families of their own, Tracey feels a mounting pressure to socialize them as good future husbands and fathers. Her attempts to socialize them (in particular in teaching them cooking skills) are strongly influenced by her own received ideals of family togetherness and shared responsibility in the home. As we have seen, these attempts may also be motivated by Tracey's own gender politics; she is keen that her sons do not reproduce the unequal gender relations she observed between her own parents. These past experiences shape both her relations with her own husband as well as her aspirations for her sons' future relationships. This highlights the power of received experiences of family life, in particular power relations between family members in shaping future ideas and expectations about 'doing family' and 'doing mothering'.

References

Bianchi S. M., Milkie, M. A., Sayer L. C., and Robinson J. P (2000) 'Is anyone doing the housework? Trends in the gender division of household labour', *Social Forces,* 79:1, 191–228.

Brownlie, D. and Hewer, P. (2007) 'Prime beef cuts: culinary images for thinking men', *Consumption, Markets and Culture*, 10:3, 229–50.

Cappellini, B. and Parsons, E. (2012a) '(Re) enacting motherhood: self-sacrifice and abnegation in the kitchen', in R. Belk and A. Ruvio (eds), *The Routledge Companion to Identity and Consumption*, London: Routledge, 119–28.

Cappellini, B. and Parsons, E. (2012b) 'Sharing the meal: food consumption and family identity', in R. Belk, S. Askegaard and L. Scott (eds), *Research in Consumer Behavior 14*, London: Emerald, 109–28.

Carrigan, M. and Szmigin, I. (2006) '"Mothers of invention": maternal empowerment and convenience consumption', *European Journal of Marketing*, 40:9/10, 1122–42.

Chodorow, N. J. (1978) *The Reproduction of Mothering: Psychoanalysis and the Sociology of Gender*, Berkeley: University of California Press.

Cinotto, S. (2006) '"Everyone would be around the table": American family mealtimes in historical perspective, 1850–1960', *New Directions for Child and Adolescent Development*, 111, 17–34.

Cody, K. and Lawlor, K. (2011) 'On the borderline: exploring liminal consumption and the negotiation of threshold selves', *Marketing Theory*, 11:2, 207–28.

Daly, K. (2001) 'Deconstructing family time: from ideology to lived experience', *Journal of Marriage and Family*, 63, 283–94.

DeVault, M. (1991) *Feeding the Family: the Social Organization of Caring as Gendered Work*, Chicago, IL: University of Chicago Press.

Deutsch, F. (2007) 'Undoing gender', *Gender & Society*, 21:1, 106–27.

Doucet, A. (1996) 'Encouraging voices: towards more creative methods for collecting data on gender and household labor', in L. Morris and E. Lyon (eds), *Gender Relations in Public and Private*, London: Macmillan.

Gillis, J. (1996) *A World of Their Own Making: Myth, Ritual and the Quest for Family Values*, New York: Basic Books.

Hays, S. (1996) *The Cultural Contradictions of Motherhood*, New Haven, CT: Yale University Press.

Hogg, M., Curasi, C. F., and Maclaran, P. (2004) 'The (re-) configuration of production and consumption in empty nest households/families', *Consumption, Markets and Culture*, 7:3, 329–50.

Hollway, W. (2006) *The Capacity to Care: Gender and Ethical Subjectivity*, London: Routledge.

Hook, J. L. (2010) 'Gender inequality in the welfare state: sex segregation in housework, 1965–2003', *American Journal of Sociology*, 1155, 1480–523.

Lindridge, A. M., Hogg, M. K, and Shah, M. (2004) 'Imagined multiple worlds: how South Asian women in Britain use family and friends to navigate the "border crossings" between household and societal contexts', *Consumption, Markets and Culture*, 7:3 211–38.

Miller, D. (1998) *A Theory of Shopping*, New York, Ithaca: Cornell University Press.

Moisio, R., Arnould, E. J., and Price, L. (2004) 'Between mothers and markets: constructing family identity through homemade food', *Journal of Consumer Culture*, 4, 361–84.

Moloney, M. and Fenstermaker, S. (2002) 'Performance and accomplishment: reconciling feminist conceptions of gender', in S. Fenstermaker and C. West (eds), *Doing Gender, Doing Difference: Inequality, Power, and Institutional Change*, New York, NY: Routledge.

Risman, B. (2009) 'From doing to undoing: gender as we know it', *Gender & Society*, 23:1, 81–4.

Sullivan, O. (2004) 'Changing gender practices within the household: a theoretical perspective', *Gender and Society*, 18:2, 207–22.

Thompson, C. (1996) 'Caring consumers: gendered consumption meanings and the juggling lifestyle', *Journal of Consumer Research*, 22, 388–407.

Warner, J. (2006) *Perfect Madness: Motherhood in the Age of Anxiety*, New York: Penguin.

West, C. and Zimmerman, D. (1987) 'Doing gender', *Gender & Society*, 1, 125–51.

West, C. and Zimmerman, D. (2009) 'Accounting for doing gender', *Gender & Society*, 23:1, 112–22.

Part IV

Consumption and contested motherhood identities

15 Mothering, poverty and consumption

Lisa Glass, Kathy Hamilton and Katherine Trebeck

Introduction

This chapter focuses on the experiences of mothers in poverty within the context of UK consumer culture. We follow a relative poverty definition, referring to those who lack the resources necessary to participate in the normal customs of society and are unable to obtain goods and services needed for an 'adequate' and 'socially acceptable' standard of living (Darley and Johnson 1985: 206). The latest Joseph Rowntree Foundation (2011) report on poverty and social exclusion indicated in 2009/10 that over one-fifth of the population lived in low-income households.[1] Lone mothers, in particular, are vulnerable to poverty and of children in one parent families, 39 per cent are in the bottom quintile of household disposable income, and only 4 per cent are in the top quintile (Department of Work and Pensions 2009: 68). Lone mothers are often subject to stigmatization, particularly in relation to 'the adequacy of their mothering' (Silva 1996: 8). May (2008) suggests being a good mother is linked to the moral presentation of self. In this chapter, we consider how discourses surrounding mothers in poverty present them as morally deficient. We discuss how low-income mothers must navigate a problematic and often harmful labour market, and interact with consumer culture – enduring, resisting, succumbing and modifying the pressures to consume experienced themselves and by their children. We illustrate the experiences of mothers in poverty, drawing on two qualitative research projects conducted in Scotland and Northern Ireland and we highlight policy implications.

Mothering in a labour market that doesn't deliver

Motherhood is a social construction and ideals of good motherhood are defined according to social norms (May 2008). Poverty makes these ideals more difficult to realize (McCormack 2005) and failing to reach socially acceptable standards of a good mother results in stigmatization and social exclusion. Mothers in poverty can be stigmatized for a variety of reasons, including lone mother status and reliance on welfare benefits.

Many lone mothers are unemployed and the 'welfare mother' is stigmatized as a non-productive citizen and a bad mother harming the life chances of her children (McCormack 2005; Wilson and Huntington 2006). For example, the lone mothers in Power's (2005) Canadian study felt they were perceived as lazy, irresponsible and undeserving. This emphasis on paid work and employment excludes the unpaid work all mothers perform (Christopher 2004). This is in line with the normalization of the idea that women belong in employment and an ideological shift against welfare dependence (Himmelweit 2004). However, reconciliation of work and family life is particularly problematic for lone mothers. According to McCormack (2005: 663), the mother experiencing poverty has to negotiate a 'contradictory set of expectations'. On the one hand, she is to seek employment and work hard to lift herself and her family out of poverty and on the other hand, intensive mothering is positioned as necessary to secure children's well-being.

Mothers, particularly those living in deprived areas or experiencing poverty, are often faced with a choice between unemployment and poor quality work (Escott 2007). Recruitment practices and discriminatory attitudes exclude many, so that labour market inequalities are perpetuated by informal recruitment methods and reluctance to employ women with caring responsibilities (Sanderson 2006).[2]

Beyond accessibility issues, the labour market is characterized by a lack of permanent jobs, limited opportunities for high quality part-time work and insufficient family-friendly policies (such as job sharing and term-time working) (Escott 2007). For example, by 2009, services constituted almost 82 per cent of all jobs in Scotland (NOMIS 2010), but these jobs (retailing, catering and increasingly, call centres) often do not represent 'quality work'; instead they are jobs taken by a growing 'precariat' – particularly women (Oxfam International 2010)–who face an 'insecure working environment characterised by casualisation, low pay and deskilled work…with high levels of turnover…fixed term contracts and the increasing use by employers of temporary staffing agencies' (Helms and Cumbers 2005: 145). Entering the labour market is therefore a dismal prospect for many mothers. Moreover, supportive assets are damaged when people can access only short-term poor quality work – social interaction, for example, is limited when people work anti-social hours or seek multiple jobs to make ends meet.

Yet government policies over the last ten or more years have pursued a 'work first' agenda. This involved 'activating' the unemployed or economically inactive, leveraging them into work (OECD 2010), invariably low skill, hence typically low wage (Goos and Manning 2007). While governments in the UK and US have introduced remedial interventions to shore up these bad jobs (most obviously through the introduction of Tax Credits to supplement low wages), there has been no attempt to prevent these 'bad jobs' in the first place. Pertinently, the work first agenda has downplayed (if not explicitly ignored) the disconnect between entry into employment and poverty alleviation (working households make up one third of all poor families (Spencer 2008)), the concentration of particular demographics in low quality employment and other social and economic roles, not least being a good mother. Moreover, gender bias in remuneration and job quality also means that jobs performed by women (particularly women from ethnic minority communities) are often the lowest paid and most insecure, yet these jobs (such as care work) are 'often those that are among the most socially valuable – jobs that keep our communities and families together' (Lawlor *et al.* 2009: 2).

Mothering in consumer culture

Pressures encountered by mothers experiencing poverty are accentuated by consumer culture in which 'a "normal life" is the life of consumers' (Bauman 2005: 38) and consumption becomes central to the 'total organization of everyday life' (Baudrillard 1998: 29). Since the introduction of conspicuous consumption (Veblen 1899), social identity centres on visibility of consumer goods and possessions (Dittmar 2008). Consumption represents a moral doctrine in pursuit of the good life (Gabriel and Lang 2006). Consequently, the desire to participate in consumer culture is not always promoted by material need but the belief that to find happiness one must be richer (Hamilton 2004). Arguably contributing to these changes has been the transformation of Western society by capitalism and the associated decline in traditional sources of meaning, such as religion or holding a fixed place in the social hierarchy (Carlisle *et al.* 2008). Self worth and purpose in life seem to be measured according to personal wealth, job status or purchasing power.

Despite the supposed benefits of living in consumer culture, an investigation by UNICEF concluded childhood well-being in the UK was the lowest of the 21 rich countries included in the research (UNICEF 2007). A follow-up report in the UK, Spain and Sweden indicated children's well-being 'centres on time with a happy, stable family, having good friends and plenty of things to do, especially outdoors' (Ipsos MORI and Nairn 2011: 1). Material possessions did not feature highly in children's descriptions of things that made them happy and were not seen as essential to well-being. The only exception to this was poor children in the UK, where parents felt compelled to keep purchasing consumer goods, sometimes to compensate for relationship problems and social insecurity, whilst struggling to spend time participating in creative or sporting activities with their children. Often this was due to work-related reasons, in particular long working hours, either due to economic necessity or the demands of the job. In comparison, parents in Spain and Sweden appeared to feel much less pressure to consume, and material goods were less central to family life. While UK parents were regular purchasers of status goods, this was almost totally absent in Spain and Sweden.

For parents in the UK, the purchase and display of consumer goods seems to be equated with good parenting. Power (2005: 654) found a similar situation in Canada and suggests the desire to fulfil the consumer aspirations of their children is 'not simply a materialistic impulse, but a fervent wish to be a better mother and a better citizen.' This illustrates how low-income mothers may experience contested identities: limited financial resources constrain consumption opportunities and increase risk of perceived social disapproval.

Living in such a society puts pressure on all groups, and even amongst those who have achieved goals of material wealth, large numbers remain unhappy and unsatisfied (Carlisle and Hanlon 2007). Poorer individuals are prevented from participating fully in consumer activities that are now so pertinent to our everyday lives and feelings of social acceptance. Purchasing the latest brands and gadgets and keeping up with fashion trends is difficult for those managing a tight budget. For families, the affordability of the 'aspirational lifestyle' is exacerbated: children are particularly susceptible to peer pressure to consume, which they then exert on their parents (Hamilton and Catterall 2006). For lone parent households the combined pressure of low income and the pressure to consume for and via children can make coping financially difficult.

Far from being passive, mothers employ various coping mechanisms to overcome the potential negative consequences of poverty (Hamilton and Catterall 2008). Strategies may include shopping in second-hand markets or relying on support from family and friends. Individuals sacrifice heating their homes to buy birthday presents for their child's friends, and prioritize new clothes for their children over much-needed items for themselves in an attempt to disguise their poverty from their children and from outsiders to the family (Jury and Bianchi 2008). Borrowing money from doorstep lenders or other institutions is another common method for allowing spending on consumer items. These actions have been described as 'masking strategies' used to hide poverty from outsiders to avoid stigma or bullying (Hamilton and Catterall 2006).

In the findings, we present the lived experience of low-income mothers in Scotland and Northern Ireland.

Reflection on methods

In the remainder of this chapter, we focus on two research projects: Hamilton's (2005) study exploring the coping strategies employed by low-income families in Northern Ireland and Glass's (2011) study focusing on poverty in Scotland.

Hamilton interviewed 30 low-income families from urban areas of Northern Ireland (all with at least one child under the age of 18). Twenty-four lone parent families and six two-parent families participated. Interviews were held within family homes to ensure a comfortable, private environment. In 21 families, the parent(s) was interviewed and in nine families it was possible to arrange an interview with parent(s) and children (aged 11–18) together. Participants were recruited purposefully via a market research agency.

Glass held four discussion groups totalling 27 individuals in community organizations in Glasgow with participants volunteering involvement in an opportunity sample. Emails were sent and notices were placed in the premises of four organizations – a community group for refugees and asylum seekers, a Muslim women's resource centre, a drop-in centre for women and a community radio station. All but two participants were female and most had children. The group environment was useful for obtaining information on a wide range of topics, although the lack of anonymity was a barrier to gaining detailed insights into personal family life. This is one instance where the studies complement each other.

Both studies adopted a thematic approach to coding. Our analysis here is based on a cross-study comparison as we brought together datasets to identify common patterns. Although some fathers were included in both studies, here we focus on only the mothers.

There were various differences in the two studies including recruitment technique (purposeful sampling via a market research agency versus opportunity sampling via existing networks), profile of informants (all white UK versus ethnically diverse), data collection method (individual/family interviews versus focus groups), location (homes versus community organization), country (Northern Ireland versus Scotland) and date of research (2005 versus 2011). It is also worth noting the different perspectives of the researchers; the Northern Ireland study was conducted by a PhD researcher (at the time) in association with an academic institution and the Glasgow study was conducted by a consultant for a charitable organization. Despite these contrasts, there are very strong parallels in the findings and both demonstrate the difficulties encountered by mothers living in poverty within consumer culture.

Findings: mothering in poverty and lived experience in consumer culture

The pressure felt to conform to consumer culture was a dominant theme in both studies. A feeling of helplessness and struggle emerged, particularly in families on benefits or the minimum wage as they struggled to cope with financial difficulties and the emotional hardship of not being able to consume at the same rate as societal norms. Consistent with evidence of a problematic labour market, the majority of participants felt remaining in the home to care for their children was the best route for them:

> …it's hard for me to get a job because I wouldn't have a babysitter so I could only work the hours that the kids would be in school and it's hard to get a job fitting around that. And because I've no transport, it's hard to find a job even if they were going to accommodate the hours you would need to get the kids to school and then go on to work.
>
> [Northern Ireland]

> I looked at a cleaning job at the weekend, you'd earn maybe £20 a week and £20 would only get you one day's dinners, you'd really need to go out and do four different cleaning jobs to get any benefit, to be honest £20 a week is not worth the hassle half the time.
>
> [Northern Ireland]

Extra pressures are placed on lone mothers as the sole potential wage-earner within the family. To illustrate, Louise, a 25-year-old lone mother with a five-year-old daughter, discussed how comparing her situation with that of her friends and family accentuated feelings of relative disadvantage:

I'm not as well off as some of them; I'm the only one that doesn't have a partner. Sometimes I would find it hard if they were all doing something and they'd say 'do you want to come and do this? Do you want to come and do that?' And even though they know you don't get very much money a week they forget because they get money and they have their partner bringing an extra wage into the house. I have to remind them of that sometimes, I'm the only one here while they have two incomes.

[Northern Ireland]

Both studies reveal some low-income consumers put a great deal of effort into fighting the negative stereotype of poverty. Attempts to disguise or mask poverty are common through portrayal of an image that minimizes visible signs of social difference. This masking strategy was found both outside and within the family. Thus the family united in attempting to reduce the visibility of poverty to outsiders, while parents also tried to shield their children from the effects of poverty. Consistent with Ipsos MORI and Nairn (2011), masking poverty from outsiders was especially important for the children in the study who did not want to appear different from their peers.

Less noted in the literature is the subsequent effect on parents' behaviour. Many discussed feeling pressure to keep up with other parents in terms of buying goods, which was reasoned to be for the child's benefit – to keep them up-to-date with their peers.

I remember my boy...he wouldnae put cheap trainers on his feet. And my man was like that, 'look he's at it', and I said 'he's no at it because that can cause a fight, coz if he's got cheap trainers he'll get slagged [teased] and they'll end up fighting so save a lot of hassle and just get him a decent pair of trainers'.

[Scotland]

If I buy them cheap stuff they won't wear them, they're only going to be laughed at in the street, you buy stuff for the kids so as they're not going to be bullied.

[Northern Ireland]

However, the idea of competing with others around them extended beyond the realms of children. It was not so much a need to be better than others, but more a case of seeking to match them, as a way of proving your worth:

...a 'keeping up with the Joneses' mentality, you know, being in competition with their neighbours or their children's friends.

[Scotland]

There always seems to be a lot of this kind of competition around now...what you're wearing, what your house is like, what food you offer guests when they come...And the bigger house, the bigger car, the bigger...everything's become a competition.

[Scotland]

These low-income consumers employed a variety of coping strategies to help them deal with and reduce the negative consequences arising from their disadvantaged position in the marketplace. Behavioural coping mechanisms included looking for discounted goods, shopping online so as to avoid the inevitable demands of children, engaging in price comparisons or using credit.

Both studies found self-sacrifice on the part of the parents: particular purchases or certain people were prioritized, with many mothers suggesting family consumption was structured around children. Some mothers suggest their own lives were on hold until their children were older. Part of this was down to the strength of so-called 'pester power', but also to a learned connection (imposed by a consumerist society) between being a good provider and being a good parent. Parents showed signs of distress and guilt at being unable to provide everything for their child and being seen as a deficient provider.

> You put yourself – especially women I think – you put yourself doon [down] all the time, you put your weans [children] and your man ahead, get them, and you can do without.
>
> [Scotland]

> I tend to buy what they eat and I would sort of skimp on my own stuff.
>
> [Northern Ireland]

> [Two year-old son] gets a lot of my shopping money, he gets a lot of clothes. I can't afford to buy clothes for me and him.
>
> [Northern Ireland]

The Glasgow study saw four community groups cited as a source of support helping them deal with many of the pressures arising from living in a consumer society. They felt they could open up to other members about their financial struggles often more than they could to their own families. That coping strategies and tips can be shared meant 'there are so many ideas going around and that helps a lot'. Contact with other members who could relate to an individual's situation was similarly beneficial. Perhaps it is because of the tendency towards social comparison that support groups like this are so effective – by comparing oneself with others who have been or are currently in the same situation, the situation is normalized and the individual no longer feels ostracized from society by their apparent failure to cope.

> We can share, so that way you don't think 'well I'm the only one, nobody else does it'.
>
> [Scotland]

> Somebody's always been there…instead of burying your head in the sand you have to say 'look, you've done it for so many years: you need to face it now, I've been there, I done that, so this is what I did'…Everyone can get a wee bit of advice because most people have been there in their years.
>
> [Scotland]

In contrast, many in the Northern Ireland study experienced feelings of isolation and few were members of local community groups. For example, Eva (aged 45), having left her husband three years prior to the interview after 25 years of marriage, now lives alone with her 12-year-old daughter:

> At the minute I'm very lonely...and when you get to my age you're nearly put on the shelf, you can't get jobs or nothing...there's nothing really for you. At the minute I'm just existing, I get her to school in the morning and I do my housework and I sit here.
>
> [Northern Ireland]

Although Eva indicated she would like to become involved in community activity, she wasn't aware of anything available that would be appropriate. Many others indicated a similar lack of awareness of opportunities for community involvement in their local areas. For others, inability to become involved in local organizations was driven by practical considerations:

> I used to go to the women's group in the community centre but they always wanted you to go away for weekends and I couldn't do that...I had no-one to mind the kids so I just left. It was free too, they were paying for it but I couldn't go.
>
> [Northern Ireland]

This was one of the central differences between the studies and raises important implications in terms of the social value created by community involvement. We discuss implications in greater detail in the following section.

Policy implications

Focusing on quality work requires encouraging payment of living wages that do not necessitate excessive hours[3] in order to make ends meet; enabling employees to undertake other activities in their communities and meet other family responsibilities; imparting the security that allows people to focus on factors of life that contribute to their wellbeing and collective prosperity; and facilitating progression. Regulation is important to compensate for unequal power – a relatively unfettered labour market has allowed in-work poverty to increase. Individuals equally need support to gain traction in the labour market – collective mechanisms such as employee ownership, trade unions or producer co-operatives help ensure standards are determined by employees themselves. Public policy needs to not only enhance women's skills so they are relevant to those demanded by quality employment, but also creatively recognize the skills women already have by virtue of being mothers – time management, problem solving, budgeting, caring, logistics management and so on.

Carlisle *et al.* (2008: 365) argue for more assistance to communities to develop their own cultural assets, identities and sense of belonging, thereby reducing desires formed according to the tastes of others, and helping people 'move beyond the glossy illusions of the good life represented by modern consumer capitalism'. Policies, such as planning policies, need to be amended to position communities and their priorities at the apex of decision-making. This means directing state revenue to areas and projects that people themselves determine. This would incorporate community priorities into decision-making, ensuring their values are met in allocating collective resources. Local environs also need to be conducive to people coming together – if there is not the physical space to share, engage and deliberate, there will never be the 'head space' for doing so. Community spaces – rather than those for shopping – need to be prioritized by planning and economic development.

Conclusion

Consumerism places pressure on mothers to make enough money to provide for themselves and their families to fully participate in society. The growth of materialism and individualism, seemingly inevitable in capitalist society, aggravates the negative impact of being relatively poor, undermining social relationships and intensifying the importance of money in measuring an individual's self-worth (Eckersley 2005). Using consumer goods for self-definition demonstrates how, in our society, consumption provides meaning and purpose in life that is not freely available elsewhere (Carlisle and Hanlon 2007). Yet promotion of a certain sought-after lifestyle through the purchase of goods may represent 'cultural fraud' as these purchases do not in fact automatically lead to happiness (Eckersley 2005). Instead they encourage aspirations and goals that are unhealthy because they are not attainable. By definition, consumerist aspirations are less achievable for those with lower disposable income, leading to acute frustration and stress in these groups. At the same time, recent discourse around 'chav' culture has added new terminology which serves to further stigmatize mothers in poverty. For example, Tyler's (2008) article, entitled 'Chav mum chav scum', describes how stereotypes about the 'chav' mum are used to 'classify bodies according to more or less desirable forms of reproduction' (p. 29). This reinforces the difficulty of achieving the identity of good mother whilst experiencing poverty.

The inequality in UK society, alongside social barriers, places a huge strain on individuals who cannot achieve the same standard of living as those who are wealthier. However, a shift to some of the policies outlined above may offer potential for this experience of contested identity to be resolved. Communities will develop and implement their own solutions more energetically when they are free from stigma. Focusing on assets rather than deficits enables a shift in how policy makers view people experiencing poverty and vulnerable communities; valuing their contribution to the economy and society (for example, through mothering), and recognizing skills, activities and roles that are not based around simply increasing one's own income. In turn, communities (not material goods) will be valued as a source of energy, resilience and identity. Future research could focus on mothers outside the mainstream who have achieved ways of identity-making that are not focused on consumerism. In line with our approach in this chapter, qualitative studies that profile alternative approaches to motherhood whilst experiencing poverty would be a welcome contribution.

Notes

1 This refers to a household income that is less than 60 per cent of the median UK household income in that year.
2 Other groups face a similar situation including the long-term unemployed, certain ethnic minorities, those whose language or appearance does not 'fit', people experiencing mental health or people with criminal records (Sanderson 2006).
3 The European working time directive – which the UK has opted out of – should be used as a benchmark for an acceptable working week. If people need to work beyond this to earn enough to live with dignity and participate in consumer culture, their wages are clearly too low.

References

Baudrillard, J. (1998) *The Consumer Society*, London: Sage.
Bauman, Z. (2005) *Work, Consumerism and the New Poor*, Buckingham: Open University Press.
Carlisle, S. and Hanlon, P. (2007) 'Well-being and consumer culture: a different kind of public health problem?', *Health Promotion International*, 22:3, 261–8.
Carlisle, S., Hanlon, P. and Hannah, M. (2008) 'Status, taste and distinction in consumer culture: acknowledging the symbolic dimensions of inequality', *Public Health*, 122:6, 631–7.
Christopher, K. (2004) 'Welfare as we [don't] know it: a review and feminist critique of welfare reform research in the United States', *Feminist Economics*, 10:2, 143–71.
Darley, W. K. and Johnson, D. M. (1985) 'A contemporary analysis of the low income consumer: an international perspective'. In C. T. Tan and J. N. Sheth (eds), *Historical Perspectives in Consumer Research: National and International Perspectives*, Provo, UT: Association for Consumer Research, 206–10.
Department of Work and Pensions (DWP) (2009) 'Households Below Average Income: An Analysis of the Income Distribution 1994/95 – 2008/09', Office for National Statistics   http://statistics.dwp.gov.uk/asd/hbai/hbai_2009/pdf_files/full_hbai10.pdf (accessed 29 November 2010).
Dittmar, H. (2008) *Consumer Culture, Identity and Well-Being: the Search for the 'Good Life' and the 'Body Perfect'*, East Sussex: Psychology Press.
Eckersley, R. (2005) 'Is modern Western culture a health hazard?', *International Journal of Epidemiology*, 35, 252–8.
Escott, K. and Oxfam (2007) 'From getting by to getting on: women's employment and local regeneration programmes', RENEW Northwest: Oxfam.
Gabriel, Y. and Lang, T. (2006) *The Unmanageable Consumer: Contemporary Consumption and its Fragmentation*, 2nd edition, London: Sage.
Glass, L. (2011) 'Consumer pressure – the influence of children and "keeping up with the Joneses"', Unpublished report, Oxfam UK Poverty Programme.
Goos, M. and Manning, A. (2007) 'Lousy and lovely jobs: the rising polarization of work in Britain', *Review of Economics and Statistics*, 89:1, 118–33.
Hamilton, C. (2004) *Growth Fetish*, London: Pluto Press.
Hamilton, K. (2005) *Low-income Families: Coping with Consumer Disadvantage*, PhD thesis, Belfast: Queen's University.
Hamilton, K. and Catterall, M. (2006) 'Consuming love in poor families: children's influence on consumption decisions', *Journal of Marketing Management*, 22, 1025–46.

Hamilton, K. and Catterall, M. (2008) '"I can do it": consumer coping and poverty,' in A.Y. Lee and D. Soman (eds), *Advances in Consumer Research* 35, Duluth, MN: Association for Consumer Research, 551–6.

Helms, G. and Cumbers, A. (2005) 'Regulating the New Urban Poor: Local Labour Market Control in an Old Industrial City'. Centre for Public Policy for Regions (ed.) Discussion Paper, Glasgow, www.cppr.ac.uk/centres/cppr/publications (accessed 25 January 2010).

Himmelweit, S. (2004) 'Lone mothers: what is to be done? Introduction', *Feminist Economics*, 10:2, 237–40.

Ipsos MORI and Nairn, A. (2011) *Children's Well-being in UK, Sweden and Spain: The Role of Inequality and Materialism*, London: Ipsos MORI.

Joseph Rowntree Foundation (2011) *Monitoring Poverty and Social Exclusion 2011*, York: Joseph Rowntree Foundation.

Jury, R. and Bianchi, L. (2008) *Heat or Eat?: Women's Experience of Poverty in Scotland Today*, Glasgow: The Poverty Alliance.

Lawlor, E., Kersley, H. and Steed, S. (2009) *A Bit Rich: Calculating the Real Value to Society of Different Professions*, London: New Economics Foundation.

May, V. (2008) 'On being a "good" mother: the moral presentation of self in written life stories,' *Sociology*, 42:3, 470–86.

McCormack, K. (2005) 'Stratified reproduction and poor women's resistance,' *Gender & Society*, 19:5, 660–79.

NOMIS (2010) *Labour Market Profile – Glasgow City*, https://www.nomisweb.co.uk/reports/lmp/la/2038432136/report.aspx?pc=G12%209UY#tabempocc (accessed 20 July 2010).

OECD (2010) *Putting in Place Jobs That Last*, Paris: OECD.

Oxfam International and European Women's Lobby (2010) *An Invisible Crisis? Women's Poverty and Social Exclusion in the European Union at a Time of Recession*, http://www.oxfam.org.uk/resources/policy/economic_crisis/economic-crisis-women-poverty-exclusion-eu.html (accessed 11 August 2010).

Power, E. (2005) 'The unfreedom of being Other: Canadian lone mothers' experiences of poverty and life "on the cheque"', *Sociology*, 39:4, 643–66.

Sanderson, I. (2006) 'Worklessness in deprived neighbourhoods: a review of evidence'. In *Report for the Neighbourhood Renewal Unit*, London: Department for Communities and Local Government, http://www.communities.gov.uk/documents/communities/pdf/151696.pdf (accessed 15 August 2011).

Silva, E. B. (1996) *Good enough Mothering? Feminist Perspectives on Lone Mothering*, London: Routledge.

Spencer, T. (2008) *Low Pay and In-Work Poverty in Scotland*, Scottish Government, http://www.scotland.gov.uk/Publications/2009/01/29150444/5 (accessed 20 July 2010).

Tyler, I. (2008) '"Chav mum chav scum": class disgust in contemporary Britain', *Feminist Media Studies*, 8:1, 17–34.

UNICEF (2007) *Child Poverty in Perspective: an Overview of Child Well-Being in Rich Countries*, Innocenti Report Card 7, Florence: Innocenti Research Centre.

Veblen, T. (1899) *Conspicuous Consumption*, London: Penguin Books.

Wilson, H. and Huntington, A. (2006) 'Deviant (M)others: the construction of teenage motherhood in contemporary discourse', *Journal of Social Policy*, 35:1, 59–76.

16 On markets and motherhood

The case of American mothers of children adopted from China

Amy E. Traver

Introduction

Adoption and markets exist in tense relationship. From cases of baby selling and bribery to the proliferation of adoption-themed baby goods, adoptive family construction is often likened or linked to markets. At the same time, adoption must also be recognized as a uniquely typical, though oft contested, means to care and kinship. As such, it is also counterposed to market forces. Consequently, adoption provides insight into what Dorow (2002) describes as the false dichotomy between familism and the market; revealing how discourses and practices of care and consumption are both informed by and reliant on each other.

This chapter builds on that insight. Drawing on original data gathered via in-depth interviews with more than 90 Americans interested or involved in an international adoption from China, it reveals how adopters: 1) employ the language and logic of markets in their adoption decision-making, and 2) engage in adoption-oriented consumption to convey care and kinship in the face of hegemonic, biological conceptions of family. To do so, this chapter focuses on White American adoptive *mothers*, who tend to lead the adoption decision-making and adoption-oriented consumption in their families (Gailey 2000), and whose status as mothers is often complicated by 'questions of faltering maternity – of failed reproduction and proper mothering' (Eng 2003:22).

To begin this chapter, I synthesize the literature on adoption and markets with the literature on consumption and maternal practice. I then review the methods employed in my research. After this, I present my data temporally; focusing first on the manner in which White American women employ the language and logic of markets in their decision to adopt from China, and then on how they consume to convey care and kinship after so deciding. I conclude with final thoughts and directions for future research.

Review of the literature

In *Pricing the Priceless Child*, Zelizer (1985) describes how children, childhood, and markets are inextricably linked in the United States. Using historical data, she traces the manner in which nineteenth century efforts to abolish child labor did little to protect American children from market forces; in fact, by stripping children of their economic agency and utility, these efforts only repositioned children as sentimental objects of unforeseen value. To exemplify this, Zelizer highlights related changes in the American system of child adoption: although laboring adolescent boys were considered most adoptable in the nineteenth century, loveable infant girls emerged as such in the early 1900s. Given the relatively small number of infants available for adoption in the United States, this transition from utilitarian to sentimental adoptions necessarily created an adoption market.

Much has been written about how the American adoption market marginalizes some children (i.e., older children, children of color, children with emotional and/or physical disabilities, and children of ill health) while it privileges parents of means (e.g., Shanley 2001; Bartholet 1999). The more sociological of these writings root this marginalization and privilege in a 'cultural logic' that renders some children and adults more deserving of family than others (Ortiz and Briggs 2003:40; see also Rothman 2005; Modell 1999).

Additional research reveals how these and other domestic market constraints have encouraged many Americans to pursue international adoption, where 'money (changes) hands, agencies are established, baby flights are chartered, (and) tour packages are assembled' across national borders in the pursuit of family (Anagnost 2000:398; see also Ortiz and Briggs 2003; Riley 1997). While most researchers in this area study the racialized macro-level inequalities that facilitate these transactions (e.g., Dorow 2006a; Rothman 2005), others focus on how international adopters distance their family building from market comparisons (e.g., Yngvesson 2003, 2002, 2000; Dorow 2006a, 2002; Briggs 2003; Ortiz and Briggs 2003; Anagnost 2000; Modell 1999).

It is worth remembering, however, that Zelizer's (1985) thesis is true of all children in the United States and that, as evidenced in the literature on care and consumption, markets have long been a means by which *all* families convey care and kinship. Significantly, given gendered expectations for behavior and the rise of the female consumer, much of the research on care and consumption focuses on women in families (Williams 2001; Collett 2005; Clarke 2004; Miller 1998; DeVault 1991).

Just as women's disproportionate consumption reveals the inequalities that exist *within* families (DeVault 1991), women's – particularly mothers' – consumption also reveals the inequalities that exist *between* families. For instance, research in this area often focuses on how variables like race and class mediate a mother's shopping (Pugh 2009; Hamilton and Catterall 2007). Also revelatory are studies of women who consume from the 'fault lines' of maternal normativity (Ragoné and Twine 2000): working mothers (Pugh 2005); mothers who have experienced pregnancy loss (Layne 2000); foster mothers (Wozniak 2004); and mothers of children with disabilities (Landsman 2004).

Methods

Like many adoption scholars (e.g., Fisher 2003; Rothman 2005), my research reflects both personal and professional interests. In the fall of 2004, my partner and I initiated an adoption from China. Searching for guidance and companionship in the flurry of required paperwork, we began to network, in our immediate area and online, with other families touched by adoption from China. Given my sociological interests in gender, race/ethnicity, identity, and family, I, like Volkman (2003), found myself intellectually and emotionally intrigued by the actions and interactions of these families.

My formal research protocol began shortly thereafter, in January of 2005. Over the course of that calendar year, I conducted semi-structured in-depth interviews with 91 Americans interested or involved in an international adoption from China. Interviewees were located via a snowball sampling technique initiated from a variety of starting points: friends and their acquaintances; calls for participants posted on adoption research sites or in adoption newsletters; and calls for participants distributed via adoption blogs, chat-groups, and listservs. In selecting these starting points, I made a concerted effort to capture the range of China adoption experiences.[1] Most relevant to this analysis is the fact that I divided my sample into three groups of interviewees, each of which symbolized a particular stage of an adoption from China: pre-adoption, in the midst of an adoption or 'waiting,' and post-adoption.[2]

Also beginning in 2005, I read a number of first-person accounts of adoption from China, including books like Karin Evans's (2000) *The Lost Daughters of China* and edited collections like Amy Klatzkin's (1999) *A Passage to the Heart.* These autobiographical texts provide additional insight – in parents' own words – into Americans' international adoptions from China.

I organized all interview transcripts and first-person accounts through a process of open-coding. The same conceptual categories or codes were applied to all data (Emerson, Fretz, and Shaw 1995).

Deciding to adopt from China: the language and logic of markets

According to Dorow (2002:150), international adoption provides a powerful lens into the ways in which 'market and nonmarket sensibilities interrelate.' In this section, I examine the market sensibilities that mediate American international adopters' family-building; focusing, most specifically, on how White American women employ the language and logic of markets as they: 1) decide to adopt internationally, and 2) decide to adopt from China. Like Dorow (2002:165), I present this data without judgment regarding familism or markets; instead, I offer it as evidence of how 'market (discourses) can "invade" care.'

Fisher (2003) reports that most American women pursue adoption after experiencing and seeking medical intervention for impaired fecundity or infertility. As Rothman (2005) indicates, this intervention is generally expensive *and* unsuccessful: despite considerable investments in time, energy, and money, only a small percentage of the women who access assisted reproductive technologies actually become pregnant. Significantly, it is often this ratio of investments-to-results that draws Americans to adoption. Renda, a White mother of two girls under the age of thirteen from China, explains: 'We went through the infertility bit and, you know, after spending a total of about $15,000, I just said, "Hey, stop right here and let's look at adoption."'

Research indicates that many White Americans begin their adoption journey by investigating the viability of a private domestic adoption, as privately-adoptable American children are thought to be the most healthy, young, and racially-similar (i.e., White) children available for their adoption (Dorow 2006b; Ortiz and Briggs 2003). Yet, because the number of White American women willing to relinquish their healthy infants for adoption has declined over the last fifty years, the White American women who *do* relinquish their children for adoption now control 'a desirable commodity in short supply' and as a result, can 'think through the terms under which they might be willing to part with' their children (Sanger 1996:490). For many White Americans interested in adoption, these terms are prohibitive and/or objectionable.

For example, in the United States, a private domestic adoption generally begins when a birthmother selects an adoptive parent(s) from a pool of potential adopters brought forth by her lawyer or adoption agency. Given that they are often older than the average American parent and/or unmarried, most of the White Americans who turn to international adoption doubt their marketability in this domestic pool; Renda again:

> As older parents, PhDs, a bunch of other things, we just weren't really in the mood to try to appeal to a 16-year-old or to put up the façade of the white picket fence, Christianity, and the little fluffy dog in our lives.

Likewise, because a private domestic adoption tends to be more expensive than an international adoption, they also doubt their ability to compete against their wealthier counterparts for a birthmother's attention. Jamie, a White mother of a one-year-old girl from China, explains: 'I didn't really like the process where the birthparents pick people. Other people were putting up bargains like, "Oh, pick me and your child will go to private school and have a pony."'

Additionally, most American birthmothers anticipate contact with their child post-placement: sometimes this expectation translates into written updates about the child; other times it extends to phone-calls and visits with the child (Modell 1999). For many potential American adopters, this contact threatens the exclusivity central to cultural conceptions of parenthood *and* traditional market-oriented transactions (Yngvesson 2003, 2002; Gailey 2000). Tracy, a White mother of three girls under the age of eight from China, explains: 'I'm not a secure person about, you know, open adoptions. Once you're mine, you're mine. We're not going to go back to your biological mother's house for Thanksgiving or Christmas. That's why we chose international.'[3]

The idea that international adoption is the most reliable means to a coherent, bounded family echoes throughout the adoption narratives of American international adopters, regardless of the sending nation from which they eventually adopt (Gailey 2000). Robin, a White mother of a five-year-old girl from China, states: 'International adoption was just a more secure method, in terms of, this is what you do, this is the timetable, and if you follow all the steps, you will have your baby.'

Yet, it might be the act of selecting a sending nation in international adoption that best demonstrates how adoption constructs children *and* parents as commodities of related and relative value. For instance, while multinational agreements like The Hague Adoption Convention have helped to standardize the international adoption process,[4] each sending nation still employs their own health, marital, sex/sexual, economic, and educational standards when evaluating a foreigner's parental fitness (Riley 1997).[5] Similarly, given the unique domestic conditions that necessitate international adoption programs, the age, race/ethnicity, health status, and/or institutional histories of the children made available for adoption tend to vary across sending nations, as well.[6] According to Bartholet (1999), these two realities turn adopters' selection of a sending nation into a veritable market transaction: prospective adopters trade on their parental rankings to gain access to the program that offers the youngest and healthiest children available (see also Rothman 2005; Shanley 2001). Misty, a White mother of a two-year-old girl from China, references her/her husband's positions in that market as she explains their decision to adopt an infant from China:

> A lot of it comes down to who will take you or who will give you closest to what you want for who you are. For us, as older parents, in a lot of programs we would have had to adopt a child who was more like three or four years old.

Given the association between 'choice' and markets, and the way family is frequently conceptualized as a haven from both, most of the White women in my sample conveyed some level of discomfort with their ability to choose a sending nation and, by proxy, a child in international adoption (see also Dorow 2006a; 2002).[7] Margaret, a White waiting parent, exemplifies this as she describes how she came to adopt from China: 'In making the decision I thought, "What kind of baby do I want?" as if I could just go to Walmart. But I thought about it and, truthfully, the answer was, "I don't care." I just want one that needs a mother, you know?'

But, it is often their appraisal of the number of children in need within a sending nation – and the subsequent size and success of that nation's international adoption program – that informs an American international adopter's choice of a sending nation. Nona, a White pre-adoptive parent, explains her family's selection of China in these terms: 'I guess it's sort of like a market-share thing, where you just know that there are a lot of children available there and, you know, we have a lot of China adoption around us.' Equally important is the perception of how such market share – or need – is generated and managed in each sending nation. Meghan, a White pre-adoptive parent, references ethical concerns as she describes her family's decision to adopt from China:

> We picked China just because of why the children become available, because they are abandoned. I know in Guatemala it was kind of dodgy a few years ago, and I didn't want to get my child off of somebody else's hardship, like if the child was stolen.

Also significant are White American women's perceptions of the reliability, cost, and efficiency of each program. In explaining her decision to adopt from China, Pamela, a White waiting parent, synthesizes all of these concerns: 'So I started researching adoption and in China there is a huge need. The program is also very organized, streamlined, and the cost is the most reasonable, too. It's very practical.'[8]

Adopting from China: care, kinship, and consumption[9]

For the Americans who choose China's international adoption program, the pursuant journey to parenthood consists of complicated paperwork, bi-national scrutiny, and extended periods of waiting. At the time of data collection, most Americans waited 12 to 18 months after initiating an adoption from China to meet and adopt their child.[10]

According to Anagnost (2004), many Americans engage in a 'jubilant flurry of shopping' as they anticipate their adoption from China. Often this shopping is directed at 'ethnically marked commodities' that both 'define the properly prepared parent-consumer' and 'signify the child's "difference"' (p.151). In this section, I extend Anagnost by examining American women's consumption of Chinese cultural objects before *and* after their adoptions from China.[11] In doing so, I evidence how 'care (can also) "invade" the market' (Dorow 2002:165).

In her study of pregnancy loss, Layne (2000:113) shows how women use angel figurines, sonogram images, and baby toys to 'assert their claim that a "real baby" existed' and to 'claim for themselves the social credit to which they feel entitled as real mothers.' After deciding to adopt from China, White American women imbue Chinese cultural objects with similar meanings. For example, absent a positive pregnancy test and a protruding belly, they consume these objects to signal to themselves and to others that they are becoming mothers. Vivian, a White waiting parent, describes how she bought and gifted Chinese cultural objects to announce her emergent motherhood:

> I decided, whoever was left to tell, I would make a big announcement at Christmas. So I bought China related gifts. I bought a bunch of Chinese tea and a China children's calendar and things like that. Then I wrapped everything in red and gold and I bought these pretty chopsticks and used them to tie the ribbon and all. I think word had gotten around the family and I'm pretty sure they pretended not to know. So I said, "This is a guessing game," but they still swear that they were surprised.

Likewise, as they anticipate their adoption, White American women also use Chinese cultural objects to represent their potential child (see also Anagnost 2004). For instance, in an essay titled *The Labor of Waiting*, one American mother of a child adopted from China explains how, during a particularly long and complicated adoption journey, a photo from a book about China came to signify the child that needed her:

(The photo) showed a group of Chinese children standing together, giggling at the photographer. I taped it to my computer and speculated daily which my future daughter might look like. ... No longer how painful the wait – and how heartless the international conditions that prolonged it – that picture promised that if I somehow maintained hope, somewhere out there a child would come to me.

(Kukka 1999:20)

In other words, prior to their adoptions from China, American women consume Chinese cultural objects to affirm their membership in the symbolic community of mothers.

Significantly, White American women continue to consume Chinese cultural objects even after a child has joined their family; however, given the presence of that child in the family, the meaning of this consumption shifts. Where once the objects, themselves, were significant, it is now the *act of displaying* these objects that is central and symbolic. This act of display is intimately bound to conceptions of good mothering; Vivian, again:

I keep thinking of those sorts of stereotypes of mothers in the '50s who were always worried that everything had to be clean and had to be, you know, 'Oh my God, what if you get in an accident and your underwear isn't right?' And I'm sort of thinking, I betcha some Chinese (adoptee) is going to become a comedian and make fun of, you know, 'My mother was so, she was always hanging up these Chinese calendars.'

While the desire to mother well is not unique to these American women, Anagnost (2000) shows how the use of de-contextualized Chinese cultural objects to express and address that desire *is* specific to them. In fact, White American mothers of children adopted from China consume these objects to signal that they are not only *good* mothers, but that they are *better* mothers than an earlier cohort of similar women: the White American mothers who downplayed issues of ethnic/ racial difference in their adoptions of children from Korea during the 1960's and 1970's. Kim, a White waiting parent, mentions this negative reference group as she explains her plans to display Chinese cultural objects in her home:

In our (adoption) agency meeting there was a woman who had been adopted from Korea and it was really wonderful to hear first-hand how, she loves her family dearly but they didn't make her culture a part of their life. I think they had a Korean flag in her bedroom, she described that, and there were a couple of other Korean things in her room, but there was nothing up in the rest of the apartment.

Additionally, as many adult Americans adopted from Korea now relay angry stories of 'growing up thinking they were White like their parents,' this referential activity can also be read as a form of intensive mothering (Trenka 2003:35).

According to Hays (1996:x, 127), intensive mothering is 'a gendered model that advises mothers to expend a tremendous amount of time, energy, and money raising their children' and that expects, as payment for this expenditure, 'the promise of ...long-term intimate ties.' Diane, a White mother of a five-year-old girl from China, defends her consumption and display of Chinese cultural objects by appealing to her daughter's eventual gratitude:

> I think that when your heart's in the right place, that makes up for a lot of stuff and I think what will happen is that twenty years from now Nina (her daughter) will probably say, 'You know, that whole you trying to be Chinese thing was so lame, but I really appreciate you trying.'

Finally, as implied in all of the interview excerpts in this section, American mothers are considered most responsible for the cohesion of the adoptive family (Gailey 2000). Such is evident not just in the actions and emotions conveyed in each excerpt, but also in the words – particularly the singular, first-person pronoun – used to convey them. According to Bourdieu (1977:68), mothers in *all* families are expected to transform family 'from a nominal fiction into a real group whose members are united by intense affective bonds' (see also DeVault 1991). Rothman (2005:39, 37) describes the function of consumption in this transformation; noting that shopping is one way American mothers create 'households as families' and 'make, display, (and) distinguish' family units. Katie, a White mother of a seven-year-old girl from China, exemplifies this as she describes her consumption of Chinese cultural objects to display with family artifacts: 'Because I have a lot of antiques from my family, I wanted to make sure I had something for Sydney (her daughter) that was an antique from her country, from her culture.' In fact, as Laura, a White mother of two girls under the age of three from China, explains, it is often a mother's decontextualized display of these objects that best captures what Bourdieu (1977:68) refers to as her construction of 'family feelings':

> It's a funny story. I decorate my house. I collected all of these cool things to put up for Chinese New Year. For a while we had a Chinese teacher coming in from the city to teach piano to my girls. Anyway, for Chinese New Year he came and my house is all decorated up. I put the Chinese flag out in front and he came in and he just shakes his head. He goes, 'You know, people don't do this in China.' I'm like, 'What? Of course they don't do that in China! It's a minimalist society! They don't carry on and decorate all over the whole house.' And he's like, 'We don't do this in China.' So I thought about it and said, 'Do I want to change that?' And I thought, 'No, because it's how *we* celebrate.'

Discussion and conclusion

Hochschild (2003:42) describes how Americans conceptualize markets and families as 'spacially divided,' 'functionally separate,' and 'culturally distinct' social entities: while markets are regarded as the appropriate space for calculative decision-making and action, families are defined by the seemingly opposite ends of emotional expressivity and care. In contrast to these cultural conceptions, this chapter focuses on the ways in which markets and families intersect in Americans' international adoptions from China. To do so, it focuses on the adoption decision-making and adoption-oriented consumption of White American *women*, who tend to direct both in their families.

Reflecting the phenomenon's temporal structure, this chapter begins with an analysis of White American women's use of the language and logic of markets in their adoption decision-making. This analysis reveals that most White American women decide to adopt internationally after careful consideration of the cost/success ratio of assisted reproductive technologies and the competitive realities of a private domestic adoption. It then shows how, given their subsequent need to select a nation from which to adopt, these women become embedded and engaged in complicated, overlapping, and global assessments of value. Throughout, this analysis demonstrates how markets and market discourses mediate the expression and provision of care in international adoption.

This chapter then segues into an analysis of the ways in which care and kinship mediate White American women's adoption-oriented consumption. This analysis reveals that, after deciding to adopt from China, White American women consume Chinese cultural objects to both claim and proclaim their oft-contested maternal positions. It then shows how, after completing an adoption, American mothers of children adopted from China consume these objects to normalize the bonds of adoptive and multi-ethnic/multi-racial kinship. Thus, this analysis also demonstrates how care mediates White American adoptive mothers' market behaviors.

There remains much to be explored in the area of adoption and markets. Issues begging for future and/or further analysis include the larger organizations and institutions (i.e., the adoption agencies and government offices) that employ market metaphors in their efforts to build families through adoption.[12] At the more micro level, research on how an adopted child's gender, or the presence of biological children, might shape an adoptive mother's consumption could also prove fascinating and fruitful.

Also deserving of further exploration are issues of a more methodological nature; particularly those that pertain to mothers researching aspects of motherhood with which they are intimately familiar. In my case, my own adoption 'provided a sensitizing perspective' to the 'issues of profound personal change' that accompany women's experiences with adoption (Katz 2001a:460). Significantly, this 'sensitizing perspective' provided more than just embodied data; it also informed my research interactions with informants as, quite often, 'a tribe will tell you its secrets if you already know them' (Fox 2004:309). Thus, while many researchers struggle to connect with a community, my intimate participation generated the equally vexing problem of maintaining emotional and objective distance from my subjects and my work (for a similar example, see Reich 2003). Additional exploration of this issue is certainly warranted.

Notes

1 See Katz (2001) for the explanatory benefits of intentionally diversifying a research sample.
2 See Katz (2001) on temporal structure in research design.
3 Dorow (2006a, 2006b, 2002) describes how the 'clean-break' policies and practices of international adoption stand in direct contrast to the increasingly open practices of most American domestic adoptions.
4 The Hague Convention on the Protection of Children and Co-Operation in Respect of Inter-Country Adoption was concluded in 1993 to both standardize and protect the interests of children and prospective parents in international adoption (see 'Overview', http://www.halfthesky.org/about/index.php, accessed 11 March 2008).
5 For example, while foreigners interested in adopting from China have long had to satisfy a range of measures of parental fitness, more stringent measures – including body mass specifications and restrictions on antidepressant use – were instituted in 2006 (Newman and Cathcart 2006).
6 Shanley (2001) explores how this variability is also reflected in a sending nation's program fees.
7 In contrast, Cartwright (2003) describes how some international adopters view this choice as one consolation for their infertility.
8 Gailey (2000) estimates that Americans' international adoptions cost within the range of $25,000–$63,000. In an article titled, 'Why we decided to adopt from China,' *Wall Street Journal* financial reporter Jeff Opdyke (2003) writes that the cost of an adoption from China falls in the *middle* of this range.
9 A version of my analysis of mothers' consumption of Chinese cultural objects was previously published in 'Home(land) décor: China adoptive parents' consumption of Chinese cultural objects for display in their homes' (*Qualitative Sociology* 30.3:201–20).
10 Upon completion, a potential foreign adopter's dossier of paperwork is sent to the China Center for Adoption Affairs (CCAA) for review. After the CCAA completes that review, the potential adopter receives a package of information on the child referred for adoption; this information includes at least one picture of the child, the child's health and development report, and a brief statement about the child's personality. This package of information is called a 'referral.' At writing, most Americans now wait five years for their referral. Adoption typically occurs, in China, four to six weeks after referral.
11 For American parents of children adopted from China, these objects typically fall into three broad categories: art created by Chinese artisans or reflecting a traditional Chinese aesthetic; standard household décor with/of Chinese cultural themes; and Chinese holiday decorations.
12 See Dorow (2006a, 2002) for examples of this research approach.

References

Anagnost, A. (2000) 'Scenes of misrecognition: maternal citizenship in the age of transnational adoption', *Positions* 8.2:389–421.
Anagnost, A (2004) 'Maternal labor in a transnational circuit', in J.S. Taylor, L.L. Layne, and D.F. Wozniak (eds) *Consuming Motherhood*. New Brunswick: Rutgers University Press, 139–67.
Bartholet, E. (1999) *Family Bonds: Adoption, Infertility, and the New World of Child Production*. Boston: Beacon Press.
Bourdieu, P. (1977) *Outline of a Theory of Practice*. Cambridge, UK: Cambridge University Press.

Briggs, L. (2003) 'Mother, child, race, nation: the visual iconography of rescue and the politics of transnational and transracial adoption', *Gender & History* 15.2:179–200.

Cartwright, L. (2003) 'Photographs of "waiting children": the transnational adoption market', *Social Text* 21.1: 83–109.

Clarke, A.J. (2004) 'Maternity and materiality: becoming a mother in consumer culture', in J.S. Taylor, L.L. Layne, and D.F. Wozniak (eds) *Consuming Motherhood.* New Brunswick: Rutgers University Press, 55–71.

Collett, J. (2005) '"What kind of mother am I? Impression management and the social construction of motherhood', *Symbolic Interaction* 28.3, 327–47.

DeVault, M. (1991) *Feeding the Family: the Social Organization of Caring as Gendered Work.* Chicago: University of Chicago Press.

Dorow, S. (2002) '"China 'R' Us"? Care, consumption, and transnationally adopted children', in D. Cook (ed.) *Symbolic Childhood.* New York: Peter Lang Publishers, 149–68.

Dorow, S (2006a) *Transnational Adoption: a Cultural Economy of Race, Gender, and Kinship.* New York: New York University Press.

Dorow, S (2006b) 'Racialized choices: Chinese adoption and the "white noise" of blackness', *Critical Sociology* 32.2–3: 357–79.

Emerson, R., Fretz, R., and Shaw, L. (1995) *Writing Ethnographic Fieldnotes.* Chicago: University of Chicago Press.

Eng, D. (2003) 'Transnational adoption and queer diasporas', *Social Text* 21: 1–37.

Evans, K. (2000) *The Lost Daughters of China: Abandoned Girls, Their Journey to America, and the Search For a Missing Past.* New York: Jeremy T. Archer/Penguin.

Fisher, A. (2003) 'Still "not quite as good as having your own"? Toward a sociology of adoption', *Annual Review of Sociology* 29: 335–61.

Fox, R. (2004) 'Observations and reflections of a perpetual fieldworker, *Annals, American Academy of Political and Social Science* 595: 309–26.

Gailey, C.W. (2000) 'Ideologies of motherhood and kinship in U.S. Adoption', in H. Ragoné and F.W. Twine (eds) *Ideologies and Technologies of Motherhood.* New York: Routledge, 11–55.

Hamilton, K. and Catterall. M. (2007) 'Love and consumption in poor families headed by lone mothers', *Advances in Consumer Research* 34: 559–64.

Hays, S. (1996) *The Cultural Contradictions of Motherhood.* New Haven, CT: Yale University Press.

Hochschild, A.R. (2003) *The Commercialization of Intimate Life: Notes From Home and Work.* Berkeley: University of California Press.

Katz, J. (2001) 'From how to why: on luminous description and causal inference in ethnography (Part I)', *Ethnography* 2.4: 443–73.

Klatzkin, A. (ed.) (1999) *A Passage to the Heart: Writings From Families With Children From China.* St. Paul, MN: Yeong and Yeong Books.

Kukka, C. (1999) 'The labor of waiting' in A. Klatzkin (ed.) *A Passage to the Heart: Writings From Families With Children From China.* St. Paul, MN: Yeong and Yeong Books, 19–20.

Landsman, G. (2004) '"Too bad you got a lemon": Peter Singer, mothers of children with disabilities, and the critique of consumer culture', in J.S. Taylor, L.L. Layne, and D.F. Wozniak (eds) *Consuming Motherhood.* New Brunswick: Rutgers University Press, 100–21.

Layne, L.L. (2000) 'Baby things as fetishes? Memorial goods, simulacra, and the "realness" problem of pregnancy loss', in H. Ragoné and F.W. Twine (eds) *Ideologies and Technologies of Motherhood: Race, Class, Sexuality, Nationalism.* London: Routledge, 111–38.

Miller, D. (1998) *A Theory of Shopping*. Ithaca, NY: Cornell University Press.

Modell, J. (1999) 'Freely given: open adoption and the rhetoric of the gift', in L.L. Layne (ed.) *Transformative Motherhood: on Giving and Getting in a Consumer Culture*. New York: New York University Press, 29–64.

Newman, A. and Cathcart, R. (2006) 'In an adoption hub, China's new rules stir dismay', *The New York Times*, December 24.

Opdyke, J. (2003) 'Why we decided to adopt from China', *The Wall Street Journal*, September 21.

Ortiz, A. and Briggs, L. (2003) 'The culture of poverty, crack babies, and welfare cheats: the making of the "healthy white baby crisis"', *Social Text* 21.3: 39–57.

Pugh, A. (2005) 'Selling Compromise: toys, motherhood and the cultural deal', *Gender & Society* 19: 729–49.

Pugh, A. (2009) *Longing and Belonging: Parents, Children and Consumer Culture*. Berkeley: University of California Press.

Ragoné, H. and Twine, F.W. (2000) 'Introduction: motherhood on the fault lines', in H. Ragoné and F.W. Twine (eds) *Ideologies and Technologies of Motherhood: Race, Class, Sexuality, Nationalism*. New York: Routledge, 1–8.

Reich, J. (2003) 'Pregnant with possibility: reflections on embodiment, access, and inclusion in field research', *Qualitative Sociology* 26.3: 351–67.

Riley, N. (1997) 'American adoptions of Chinese girls: the socio-political matrices of individual decisions', *Women's Studies International Forum* 20.1:87–102.

Rothman, B. (2005) *Weaving a Family: Untangling Race and Adoption*. Boston: Beacon Press.

Sanger, C. (1996) 'Separating from children', *Columbia Law Review* 96.2: 375–517.

Shanley, M. (2001) *Making Babies, Making Families: What Matters Most in an Age of Reproductive Technologies, Surrogacy, Adoption, and Same-Sex and Unwed Parents*. Boston: Beacon Press.

Trenka, J.K. (2003) *The Language of Blood: a Memoir*. Minneapolis, MN: Borealis Books.

Volkman, T. (2003) 'Embodying Chinese culture: transnational adoption in North America', *Social Text* 74.1: 29–55.

Williams, J. (2001) *Unbending Gender: Why Family and Work Conflict and What to Do About It*. New York: Oxford University Press.

Wozniak, D.F. (2004) '"What will I do with all the toys now?" Consumption and the signification of kinship and fostering relationships', in J.S. Taylor, L.L. Layne, and D.F. Wozniak (eds) *Consuming Motherhood*. New Brunswick: Rutgers University Press, 72–99.

Yngvesson, B. (2000) '"Un niña de cualquier color": race and nation in inter-country adoption', in J. Jenson and B. de Sousa Santos (eds) *Globalizing Institutions: Case Studies in Regulation and Innovation*. Burlington, VT: Ashgate Publishing Company, 169–204.

Yngvesson, B. (2002) 'Placing the "Gift Child" in transnational adoption', *Law and Society Review* 36.2: 227–56.

Yngvesson, B. (2003) 'Going "Home": adoption, loss of bearings, and the mythology of roots, *Social Text* 21.1: 7–27.

Zelizer, V. (1985) *Pricing the Priceless Child: the Changing Social Value of Children*. New York: Basic Books, Inc.

17 Spectacular pregnancy loss

The public private lives of the Santorums and Duggars at the intersection of politics, religion and tabloid culture

Linda L. Layne

Introduction

In *Transformative Motherhood: On Giving and Getting in a Consumer Culture* (Layne 1999) and *Consuming Motherhood* (Taylor, Layne and Wozniak 2004), the examples of 'non-normative motherhood' we studied were contested because the mothers were judged to be lacking in some way. They did not count as 'real' mothers because their children were not genetically related to them (adoption, fostering, gestational surrogacy); because they received remuneration for their mothering (fostering); because their children didn't measure up because they had died before or shortly after birth; or because they were born with disabilities. In this chapter, I focus on two celebrities, Karen Santorum and Michelle Duggar, whose motherhood has been contested, not for falling short of the norm, but for exceeding it – for going too far, for crossing the line. These women have been criticized in the press and in the blogosphere for alleged maternal excesses including their excessively large families. Karen has eight children, Michelle 19, compared with the US average of 2.06 in 2011.[1] They have also been criticized for not knowing when enough is enough, continuing to get pregnant in their late forties thereby increasing the likelihood of reproductive harms. As a result of their late-in-life pregnancies, both women faced life-threatening illnesses and both produced babies with severe health problems. Karen Santorum's eighth child, Bella, was born when Karen was 48, with Trisomy 18, a severe birth defect, the primary cause of which is advanced maternal age; Michelle was 44 when her 19th child had to be delivered at 25 weeks gestation, weighing only 1.6 oz. In addition to these births, both women suffered a second-trimester pregnancy loss. It is the criticism they received for the hyperbolic way they (and their husbands) handled their pregnancy losses and for their willingness to make their family life public on which I focus in this chapter. I employ the concepts of 'the canny', 'the uncanny', and 'tabloid culture' to help explain why the practices they engaged in following their losses evoked such strong, mostly negative, feelings. I conclude by considering whether such spectacular losses enhance public understanding of pregnancy loss or reinforce social taboos.

'"Tabloid culture", characterized by an "emphasis on spectacle and excess", has permeated "television and online media which generate much of the everyday news coverage"' (Biressi and Nunn 2008:2). Tabloid journalism in its many forms 'personalises', 'thrives on sensation and scandal', and privileges the visual (Örnebring and Jonsson 2008:23). Some of the sensations capitalized on by tabloid culture are the same as those evoked by 'the uncanny' – things, events, or circumstances which we experience as 'eerie, creepy, and weird'. 'The uncanny' *(unheimlich)* refers to things which are experienced as 'unhomey, unfamiliar' (Freud n.d.:375), whereas 'the canny' *(heimlich)* refers to 'belonging to the house or the family...familiar, intimate....arousing a sense of peaceful pleasure and security' (Freud 1949:371–2). Paradoxically, the notion of 'the canny' also refers to that which is 'concealed, kept from sight', such as those intimate things inside one's house that cannot be seen by outsiders (1949:129). The Santorums' and Duggars' pregnancy losses are remarkable primarily because of the extent to which they brought them out of the secret confines of intimate home (and hospital) life, into public view.

Miscarriages and stillbirths exemplify many qualities of the 'uncanny'. Freud noted that 'uncanniness' is often experienced to the highest degree in relation to death and dead bodies. Babies are perfect exemplars of the 'cosiness' and 'intimacy' of that which 'belongs to the house' (Freud 2003:127). Dead babies are the anything but cosy. Furthermore, in societies like ours which attempt to conceal such unpleasant eventualities, pregnancy losses are especially frightening because they are unknown. Although pregnancy loss occurs in between 10–20 per cent of confirmed pregnancies, because of the cultural taboo surrounding death, until one has a loss, most people have very little familiarity with them. In the US, pregnancy losses and dead babies are generally experienced as disturbing and unseemly by those not directly involved in the loss, and there is great social pressure to keep them concealed. Pregnancy loss support organizations have been fighting this pressure since the mid-1970s. My earlier work involved long-term ethnographic research with a number of these organizations and their members (Layne 2003). In the wake of the post-1960s social movements including the women's, civil and disability rights movements which maintain that people should not be discriminated against because of physical differences, bereaved parents have been asserting that just because their babies differ physically from other people's in that they are born dead or die shortly after birth, they are of equal value to other children and still loved.

Rather than whisking the dead baby away in an effort to spare the mother, as was done in the past, hospital staff now encourage American families to spend time bathing, dressing, holding, speaking and singing to the dead baby. Nurses and/or social workers take pictures of the baby for the family to keep and prepare memory boxes filled with mementoes (Layne 2000a, b, 2001, 2004). Pregnancy loss support organizations encourage bereaved parents to name their baby, no matter how early the loss, and encourage members of their social network to use the name (Layne 2006). After the loss, many families express their grief and assert kinship ties by writing letters or poems to or from their baby and by purchasing consumer goods or services that serve as reminders of, or as surrogates for, the child. I will now describe how the Santorums and Duggars engaged in these recommended practices, in what regards their behaviour differed from the norm, and how their celebrity contributed to the vitriol they encountered.

The Santorums

Karen Garver married the conservative Catholic, Rick Santorum in 1990, the year he was elected to the House of Representatives (1991–1995). This relationship followed a six-year affair Karen had had with the ob/gyn who had delivered her, a man who routinely provided abortions as part of his practice. Although prior to running for Congress, 'Santorum considered himself pro-choice on abortion' (*Huffington Post* 2012), he subsequently became one of its most outspoken opponents, condemning it even in cases of incest or rape. In 1995 he was elected to the Senate (1995–2007) and in late September 1996, while at home with her children (ages five, four, and 15 months), Karen, who was once again pregnant, watched the televized Senate debate where her husband was leading the fight to ban 'partial birth abortion'. When one of the senators opposing the ban explained that it was unjust for 'the men of the Senate' to rule on something they would never have to go through, 'a chill went down [her] spine' as she suddenly realized that as a pregnant woman, it was indeed something she might face (Santorum 2012:26). Less than two weeks later, at a routine ultrasound, with her husband and children present, she learned that the baby she was carrying was a boy who had 'a fatal defect' – a valve in his urethra was not working and so there was no amniotic fluid. She realized this meant hers was 'a pregnancy not unlike the cases used to defend partial birth abortion' (2012:41).

The next day, Karen underwent a painful in-utero fetal surgical procedure that revealed that the baby's kidneys were not working. That evening Karen and Rick decided to name him Gabriel Michael, 'after the two great Archangels…' Thereafter, the family spoke of him and prayed for him by name.

Despite the fact that there is a '100 per cent mortality rate' associated with the condition he had (2012:46), Karen agreed to further painful, unanaesthesized, experimental in-utero fetal surgery. The surgery resulted in an infection which threatened Karen's life, the only cure for which was delivery of the baby who, at 20 weeks, was not viable. He lived 'two whole hours' after being delivered and the Santorums kept him with them in their hospital room the rest of the night, making the most of the short time they had to love and care for him. That night, and the next day at home, the Santorums engaged in all of the recommended practices for dealing with such a loss, practices Karen very likely encountered during the nine years she had worked as a neonatal intensive care nurse.

Pregnancy loss support organizations advise parents who are able to spend time with their dead baby in the hospital to 'speak to your baby. Tell him or her how you feel' (SHARE n.d.). In her memoir, Karen reports, 'we bundled you in a blanket and put a hat on your head to keep you warm. We held you ever so close, sang to you, spoke softly into your perfect little ears, and held your perfect little hands and feet. …We took many pictures and made little hand and foot prints' (2012:80).

The Santorums had the wherewithal to insist on keeping the baby with them from the moment of his birth until his burial the next day – refusing to allow him to be taken to the morgue or picked up by the funeral home. The morning after his birth/death they 'left the hospital with you in our arms'. They took him to Karen's parents' home where they 'spent the entire afternoon …with you in our arms. We talked with you about so many things' (2012:84). Elizabeth (age five) and Jonny (age four) took turns holding him and 'whispered sweet things in your ears, and sang you lullabies'. Karen took pictures of the three children (including Daniel, age 18 months) with their little brother. Allowing their young children to spend time with him was one of the things that most disturbed critics.

One of the reasons bereaved parents want a photo of their dead baby is so that they can hang it in their home amidst their other children's portraits (Layne 2006, 2012) as an assertion of family membership. This was the case for the Santorums. A year after his birth/death, Karen Santorum wrote to Gabriel to assure him that even though she was pregnant again, he would not be forgotten: 'Your pictures will always remain next to your siblings throughout our house' (2012:126).

Clothing is another means of constructing and remembering the personhood of a longed-for baby (Layne 2000a, b, 2001, 2004). Karen reports that though Gabriel never opened his eyes or cried, he was born 'pink and warm'. Keeping him warm became something of a preoccupation for her. In the hospital, she recalls '[we] bundled you in a blanket and put a hat on your head to keep you warm' (2012:80). At home, 'Elizabeth wanted to change your clothes and get you dressed up for your Mass of the Angels. I told her that we had to keep you warm and bundled' (2012:84). The fact that he was clothed made it harder to believe he was dead. Karen describes opening the casket for 'one last look' and how 'seeing you lying there wearing your little blue hand knit hat and sweater made all of this seem as if it were not real' (2012:86). Clothing is also frequently used as a keepsake, a means for keeping the absent, longed-for child present (SHARE n.d.). In the days following the funeral, Karen reports 'holding your blanket as if to feel a part of you' and lists among her 'treasured keepsakes' 'your little hat, undershirt and blanket' (2012:105).

In addition to items like these, that had a direct connection with the child, many bereaved parents report buying or making items after the loss which symbolize their baby, as a way of keeping the missing family member present in their home. Christmas ornaments representing the children are especially common (Layne 2003). Karen placed 'two very special ornaments hanging on the Christmas tree' to 'honour' Gabriel – one a picture of him, 'the other…St. Gabriel the Archangel' (2012:117). Karen also 'put a lot of time into making' a 'beautiful angel wreath' for his grave, recognizing that it was 'the only way [she could] mother' this son (2012:110).

Sometimes, as in the case of the gifts that the Santorums gave each other that Christmas, memorial items are used to place the child into the generational stream of ethnic patrimony (Layne 2000a, b). Karen describes how 'we bought each other St. Gabriel and St. Michael statues in honor of your life. They are extremely beautiful and one of a kind. Both were handmade in Northern Italy, close to PopPop's hometown' (2012:118).

In addition to speaking with the baby while together, many continue to address their babies through letters or poems, many of which are published in pregnancy loss support newsletters. Karen Santorum's book, *Letters to Gabriel*, is a series of letters she wrote to him during the pregnancy and after his birth/death. Some families also believe that their angel baby communicates with them from heaven, usually via signs, often in the form of mundane natural occurrences (Layne 2012). Karen says she feels Gabriel's spirit 'in the gentle breeze that cools us and the sunshine that warms our faces' and little Elizabeth pointed out a 'Gabriel cloud', one with wings (2012:123). Like many members of pregnancy loss support groups, the Santorums believe that their dead baby now acts as a guardian angel for the family. Karen reports 'pray[ing] that you will be there to comfort your Daddy and me' (2012:89). Her other children are glad they now have 'an extra [guardian angel] watching over them'. Elizabeth reported that when she awoke having a bad dream, Gabriel 'helped me not to be afraid and to fall back to sleep' (2012:107–8).

The Duggars

The Duggar family are the stars of a reality television show, *19 Kids and Counting* (formerly *17 Kids and Counting* and *18 Kids and Counting*), which has aired on the TLC[2] channel since 2008 and averages '1–1.5 million viewers…every week' (Duggar 2009:88). Jim Bob (a Republican representative of the Arkansas House of Representatives 1999–2002[3]) and Michelle married when Michelle was 17 and he was 19. They practiced birth control for several years but when she became pregnant while on the pill following the birth of their first child and then miscarried, they decided to leave the number of children they have in God's hands. The result is 'TV's largest family'.

The entire family appears regularly on the *Today Show* (ten appearances as of 2012) and in November 2011 they announced that Michelle was expecting their 20th child in April. On December 8, a 'routine ultrasound' at 19 weeks gestation revealed that the baby had died (probably at about 16 weeks gestation). The TLC camera crew zoomed in on Michelle's tears as she lay on the examination table hearing this news. Footage of Michelle and her husband breaking the news of this loss to their children was used in the fifth season's finale and the footage of her crying during the ultrasound was used in the next season's premiere and aired on the *Today Show.*

According to *People* magazine, 'Michelle's doctor recommended that she allow the miscarriage to occur without using the standard medications that would cause her uterus to contract', i.e., the same medications used for abortion (Dennis 2011a). On December 11, Michelle miscarried at home where, like the Santorums, the family had a private service. Also like the Santorums, and so many members of pregnancy loss support organizations, they named their baby, addressed her orally and in writing, had her photographed, and acquired consumer goods that would remind them of her.

They named her Jubilee Shalom, and like Karen Santorum, Michelle Duggar wrote a letter to her baby. Both the written text and a recording of Michelle reading the letter that was played at the memorial service are posted on the Duggar family website.[4] The Duggars enlisted the services of 'Now I Lay Me Down To Sleep', an organization that recruits professional photographers to take studio-quality photos of dead or dying babies. Two pictures which show what one critic described as the baby's 'mouse-sized appendages' were posted on Twitter by a Duggar cousin and found their way onto a celebrity news website. In one, Michelle is holding the baby's miniscule feet between her thumb and index finger and the slogan, 'There is no foot so small that cannot leave an imprint on this world' is superimposed upon it. The other is captioned 'Michelle holding Jubilee's hand!' In fact, the hand is far too small to hold. It is shown resting upon a portion of the pad of one of Michelle's fingers.

It was these photos that created a public outcry. In the wake of this negative publicity, a family representative told *People* magazine 'the photos were intended for private use only and... were released without the Duggars' consent' (Dennis 2011b). However, copies of these photographs were handed out to the over one hundred people who attended the memorial service and the photos were projected onto a big screen during the event. Michelle also posted the picture of the hand on her blog and told Jubilee in the letter that she plans on hanging the photo (of her hand) 'with all of your siblings' pictures on our baby wall'.

Michelle mentions other memorial goods on her blog. In a hand-written note she explains, 'We have chosen the butterfly to represent our precious baby...She is the quiet, gentle, peaceful picture of new life leaving the cocoon and taking flight to heaven'. The note is illustrated with a pink butterfly and displayed on a background of butterfly-patterned fabric. Michelle also describes the butterfly necklace she now wears and includes a picture of a blanket on which Jubilee's name is embroidered along with several pink butterflies.[5]

Tabloid culture and the uncanny

Tabloids are known as 'scandal sheets' because they publicize behaviour that offends 'propriety', that which is considered, at any given place and time, 'good and proper behaviour'. Both of the pregnancy losses examined here were scandalous. Tellingly, one of the cultural norms the Santorums and Duggars spurned is the same one that tabloids by definition break: they brought to light that which is considered unseemly and improper. In other words, these two celebrity families and the tabloid infrastructure which covers them, moved their dead babies from the realm of 'the canny', that which is 'locked away' and 'inscrutable' (Freud 2003:133), into the realm of 'the uncanny', thereby creating feelings of disquiet and repulsion.

By making the details of how they handled their dead babies public, they created spectators of mass-mediated audiences. Much like reality TV participants, such as the Duggars, the Santorums 'knowingly...display[ed] themselves – or rather images of themselves – to a mass and invisible audience' (Deery 2004:9). These scandals aired not just on 'trash' news outlets (Glynn 2000) but also on 'soft news outlets' (Cashmore 2006:210) and allowed 'viewers the thrill of seeing something intimate and taboo' (Deery 2004:9). In addition, as Deery has noted with respect to reality TV viewers, 'unlike the classic voyeur', who peeks alone, one of the attractions of such mass-mediated displays is that they will be viewed by millions, thus enabling sharing the pleasures of 'water-cooler' gossip and moral outrage (Deery 2004:4, 8).

Tabloid culture thrives on generating feelings – of horror, disgust, moral outrage, disbelief, but also of pity, sympathy, and schadenfreude, relief that it is others, not us, who suffer so. All of these reactions are evident in the public's response to the Santorums' and Duggars' spectacular losses.

The Santorums were criticized shortly after their loss for the way they handled Gabriel (Goldstein 1997) and the story resurfaced in the press from time to time because of Rick's continuing anti-abortion efforts. This horror-inducing story was reintroduced during the US Republican Primaries in 2012 following Santorum's unexpected success in Iowa. Critics focused on the two elements they found most troubling – that 'they slept that night in the hospital with their lifeless baby between them' (Sokolove 2005), and that they brought the dead baby home and allowed their young children to interact with him as they would a living new-born.

During a live Fox television news show, Alan Colmes, a 'liberal' commentator on this conservative television station's payroll, predicted voters would not support Santorum once they learned 'of some of the crazy things he's …done, like taking his two-hour-old baby when it died right after child birth home and played with it so that his other children would know that the child was real' (Santarelli 2012). On MSNBC, the liberal counterpart to Fox, the Pulitzer Prize-winning columnist Eugene Robinson deemed the way they mourned their stillborn child as 'not just weird, but very weird'.

Both the details of what the Santorums had done with their dead baby, and the 'cheap shots' taken by the pundits, generated lots of further publicity for this candidate and provide an excellent example of the symbiotic relationship between celebrities and tabloid culture. Just as brokers churn stocks to generate profits for themselves, the multi-media activity which followed illustrates how 'interest is manufactured around [celebrities] as a means of promoting …media products' (Turner 2004:22).

Santorum appeared on Fox television the same day Colmes insulted him to discuss his acceptance of Colmes' apology (announced on Twitter), and described again what they had done following their baby's death. He repeated this story yet again on camera, with tearful Karen by his side, despite the fact she made it clear she thought it was 'so inappropriate', at a campaign event in Iowa, where he took the opportunity to pitch 'her amazing book' (published in 1998 and reissued in 2012 following the furore stirred up during his campaign). The Santorums, along with their four eldest children, also appeared on the CNN talk show, *Piers Morgan Tonight*, to defend having let these children hold their dead brother.

Rick's 'retelling the story of… the family's unconventional response – taking the body home from the hospital and allowing their other children to cuddle the corpse and say goodbye… evoked squeamishness' (James 2012), i.e., emotional reactions associated with 'the uncanny'. The Internet 'lit up with comments', many describing 'Santorum's story as "weird" or "horrifying"' (James 2012). Comments posted on ABC's website (Fisher 2011) included one that said,

It was the bit about taking a cadaver home from the hospital with them so that their kids could see a dead body and hurt even more than just the knowledge that it died that made him unacceptable presidential material. That's just not normal. It's not what I would consider sane.

Many asserted that everyone is entitled to grieve as they wish but some noted that openness to diversity in private matters (such as ending an unwanted pregnancy or engaging in homosexual acts) is not something the Santorums endorse. For example, one wrote,

> how he and his wife chose to handle the loss of their child, and whatever bizarre method they might have had to handle their grief, it is not right to attack him on this issue. We should accord him the respect to follow his own instincts in this matter. He is not the type to allow other folks this luxury … which is why he is not fit to hold public office!

Others wrote to share details of their own losses and/or chastise critics for their hard-heartedness.

In fact, as we have seen, in holding, speaking to, dressing and taking photos with their dead baby, the Santorums engaged in practices that are encouraged in US hospitals. The only thing they did that was unusual, and no doubt redounds to the privileges of power, was to engage in those practices in the privacy of their own home. Ironically, it was what they did in private that they subsequently described so often in public that led to their pillorization.

One of 126 commentators on the *Daily Beast* website on January 3 expressed this sentiment, 'The whole thing became a grotesque spectacle … the whole bizarre incident should have remained private' (Fernandez 2011). What had been and should have remained 'canny', had moved into the realm of 'the uncanny'. It was the public exposure of that which should be kept secret – the frightening mysterious power of a corpse, but not just any corpse, but that of a new-born, and not just any new-born, but an out-of-place one, one that should have still been safely hidden in the 'secret places of the human body' (Freud 2003:133), the dark confines of its mother's womb, which evoked such horror. But 'the uncanny' is in the eye of the beholder. Gabriel, we can assume, was not experienced in this way by the family members who slept with him and/or held him. Feelings of horror and disgust were evoked in others, in outsiders, the public, who heard about it and conjured the scene in their imaginations.

In reviewing 'the persons and things, the impressions, processes and situations that can arouse an especially strong …sense of the uncanny in us', Freud (2003:135) noted that one of the clearest examples are those settings that cause 'doubt as to whether an apparently animate object is really alive and conversely, whether a lifeless object might not perhaps be animate' (Freud 2003:135). It is precisely this ambiguity which evoked abhorrence (the idea of sleeping with a corpse or allowing children to play with one, i.e., the treating a corpse as if s/he were still animate).

In addition, some, including myself, felt disgust by the way this loss was used for political gain – by those who opposed Santorum's candidacy, and by the Santorums themselves, who seemed so willing to tell the gory details in order to gain publicity and promote their political agenda. This is another line between private and public lives which, when breached, can evoke feelings of revulsion.

The Duggars also actively generated media attention for their loss. Like the Santorums, they discussed their loss repeatedly on the air. They appeared on *The Today Show* eight weeks after the miscarriage to discuss their loss and promote the premiere of their new season. A video montage was shown that included clips of when they had announced the pregnancy on the show and footage of Michelle crying when the ultrasound revealed the baby had died (MSNBC.com). *People* magazine, one of the Duggars' preferred media outlets (94 articles on the family as of May 2012), published regular updates on the miscarriage – when the demise was discovered, the miscarriage took place at home, when the memorial service was planned, and then held, and their Valentine's Day appearance on *The Today Show* where they discussed the loss.

In the Duggars' case, it was the public display of the photos of Jubilee which generated the strongest reactions with headlines like, 'Who would take photographs of their dead baby daughter, and release them?' (Celebitchy 2011). Mainstream outlets and celebrity news sites invite readers to post their responses. As with the Santorums, reactions were polarized. Many found the images disturbing, offensive, out of place. One of the 194 comments posted in response to Celebitchy's article 'Duggar family shares pics at miscarried baby's memorial showing her tiny hands & feet' expressed the following:

> Not just morbid, downright creepy and weird. For those who dispute this, forget the fact it's a miscarried baby, and think: if this was a funeral for one's recently deceased aunt, would it be appropriate to put a picture of the dead person's body on the front of a card?[6]

In addition to a visceral reaction to the images, many of the 1,399 comments posted in response to the *People* magazine article (Dennis 2011b) on the Duggar's memorial service were outraged by what they saw as the family's exploitation of their loss to increase publicity.

> A dead baby is great publicity for your show! I bet a lot of people will watch and you'll make a lot of money. Is pimping out your kids to make money in the Bible? No, it's not. These people make me sick.

Another person agreed, adding, 'People who profit from the death of a baby are disgusting pigs!'. Even supporters worried whether they were 'going to air any of this…on their TLC show'. Of the notorious photos which at the Duggars' behest, cousin Amy deleted from her Twitter feed, this commentator confessed to:

wonder[ing] if they were trying to save those to reveal on their reality show....
It just seems like as nice as these people may be and as much of a tragedy
they're suffering, they're reality stars and that trumps everything. Even if
they don't mean for it to, you know?

(Celebitchy 2011)

Is tabloid culture a good means of raising awareness about pregnancy loss?

In the years since January 16, 1987 when I miscarried at 13 weeks gestation,
I have worked through my scholarship to 'break the silence' (1997) and make
socially visible miscarriage, stillbirth and early infant death. I have done so with
my book, *Motherhood Lost* (2003) and even more explicitly through an 11-
part educational TV series (*Motherhood Lost: Conversations*), two episodes of
which focus specifically on the need for raising public awareness. In *Normalizing
Miscarriage Through Popular Culture*, in conversation with novelist Heather
Swain, we discuss why Heather, and her fictional stand-in, were so ill-prepared
for their miscarriages, why graphic descriptions of miscarriage like the one she
brilliantly renders in her book are necessary, and the pros and cons of her press's
decision to hide the fact that her novel was about a pregnancy loss. In *Making
Loss Visible*, in conversation with artist Joanne Leonard, we discuss the artwork
Joanne created following a first-trimester loss including some which incorporated
blood from the miscarriage, the strong reactions people had to this work, the
dearth of visual representations of pregnancy loss, and the importance of bringing
pregnancy loss into the light.

Given this, one might think I would be pleased with the attention these two
celebrity losses generated, but the way these losses were spun and churned by a
thoroughly tabloidized media industry (with full cooperation of the protagonists)
makes such mass-mediated losses a double-edged sword.

On the one hand, they did generate some solid reporting on pregnancy and
early infant loss which conveyed statistics on the estimated number of losses that
take place each year in the US, the most frequent causes, and consulted mental
health experts regarding recommended practices following a loss. In addition,
two columnists shared accounts of their own losses. Charles Lane (2012), of the
Washington Post, hoped the media attention to the Santorums' loss had created 'a
teachable moment about neonatal death and stillbirth — and the special grief that
these not-uncommon, but obviously insufficiently understood, tragedies inflict
upon parents'. In this spirit, he shared his own experience nine years earlier of a
stillbirth. He reports that though he had been hesitant 'to hold the lifeless body,
which nurses had wrapped in a blanket and cap like a newborn', he eventually
'cradled Jonathan in his arms and said goodbye'; and was glad to have done so.
He added that 'We, like the Santorums, took a photograph of the baby – lying, as
if asleep, in Cati's arms. We have a framed copy in our bedroom. It's beautiful'.
Jessica Heslam (2012), of the *Boston Herald*, also responded to the attacks on
the Santorums by writing about her devastating loss at 26 weeks gestation. Even

though she was terrified, at the nurse's urgings, she held her daughter, something for which she is 'eternally grateful'.

The widespread coverage on the internet also created opportunities for ordinary people to share their losses and receive sympathy and support. For example, one woman revealed that she had miscarried twins:

> It was difficult having to go through the physical pain but the emotional pain was worse. There is no way in hell I could put my baby's body on display like that for the world to see – especially soon after it happened. I still think about them, have their ultrasound picture and have talked about it with a very close set of friends.

Posts such as this one inevitably generated sympathy.

People also shared their stories of loss directly with Karen and Michelle. One of the reasons Karen Santorum gives for 'revealing this very personal part of our lives' is 'to comfort other parents in their grief' because she and her husband were 'enormously comforted and strengthened by …parents who shared their stories of grief in books and personal letters to us'(2012:12). During their appearance on the *Piers Morgan Show*, Rick, once again plugging Karen's book, asserted, perhaps correctly, that her book 'was so healing for *so* many people in this country, thousands of letters we've gotten' (emphasis original).

Michelle reports that following the memorial service, 'a lot of people shared their experiences with us'

> because sometimes experiencing a miscarriage is swept under the rug. So often people get excited when they hear that you're expecting but then when they hear that you lose the baby ….everybody's just acting like nothing happened. And it's a really hard thing to go through'
>
> (Duggar 2012)

In each of these ways, the star-status of the Santorums and Duggars probably did help raise awareness and increase support for Americans whose wanted pregnancies end without a live baby to bring home.

But the Santorums and Duggars are extremists. That is why they make such good news copy. In fact, over time both families have moved further and further right, and have been rewarded each step of the way with more fame and the opportunities that come with it.

As we have seen, there are striking similarities between politicians and reality TV stars (see also McGinniss 1988). Critics of reality TV often note that participants agree to 'an unusual degree of intimate exposure in the hopes of some monetary gain'. To a certain extent, in both of these cases, 'the family' has become the business. This is especially clear in the Duggars' case. In addition to the TV series, they have two books, a website which sells the books and DVDs of their shows, contains many product endorsements (e.g., for the shoulder to knee swim wear their daughters wear), and advertises the workshops and retreats they run.

But it would be inaccurate to say that monetary gain is their only, or even primary motivation. They are true believers and what motivates them is the opportunity to proselytize, most importantly about their beliefs about abortion. By their own account, 'the challenges of being in the spotlight would be worth it if someday we hear that one girl who was considering an abortion heard us say that children are a blessing from God and decided to keep her baby' (Duggar 2009:85).

The Santorums, too, have blurred the line between family and work. After marrying Rick, Karen gave up her job and, like Michelle, Karen home-schools the children. One result of this is that both families can easily take their children along with them for campaign and/or television appearances. While the Santorums are less frequently criticized for exposing and exploiting their family for money, the monetary gains of holding, or having held, high political office are great. After leaving the Senate in 2007, Santorum 'made more than $3.6 million...as a Washington consultant' (Eggan and Helderman 2012, see also Lewis 2000).

Some reporters remarked upon the political gain Santorum seemed to receive by forefronting his severely disabled youngest child. One attributed the surge he was enjoying in the polls to 'the Bella bounce' following her 'brief hospitalization. It cemented Santorum's "family man" image, and softened some criticisms' (Marlantes 2012). One commentator noted, 'The raw truth is that politicians use whatever tools they have handy to increase their electability – and Rick Santorum is a politician! ... Expect to see lots more of Bella'.

Nonetheless, the Santorums, too, appear to be ardent believers. Karen explains that one of the reasons she decided to publish her book, given the fact that she 'constantly seeks[s] to protect the privacy of our family because of my husband's role as a United States senator and the public life it creates' was because 'if sharing this story can comfort other parents in their grief, then revealing this very personal part of our lives is worth any loss of privacy' (2012:11,12). The other reason was to try to convince other parents who learn that their baby has a fatal defect not to terminate the pregnancy. Though Santorum has said that it is acceptable to have an abortion to save the woman's life because the Bible says it is alright to kill another in self defence (Gross 2004), Karen's published account maintains that she chose not to follow her doctor's advice to take Pitocin to bring on labour, even though her temperature was perilously high, because she felt that even a few days of the terminally ill fetus' life was worth the risk of dying and leaving her three young children motherless. This is the behaviour she wants to model for others:

If parents facing similar, heart-wrenching circumstances can take enough strength and hope from this story to embrace life, then our loss can be transmuted into new life. Through the story of Gabriel's death, perhaps others can live.

(Santorum 2012:13)

Rick Santorum shares this view of the purpose and value of her book. In the *Piers Morgan* interview, he said there are 'people who I know went through with difficult pregnancies because of [the book] and now have little children and older children now as a result of that life that Karen shared'. The story for them, then, is not so much about having and grieving a terminally ill baby, but about convincing others never to terminate a pregnancy even if it is doomed and threatens the mother's life.

For the Santorums and Duggars, it may well be true that there is 'No Such Thing as Bad Publicity'. The extensive media coverage they enjoyed as the result of the controversial ways they handled their pregnancy losses provided a bully pulpit for their political/religious beliefs regarding the evils of birth control and abortion. But if the goal is to increase public awareness about and social support for pregnancy loss, this type of publicity is likely to do as much harm as good. Tabloid culture, which exploits 'the uncanny' for profit, creates greater distance between those who have experienced pregnancy loss and those who have not. The publicity generated around these two celebrity losses was in large measure aimed at attracting readers and viewers by generating feelings of disgust and repulsion. Such publicity is likely to reinforce rather than change social taboos. Unfortunately, given how successful these two families were in garnering multi-media attention by exposing their losses, it seems likely there will be more spectacular losses in our future.

Notes

1   http://www.indexmundi.com/united_states/total_fertility_rate.html (accessed May 18, 2012)
2   See Stephens (2004) on two of TLCs other pro-marriage/pro-family shows and Cashmore (2006) and Jensen (2010) for analyses of other family-focused reality programmes.
3   He decided to run for office after the bill to ban partial birth abortion was voted down in Arkansas (Duggar 2009:82). Shortly after their loss, in the midst of the rekindled controversy regarding the Santorums' loss, the Duggars publicly endorsed Rick Santorum's candidacy.
4   http://www.hollywoodlife.com/2011/12/22/michelle-duggar-jubilee-letter/?v02
5   http://duggarfamily.com/content/article/31215
6   Others discussed the common practice of post-mortem photography during the Victorian era, or argued this was no less creepy than having an open casket.

References

Biressi, A. and Nunn, H. (2008) 'Introduction – origins, definitions and debates: talking about the tabloids', in A. Biressi and H. Nunn (eds) *The Tabloid Culture Reader*, Berkshire: Open University Press, 1–12.

Cashmore, E. (2006) *Celebrity/Culture*. New York: Routledge.

Celebitchy (2011) 'Duggar family shares pics at miscarried baby's memorial showing her tiny hands & feet', December 15,http://www.celebitchy.com/197672/duggar_family_shares_photos_at_miscarried_babys_memorial_showing_the_babys_tiny_hands_feet_pics_are_not_here/#comment-8601529 (accessed May 20, 2012).

CNN (2012) 'Santorums brought baby home to bury him', *Piers Morgan Show*, January 20, http://www.youtube.com/watch?v=GFuQGIhLm1A (accessed May 25, 2012).

Deery, J. (2004) 'Reality TV as advertisement', *Popular Communication*, Feb. 2:1, 1–19.

Dennis, A. (2011a) 'Michelle Duggar resting at home, plans to name child', *People*, December 9.

Dennis, A. (2011b) 'Hundreds attend Jubilee Duggar's memorial, *People*, December 15.

Duggar, M. (2012) 'Healing the family after a miscarriage', March 30, http://parentables. howstuffworks.com/family-matters/healing-family-after-miscarriage.html (accessed May 20, 2012).

Duggar, M. and Duggar, J.B. (2009) *The Duggars: 20 and Counting! Raising One of America's Largest Families–How They Do It*. New York: Howard Books.

Eggan, D. and Helderman, R. (2012) 'Santorum reports millions in income as Washington consultant', *Washington Post*, February 17.

Fernandez, M. (2011) 'The Duggars' photo of their stillborn baby ignites debate', *The Daily Beast*, December 16, http://www.thedailybeast.com/articles/2011/12/16/ the-duggars-s-photo-of-their-stillborn-baby-ignites-debate.html (accessed May 15, 2012).

Fisher, L. (2011) 'Photo of Duggars' stillborn baby released', ABC Newsblogs, December 15, http://abcnews.go.com/blogs/entertainment/2011/12/photo-of-duggars-stillborn-baby-released (accessed May 15, 2012).

Freud, S. (1949) 'The Uncanny', in *Sigmund Freud: Collected Papers, Volume IV*. Trans. J. Riviere. London: Hogarth Press, 368–407.

Freud, S. (2003) *The Uncanny*. Trans. D. Mclintock. New York: Penguin.

Freud, S. (nd) 'The Uncanny', http://www-rohan.sdsu.edu/~amtower/uncanny.html (accessed December 2006).

Fuller, B. (2011) 'Michelle Duggar's heartbreaking letter to miscarried baby Jubilee – listen here', *Holywood Life*, December 22.

Glynn, K. (2000) *Tabloid Culture: Trash Taste, Popular Power, and the Transformation of American Television*, Durham: Duke University Press.

Goldstein, S. (1997) 'Issue turns personal for Santorums: the Senator and his wife had to consider an abortion as she lay near death, *Inquirer*, Washington Bureau, May 4.

Gross, T. (2004) 'Senator Rick Santorum on abortion', August 30. *Fresh Air*, NPR.

Heslam, J. (2012) 'Our bereavement is our own, *Boston Herald*, January 7.

Huffington Post (2012) 'Santorum in '95: 'I was basically pro-choice all my life, until I ran for congress', http://www.huffingtonpost.com/2012/02/21/rick-santorum-abortion_n_1291634.html?ref=politics (accessed May 11, 2012).

James, S. (2012) 'Experts: Rick Santorum grief is typical, but taking body home, unusual' January 6, http://abcnews.go.com/Health/rick-santorum-dead-baby-critics-lambasted-families-grieve/story?id=15306750 (accessed May 11, 2012).

Jensen, T. (2010) 'What kind of mum are you at the moment? *Supernanny* and the psychologyzing of classed embodiment', *Subjectivity* 3:2, 170–92.

Lane, C. (2012) 'Rick Santorum's baby – and mine' *Washington Post*, January 6.

Layne, L.L. (ed.) (1999) *Transformative Motherhood: on Giving and Getting in a Consumer Culture*. New York: New York University Press.

Layne, L.L. (2000a) '"He was a real baby with baby things: a material culture analysis of personhood and pregnancy loss', *Journal of Material Culture* 5:3, 321–45.

Layne, L.L. (2000b) 'Baby things as fetishes?: Memorial goods, simulacra, and the "realness" problem of pregnancy loss', in H. Ragone and F.W. Twine (eds) *Ideologies and Technologies of Motherhood*. New York: Routledge, 111–38.

Layne, L.L. (2001) '"I remember the day I shopped for your layette": goods, fetuses and feminism in the context of pregnancy loss', in D. Miller (ed) *Consumption*. London: Routledge, 251–278.

Layne, L.L. (2003) *Motherhood Lost: a Feminist Account of Pregnancy Loss in America*. New York: Routledge.

Layne, L.L. (2004) 'Making memories: trauma, choice, and consumer culture in the case of pregnancy loss', in J. Taylor, L. Layne and D. Wozniak (eds) *Consuming Motherhood*. New Brunswick: Rutgers University Press, 122–38.

Layne, L.L. (2006) '"Your child deserves a name": possessive individualism and the politics of memory in pregnancy loss', in G. vom Bruck and B. Bodenhorn (eds) *Tropes of Entanglement: Towards an Anthropology of Names and Naming*. Cambridge: Cambridge University Press, 31–50.

Layne, L.L. (2012) '"Troubling the normal": dealing with the canny/uncanny absent presences of "angel babies", in S. Earle, C. Komaromy and L. Layne (eds) *Understanding Reproductive Loss*. Farnham: Ashgate Press, 129–142.

Lewis, C. (2000) *The Buying of the President 2000*. New York: Avon.

Marlantes, L. (2012) 'Is Rick Santorum benefiting from a Bella Bounce?' *Christian Science Monitor*, February 16.

McGinniss, J. (1988) [1969] *The Selling of the President: a Classic Account of the Packaging of a Candidate*. New York: Penguin.

Örnebring, H. and Jonsson, A. (2008) 'Tabloid journalism and the public sphere: a historical perspective on tabloid journalism', in A. Biressi and H. Nunn (eds) *The Tabloid Culture Reader*. Berkshire: Open University Press, 23–33.

Santarelli, C. (2012) 'Alan Colmes called out for "cheap shot" comments about how Santorum dealt with death of baby', theblaze.com, January 2.

Santorum, K. (2012) [1998] *Letters to Gabriel: the True Story of Gabriel Michael Santorum*, San Francisco, CA: Ignatius Press.

SHARE (n.d.) 'Creating memories to last a lifetime', http://www.nationalshare.org/lifetime-memories.html.

Sokolove, M. (2005) 'The Believer', *New York Times Magazine*, May 22.

Stephens, R. (2004) 'Socially soothing stories? Gender, race and class in TLC's *A Wedding Story* and *A Baby Story*', *Understanding Reality Television*. London: Routledge, 191–210.

Taylor, J., Layne, L. and Wozniak, D. (eds) (2004) *Consuming Motherhood*. New Brunswick: Rutgers University Press.

Turner, G. (2004) *Understanding Celebrity*. London: Sage.

18 Pregnancy, privacy and personhood in the consumer socialization of expectant mothers

The VOICE Group[1]
Voicing International Consumer Experiences

Introduction

Many scholars have highlighted the moral discourses surrounding motherhood and mothering. Various studies, including those discussed elsewhere in this section, have explored how a woman's particular *characteristics*, such as income, sexuality, employment, age, or even biological relationship to her children, are translated into judgments about her moral *character* as a mother, or indeed whether she is a 'proper' mother.

Much of this research has focused on mothers already involved in the process of raising children, and from social positions which have been marginalized or stigmatized in some way. In contrast, this chapter explores how contested motherhood identities were experienced as part and parcel of pregnancy for the 'ordinary', heterosexual, middle-class women in Europe and the USA who took part in our interpretive study. We suggest that the public, visible nature of pregnancy serves as a catalyst for transitional tensions, which are part of broader, longer-term socialization processes into the domain of motherhood.

In the remainder of this chapter, we review prior research related to the transition to motherhood and consumer socialization issues around this pivotal stage in a woman's life. We provide a brief outline of our study before presenting findings related to expectant mothers' experiences of the challenges to their own sense of self from other people's assumptions and judgments about them based on their pregnancy.

Theoretical background

Much attention has been paid to children's socialization into the adult world, including that of consumption (Roedder John 1999; Wooten 2006). Less attention has been paid to socialization processes and experiences in other lifecourse stages, even though adults too are human becomings as well as human beings (Ekström 2006), sometimes involved in quite dramatic family lifecycle transitions (Commuri and Gentry 2000; Gentry *et al.* 1995; Hogg *et al.* 2004).

The transition to motherhood appears a rich site for exploration of these issues. Although socialization agents including books, dolls and younger siblings may help girls imagine their mothering selves from an early age, pregnancy remains a 'journey into the unknown' (Oakley 1979), with the transition shaped by interaction with multiple socialization agents. These include but are not limited to medical professionals and experts (Miller 2005); personal networks of family and friends (Fisher *et al.* 2006); online networks (O'Connor and Madge 2004), media offerings such as advice books (Douglas and Michaels 2004; O'Malley *et al.* 2006) and women's magazines (Johnston and Swanson 2003); and the market more broadly (Rothman 1989; VOICE Group 2010a).

The general message from these disparate socialization agents is that there exist 'appropriate, morally underpinned and socially acceptable ways of preparing to become a mother' (Miller 2005). Thus, pregnancy is bound up with issues of identity and conformity as well as excitement and anxiety about the development of new life and responsibility for it. Bailey (1999) refers to pregnancy as a 'narrative pivot' which may reaffirm or change a woman's sense of self, while Banister and Hogg (2006) refer to the different possible selves, some desired and others undesired, ushered in by pregnancy.

Consumer culture theorists have highlighted the embodiment of self (Thompson and Hirschman,1998), and the range of body projects undertaken through practices such as grooming, styling, diet, physical exercise, tattooing and cosmetic surgery (Askegaard *et al.* 2002; Crossley 2006; Murray 2010; Patterson and Schroeder 2010).

Thus, the significant changes to women's bodies wrought by pregnancy may change their relationship with their body, either positively or negatively (Kukla 2005; Ryan *et al.* 2011; Warin *et al.* 2008). Furthermore, such changes to their shape and sense of self do not happen privately, but are witnessed and often commented on by others (O'Malley 2006).

Given these high stake changes, it is hardly surprising that many women 'practice their pregnant selves' through extensive reflection and preparation for birth and consultation (Bailey 1999; O'Malley *et al.* 2006; O'Connor and Madge 2004). Since consumer culture highlights the materiality of experience (Miller 2009), Clarke (2004: 55) notes that:

> From the onset of pregnancy, the conceptualization of motherhood is bound up with facets of provisioning and consumption choices that mark imagined trajectories for both women and infants.

In this context, several studies have highlighted how the consumption choices made as mothers, particularly as women approach the birth of their first child, reflect and generate emergent maternal identities and anxieties (Prothero 2002; Jennings and O'Malley 2003; Thomsen and Sørensen 2006). In this chapter we explore how identity struggles and anxieties are part of women's consumer socialization into motherhood.

Method

This chapter draws on a broader interpretive research project exploring motherhood consumption and experiences, focusing on the transition to motherhood. Our study was undertaken across four countries (Denmark, Ireland, the UK and the USA). It began with each mother-researcher writing an introspective account of her own transition to motherhood and sharing these within the group to sensitize ourselves to the different personal, social and cultural contexts for our experiences, as consumers and mothers-to-be (VOICE 2008). Perhaps unsurprisingly, sharing these introspections also sensitized us to how research participants might feel if consumption issues touched on difficult personal experiences or family relationships. Drawing on reflections from these introspections, interviews were conducted with twenty-five women making the transition to motherhood. Ranging in age from mid twenties to late thirties, most were white, and all were middle-class and in stable, heterosexual relationships.

Participants kept a diary of their pregnancy and baby-related product acquisitions during this time, and also provided photographs of their acquisitions. These diaries and photographs helped to set the agenda for the interviews, conducted towards the end of each woman's pregnancy and then several months after the birth of their first child. These interviews were typically conducted in participants' homes, and this often led to our being shown rooms set aside for the baby and particular baby-related items. Further details of the methodology and other findings are presented elsewhere, including VOICE Group (2008, 2010b). This chapter is based on the pre-birth experiences from the interviews and the authors' introspections, with pseudonyms used throughout.

Findings

Perhaps not surprisingly, the women who were willing to share their stories talked about much-wanted babies, generally from the vantage point of good health, material comfort and stable relationships with the fathers-to-be. Participants' stories also tended to feature broadly supportive family and friends, and some acknowledgement of their economic, social and cultural capital. For example, some participants described how they enjoyed the attention and the public affirmation of their status as mothers-to-be:

Yeah, it's been great, I felt like a VIP. I mean even in a pub, you kind of forget that you even look pregnant and if you're going to the toilet fellas will move out of the way and go 'After you', or women will be 'Oh, you first'. So that was a real novelty, I'm not used to that. You know people's attitude has been really great, you know, 'You sit down' or whatever. I might be feeling fine, but they are just being considerate. That was really nice.

[Sadie, Ireland]

Caroline [UK] also talked about how her pregnancy triggered a gift of second-hand maternity clothes from a relatively distant male colleague whose girlfriend had given birth the previous year.

> That was really sweet…I just thought it was nice…You can understand with family and friends, but when it's a colleague that you're not, I suppose, that close to, then I did think that was really sweet…and it was very nice of them to do it…

As illustrated above, during the interviews, participants expressed a great deal of pleasure and excitement as well as anxiety around becoming a mother. Thus, it is important to emphasize that the following accounts, which focus on the tensions and frustrations our participants experienced, reflect only part of their transition to motherhood. These tensions are presented below in terms of participants' difficulties in accepting discourses of expectant mothers as sacrificing privacy and as one-dimensional, lesser beings whose autonomy and sense of personal style had diminished as their body grew.

Pregnant women as sacrificing privacy

Pregnancies tend to be made public by both the changing shape of a woman's body and an announcement, typically around the end of the first trimester, to family, friends and colleagues. Our participants' stories suggested that being visibly pregnant changed the boundaries between private and public for others more than for mothers: there were various references to people crossing the line, and to 'women's bodies becoming public space' through intrusive comments or unsolicited touching. In some cases these boundaries were crossed at work. Aileen [UK] described how a pregnant woman was an unfamiliar sight in her workplace, leading to a fascination with her size:

> You know, just like 'wow, you're huge!' – don't want to hear it (laughs). And you know like repeated comments about how giant you are, you're just like 'Yes, you mentioned that last week, can you let it go?'

Lotte described her resentment at physical intrusions on her private space at work, especially:

> …this thing about so many people wanting to touch my belly. They don't normally do that…And then one of my male colleagues patted me on my belly a little too often, and I thought 'What do you think I am?' So one day, I patted him on his belly and said: 'Mine is firmer than yours' and he never did it again. Because that's where I draw the line. I didn't like it when 'strangers' – in inverted commas – do that, that is just too intimate. Then you had damn well better ask permission.
>
> [Lotte, Denmark]

When Caroline's husband was given the book *You're Pregnant Too, Mate!* by his friend, she felt her changing body had become subject to an intrusive and unexpected male gaze:

> ...it's written for a guy. It's not something that I would say go and read, because it's written like they're down the pub and they're chatting, and you know the way lads will have a few pints...I was surprised, initially, that he enjoyed it. You know lads laughing at you... and then I look at the bit he's just read and think, OK. It's not the most polite about us girls, but, yeah... the fact that even though it's quite coarse in places, or appeared a bit as I saw it, he thought they were, oh, 'This is fine and this is funny and this is what you do, mate, and this is what happens'.

> [Caroline, UK]

While comments such as these suggested that the visibility of pregnancy allowed others to intrude on their personal space, there was also a sense in which becoming pregnant exposed them to the marketer's gaze and defined them as a target market, even if a reluctant or unsuspecting one. Online purchasing patterns, for example, allowed marketers to profile and target them:

> I've got a Google Mail account and I noticed that all the sort of advertising around is all about babies. It's as if they know that I'm pregnant, that's a bit weird – monitoring my emails?

> [Jenny, UK]

Jenny's uneasiness resonates with recent industry suggestions that consumers' concerns about privacy increasingly focus on companies treating personal data and behavioural data patterns as 'a commodity to be farmed' (Beveridge *et al.* 2012).

Several participants provided examples of how the market had intruded on their personal, intimate or even medical pathways to motherhood; British participants talked about how antenatal classes were 'really a sales pitch for formula', for example, or how preparatory hospital tours emphasized pay-per-view TVs in the ward, while Aileen, an American living in Britain, noted that childbirth in the USA is 'privatised and for profit and intervention is so much more routine' than in the UK.

For some participants, it was not just marketers who framed them as consumers by virtue of their pregnancy; as Mhairi [UK] noted, when people asked her if she was prepared, they were asking what she had bought. She resented this, not only because she had not acquired much earlier in her pregnancy, but also because she didn't share their understanding of what was required:

> ...I suppose preparation can either be buying things or just acquiring things but it's, I think it's also about transition, and how you feel about how your life is going to change.

Pregnant women as less autonomous

In addition to breaches of their personal space, participants described occasions where they felt that being pregnant led to their personal autonomy being undermined by others. While Aileen had less sense of 'strangers monitoring you' in the UK than in her native USA, she still felt self-conscious in a pub with friends, expecting 'someone to give you the old "you shouldn't be here" or, you know, "you're not allowed"'. She provided several examples of 'the kind of well-intentioned, you know, "oh you can't do that" conversations' that she encountered at work. One of her colleagues

> ...kept chickens in her back-yard and she would bring the eggs into work and you could buy them off of her, which was great. So I used to buy eggs from her. But the first time I bought eggs from her [after announcing her pregnancy] she gave me this scary, kind of like finger-waggy 'well you better make sure that you cook those all the way through'!

On another occasion, she was scheduled to visit a farm for work. This upset a colleague with responsibility for health and safety because of 'toxoplasmosis, the risk from lambing':

> And that was fine, I didn't even realise there was a risk. So once I was told...I was ready to kind of work within the boundaries of that, but I still wanted to go, there was no reason not to go. And we really, like, we got into a kind of contentious situation because she wasn't going to let me go and she went so far as to suggest that her best interest, like she was more interested in the welfare of this baby than I was, and I was just like 'lady, you have to watch it', like I was *so* raging... in the end it was fine and I got to go. I made this agreement with her that I would avoid the sheep. But, you know, it was stupid. It was a month before lambing season anyway...

Helen [Denmark] described how she was treated as irresponsible for continuing to play sport during her pregnancy:

> I played volleyball at a reasonably high level until the sixth month. My coach tried to restrict me, he didn't like to let me play the games. I thought he was stupid. I was a grown up woman. I could care for myself. I continued to do fitness training till the day before the birth.

Perhaps not surprisingly, participants talked about challenges to their autonomy in terms of what to consume, or not to consume. Abigail [USA] had been sick a lot during her pregnancy, and:

> ...I just kind of got sick of everyone, you know, everyone had advice. 'Eat this, don't eat that'. 'Do this, just ignore it', 'It's in your head'. It's not in my head [having to be sick]; I have to use the bathroom.

Jenny [UK] talked about how instructions about what to eat made her 'a bit neurotic actually'. For example, she worried about having eaten peanuts before reading guidance to avoid nuts during the early stages of pregnancy in particular. Although she considered some advice 'overcautious' and associated it with 'that nanny state feeling', she also found it hard to ignore.

Despite the rhetoric of choice and empowerment in maternity services (Geiger and Prothero 2007), some participants felt their autonomy was challenged or undermined by encounters with medical practitioners. Terry [USA] was astounded when the nurse-practitioner boyfriend of an employee took it upon himself to tell her how to behave once the baby arrived:

> ...[he] basically said I should breastfeed for a year, and at least a year. And I'm like, who – who are you, you know? You know, you are -- you don't even have breasts, you're not going to be doing this, and I'm going to do the best I can, you know.

Laura highlighted what she described as a paternalistic attitude underpinning the treatment of pregnant women in the Irish medical system. For example, she remembered:

> On meeting the consultant, after numerous tests by different midwives, a production line experience, his first words to me were 'Lie up on the bed and pull your trousers down'. My response: 'Would you like to tell me who you are first?'. His, 'Well, who do you think I am?' Me: 'The hospital porter'. From there on in it got worse.
>
> [Laura, Ireland]

Pregnant women as lesser, one-dimensional beings

Some participants talked about occasions when they felt the multifaceted nature of their identity denied by others due to their pregnancy. Thus, some women described how their professional identities seemed to be swamped by their identity as mothers-to-be. Lotte [Denmark], for example, worked in investment banking and noted that:

> Just because I'm pregnant, doesn't mean that I no longer think that it's interesting to make capital increases. There is so much focus on the fact that you are going to have a child. People kind of forget that you still have a brain, and that you are actually interested in other things. And that's been really annoying and I have very much felt that my worst fear is to be discriminated against at work. That interesting assignments would be taken from you. That's been my biggest fear. That you are put in a pigeonhole, and that's the only thing. This baby thing. And that's really not enough. It hasn't been enough for me, yet. Maybe in two weeks I will feel differently, but so far it is not the only thing in my life.

Mandy [UK] found her employers reluctant to engage in reasonable consultation about workplace changes because they made assumptions about her post-birth career expectations.

> You know, there's a big reorganisation, I'm not happy with my job, blah, blah, blah... But when I raise that sort of issue, it's 'But never mind, you're having a baby'.
>
> [Mandy, UK]

Although she was used to working in an environment which was 'quite masculine', she was shocked to be treated in this way and frustrated that she found asserting herself more difficult than usual because 'you're feeling sleep deprived and you're feeling rubbish anyway'.

It was not only in the workplace that participants felt their identities had been reduced to that of expectant mothers:

> I think what I found starting to happen and what I am fearful of happening after the baby is born is that I am seen as pregnant woman rather than what I do and who I am and all the things that I am used to being.
>
> [Mhairi, UK]

Being defined primarily in terms of their pregnancy sometimes meant that they received less respect from others. Various participants shared horror stories about their encounters with sales assistants fitting them with nursing bras, chiding them for coming too early, 'bossing' or 'bullying' them in the fitting room, and even infantilizing them; as Mhairi [UK], a senior legal professional, noted with incredulity, 'She called me "Toots"!'. She also described how her midwife irritated her by:

> ...encouraging me to write things down because I would forget them... pregnant women often forget things and there would be so much to remember...And I remember thinking, I'm quite good at remembering things (laughs). People tell me things all the time and I seem to cope. And yes, I will write things down if I have to but you don't need to patronise me.

For Nina [Denmark], the advice pages in *Mama*, a magazine for expectant and new mothers, offended her because they addressed her not as a feminist in an egalitarian relationship, but as a woman who would naturally have primary responsibility for her baby:

> Something like: 'if you feel tired and worn out in the evening, have your husband look after the baby, lift your feet, have a happy cocoa and you'll feel much better'. And I just felt like: No, stop! I have no use for that; that I can figure out myself if it comes to that. To me, it's a bit of an old-fashioned view of women. As a mum you're in charge of the child? I have a husband, too, and he is also in charge of the child.

Even close relatives could render pregnant women as less than their full adult selves, as Caroline [UK] described her husband doing:

> ...they've all said it's going to be a girl, so now he's like going around, 'Oh, I'm going to have another one in the house with boots and tights and skirts and berets. Girls, another little girl in the house'.

Pregnant women as sacrificing personal style and taste

While the comments above suggested that participants struggled with the way that pregnancy reduced their social identity to a single dimension, they also talked about the difficulties of creating continuity between their pre-pregnant and pregnant wardrobe. Some participants were not particularly concerned about their wardrobe and were happy to spend a lot of time in loose-fitting casual wear, but others noted that affordable maternity clothes were 'too casual', more like 'weekend-wear', catering 'more to the younger range', or 'made of polyester, nylon stuff'. Megan's [Ireland] employer supplied her with a maternity uniform that was 'absolutely horrendous':

> ...I kind of felt that I looked massive in it and I felt it was uncomfortable, especially the trousers...there were two buttons that you pulled, and there were knots at the back of the buttons, and they were just digging into me. It was just so uncomfortable.

Although frustrations about the limited range of styles available in maternity clothing were not a major preoccupation for participants, some did talk about how this disrupted their sense of self, to the extent that they would need to 'undergo some sort of character change' in order to wear what was readily available. This is hardly surprising, since clothing is a highly visible and routine way of performing one's identity (Thompson and Haytko 1997). Thus, Mhairi [UK] commented that she always chose natural fibres for herself, and did not see why she should now be satisfied with 'nasty, stretchy stuff' during her pregnancy. Similarly, Nina [Denmark] remembered how:

> ...when I was shopping for pregnancy clothes I felt like – it has to be unbelievably feminine. Now I wear practical clothes but in many shops there are flowers and lace all over the clothes. It's like – it has to be unbelievably feminine like 'because now you're pregnant'. I don't like that. It makes me move in the opposite direction.

Discussion and conclusions

The expectant mothers participating in this study talked about many positive aspects of their pregnancy, including the support they received from a range of others. Nonetheless, the stories they told also suggested that the public, visible nature of pregnancy exposed them to various discourses which had implications for their sense of self. These discourses suggested that pregnancy entails sacrifices of privacy, autonomy and personal style, and constitutes mothers-to-be as one-dimensional, lesser beings. The discourses seemed to circulate across the four countries in our study, at least within the middle-class enclaves to which our participants belonged. They also appeared to be part of broader socialization processes into motherhood and mothering.

Consumption practices were embedded in the socialization processes explored in this chapter. Friends, family, colleagues, sales staff, media offerings and medical practitioners served as socialization agents, offering advice or instructing participants about what they should or should not buy or consume, and how they should or should not behave. They also addressed pregnant women in ways that projected particular identities or preoccupations on them. Some of these clearly had a moral and future-orientated character, such as injunctions to avoid food, substances or environments that might have an adverse effect on their unborn baby's health. Other projections had less to do with pregnant women as protectors of their unborn children, and more about pregnancy as a biological or hormonal state which led to functional or intellectual impairment and obliterated any need for continuity in the styling of self.

Participants generally contested these discourses and resisted the identities imposed on them as expectant mothers. In some cases, such as Laura's encounter with the consultant, they challenged them directly and explicitly. In other cases they talked about compromise and negotiation, but they frequently articulated their objections to themselves rather than to others; politeness seemed to be deeply ingrained and many talked about resisting the temptation to be rude to others, even if they felt offended or belittled by them.

By exploring the discourses circulating around a group of middle-class, mainstream expectant mothers in Western Europe and America, this chapter highlights how the processes of constructing and contesting motherhood identities begin before a woman gives birth and extend beyond mothers in marginalized social positions. It has also highlighted the role of consumption in lifecourse socialization processes. This suggests that studies of consumption experiences can serve as a gateway to explorations of broader socialization processes. In this regard, we found the concrete examples provided by acquisition diaries and photographs very helpful in eliciting rich stories of how individual participants' experiences related to broader social and cultural contexts.

Looking beyond this study, there is certainly scope to explore the discourses and consumption practices involved in the socialization of expectant mothers in other cultures and in less privileged circumstances. Indeed, consistent with scholarly interest in anticipatory socialization (Waerdahl 2005), it may also be interesting to explore the discourses of pregnancy that circulate within consumer culture among adolescents and young women before they enter this liminal state themselves.

Note

1 This paper is the result of collective, collaborative research undertaken by members of The VOICE Group – *Voicing International Consumer Experiences*. The members of this group, in alphabetical order, are Andrea Davies, Susan Dobscha, Susi Geiger, Stephanie O'Donohoe, Lisa O'Malley, Andrea Prothero, Elin Brandi Sørensen and Thyra Uth Thomsen.

References

Askegaard, S., Gertsen, M.C. and Langer, R. (2002) 'The body consumed: reflexivity and cosmetic surgery', *Psychology and Marketing*, 19: 793–812.

Bailey, L. (1999) 'Refracted selves? A study of changes in self-identity in the transition to motherhood', *Sociology*, 33: 335–53.

Banister, E. and Hogg, M. (2006) 'Experiencing motherhood: the importance of possible selves to new mothers', in C. Pechmann and L. Price (eds) *Advances in Consumer Research*, 33: 343–4.

Beveridge, A., Cook, C. and Stubbings, A. (2012) *Privacy: From Data to People*. The Futures Company trends: future perspectives.

Clarke, A. (2004) 'Maternity and materiality: becoming a mother in consumer culture', in J.S. Taylor, L.L. Layne and D. Wozniak (eds) *Consuming Motherhood*, New Jersey: Rutgers University Press, 55–71.

Commuri, S. and Gentry, J. (2000) 'Opportunities for family research in marketing', *Academy of Marketing Science Review*, http://www.ansrev/theory/commuri08-00.html. Accessed 31 August 2012.

Crossley, N. (2006) 'In the gym: motives, meaning and moral careers', *Body & Society*, 12(3): 23–50.

Douglas, S. and Michaels, M. (2004) *The Mommy Myth: the Idealization of Motherhood and How it has Undermined all Women*, New York: Free Press.

Ekström, K.M. (2006) 'Consumer socialization revisited', *Research in Consumer Behavior*, 10: 71–98.

Fisher, C., Hauck, Y. and Fenwick, J. (2006) 'How social context impacts on women's fears of childbirth: a Western Australian example', *Social Science & Medicine*, 63: 64–75.

Geiger, S. and Prothero, A. (2007) 'Rhetoric versus reality: exploring consumer empowerment in a maternity setting', *Consumption, Markets and Culture*, 10: 375–400.

Gentry, J.W., Kennedy P.F., Paul C. and Hill, R.P. (1995) 'Family transitions during grief: discontinuities in household consumption patterns', *Journal of Business Research*, 34: 7–79.

Hogg, M., Folkman C., Curasi, C. and Maclaran, P. (2004) 'The (re-)configuration of production and consumption in empty nest households/families', *Consumption, Markets & Culture*, 7: 239–59.

Jennings, R. and O'Malley, L. (2003) 'Motherhood, identity, and consumption', in S. Brown and D. Turley (eds) *European Advances in Consumer Research*, 3: 221.

Johnston, D. and Swanson, D. (2003) 'Invisible mothers: a content analysis of motherhood ideologies and myths in magazines', *Sex Roles*, 49: 21–33.

Kukla, R. (2005) *Mass Hysteria: Medicine, Culture, and Mothers' Bodies*, Lanham, MD: Rowman & Littlefield.

Miller, D. (2009) *The Comfort of Things*, Cambridge: Polity Press.

Miller, T. (2005) *Making Sense of Motherhood: a Narrative Approach*, Cambridge: Cambridge University Press.

Murray, S. (2010) 'Women in/under control? Embodying eating after gastric banding' *Radical Psychology Online Journal*, 8(1), available at http://radicalpsychology.org/index.html. Accessed 3 September 2012.

Oakley, A. (1979) *Becoming a Mother*, Oxford: Martin Robertson.

O'Connor, H. and Madge, C. (2004) '"My mum's thirty years out of date": the role of the internet in the transition to motherhood', *Community, Work and Family*, 7: 351–69.

O'Malley, L. (2006) 'Does my bump look big in this?', *Advertising & Society Review*, 7(3), available at http://muse.jhu.edu/journals/asr/v007/7.3omalley.html. Accessed 3 September 2012.

O'Malley, L., Patterson, M. and Ni Bheachain, C. (2006) 'Paperback mother', in S. Brown (ed) *Consuming Books: The Marketing and Consumption of Literature*, London: Routledge, 83–95.

Patterson, M. and Schroeder, J. (2010) 'Borderlines: skin, tattoos and consumer culture theory', *Marketing Theory*, 10: 253–67.

Prothero, A. (2002) Consuming motherhood: an introspective journey on consuming to be a good mother, *Proceedings of the 6th Conference of Gender, Marketing, and Consumer Behaviour*, Dublin, June, 211–25.

Roedder John, D. (1999) 'Consumer socialization of children: a retrospective look at twenty-five years of research', *Journal of Consumer Research*, December, 183–213.

Rothman, B.K. (1989) 'Motherhood under capitalism', in B.K. Rothman (ed.) *Recreating Motherhood: Ideology and Technology in a Patriarchal Society*, New York: Norton, 39–50.

Ryan, K., Tordes, L. and Alexander, J. (2011) 'Calling, permission and fulfilment: the interembodied experiences of breastfeeding', *Qualitative Health Research*, 21: 731–42.

Thompson, C. and Haytko, D. (1997) 'Speaking of fashion: consumers' uses of fashion discourses and the appropriation of countervailing cultural meanings', *Journal of Consumer Research*, 24: 15–42.

Thompson, C. and Hirschman, E. (1998) 'An existential analysis of the embodied self in postmodern consumer culture', *Consumption Markets & Culture*, 2: 401–47.

Thomsen, T.U. and Sørensen, E.B. (2006) 'The first four-wheeled status symbol – pram consumption as a vehicle for the construction of motherhood identity', *Journal of Marketing Management*, 22: 907–27.

VOICE Group (2008) 'Reflections on collaboration in interpretive consumer research', *Qualitative Market Research: An International Journal*, 11(2): 147–65.

VOICE Group (2010a) 'Motherhood, marketization and consumer vulnerability', *Journal of Macromarketing*, 30(4): 384–97.

VOICE Group (2010b) 'Buying into motherhood? Problematic consumption and ambivalence in transitional phases', *Consumption, Markets and Culture*, 13(4): 373–97.

Waerdahl, R. (2005) '"Maybe I'll need a pair of Levi's before Junior High?" Child to youth trajectories and anticipatory socialization', *Childhood*, 12: 201–9.

Warin, M., Turner, K., Moore, V. and Davies, M. (2008) 'Bodies, mothers and identities: rethinking obesity and the BMI', *Sociology of Health & Illness*, 30: 97–111.

Wooten, D.B. (2006) 'From labeling possessions to possessing labels: ridicule and socialization among adolescents', *Journal of Consumer Research*, 33: 188–98.

Index